The Druze & Their Faith in Tawhid

 CONTEMPORARY ISSUES IN THE MIDDLE EAST

The Prophet Muhammad (570–632 C.E.)

Abu Bakr (d.634 C.E./A.H. 13)
Omar (d. 644 C.E./A.H. 23)
Uthman (d. 565 C.E./A.H. 35)

Ali ibn Abu Talib (d. 661 C.E./A.H. 40)

al-Hasan ibn 'Ali (d. 669 C.E./A.H. 49)   al-Husayn ibn 'Ali (d. 680 C.E./A.H. 61)

'Ali Zayn al-'Abidin (d. 714 C.E./A.H. 95)

Muhammad al-Baqir (d. 732 C.E./A.H. 114)

Ja'afar al-Sadiq (d. 765 C.E./A.H. 148)

Musa al-Kazim (d. 799 C.E./A.H. 183)	Isma'il ibn Ja'far (d. 754 C.E./A.H. 136)
'Ali al-Ridha (d. 818 C.E./A.H. 202)	Muhammad Ibn Isma'il
Muhammad al-Jawad (d. 835 C.E./A.H. 220)	Abdullah
'Ali al-Hadi (d. 868 C.E./A.H. 254)	Ahmad
Hassan al-Askari (d. 874 C.E./A.H. 260)	al-Husayn
Muhammad al-Mahdi al-Muntazar (disappeared c. 879 C.E./A.H. 266)	Ali
	al-Mahdi (d. 934 C.E./A.H. 322)
	al-Qa'im (d. 946 C.E./A.H. 334)
	Isma'il al-Mansur (d. 953 C.E./A.H. 341)
	al-mu'izz Li Din-Allah (d. 975 C.E./A.H. 365)
	al-'Aziz bi Allah (d. 996 C.E./A.H. 386)
	al-Hakim bi Amr Allah (d. 1021 C.E./A.H. 411)
	'Ali al-Zahir (d. 1036 C.E./A.H. 427)

The Druze &
Their Faith in Tawhid

A N I S   O B E I D

With a Foreword by Sami Nasib Makarem

SYRACUSE UNIVERSITY PRESS

Library of Congress Cataloging-in-Publication Data
Obeid, Anis I.
The Druze and their faith in tawhid / Anis Obeid.
p.   cm.
Includes bibliographical references and index.
ISBN 0-8156-3097-2 (hardcover (cloth) : alk. paper)
1. Druzes—History.   2. Druzes—Doctrine.   I. Title.
BL1695.O24 2006
297.2'045—dc22

2006012978

Manufactured in the United States of America

In memory of my sister,
Jamal Obeid,
whose love, kindness, and spiritual wisdom
touched the lives of many.

Anis Obeid was born and raised in Lebanon, where he received his medical education at the American University of Beirut. He then pursued postgraduate training in cardiology in the United States, and currently serves as clinical professor of medicine at Upstate Medical University and director of echocardiography at Crouse Hospital in Syracuse, New York. He is also a founding member of the New York Heart Center, serving most of Central New York, and has written a book and many articles on medical subjects.

Dr. Obeid is a member of several scientific and professional organizations, including the American Heart Association, the American College of Cardiology, and the American Society of Echocardiography. He has been given distinguished service awards by the Onondaga County Medical Society and the Auxiliary of Crouse Hospital.

He is a founding member of the American Druze Foundation, whose aim is to preserve the cultural and religious tenets of the Druze faith among American Druze and to promote interfaith understanding and tolerance. Dr. Obeid has a special interest in Arabic literature and poetry and has published *Sada al-Sinin* (1999), a book of Arabic poetry. He resides in Fayetteville, New York, with his wife, Nawal, and his sons, Omar and Kareem.

Contents

Foreword

IN HIS CONCLUDING REMARKS to this book, Dr. Anis Obeid has clearly stated his twofold purpose in writing it: "to lay out the core concepts of the Tawhid faith of the Druze within the historical context of its emergence from . . . Islam in the era of the sixth Fatamid caliph, al-Hakim bi Amr Allah" and "to stimulate the Druze community to take a close look at what they have and initiate a process of dialogue with reform in mind." Dr. Obeid's thorough, scholarly narrative succeeds admirably in this double aim, informed by his sincere concern and his deep understanding of both the Druze faith and Western culture. Not only does he logically explore the origins and development of his Druze faith in lucid prose, but he sets out the challenges its followers currently face.

Demonstrating his profound comprehension of the problems facing both the Druze faith and the Druze themselves in the West and Middle East alike, Dr. Obeid rightly identifies the key to the survival of both: how the Druze are to deal with modernity. The Druze, Dr. Obeid explains, should neither lose the identity of their religious faith for the sake of modernity nor lose modernity for the sake of traditional religion, especially when the Druze faith developed as an intellectual revolution within Islam against traditions its adherents saw as contravening the essential spirit of Islam.

By tracing the evolution of the Druze faith over its long history, Dr. Obeid illuminates its nature, allowing the Druze to seek a true understanding of their faith while keeping abreast of modernity in its essential rather than its superficial sense. Very few studies of the Druze have displayed such farsightedness. Thank you, Dr. Obeid, for this most interesting and needed book.

Sami Nasib Makarem
Professor
Department of Arabic and Near Eastern Languages
American University of Beirut

Preface

SEVERAL FACTORS led me to undertake this endeavor at this time. These include my firm belief that knowledge is a prerequisite for interfaith understanding and cooperation and for reducing mistrust and misconceptions that generally arise out of ignorance. The benefits of knowledge are especially apparent when the subject is the religious path of a minority known as the Druze, a subsect that evolved from the Isma'ili branch of Shi'a Islam in the early part of the eleventh century. The faith that the Druze adopted is known as Tawhid. Tawhid is a faith or a path (*mislak* or *madhhab*) that has not been open to the outside world for hundreds of years. Its basic tenets, enshrined in Druze religious epistles, have not even been accessible to most members of the Druze community, who are, or should be, entitled to them by right of birth. *Tawhid* is an Arabic term that refers to unity or oneness. In this case it is the oneness of God and the unity of all in the oneness of the one and only God. The tenets of Tawhid and the complexity of the faith are the subjects of this book.

Fear of persecution is among the reasons for the closed nature of the Druze faith. The Druze, like their predecessors in the Shi'a Isma'ili traditions, have been subjected to persecution almost from inception. However, persecution has not been the only reason for circumspection. Other reasons relate to the nature of the doctrine itself, which, being esoteric, is not easily understood by the unprepared or uninitiated members within the faith, and still less by those outside the closed Druze circle. Circumspection leads to secrecy, which, in the extreme, results in disconnection of the majority of the faithful from the theosophical principles on which their faith is based. When a select few are admitted to the inner sanctum of real knowledge of the faith, and then only after a long and arduous preparatory journey, the majority of believers remain on the periphery and have to contend with a minimum of exposure to the tenets of their faith. As for those outside the faith, they have no chance at all for an encounter.

Fear of the misunderstanding that may result from exposure of the unprepared or uninitiated to the doctrine is not restricted to the Druze. Admonitions for caution in indiscriminate exposure to the tenets of religion is a characteristic that is present in many faiths.

Circumspection, however, comes with a price, and the veil of secrecy has had its downside for the Druze. It has contributed to a state that limits the Druze integration in a religious sense with members of the larger communities with whom the Druze coexist. Ultimately, religious secrecy defeats the purpose for which it was instituted and increases vulnerability to ignorance and distortion.

Another reason for writing this book is the possibility that the Tawhid faith that the Druze have adopted may harbor within its closely guarded and relatively untouched boundaries certain philosophical and metaphysical concepts that deserve a closer look, particularly in relation to modern life and the evolving understanding of religion. It would be unfortunate to allow neglect and deterioration to swallow a potentially significant component in the story of mankind's quest for spirituality and truth. The neglect, which may have been partly by design in the past, can no longer be regarded as a form of preservation, even if there are real risks. Exposing the basic tenets of the Tawhid faith of the Druze to further study and analysis may in fact be to its advantage as well as to the advantage of those who seek to resurrect its tenets from the atrophic consequences of neglect and the annals of ignored history.

Perhaps my own most compelling reason for writing this book is my personal need to understand and clarify the religious doctrine into which I was born and which has had a significant impact on my life. Most human beings come to a certain religion by being born into it, absorbing its tenets and influence at the earliest stages in their formative years. At this early stage there is usually no choice except in families that do not indoctrinate their children early on in life. Most people are raised into one faith or another as a matter of "religious heredity." It is therefore an awesome responsibility to raise a child in a particular religion. Religious affiliation is generally a predetermined and lifelong commitment that impacts many aspects of daily life. Of course, one could change one's mind later, and many do, but these individuals base their decisions on careful and deliberate choice. After all, change of religious affiliation carries the potential trauma of disconnection from one's roots and the potential instability that attends a change in identity.

Religion is not an easy subject to deal with, particularly for someone whose training and orientation has been in medicine and biology rather than theology and metaphysics. Thus, in a technical sense, this book may be looked on as an outsider's intrusion into the domain of the scholars in the field, or into the arena of those who practice and preach religion as a profession. Moreover, the approach in presentation of the subject matter is somewhat different from the approach of the scholars or the traditionalists. My reliance on many secondary sources may not please the scholars, while reflections of my own understanding of the subject may be at variance with some of the views of the traditionalists. In addition, there will inevitably be others who do not agree with the opinions that I put forth, or with the conclusions that follow. They are entitled to express their views freely, as I have expressed mine. In any event, I am fully prepared to consider criticism of my approach—and to readjust my views in response to arguments based on compelling evidence. Preparation of this work represented a major reward in itself, and my satisfaction with the effort became an incentive to share it with others of both similar and dissimilar backgrounds.

It is a fact that for most Druze people, identity is defined more by family values and traditions than by the tenets of their faith. Most of the religious activities among the Druze have been the domain of a traditional order of self-appointed wise and pious men (*'uqqal*), who have kept the tenets of the Druze path in Tawhid in safe custody, away from the majority of its uninitiated members (including those with high levels of education and learning) and from people outside the Druze community. Although this tradition protected the tenets of the Druze faith, it also kept them static and held them apart from most members of the Druze community—a state of affairs that many secular Druze have regarded as a valid alibi for noninvolvement. After all, the secular class, being more educated, was never in the inner circle of the religious order. With few exceptions, the educated class was never close enough to the faith to feel the stimulation for a proactive stand. Their sense of identity is based mostly on the traditions of the community rather than the tenets of the faith. The ensuing ignorance has resulted in ambiguity and confusion both within and outside the Druze community, leaving the faith vulnerable to speculation, misinformation, and, in many instances, outright distortion.

In the East, religious feelings run more intensely than in most modern Western societies. Religious identity and allegiance can be used as a powerful tool for beneficence or mischief, and the enshrouded state of Druze doctrine leaves it particularly vulnerable to misinterpretation and speculation.

This state of affairs reinforced my urge to explore my religious heritage on my own with as much objectivity as possible, seeking a clear view of the basic tenets of my faith. While recognizing that one can never achieve total objectivity in such matters, I have tried to avoid dogmatic views and to steer clear of blind allegiance to the established traditions of the community. I have likewise tried to clear away the tangled web of identities that have been ascribed to the Druze faith by non-Druze sources in religious and theosophical discourse, identities that range from the reasonably accurate to the totally erroneous. Some of these profiles were deliberately created for political or propaganda purposes as sources of misinformation or disinformation, particularly with respect to the Druze-Islamic relationship. Such attempts compelled me to try to sort out fact from fiction by delving into the real meaning of the message of Tawhid and deciphering its complexities.

These are the reasons behind this book. I wrote it not as a scholarly thesis nor as a major theological reference but as a personal exploration, laying out my own perspective on the Druze faith and the concept of Tawhid as I have come to understand them.

The decision to write this book was not made without hesitation or trepidation. All my life, I have been sensitized to the negative aspects of organized religion. As we all know, religion can be manipulated into an instrument of politics and divisiveness, and it often is. In addition, my own spiritual impulses run primarily along introspective and mystical lines, rather than toward overt expressions of religiosity. Consequently, I have never felt the need for complex ritualistic practices. As I delved into the Druze path in Tawhid, I found it to be more consistent with my own inclination—which is close to the approach of secular humanism—than with a more formalized approach. Moreover, secularism does not negate the feeling of spirituality that is, I believe, deeply ingrained in the nature of human beings.

Discussion of religion may lead to enlightenment and understanding within a given faith and among different faiths. However, it neither does nor can be expected to lead to unanimity of opinion, consensus, or agreement on interpretation of the religious message. Diversity and not unanimity is the hallmark of religious expression in human societies. And it is within this diversity that ideas can and should flourish, interacting and evolving to the betterment of mankind. Thus, far from being a liability, different opinions and approaches are an asset that, when used properly, will lead to tolerance and mutual respect. It is with this aim in mind that I took on this endeavor, and it is in this spirit I hope it will be viewed and understood. I believe that the main purpose of religion is to make life more meaningful in the present world and more hopeful as to the next. It cannot and should not be an impediment in people's lives; otherwise, it loses relevance and becomes an empty shell to be discarded and replaced by a new and more meaningful alternative. The roads of history are littered with the remains of once viable and vibrant faiths. In most instances of this kind, it was the inability of the faith, any faith, to evolve and adjust to the human needs of the time that sealed its fate.

The Druze path in Tawhid challenged accepted religious dogmas of the day and subjected these dogmas to the critical test of reason. When the expected backlash took place, the faith was forced to turn inward for almost a thousand years. It has been virtually frozen almost all this time without the benefit of change or development in response to the changing conditions in daily life.

Now, however, the Druze path in Tawhid faith stands at a crossroads. The compelling conditions of modern life present the followers of the Druze faith with the imperative of choice between two major paths. One is the traditional path: to maintain the status quo and preserve the tenets of the faith in the nascent form in which they were articulated, with little or no evolution over a thousand years. The other is to choose the road of openness and evolution, knowing full well that change will not come without a price. Many members of the faith, particularly in the West but also in the East, are of the opinion that the need to evolve is urgent and the option of reform, unavoidable. They believe that the Druze path in Tawhid deserves to be interpreted and understood in a more scholarly historical context than has occurred thus far. Closure and secrecy, whatever the reasons prompting them in the past, are no longer protective in today's world. The Tawhid path was built on evolution of religious thought across the entirety of human existence and on the exercise of free choice by the individual human being. The present work is an indication that I cast my lot with those who believe in openness and evolution.

A brief remark on source material and style of presentation is in order. The primary source of this material is unpublished manuscripts that contain the tenets of the Druze faith, in the form of letters or epistles (*rasa'il*, sing. *risalat*), compiled into what is known as the Kutub al-Hikma (Books of Wisdom). These manuscripts have been preserved by religious figures in various families, and it is from one such collection, held by my family as far back as my great-grandfather's time, that the material discussed in this book was obtained. Collections of these books in manuscript form are found in major libraries throughout the world. A printed version of the Books of Wisdom, put out by unknown publishers (most likely non-Druze authors under assumed names), appeared during the Lebanese civil war. While Druze scholars and religious leaders have not commented on the veracity of that printed version, many believe that it is close to what exists in manuscript form, considering that, to my knowledge, there is no single, standard authenticated manuscript. What we have is instead a collection of hand-copied material in the form of epistles, passed from one generation to the next over a period of almost a thousand years. There are no ordained Druze clergy or formal religious authorities to authenticate these books. This seeming drawback paradoxically allows considerable latitude in interpretation. More recently, other manuscripts were discovered that pertain to the tenets of the faith and probably complement the Books of Wisdom. These manuscripts are discussed in chapter 5.

All these materials, including the epistles in the Books of Wisdom, are the work of human beings, and they do not enjoy the status of divine revelation accorded the Qur'an. As such, they are open to greater latitude in interpretation, discussion, and editorial analysis than is the Qur'an.

Transliteration of names from Arabic to English conforms to accepted norms, with minor modifications to aid the Western reader, including the elimination of all diacritical marks except the ayn and the hamza. All quotations from the Qur'an were taken from Arthur John Arberry's translation, *The Koran Interpreted* (London: Allen & Unwin and New York: Macmillan, 1955; reprinted, New York: Touchstone, 1996). Dates are given primarily in accordance with the Western calendar, although in certain instances I have also given the corresponding Islamic (Hijra) year when indicated.

This book is divided into eight chapters. The material in the first four chapters provides the background necessary for understanding the material to follow. Chapter 1 is a brief introduction to religion in general, with a glimpse of the Druze ethnicity and their concept of Tawhid. Chapters 2 and 3 deal with the Islamic history and the emergence of different sects in Islam. The rise of Islam as a worldly realm in addition to a religious movement, with the accompanying political and intellectual ferment, is touched upon as a prelude to the emergence of the Isma'ili doctrine and the establishment of the Fatimid Empire. The Druze concept of Tawhid was crystallized and made public during the reign of the sixth Fatimid caliph, al-Hakim bi 'Amr Allah. Chapter 4 is devoted to the rise of the Fatimid caliphate and imamate. Because of the centrality of al-Hakim in the Druze concept of Tawhid, his role is discussed in this chapter as well as in the rest of the book.

Chapters 5 and 6 are devoted to presentation of the basic tenets of the Tawhid faith as conceptualized by the Druze. The core tenets are presented in chapter 5, and the behavioral prerequisites and determinants of these tenets in the conduct of daily life are presented in chapter 6.

Chapter 7 deals with the challenges of modern life that confront the Druze as individuals and as a community. Although the emphasis is mainly on the challenges of life in the West, the discussion may be applicable, with some modifications, to conditions of life that the Druze face wherever they live. After all, the impact of geographical boundaries in shaping human behavior is rapidly declining in the global village. Thus closed communities such as the Druze can no longer survive and function without proper adjustment to the conditions of the day, and embarking on reforms that facilitate such adjustment.

Concluding remarks in chapter 8 bring the book to a close.

Devoting a relatively large space to the Islamic background in the first four chapters is an indication of, first, the importance of this historical background in understanding the evolution of the Tawhid faith of the Druze, and second, the ignorance of a significant segment of the Druze community about the importance of this heritage. Although the information on the Islamic heritage provided in this book may seem redundant or simplistic for the informed reader, I have included it for two reasons. First, I wish to emphasize the relationship of the Druze faith to the main trunk from which it emerged—and that is Islam. Second, I believe that an understanding of this heritage is vital to an understanding the Tawhid faith of the Druze.

Acknowledgments

THIS WORK is in large measure the result of years of deliberation among concerned and well-informed friends and colleagues within and outside the Druze community. Several years ago, the Committee on Religious Affairs (CORA) of the American Druze Society, under the dedicated leadership of the late Dr. Wahbah Sayegh, provided the germ seed for this book. Samah Helal, Hassan Izzeddin, Dr. Nadim Kassim, Dr. Abdallah Najjar, and I were major participants in that committee. Later on, members from the same team, with the addition of Dr. Ghaleb Maher and Dr. Melhem Salman, were incorporated into the Committee for Religious Reform (CORR) in the newly formed American Druze Foundation. The shortage of material on the Druze faith that is available to those born and raised in the West, particularly in the United States, was obvious and needed to be addressed. It was mainly in the course of discussions among members of this committee that the idea evolved for the production of the present work. Major credit, therefore, is due to the members of CORR: Samah Helal, Dr. Nadim Kassim, Dr. Ghaleb Maher, Dr. Abdallah Najjar, and Dr. Melhem Salman. To them, collectively and individually, I owe a debt of gratitude. I particularly wish to acknowledge Melhem Salman for his critical review and challenging comments, most of which were incorporated into the text. I am also indebted to the board of directors of the American Druze Foundation, under the able leadership of Ghassan Saab, for their continuous support and encouragement. Without such support and encouragement, this work would not have been possible.

This book is in a sense the fulfillment of a dream of the late Jack Hamady, founding father of the American Druze Foundation and a community leader and philanthropist who never lost pride in his heritage. In this regard I tried to pursue the pioneering work of Samah Helal, Dr. Naji Jurdi, Mustafa Moukarem, Dr. Sahar Mua'kassa, and Dr. Abdallah Najjar. These scholars and many others in the American Druze community have been engaged with these issues over a period of several decades. Their contributions in writing and through personal interactions have played a big role in shaping my own thinking on the subject and in refining my approach.

I wish to acknowledge the contributions of many friends and scholars in addition to those mentioned above, whose publications and discussions have been a major resource in my understanding of the complexities of the Druze faith. For the sake of brevity I cannot list them individually here, but this omission in no way signals a lack of appreciation of their impact on my thought and the development of this work.

I am grateful to Drs. Anwar Abi-Khzam, Nejla Abu-Izzeddin, Kais Firro, Sami Makarem, Abbas Abu Saleh, and Sami Swayd for the source material in their scholarly publications. Advice and encouragement from Dr. Adil Abu Asi, Nadeem Makarem, Najla Abu A'si Shouhayeb, and the late Shaykh Naim Shouhayeb, to name only a few, was valuable and appreciated. To them and many others whose encouragement and challenge helped me bring this work to fruition, I owe a debt of gratitude.

Eyad Abu Shakra, a long-time friend and scholar in Druze and Islamic affairs stationed in London, was kind enough to review this manuscript and offer valuable and critical suggestions that are gratefully acknowledged. His contributions were of enormous help in style and substance. I wish to thank Ahmad al-Hindi for introducing me to Syracuse University Press, whose editorial staff contributed to the refinements of the finished product. I am particularly grateful to Mary Selden Evans, executive editor of the press, for her continuous encouragement and guidance. I also wish to thank Carolyn Russ for her thorough copyediting of the manuscript.

I wish to recognize the encouragement and support of my brothers and sisters: Asma Obeid, Nadia Obeid Abul Hosn, the late Jamal Obeid, and Sami and Said Obeid, and their families. Their involvement and emotional support eased the stress associated with this work.

Finally, on the home front, special thanks go to my wife, Nawal, for critical comments and suggestions that enhanced the presentation of this work. She would not be satisfied until passages that were vague or ambiguous were clarified and focused. Likewise, my sons Omar and Kareem encouraged and supported me throughout the long period of preparation for this book. Thus the time spent in preparation of this work was theirs to contribute generously and cheerfully.

The contributions and refinements of all those mentioned above notwithstanding, I assume full responsibility for the material in this book, including the opinions, explanations, approaches, and recommendations expressed herein. My aim is to explore the basic philosophy of the Tawhid faith of the Druze and to share the fruits of this labor.

The Druze & Their Faith in Tawhid

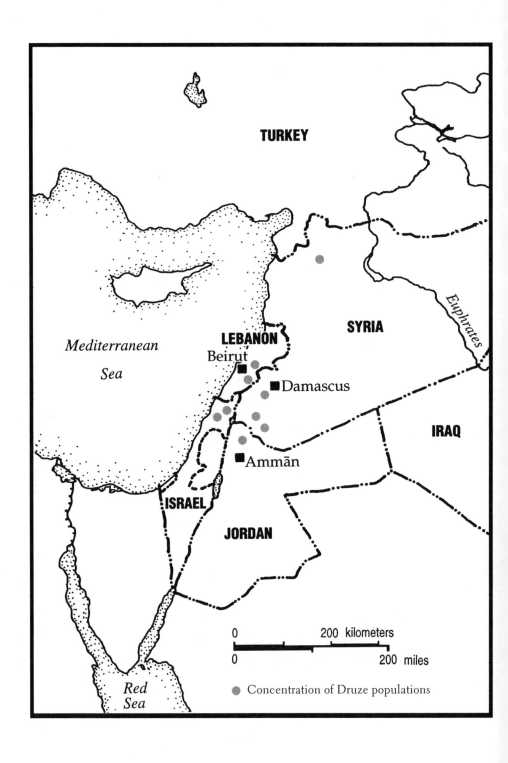

TURKEY

Euphrates

SYRIA

LEBANON

Beirut

Damascus

Mediterranean
Sea

IRAQ

Ammān

ISRAEL

JORDAN

Red
Sea

0   200 kilometers

0   200 miles

● Concentration of Druze populations

1 *Introduction*

AMONG THE BIOLOGICAL DIVERSITY of this planet, human beings occupy the apex of the pyramid, in that their urge to explore and learn is as irresistible as their formidable intellectual capacity allows. This urge cuts across all ages and stages of life. We only have to watch a child probing his or her environment and engaging in what we may call mischief, or an elderly person in the twilight years engrossed in a book, straining his poor eyesight to join the author in looking for answers, to realize how profound this inquisitive instinct is in the human race. What is characteristically human, in addition, is the capacity to learn and build on previous experiences, and to transmit the acquired knowledge (cultural heredity) to future generations.

Since the dawn of human history, the accumulation of knowledge has proceeded in fits and starts, surviving natural and self-induced disasters to reach present-day levels of globalization. From all indicators the march is likely to continue and to accelerate, with new innovations eclipsing the preceding ones. Moreover, as long as the human race continues on its present course, the struggle to explore and to find answers will only intensify. This cumulative knowledge—termed the *noosphere*, by Pierre Teilhard de Chardin "to denote the sphere of mind, as opposed to, or rather superposed on, the biosphere or the sphere of life, and acting as a transforming agency promoting hominisation"—is getting thicker and more extensive as it envelops the globe, leading to progressive expansion of human horizons.[1]

The multiplicity of pathways that human beings use to explore and gain knowledge generally can be grouped under two major headings. The first is the empirical method, based on direct observation and experimentation leading to the discipline of the sciences. The second pathway to knowledge is based on contemplation and intuition that transcend the limitations of the physical senses and project to the realms of metaphysics and spirituality. Along with philosophy and mysticism, religion is the main vehicle for spiritual expression in human societies,

1

and as such it exerts enormous influence in the lives of human beings. The relation between the two poles, those of science and religion, has oscillated between confrontation and cooperation across the span of human history, touching on all the grades in between.

The main emphasis in the discipline of science is on a body of knowledge obtained by the scientific method. Empirical observations in science obtained through the use of the physical senses, directly or by extension, are subjected to testing and to tangible proof by accepted logical criteria. The results of innovations or interventions are likewise subjected to rigorous criteria of evaluation and assessment without bias or distortion. Consistent outcomes lead to the formulation of natural laws that are based on the predictability of such observations.

The spectacular strides achieved by this mode of discovery are portrayed in all that surrounds us, from the fruits of technology in daily usage to the exploration of the secrets of the universe. Hardly a day passes before some old and presumably established scientific dogma succumbs to a younger and more robust theory that, in turn, is shattered before it arrives at the level of dogma.

The spectacular strides in technology, however, have widened the gulf between the explosive growth in the physical sciences with their impact on daily life, and the slower developments in social sciences that reflect the pace of evolution of human behavior. The strain of this mismatch between material and social dimensions is demonstrated by the tremendous pressure that modernity exerts in the daily lives of ordinary people. The speed of the treadmill in everyday life does not let up, nor does it keep a predictable pace; it rather continues to increase in magnitude and intensity. The process is inexorable and, short of some cataclysmic event, irreversible.

That the fruits of familiar scientific advances subject the ethical and metaphysical repertoire of human society to an exorbitant level of stress is a known fact. More challenging is the fact that many of the scientific discoveries are totally new, thus, there is no precedent for guidance. The use and abuse of the power of the atom is one such example; another would be the use of fetal tissue in medical research, and yet another the looming challenge of human cloning. There is no shortage of breakthroughs in all the disciplines of science that pound on our doors every day, demanding a response from society. The widening gulf between the exponential progress in the physical and scientific domains, on the one hand, and the linear progress in the social and humanistic domains, on the other, gives the impression that the human race is actually regressing. This impression is erroneous, since modern societies are more equipped to respond to the challenges of modern life than previous societies were to theirs. This is in part a result of the contributions of science-generated means of analysis, record keeping, duplication, exchange, communication, and dissemination of information in all disciplines. Other contributors include the encouragement and facilitation of free thinking in modern cultures and innovative approaches to the puzzles of life in whatever form they may present. In modern cultures, subjects considered taboo only a few decades ago are no longer seen as untouchable or outside the limits of probing and inquiry. While in some cultures, the limits of inquiry remain rigid, threatening trespassers with various forms of backlash or retribution, the process of inquiry is inevitably an irreversible one. There is no discipline nowadays that can be sheltered from analysis and dissection. Were it not for the dynamic interaction between scientific achievements and societal adjustment, we would not have the complex web of organizations, laws, regulations, economic interdependence, and other interactions that exist in our world today. Without such developments modern life could not be sustained. The subtle but equally important interest in cross-cultural exchanges and attempts at understanding the theological and philosophical underpinnings of the various segments of the human race are to a large degree fruitful by-products of scientific and technical innovations.

Pessimists point to the destructive impact of the sciences on human societies—and there is no shortage of evidence to back those claims. From the assault on the environment to the depletion of renewable and nonrenewable resources, the human capacity for consumption seems insatiable. The basis of such pessimism is generally rooted in the premise that human nature is inclined to follow the path of material indulgence and technical innovation regardless of the collective costs, even when we know that sooner or later these costs will have to be paid. Oblivious to the laws of entropy, human beings seek power, and the more power they acquire the more likely they are to abuse it. "Now our world view and social system are falling victim to the very process of their creation," comments Jeremy Rifkin. "Each day we experience the truth that . . . an organism cannot long survive in a medium of its own waste."[2] At the crossroads the human race has to make painful decisions.

Scientific achievements, mighty as they indeed are, can only go so far toward solving the secrets of life. Science can address issues that fall within the scope of rigorous procedures and systems of logic. However, it is not equipped to tackle questions of an ethical or metaphysical nature because these and other related issues fall outside the scope of the scientific method. To quote Sir Peter Medawar, a towering figure in the modern biological sciences: "It is not to science, therefore, but to metaphysics, imaginative literature or religion that we must turn for answers to questions having to do with the first and last of things. Because these answers neither arise out of nor require validation by empirical evidence, it is not useful or even meaningful to ask whether they are true or false."[3]

Religion sits at the crossroads of human concerns because it deals with issues that are beyond the reach of scientific investigation and beyond the boundaries of human observation and control. In addition, religion is the only discipline whose domain crosses the threshold of death and whose concern extends to the uncharted territory beyond the grave. Religion is the main (though not the only) vehicle through which society addresses the spiritual needs of human beings. Since the dawn of human awareness, religion has been a faithful accompaniment of human societies and human evolution. "Human beings are spiritual animals," declares Karen Armstrong, coining the term *Homo religiosus* for Homo sapiens.[4] In fact, there is no era of human history that is devoid of religion and no society that has not included religion in its fabric.

From the beginning of history men and women worshipped a variety of gods and goddesses and elaborated a complex system of rituals that were performed to appease or to seek favors from their gods. It was in some ways an attempt to find meaning and to establish security in a world that their senses could neither totally comprehend nor, to any significant degree, control. The awe and wonder of primitive human beings at the powers of and their vulnerability to the caprices of nature led to the search for supernatural forces in which to seek refuge and security.

Initial concrete expression of religious concepts evolved into more abstract forms as human civilization progressed. This evolution was related to humans' increasing ability to understand and to a large extent control natural forces, and to remove the veil of mystery from such forces. Eventually religious beliefs culminated for most people in the concept of a single absolute and almighty God.

Although humankind's impressive scientific accomplishments have negated religion altogether in some scientific circles, religion remains central to a vast majority of people, and it is safe to assume that as long as the entirety of existence is beyond the reach of human comprehension and control, religion will remain one of the obligatory aspects of human life. It may well be the most important constant in human existence. "Since material solutions fail to account for our experienced uniqueness, I am constrained to attribute the uniqueness of the Self or Soul to a supernatural spiritual creation," declared the distinguished neuroscientist Sir John Eccles. "This conclusion is of inestimable theological significance. It strongly reinforces our belief in the human Soul and in its miraculous origin in

Divine creation. There is recognition not only of the Transcendent God, the Creator of the Cosmos, the God in which Einstein believed, but also of the loving God to whom we owe our being."[5]

The complexity of religious experience across the vast span of human history is best portrayed by the enormous proliferation of religions, denominations, and sects, each with its own tenets, rituals, programs, publications, and institutions devoted to furthering its cause. This complexity also finds expression in the efforts of numerous scholars and scholarly institutions to unravel the history and mystery of religions, as well as the efforts of religious professionals to defend and propagate their particular faiths. In the final analysis, however, a religious experience is highly personal, a communication between individuals and a higher power as each apprehends that entity. Broad concepts and values may be shared by most religions and are frequently expressed in the collective conscience of group affiliation and identity, but the human relationship with God in its essence remains private, intimate, and highly personal. This aspect of religion may be viewed as transcendental in nature and, as such, does not have polarizing or political overtones.

There is another aspect to religion, however, commonly referred to as organized religion, which is built on a relational connection among individuals with similar visions, beliefs, values, and rituals who hold a sense of shared destiny. Such groups of the faithful congregate in houses of worship and community centers and develop organizational structures that vary from simplicity and autonomy to highly centralized systems with extensive and efficient bureaucracies. For most people the two aspects of religion, the transcendental and the organizational, complement each other and buttress the validity of the faith. Thus, there is a synergistic relationship between the transcendental connection of an individual with a higher power, a connection on the purely spiritual plane, and the group connection among individuals who congregate around a shared vision. This shared commonality extends by its very nature into modes of behavior and interest in affairs of the mundane. While the trancendental (spiritual and individualistic) aspect of religion does not in itself carry any major repercussions with respect to society as a whole, the institutional aspect of religion profoundly affects everyday aspects of human life. The identity of religious persuasion can be as ingrained as any other major societal trait. The importance of religious group identity may supersede those of color, race, and social and economic status, as well as the effects of political upheavals and environmental catastrophes.

The strength of religious affiliation, however, has been and remains a double-edged sword that brings out the best and the worst in human behavior. Whereas the spiritual side of religion has not caused much divisiveness among people of different faiths and therefore cannot be blamed for the failings of religion, the same cannot be said about religion as an institution or an organization. We are all aware of the shortcomings of organized religion when it provides justification for bigotry, exclusion, hatred, and vilification of the other simply because the other is not like me or us, and for condoning the use of force in the devastating wars unleashed under its banner. When misused, organized religion has been a major force in the alienation of one group of humanity from another. Religion is particularly vulnerable to criticism when atrocities are committed in its name, because of the paradox between what religion teaches and what is practiced by its adherents in its name. Thus violence acquires a perverted legitimacy in the name of altruism, divisiveness in the name of unity, and hatred in the quest for love. Perhaps the nature of religion—the absoluteness of its doctrines and the extension of its scope to the domain of the afterlife—makes it particularly vulnerable to criticism when its adherents succumb, in its name, to the same ills that religion is supposed to cure. Pessimism, cynicism, and loss of faith are logical by-products of such disappointment.

Yet there is a positive side to organized religion, reflected in the shared values and interests of the community and in the dedication of its members to high ideals of morality and justice. The impressive number of religious institutions and countless numbers of people of faith whose entire reason for existence is to provide succor to those in need, expecting nothing in return except the fulfillment of religious pledge and the satisfaction of inner peace, are there for all to see. Even in societies where a clear division exists between church and state, the impact of religion is deeply felt as the foundation of morality and one of the major sources of codes of behavior.

Thus, to dismiss religion as an archaic institution that is at best reactionary and divisive and that has compounded rather than relieved human suffering is both mistaken and naïve. The complexity of human nature and the multifaceted underpinnings of behavior should caution us against sweeping and absolute judgment, especially concerning a subject as profound and as complex as religion. This does not absolve religion, any religion, from the many sordid chapters that have been written in its name by misguided zealots, whose philosophy is based on aggressive competition with other religions, who believe that the ends justifies the means and condone whatever methods are required—even including torture and death—for their side to win. Such acts of barbarism should be condemned on their merits, but not through a sweeping condemnation of religion itself: that would be throwing out the gemstones with the contaminents.

The failings and successes of religion, when all is said and done, are the failings and successes of the human race. After all, the ability to believe—one of the most abstract forms of thought and imagination—is vested solely in the human being. What is done with faith is, therefore, the prerogative and responsibility of those who embrace it. The value of faith is then directly reflected in how it influences the individual's actions in daily life. Whether these actions are concordant with or at variance from the true meaning and intent of faith is a measure of the depth of reception of the true message of the faith by humans and a reflection of the level of human spirituality. True faith can never breed hatred of others or tolerate bigotry and suspicion. True faith leads to true knowledge, a genuine gnosis of the Creator and the mysteries of the universe. Bigotry, hatred, and suspicion are manifestations of perversion of faith and not its defense. The responsibility lies with those in the know to break the cycles of ignorance and bias that transform "comparative religion into competitive religion," to use Huston Smith's expression.[6] In the extreme, xenophobic attitudes paint the "other" as an alien creature who is reluctantly endured and, in times of stress, expelled or liquidated. In the words of Andrew Knoll: "On this planet, at this moment in time, human beings reign. Regardless of who or what penned earlier chapters in the history of life, we will write the next one. Through our actions or inactions, we decide the world that our grandchildren and great-grandchildren will know. Let us have the grace and humility to choose well."[7]

In order to break down the boundaries inherent in segregated thought, we have to accept and undertake a more wholesome approach to understanding one another and respecting the special traits that each one brings to the table. "We cannot undertake the restoration of ourselves and of our environment before having transformed our habits of thought," declares Alexis Carrel.[8]

It is when we accept the prerogative of others to pursue whatever form of belief makes sense to them and addresses their needs, only when we internalize the legitimacy of this conviction, that the boundaries between "us" and "them" are transcended or melt away altogether. In addition to being the right thing to do, the alternative to mutual understanding and tolerance is unthinkable in our world of today.

This book is about the Druze, a small sect that emerged from Islam some thousand years ago, took hold in the region of Greater Syria, and survived to this day by closing in on itself as a religious community, with its own personality. Religious closure did not stand in the way of involvement of the Druze in secular affairs. In fact the Druze have been, despite their minority status, quite visible in the social and political life of the larger communities in which they live. The Druze have assumed leadership positions, such as in governance of Mount Lebanon, for centuries. Renowned for fierce defense of their freedom and independence, the Druze rulers in Lebanon, throughout its history, have fostered an atmosphere of tolerance and hospitality to other groups, particularly the Christians, who were under duress during the period of Ottoman rule. The reign of the Druze prince Fakhr al-Din II (1590–1635 C.E.) is considered to be one of the most progressive in the history of Lebanon and the Levant in general. Had his liberal and pluralistic policy succeeded against the rigid autocracy of Ottoman rule, the history of the whole area would have been different.

In modern Syria the Druze have been at the forefront of the struggle for Syrian independence from the French mandate. The great Syrian uprising against the French mandate in 1925 was inspired by the courage and fortitude of the Druze chieftain Sultan al-Atrash, who inspired his people to feats of bravery and sacrifice that astonished the French authorities and earned the admiration of the world powers.[9] Consequently, the impact of the Druze on and their contribution to the political and social activities of their environment have exceeded expectations based on numerical considerations. Having no agenda to spread their particular religious faith through the conversion of others, the Druze were largely free from pressures associated with proselytizing and preaching. This is partly because the path they have chosen, the Tawhid path, places a premium on the substantive aspect of the religious message and on seeking its essence, while paying less attention to external manifestations and ritualistic practices. This liberal attitude has allowed the Druze to be more culturally receptive to new and fresh ideas than followers of the more traditionalist religions around them. Consequently, the Druze have been able to adapt to emerging situations in innovative and creative ways.

The closure of the Druze religion occurred partly for self-preservation, in response to the persecution and antagonism to which the Druze were subjected shortly after public disclosure of the tenets of their faith. To some, however, this reason was only a pretext. Religious closure, or rather extreme circumspection in the disclosure of the faith, was also prompted by concern that certain aspects of the esoteric and philosophical doctrine of the Druze would be misunderstood in the absence of considerable preparation prior to initiation into the faith. A protective posture to safeguard valuable information from falling into the wrong hands is a feature not confined to the Druze; it exists in one form or another in many faiths. In the case of the Druze, religious circumspection worked its way into a state of closure that, by tradition, became imbedded in the religious practices of the community.

The word *Druze*, by which this sect is known, is in fact a misnomer, but through long use the name came to refer to certain religious communities that originated in southern Lebanon, Syria, and northern Palestine-Israel. The vast majority of the Druze continue to inhabit these areas to this day.

The doctrine followed by the Druze is known as *Tawhid*, which roughly means "belief in the oneness of God and the manifestation of this oneness in the totality of creation." The name by which the Druze would like to be known is Muwahhidun, that is, "believers in the concept of Tawhid." It is of major interest that *Druze* refers only to the religious communities mentioned above, while the concept of Tawhid that this community claims as its canon is universal in scope. This and other features form the subject of this book.

Ethnically, the Druze are Arabs. Many Druze families trace their lineage to a few tribes and confederacies that migrated mostly from southern Arabia at different times in history. Driven by climatic and living conditions in the Arabian Peninsula, tribes have migrated in search of water, pasture, arable lands, and other necessities of life. The lands of the Fertile Crescent, a swath that stretched from Mesopotamia to the eastern Mediterranean, provided such opportunity. Different waves carried these Semitic people from central and southern Arabia throughout history, such that by the time Islam came on the scene in 622 C.E., most of the inhabitants of Greater Syria—that is, the geographic region consisting of modern-day Syria, Lebanon, Palestine-Israel, and Jordan, were Arabs.[10]

After the Islamic conquests, more waves of migration (such as the Tanukh confederacy that played a major role in the history of Lebanon) were dispatched by the caliphs of the day to protect the Syrian coast and the overlooking mountain ranges from external forces such as the Byzantines.[11] Thus, several tribes were sent during the Umayyad and Abbasid dynasties to various regions in Greater Syria with that purpose in mind. Upon settling in the mountains of Lebanon and other strategic places in modern-day Syria and Palestine-Israel, these tribes were given administrative authority and assigned military duties to govern and defend their turf. Many of these tribes and families would later on embrace the Tawhid doctrine. The descendants of these families and tribes constitute what is known as the Druze people of today.[12]

Different theories about the origin of the Druze have been proposed at one time or another, some based on speculation and some on superficial accounts by travelers and explorers during the Middle Ages. Some even speculated that the Druze were somehow related to the Crusaders, when in fact the call to Tawhid that the Druze embraced preceded the Crusades by several decades. Others speculated that the Druze represented remnants of a lost Jewish tribe. Still others theorized that the Druze were an amalgam of Persian and Iraqi elements that infiltrated Islam.

All these theories have been disproved by the simple fact that most Druze families can trace their lineage to known Arab tribes.[13] Furthermore, the dialect spoken by the Druze is one of the purest of the Arab dialects. Finally, Druze leaders in Syria and Lebanon, Druze intellectuals, and the community at large are unanimous in attesting to the Arab ethnicity of the Druze people.[14] According to the modern Druze historian Ajaj Nuwayhid, the word *Druze* was never mentioned in any of the classical history books until the advent of Ottoman rule of the Levant in the sixteenth century.[15] Muhammad Kamil Husayn writes:

> We can conclude that these [people] who adopted the creed of Tawhid and who are erroneously identified as the Druze are from Arab tribes with lineage that is known across the span of history. They have always been and continue to be in unison with their Arab brethren in their political struggles. They fought with the Arabs against the Crusades and against the Tatars [Moguls] and subsequently against the imperialist European British and French forces [in the aftermath of dissolution of the Ottoman Empire]. And their history bears testimony to their heroism in all the battles that they fought alongside their Arab brethren. They [the Druze] are proud of their Arab heritage.[16]

In an era of political turmoil and in one of the most volatile areas of the world, misinformation or disinformation can be fraught with grave consequences, particularly when it involves a relatively small community such as the Druze.

According to the Druze interpretation, the seeds of Tawhid were sown at the beginning of human creation and continued to develop and evolve across the span of human existence. This evolution occurred in tandem with the human capacity to absorb and comprehend. The Druze path in Tawhid, along with other esoteric *(batini)* approaches, grew into maturity in the womb of Islam, specifically in the era of the sixth Fatimid Isma'ili Shi'ite caliph al-Hakim bi Amr Allah. Islam, through revelations in the Qur'an, is the foundation on which the philosophy of Tawhid is based and the gateway to such knowledge. Tawhid also drew from other sources, mainly from monotheistic faiths but also from philosophical and mystical practices that preceded or were outside the scope of traditional Islam.

It will become apparent as we go along that the Tawhid doctrine is characterized by cyclical recurrences that span a much longer historical time period than that occupied by Druze history alone. In fact, the concept of Tawhid, which reaches as far back as creation itself and projects forward to the end of time, cannot be conceptually limited by temporal or spatial boundaries, nor can it be restricted to any sector of humanity. On the other hand, the Druze, as self-appointed standard-bearers of Tawhid have a much more definable history. The history of the Druze constitutes one chapter in the history of Tawhid, certainly not the first and in all likelihood not the last.

The main emphasis in this publication is on the exploration of Tawhid as seen through the eyes of the Druze themselves, at least through the eyes of one such member of the Druze community. As such it relates to the most recent chapter, when the call to Tawhid was launched in the era of the sixth Fatimid caliph, al-Hakim bi Amr Allah, almost one thousand years ago. Al-Hakim was not only the caliph of an Islamic empire but also the highest religious authority (imam) of an important branch of Islam, that of the Isma'ilis. Since the most recent chapter of Tawhid is intimately connected with Islam, our purpose will be served well if we start with a brief review of the historical background that led to the emergence of the Druze as a sect from Islam.

It is important to note that the concept of Tawhid that the Druze adopted was launched approximately four centuries after the emergence of Islam from the heart of Arabia. By that time the Islamic civilization had interacted with, absorbed, and integrated most major civilizations of the time. The result was an intellectual ferment and a cultural cauldron seldom seen by the world before or since, until the age of modernity. Such an atmosphere provided the milieu for bold and daring initiatives in all fields of study, including innovative approaches in philosophy and religion. It is against this backdrop that the Druze concept of Tawhid can be analyzed and understood. We shall trace in some detail the sequence of events that started with the beginning of Islam as revealed to the Prophet Muhammad in the Qur'an until the emergence of the Druze some four hundred years later. By the time the Fatimid Empire reached the height of its power in the era of the sixth Fatimid caliph and imam al-Hakim bi Amr Allah, Islam had evolved considerably from the days of the Prophet. It had become a major—perhaps the major—power in the world of its time. It had interacted with, absorbed from, and was influenced by multitudes of races, religions, ideologies, and cultures. It had split into two major factions, with each faction subdividing into further groups and sects. It is from one of the subsects of the Isma'ili Shi'a branch in Islam that the Druze emerged and adopted the concept of Tawhid. Our story will, therefore, begin with the advent of Islam.

2 Historical Background

The Prophet's Message and Lifetime

In 610 C.E. a forty-year-old merchant from Mecca, in the heart of the Hijaz in Arabia, experienced a dramatic event. His name was Muhammad. Muhammad was born in 570 C.E. to a prestigious (but not wealthy) branch of the powerful tribe of Quraysh, known as the branch of Hashim. Muhammad's father, Abdullah, died before Muhammad was born, and his mother died when he was six years old, leaving him a double orphan. As was (and in many ways still is) the custom in Arabian tribal societies, Muhammad was reared by his grandfather, an old and distinguished man by the name of 'Abd al-Muttalib. When his grandfather died, Muhammad moved to the custody of his uncle, Abu-Talib. Both his grandfather and his uncle treated Muhammad with love and affection, and he grew up to be a liked and trusted man. Muhammad soon earned the appellation of al-Amin, or "the trustworthy." Eventually he married a rich widow, also from the tribe of Quraysh, whose name was Khadija bint Khuwaylid, that is, the daughter of Khuwaylid.[1] Muhammad's life with Khadija was blissful, and even after her death he cherished her memory for the rest of his life. For several years before they married, Khadija had entrusted Muhammad with her caravan business. The caravan operated on the trade route between Mecca and Damascus. In addition to providing Muhammad with a major source of income, the trips to Damascus made a profound impression on his agile and deliberative mind. Damascus at the time was rich and verdant, with flowing water, fruit orchards, elegant gardens, and a long history of culture and cosmopolitanism that stood in sharp contrast with the harsh and simple Bedouin life of Arabia.

In Arabia, and en route to Damascus, Muhammad also came into contact with learned men and religious figures from the Jewish and Christian faiths, as well as pious people known as the Hanifs (al-Ahnaf). The Hanifs belonged to a movement based on Abrahamic monotheism and mysticism, and they rejected

13

many ritualistic practices as a form of idolatry. They were noted for emphasizing learning and education within a largely illiterate society.[2] The Hanifs were therefore receptive to the Islamic message once it was announced. The idea of a single, omnipotent God was beginning to germinate in the midst of polytheistic Arabia. Muhammad, along with many of the Arabs in the Hijaz, viewed the two monotheistic faiths with admiration and respect. Yet he did not feel that the books of the Jews or the practices of the Christians were especially suited to his own people, the people of Arabia. Despite the plethora of pagan gods and goddesses in their midst, the Arab Bedouins felt that somehow they had been left out of a divine scheme. Muhammad's inquisitiveness and innate interest in spiritual matters made him absorb and internalize whatever he could learn from his contacts. These initial contacts apparently made up for his lack of formal education, because Muhammad was reported to be illiterate.

As he grew older, Muhammad spent more and more time in spiritual reflection and meditation. He felt compelled to address the deplorable state of social injustice and spiritual deprivation in Arabia. The mercantile lifestyle of Mecca allowed the wealthy tribe of Quraysh to establish hegemony in the city and to exert influence over the other tribes of the Hijaz. Quraysh was polytheistic, with hundreds of gods and goddesses (idols) that were honored in the Ka'ba in Mecca. Three hundred sixty gods were positioned around the Ka'ba.[3] These gods were accorded an array of functions ranging from the esoteric to the mundane. Gods at that time were not exalted but rather were given human characteristics. They also performed functions limited to a certain space or a given time or occasion. Some gods, in fact, were chastised for letting people down in time of need or for failing to respond to the demands of the moment. Some gods were fired, to be replaced with gods deemed more supportive. In this context the gods of pagan Arabia were much more like humans than like the Supreme Deity the Arabs would worship with the coming of Islam.

Hubal occupied center stage in the Ka'ba, the most important shrine in Mecca and in all of Arabia. A black stone, probably a meteorite, sat in one of the corners of the shrine. This black stone had been revered since the dawn of history in Arabia. The Ka'ba with its gods and godesses made Mecca a special place in ancient Arabia, a place that the Prophet would later affirm but in a diametrically different context. Tribes converged on Mecca from all over Arabia for trade, for poetry contests, and also for religious pilgrimage. Such occasions can be likened to the state fairs of modern times. During the season of pilgrimage, a truce was automatically honored among warring factions. The truce mandated suspension of all hostilities until the end of the season.

Lacking central authority or government, the tribes of Arabia lived and died by codes of behavior that were suited to the harsh life of the desert and the meager resources of nomadic life. There were a few urban settlements, the most prominent of which was Mecca, that grew and thrived on trade and services, but these were the exceptions and were ill suited for nomads, for whom confinement and manual labor were anathema. Mecca thrived primarily because it filled a vacuum in the social and economic structure of Arabia. As expected, Meccans took advantage of this position and used it as any mercantile society would have done under the prevailing circumstances. Mecca's social and economic structure was cruel and exploitative, particularly to the poor and the disenfranchised. Some of the practices regarding treatment of women in general, and newborn girls in particular, were revolting, whereby it was permissible to kill girls *(wa'd al-banat)* at birth rather than risk their being captured by potential enemies.

Muhammad was keenly aware of these and other cruel practices. He longed for reform and agonized over how to bring it about. Muhammad wanted his people to have a status like that enjoyed by people in the civilized world, with whom he had intimate interactions during his trips to Damascus. Periodically, he would go into seclusion for periods of time in the caves dotting the treeless brown mountains around Mecca. Muhammad may have been influenced in such retreats by the practices of ascetic monks whom he encountered during his many trips into the Syrian desert. There, the mainly Christian hermits contemplated the state of being alone with the Alone. Some of the Christian sects, such as the Nestorians, were considered heretic by the Orthodox Church but were able to survive in their remote outposts in the Arabian Desert. Therefore and in spite of widespread paganism in Arabia, the belief in one supreme God (Allah) was not altogether foreign. In fact, the first name of the Prophet's father was Abdullah, meaning "the servant (slave) of God."

The practice of solitary contemplation that became well established in the life of Muhammad culminated in 610 C.E. in a major event that shook Muhammad out of a trance during one of his states of deep contemplation, in a desolate cave known as the cave of Hira'.

"Recite [or read]," said a voice, waking him from his trance. Perplexed, Muhammad replied, "I cannot read." The voice repeated more forcefully, "Read," to which the dazed Muhammad gave the same reply. It was the voice of the angel Gabriel, who once again overwhelmed Muhammad with the same command. Shaken and exhausted, Muhammad asked what he could read, considering his state of illiteracy. With that, the word of God, in the form of verses, was communicated by the angel Gabriel to Muhammad:

Recite: In the Name of thy Lord who created,
created Man of a blood-clot.
Recite: And thy Lord is the Most Generous,
who taught by the Pen
taught Man that he knew not. (Qur'an 96:1)

Upon regaining his composure Muhammad left the cave and hurried home, fearing for his sanity. Finding Muhammad trembling and exhausted, his wife, Khadija, wrapped him with blankets and listened intently to his story.

"Rejoice," she said. Far from being angry, she told him that he had been chosen to be the bearer of God's message to the Arabs and indeed to all humanity. Waraqa ibn Nawfal, a Christian man of wisdom and faith who was also Khadija's uncle, reassured Khadija that her assessment was correct and that her faith in Muhammad's message was valid. The angel that appeared to Muhammad, Waraqa told Khadija, was the same one who had appeared to Moses and other prophets.[4] Encouraged, Muhammad proceeded to recite the revelations to a widening circle of followers. As expected, Islam started with only a handful of believers. In addition to Khadija, foremost among the early converts were Abu Bakr (Abdallah ibn Abi Quhafa), an old friend and respected merchant; 'Ali (Ibn Abi Talib), Muhammed's first cousin; and Zayd ibn Haritha, a slave to be freed later. Both Abu Bakr and 'Ali would play major roles in future events. The word of God was thus spoken for the first time directly to the Arabs in their own tongue and by a man from their midst.

The first few years were a period of development, as revelations continued to descend periodically on Muhammad. He would then recite them to a slowly growing body of faithful followers. The followers would commit the revelations to memory and spread the word.

The revelations were collected and written down shortly after the death of the Prophet, in a document known as the Qur'an. Within a short time (less than twenty years) after the Prophet's death, a single final edition of the Qur'an was assembled and accepted by the Muslim community. Thus the word of God was transmitted to the Arabs and to the whole world. It was quickly documented and preserved in perpetuity. Unlike previous revelations, such as those in the books of the New Testament, which were written a long time after the event, the Qur'an was recorded essentially as it was revealed. Its accuracy was verified by the Prophet himself and confirmed by the concurrence of those who had heard it for the first time from him. Although there are questions about some items that may have been omitted, either accidentally in the long process of revelation or doctrinally (such as the controversial satanic verses), the fact remains that the document we have today is as true to the original message as is humanly possible.

The Qur'an did not come all at once in a single dramatic outpouring but through a gradual and often situation-inspired sequence. The way the verses (*ayat*) were finally assembled in chapters (suras) did not follow a historical sequence, although they do address historical events and the expected human response to these events. The suras are arranged according to the number of verses each contains, starting with the longest and continuing in descending order, such that the last few suras are composed of a handful of verses.

In composition and style, the Qur'an is unlike anything ever heard by the Arabs. Its rhythmic cadence, oscillating between poetry and prose, could not have been created by a seemingly illiterate man like Muhammad. Such linguistic complexity and eloquence can be explained only by invoking supernatural forces and divine inspiration. Recitation of the Qur'an in the modulated intonation of trained readers envelops the believer in an atmosphere of peace and serenity, bestowing the feeling of safety in total submission to God and acceptance of his will. Add to this the beauty and charm of the Arabic language, with its rich repertoire of derivations, vocabulary, syntax, and grammatical nuances, and one has an idea of how exhilarating Qur'anic recitations can be. One of the best-known and most moving verses is "Al-Fatiha" (The Opening):

> In the Name of God, the Merciful, the Compassionate
> Praise belongs to God, the Lord of all Being,
> the All-merciful, the All-compassionate,
> the Master of the Day of Doom.
> Thee only we serve; to Thee alone we pray for succour.
> Guide us in the straight path,
> the path of those whom Thou hast blessed,
> not of those against whom Thou art wrathful,
> nor of those who are astray. (Qur'an 1:5)

To the Westerner, the Qur'an may appear redundant, repetitious, and somewhat less spiritual than a holy book should be. Part of the problem lies in the difficulty of translation from the Arabic language, which has a syntax that is impossible to fully represent in another tongue. The cultural specificity of the content is another factor; the real meaning of a message can only be fully appreciated in the context of the experience of the people for whom the message was sent.

We should also recognize that the Qur'an dealt with affairs of daily life and with regulatory issues that the fledgling community of Muslims (the *umma*) faced every day. These issues demanded and received immediate attention. After all, what was taking place in the midst of the tribal societies of Arabia was unprecedented in scope and substance. In that respect the Qur'an is comparable to the books of the Old Testament.

After a lapse of roughly four years, Muhammad started to publicly preach the word of God. He attracted the attention of the rebellious and the disenfranchised elements in society. He also attracted the allegiance of some members of the establishment, who pledged material and moral support. The leaders of the Quraysh initially looked the other way in neglect and derision, thinking that it was a passing fad from a neophyte who would soon be forgotten. After all, many earlier messages had disappeared in the shifting sands of Arabia. But Muhammad persisted, gaining confidence and momentum and an increasing number of converts to the new faith. As a result, the established order in Mecca (the leadership of the powerful tribe of Quraysh) began to awaken to the potential danger of this new faith, which threatened their traditional pagan beliefs and, even more, their profitable mercantilist and exploitative way of life. As the Quraysh could no longer ignore the new threat, the powerful tribe started harassing Muhammad and his followers. They were subjected to cajolery, bribery, and all sorts of inducements to abandon Islam and return to the safety of traditional practices. A small number did just that, but the majority held on. The Quraysh tried to dissuade Muhammad from his inflexible demand of total and unequivocal submission to the one and only God. They hoped for a compromise that would leave to the Meccan establishment the option to maintain the idolatrous practices of their fathers and forefathers, but to no avail. The central and supreme message of the Qur'an was a public declaration and an inner conviction that "there is no god but God and Muhammed is his messenger."

This testimony, the *shahada*, was not subject to negotiation or compromise. As a gifted diplomat Muhammad was willing to yield on many issues that did not compromise the central message. He wished no confrontation with the Quraysh—or with anyone, for that matter. But he was a man with a mission from God and he had to do what he was commanded to do regardless of the consequences.

The Quraysh were not about to capitulate, and their response was swift and merciless. Muhammad would have been eliminated had it not been for the support of men like Abu Bakr, 'Ali, and 'Uthman ibn 'Affan, a wealthy and respected old man from the Quraysh.

All three men—Abu Bakr, 'Ali, and 'Uthman—would later wear the leader-ship mantle of the Prophet and become his successors, that is, caliphs of Islam *(khulifa' al-muslimin)*. In Arabic, the term *khalifa* (caliph) refers to the one who succeeds the Prophet in the leadership of the community of believers and upholds the word of God as imparted to the Prophet Muhammad. The caliph is not a suc-cessor to the Prophet in religious terms, since divine revelations were addressed to Muhammad only and completely ceased after his death. Furthermore, Muham-mad was to be the last in the long line of prophets dating back to the Old Testa-ment—hence the title Seal of the Prophets. We should note that the office or institution of the caliphate was not formally designated by the Prophet but evolved after his death. The Prophet only recommended a process of advice and consent *(shura)* among the followers in managing the affairs of the Muslim com-munity. In fact, his precipitous death left his followers scrambling to fill the vac-uum. In their haste to nominate a successor they selected Abu Bakr as the first caliph. The transition of authority was smooth and uncontested, but the invisible seeds of discontent were already sown.

At this stage, however, Muhammad was very much alive and a source of in-creasing discomfort to the Meccan establishment. The leadership of the Quraysh struggled with how to silence Muhammad or even to get rid of him but found they could do neither without serious risks that they were unwilling to take at that point. They could and did escalate the level of harassment. Some of Muham-mad's followers had to flee town. A number of them went to Abyssinia, where they found safe haven in the land of the Christian emperor. It was an experiment to be repeated later. The Prophet, however, remained in Mecca and pursued his mis-sion as peacefully and nonbelligerently as he could, gaining more sympathy and popular support. His mission was paradoxically helped by the vociferous and out-wardly unjustified response of the Meccan establishment.

One of the most ardent opponents of Muhammad and his mission was a highly respected and feared man by the name of Omar ('Umar ibn al-Khattab). Omar was well connected by birth and by allegiance to the leaders of the Meccan establishment. A man of action, Omar had no use for the inability of the Quraysh to get rid of an impostor. Therefore, he took it upon himself to kill Muhammad and rid the Quraysh once and for all of this menace. When Omar informed one of his friends of his intentions, the friend suggested that it might be difficult to kill a man whom Omar's favorite sister believed in and whose message she willingly ac-cepted. Infuriated, Omar went to his sister's house intending to confront her with what he had just learned. As he approached his sister's house and before he had the chance to confront her, Omar heard his sister chanting verses from the

Qur'an. Unable to hold his temper, Omar burst into the house and struck his sister with his sword, intending to kill her. With her face covered with blood, she informed Omar that whatever he wanted to do would not shake her faith in God or God's messenger. Impressed by her composure Omar asked his sister to show him the verses she was chanting. After a quick glance Omar requested to borrow them for study. The next day Omar went to Muhammad, unarmed, and professed allegiance to the new faith.

The conversion of Omar was a major boost for the Islamic side, considering Omar's stature, prowess, and aristocratic birth. In some ways it may be equated with the impact of the conversion of Saul of Tarsus to Christianity, when his mission turned from enmity to submission to the new and then-heretical Jewish sect. The conversion of Omar from militant hatred to intense loyalty marked a significant milestone for the Prophet and for the message of Islam. It is said that the Prophet himself was so gratified by this event that he equated Omar's conversion to Islam with that of all the other believers up to that point. But there was a price to be paid for Omar's conversion. The Quraysh became even more vehement in their attempt to liquidate this movement before more harm was done. Muhammad tried to stay one step ahead, initiating another wave of migration to Abyssinia. This wave was larger and more important than the first and was led by 'Uthman ibn 'Affan. The purpose was to ensure continuity of the message should the messenger (the Prophet) be killed. And killed he came very close to being. Muhammad had to go into hiding and seek protection from his uncle, Abu-Talib, to buy time. The Quraysh responded by excommunicating the whole branch to which Muhammad belonged, a technicality that made him and his followers free game in Mecca.

This war of nerves continued for several years, with Muhammad hiding most of the time except during the season of pilgrimage to Mecca. Taking advantage of the customary truce, Muhammad would emerge from hiding and publicly preach his message. Back in hiding when the pilgrimage ended, Muhammad continued to organize the faithful, preach the virtues of loyalty to the faith, reinforce the message, and recite new revelations. The revelations at this time grew sterner and more pointed, demanding complete and unconditional surrender to God. Rich rewards awaited those who accepted the new faith, and swift and just retribution awaited those who professed enmity and exercised hostility. Those who chose not to become Muslims but were not belligerent were left alone. Likewise, Christians and Jews ("people of the Book") were not targeted for conversion. Furthermore, there was no attempt to convert anyone by force. The acceptance of Islam had to be based strictly on free choice and solid conviction.

Holy struggle (jihad) was not meant to force people to become Muslims. The assumption that Islam imposed itself by force on a large scale is a misconception that persists to this day. Holy struggle meant self-defense from external aggression. It also meant the relentless quest for belief in God. Swift retribution was not directed against nonbelievers if they stayed neutral, or against those who were not sympathetic, as long as they expressed their feelings by peaceful means. Rather, it was directed those who actively tried to destroy Muhammad and discredit his message, or against the apostates who reneged on their pledge.

Muhammad's primary mission was not to destroy the Quraysh but rather to proclaim a holy message that he was commanded by God to deliver. If doing so impacted the Quraysh adversely, this was a by-product he did not intend. But neither could he desist for that reason. The dilemma that the Quraysh faced was equally daunting. Muhammad's movement was by now viewed as a very serious threat to the social and economic structure of the tribe. The Quraysh, in fact, reacted as any established order would react to an emergent threat, real or perceived. And Muhammad's message definately posed a threat to the way of life and social and economic practices of ancient Arabia.

One can glean how Islamic societies viewed life before Islam in Arabia. The designation of the pre-Islamic era as the age of ignorance, the age of Jahiliyya, gives us an indication that Muslims do not and did not accord a high level of recognition to the mores and morals of Arabian societies before the advent of Islam. Although parts of Arabia had a flourishing civilization before the advent of Islam, they were not considered worthy by the emerging new order.

Resistance to a reform movement is generally proportional to the potential impact of that movement on the prevailing social structure and the magnitude of its threat to the interests of those in power. Muhammad's movement was threatening on both counts. The message was activist. It linked promise of rewards in the hereafter to actions and performance in this world. It was a message that regulated a considerable portion of people's lives on earth and related heavenly fortunes to the degree of conformity with these regulations. Thus, the establishment's hostility and rejection should not have come as a surprise. Muhammad did not expect otherwise. He gradually developed mechanisms to cope with and neutralize his opponents. This he accomplished by variations of the carrot and the stick, and by his extraordinary political and diplomatic skills. The Prophet also had the guidance of the Almighty in the form of revelations that illuminated the dark alleys of despair and clarified doubts and ambiguities.

The stress of the protracted stalemate on Muhammad and his followers was compounded by the deaths of his wife, Khadija, and his uncle Abu-Talib within a few days of each other. Muhammad left Mecca for Ta'if, a temperate and agricultural mountainous region just south of Mecca, where he had spent happy times during childhood. There he hoped he would find a warm welcome. Instead, he was jeered and practically driven out of town. Back in Mecca, Muhammad again bided his time until the season of pilgrimage, which gave him a window to get out and publicly preach his message.

It was during one of those seasons, in 620 C.E., that Muhammad met pilgrims from a settlement some two hundred miles to the north of Mecca. It was an agricultural as well as a trading town by the name of Yathrib. The name of the city was later changed to Medina (Madinat al-Rasul or al-Madina al-Munawwara). *Madina* means "city" in Arabic, and specifically "the city of the Prophet" or "the illuminated city." Yathrib was at that time inhabited by several Jewish tribes and some pagan Arab tribes, with ongoing ideological friction and economic competition over limited resources.

Muhammad's message was received eagerly by the pilgrims from Yathrib, most of whom belonged to the Khazraj tribe and were related to Muhammad on his mother's side. They promised their full support. The chance to emigrate to Yathrib came at an opportune time, as it broke the stalemate in Mecca and provided safe haven for the Prophet and the core supporters, whose lives were in real danger and whose fortunes had been largely depleted. In 622 C.E., the plan went into effect, and Muslims began making the relocation to Yathrib as inconspicuously as possible. Eventually, the Quraysh were alerted and plotted to kill Muhammad before he had the chance to join his followers. After all, Muhammad could cause more mischief from afar than if he stayed in Mecca under their watchful eye. Once again, Muhammad, with unshakable faith, was able to escape through circuitous routes, hiding in caves and changing course until he was out of harm's way.

In Yathrib, renamed Medina, there were two groups of supporters. One group was from Medina; they had invited the Prophet and his company to their city and had prepared the ground for their arrival. This group was known by the Arabic name of *al-ansar* (the supporters). The other was the group of believers who had fled Mecca and accompanied the Prophet in this emigration. These are known in Arabic as *al-muhajirun* (the emigrants). The act of emigration, known as the Hijra (or Hegira, in English), was accorded so much significance by the budding community that in that year, 622 C.E., was designated as the beginning of the Muslim calendar. An act of extraordinary significance, it marked a new phenomenon in

Arabia wherein the traditional loyalties to tribe and clan were replaced with loyalties to the believers in the message of God regardless of which tribe they came from. This allegiance cut across social and economic strata as well as family and tribal lines long held sacrosanct in Arabia. The Hijra acted as a cementing influence among members of the newly created extended family in Islam, the *umma*. The nucleus was now visible for all to see; the doors to join the *umma* were wide open. One sura in the Qur'an shows how important the Hijra was to Islam:

> And those who believe, and have emigrated
> and struggled in the way of God.
> those who have given refuge and help—
> those in truth are the believers,
> and theirs shall be forgiveness and generous provision. (8:75)

Medina, like Mecca, was a trading post on the caravan route. However, it was different in that Medina had arable land suitable for agriculture. It also had its own internal feud between its pagan Arab tribes and Jewish tribes, the largest of which were the Banu Qurayza and Banu Qainaqa'. There was another feud between the city itself and the larger and more powerful city of Mecca some two hundred miles to the south of Medina. While Muhammad's followers were a new and untested entity in the tribal perspective of the day, they held firm and formed a cohesive group. The group became more integrated as they faced the emerging challenges. And there was the resource of the timely revelations that continued to guide the hand of the Prophet and illuminate his path. Thus, in spite of the challenges and the risks the new community faced, they forged ahead with their mission, which by now had acquired a new dimension, that of governance.

At the outset, the Prophet had to attend to regulating the chores of survival and the demands of daily life. Then there was the inevitable friction between the establishment in Medina and the new and somewhat intruding alien organization. The initial welcome by some tribes and the passive tolerance by others changed to suspicion and even hostility. The Jewish tribes in particular, whose religion Muhammad greatly admired, were tolerant at the beginning, never thinking that this novice movement would grow and prevail as it did. They thought that Muhammad's movement could be used to advantage in the internal politics of Medina. Such notions quickly changed when they realized that, far from being a passing fad, Muhammad took his mission seriously and his followers were as devoted as any genuine faith-based group could be. The Jewish tribes quickly turned hostile and found natural alliance with the Quraysh.

Rejection by the Jews was especially painful to the Prophet, whose behavior toward the sons of Israel turned from endearment to chastisement. It was not the faith of the Jews that Muhammad doubted but rather what he saw as the failure of the Jewish tribes in Medina to accept the legitimacy of Islam in accordance with the predictions in their holy books. There were a few converts and supporters from the Jewish community in Medina who helped expand the Prophet's knowledge of Jewish history and religion. The majority of the Jews, however, as well as the Jewish leadership, acted otherwise. They in essence were violating the sacred trust of God's message by not believing the Prophet to whom their books alluded and who was now in their midst:

> Children of Israel, remember My blessing
> wherewith I blessed you, and fulfil My covenant
> and I shall fulfil your covenant; and have awe of Me.
> And believe in that I have sent down, confirming
> that which is with you, and be not the first
> to disbelieve in it. And sell not My signs
> for a little price; and fear you Me. (Qur'an 2:35)

References that attest to the legitimacy of previous messages and the veracity of previous messengers and biblical prophets are found in numerous places in the Qur'an. Thus, the lack of acceptance by the powerful Jewish tribes and their hostility were a source of anguish and disappointment for the Prophet. The Prophet had no choice but to organize and institute a virtual government to protect his community and propagate the message. Self-defense was absolutely essential for survival. Thus we see that Islam in Medina gradually acquired two functions, those pertaining to affairs of religion and those pertaining to affairs of state.

Unlike Christianity, which was the creed of a persecuted community for hundreds of years until it achieved worldly success, Islam depended on worldly success from inception. Jesus came into a society steeped in the art of governance for millennia in the ancient cultures of the Middle East, and into the worldly empire of Rome. In contrast Muhammad had no comparable political order. Thus he had to create a new order to be able to survive in the harsh tribal climate of ancient Arabia. One can only conjecture as to what would have been the fate of Muhammad and his message had they stayed as an underground and persecuted movement. It is doubtful that such an approach would have resulted in the survival, let alone the growth, of Islam as one of the major religions of the world. Many other religious movements before and since have disappeared without a trace. But it was

God's will for Islam to survive and for the Prophet to lay the cornerstone of a religious message that would quickly spread to the four corners of the world.

Statehood carried a different set of ideals than religion, and the Prophet had to improvise and employ great political and administrative skills to keep the two together. Throughout, the Prophet never lost sight that all the new laws and regulations must be anchored in God's revealed message. Thus, he also had the guidance of timely revelations that dealt with regulatory functions of the community. These revelations were extensive, providing codes covering a wide spectrum of human activities ranging from prayer to marriage to inheritance. They also laid out appropriate responses to conflict, allowing self-defense but strictly prohibiting aggression:

> And fight in the way of God with those
> who fight with you, but aggress not: God loves
> not the aggressors. (Qur'an 2:185)

Struggle in the cause of Islam (jihad) was legitimate, and struggle for righteousness was mandated. This and not mere conquest is the true meaning of jihad. Help to the poor and the needy, the orphans and the wayfarers, was described in some of the most tender passages in the Qur'an. Likewise, forgiveness for past transgressions is advocated when there is a genuine effort at repentance. Usury was strictly forbidden. Abstinence from alcohol and certain foods, like pork, was instituted in stages. Codes on many other matters, including marriage, divorce, inheritance, and criminal justice, were gradually revealed, usually in the context of an emerging crisis or in anticipation of one. Many of these new regulations were at variance with established customs, yet some old customs could not be totally dismantled. The Prophet deftly navigated this fine line between the new and the old while simultaneously fighting for survival and pressing on with his message. His success was creating a reality that his enemies could no longer tolerate, however. Despite Muhammad's removal from Mecca, his presence on Arabian soil was still regarded as a threat by the Quraysh. Besides, Medina was astride the trade route from Mecca to Damascus, a route that Muslims could threaten at any time.

Several battles took place between the Quraysh and the Muslim forces in Medina. Most of these battles were won by the Muslims despite overwhelming odds. The few setbacks were not fatal. In fact, they energized the Muslims and led the community to greater determination and sacrifice. Perhaps the most decisive of the battles at this time was known as the Battle of the Trench (al-Khandaq), during which Salman al-Farisi (the Persian) played a significant role. (Salman is also a central figure in Druze theosophy in the long march of humanity to the goal of Tawhid.)

For that battle the Quraysh had amassed a large army, intending to utterly destroy Islam in Medina. The vastly outnumbered defenders were hard-pressed to come up with a plan to avoid disaster. At this time Salman suggested a novel idea, imported from Persia, his native country. The plan consisted of digging a defense line in the form of a trench along the vulnerable border of Medina to create a natural barrier between the opposing forces. The trench would facilitate defense by creating an obstacle with which the attackers, accustomed to desert warfare, were not familiar. The maneuver worked perfectly well, as it discouraged the warriors of the Quraysh from mounting the customary charge of desert warfare. The trench bought the defendants time to prepare and organize.

Restlessness is the nemesis of warriors accustomed to quick attacks and lightning victories, and the morale of the attackers began to sag. The battle turned into a war of nerves for which the Muslims were far better equipped than their adversaries. Finally, a storm blew in the face of the Quraysh (and their allies from the pagan tribes of Arabia), blinding their warriors and uprooting their tents. The battle was never fought, and the whole episode was considered a form of divine intervention in support of those who were following God's commands. The Quraysh and their allies were fighting for material possessions and political hegemony, while the Muslims were fighting for the righteous cause of serving God and establishing a just and pious society.

> God
> there is no god but He, the
> Living, the Everlasting.
> Slumber seizes Him not, neither sleep;
> to Him belongs
> all that is in the heavens and the earth. (Qur'an 2:255)

The centrality of God is expressed in addressing worldly problems such as the increasing number of orphans and widows in the ranks of the Muslim community, as its men, diverted to the task of protecting the community, were being killed or wounded in battle. What would be more pleasing in the eyes of God than taking care of the needy, and those who were left without family support? We must remember that there was no safety net left for these people as the old tribal blood links were severed; new codes of behavior were needed to replace them in the Muslim community:

Give the orphans their property, and do not
exchange the corrupt for the good; and devour not
their property with your property; surely
that is a great crime.
If you fear that you will not act justly
towards the orphans, marry such women
as seems good to you, two, three, or four;
but if you fear you will not be equitable,
then only one. (Qur'an 4:3)

The importance of these and other regulatory measures challenged future generations of Muslims, especially in their ability to adapt to an ever-changing world. But that is for later. For the moment we must keep in mind that Islam as a political entity emerged from the needs of a budding community for organization, governance, and control. Such organization was a must in a harsh environment with primitive tools of governance. The flourishing and advanced neighboring civilizations, specifically those of Persia and Byzantium, had not yet been discovered by the Arabian tribes that carried the nascent banner of Islam. In Medina the world revolved around a small and closely knit group centered around the Prophet and his cumulative edifice of revelations. The strength of the message and the veracity of the messenger allowed this small group to prevail despite overwhelming odds.

Within a short period of time the Quraysh were totally demoralized and grudgingly gave up the idea of getting rid of Muhammad and destroying Islam. The hostility of the Jewish tribes was quickly neutralized through banishment or submission, and the Prophet became the de facto ruler of Medina and its environs. But his plans centered on Mecca.

The Quraysh may have failed in liquidating Muhammad and his message, but they were still far from being defeated. The powerful tribe continued to control Mecca, the major trade routes, and the annual pilgrimage to the Ka'ba, the holy shrine for all of Arabia. The momentum, however, belonged to the Muslims, and they proceeded to capitalize on the gains on the ground. Through a mixture of diplomacy, propaganda, and psychological warfare, the Prophet finally succeeded in entering Mecca peacefully, in triumph, and in establishing Islam as the dominant power in the holy city. Most members of the Quraysh either accepted Islam by conversion or were left to themselves as long as they did not challenge the authority of the Prophet or the regulations of the new Islamic state.

Success carries with it a momentum that attracts different groups of people.

Thus, in addition to those who joined Islam out of conviction and solid belief in a just and egalitarian system, there were some who were motivated by the rewards of associating with the winner. Others began to join when they recognized that tribal interests would be served best by accepting Islam and living by its rules. Still others joined for personal gain, with scant regard for ideological principles. Such diversity is inevitable in an emerging dynamic power, as Islam was at that time. The price of this rapid growth was the threat of fracture when the system faced the challenges posed by success.

Upon entry to the holy shrine, the Ka'ba, Muhammad ordered the destruction of the 360 idols that surrounded the site and publicly declared the central message of Islam: the oneness of God and submission to him. Paganism was thus eliminated from the cultural, economic, and religious life of the most important city in Arabia. Muhammad was suddenly catapulted from being a fugitive to being the leader of a dynamic religious and political movement that had no boundaries and that transcended the traditional tribal confines of the day. More conflicts were to arise with other tribes and cities in Arabia, but these posed no real threat to the new and dynamic power.

Before long, the new phenomenon in Arabia began to attract the attention of the two powerful neighboring empires, Persia to the east and Byzantium to the north and west. The leaders of both empires at first reacted to the new movement with curiosity mixed with disdain. This was followed by alarm and panic, which culminated in the destruction of the Persians almost immediately and the weakening of the Byzantines, leading to their eventual destruction. The Prophet had invited both neighbors and the governor of Egypt to submit to God and accept God's messenger. The offer was treated with reactions that ranged from contempt by the Persian rulers (of a superior civilization challenged by an uncouth transgressor from the backward tribes of the Arabian desert) to genuine admiration from the governor of Egypt. Little did the emperors know how vulnerable their realms had become, through exhaustion as well as a long record of oppressive rule and corruption. The reverse was also true. Contact with the dominant civilizations of the day exposed the early Muslim puritans to wealth and splendor they had never dreamed of and for which they were not prepared. Unnoticed during the Prophet's lifetime, the corrupting influence of wealth and power would become a problem to the Muslim *umma* soon after his death.

Having fulfilled his mission of bringing Mecca to the Islamic fold, the Prophet eventually returned to Medina. By now he was weak from years of intense struggle. The passion of the mission and the exposure to God's message during repeated states of exhausting trance had taken their toll. In 632 C.E., shortly after his return to Medina, Muhammad died, exactly ten years after his emigration from Mecca as a fugitive. He was aware that the end was near and repeatedly asked God's forgiveness. He exhorted his followers to remain resolute and follow the revelations in dealing with the difficulties to come. Whether by default or by design, the last prayer that the Prophet attended was led by Abu Bakr at the request of the Prophet. Abu Bakr, by now an old man who usually wept during recitation of the Qur'an, had been one of the earliest believers in Islam. He was also the father of 'A'isha, the youngest and most favored of the Prophet's wives. The relevance of this "who's who" in the company of the Prophet would be of critical importance in subsequent years.

By the time of his death the Prophet had laid the firm foundations of Islam as a religion addressed to all humanity. Islam rested on five major commandments, commonly known as the Five Pillars of Islam. These are:

1. *Shahada* (or *al-shahadatan*)—a declaration and belief required from every Muslim that there is no god but God and that Muhammed is his messenger;

2. *Salat*—prayer five times a day;

3. *Zakat*—payment of alms in the form of a tax for the welfare of the poor;

4. *Sawm*—abstention from food, drink, sex, smoking, and so on from sunrise to sunset during the holy month of Ramadan; and

5. *Hajj*—performance of pilgrimage to Mecca at least once in a lifetime for those who are able to do so.

Two more pillars were later added by the Shi'a. They are:

6. *Jihad*—holy struggle in the cause of God; and

7. *Walaya*—allegiance to 'Ali.

Despite multiple references to 'Ali as the Prophet's favorite friend, supporter, companion, cousin, and son-in-law, the Prophet, according to the majority of Muslims (the Sunni), did not specify in a clear and unequivocal manner that 'Ali or, for that matter, anyone else should succeed him as the caliph of Islam. The caliphate in Islam came after the death of the Prophet and evolved into a system of governance for the Muslim *umma* (state) that spread over a large area. The notion of a "state" in the Western sense did not exist in Islam.

'Ali's followers would cite numerous instances when the Prophet made remarks that clearly pointed to 'Ali as a successor. The leadership of the Muslim *umma*, however, did not interpret these as a clear and unambiguous order that specifying succession of the caliphate to 'Ali. We can only conjecture as to whether this omission was intentional or a mere oversight on the part of the

Prophet. Perhaps the age of 'Ali, in his early thirties at the time of the Prophet's death, worked against him. Choosing one of the older men among the Prophet's trusted supporters may have appeared more acceptable to a wider group of the *umma* or the closer companions of the Prophet at that time. Furthermore, the egalitarian message of Islam, with its universal appeal that cut across traditional barriers, may have stood in the way of 'Ali's succession precisely because of his close blood ties to the Prophet. All we know is that, despite his ample qualifications, 'Ali did not become the first caliph *(khalifa)* to succeed the Prophet and to wear his mantle, although he did become the fourth caliph.

The Rashidun Caliphate

Within moments of the death of the Prophet, the inner circle of his followers began to gather at a council hall in Medina to deal with the crisis. The group consisted of members who had supported the Prophet in Mecca and then accompanied him during the emigration to Medina *(al-muhajirun)*, together with those who had invited him to Medina and supported him in his mission *(al-ansar)*. Together these two groups were known as companions of the Prophet *(sahaba)*. Abu Bakr, the Prophet's old and venerable companion and father-in-law, was the first to publicly announce his death to a jittery crowd that began to mill around the place. With sword in hand Omar reportedly threatened to kill anyone who circulated or listened to rumors of the death of Muhammad. The tragedy was simply too overwhelming to bear. Yet the Prophet's death was quickly accepted following a short address by Abu Bakr.

"O men," Abu Bakr declared, "those among you who came to worship Muhammad, know ye that Muhammad is dead, and those of you who came to worship God, know that God is everlasting. . . . Muhammad is no more than a messenger. Many were the messengers who passed away before him. If he died or were slain, will ye turn back on your heels."[5] This dramatic declaration and the continuous reminders from the Prophet during his lifetime that he was merely a human being, albeit blessed by God's message, facilitated the acceptance of the death of the Prophet by Muslims. The Muslim *umma*, however, was suddenly faced with a future without Muhammad, and they were ill prepared for that.

While 'Ali—Muhammad's cousin, son-in-law, and, for many in the Islamic community, the legitimate heir to the Prophet's mantle—was performing the duty of washing the Prophet's body in preparation for burial, the process of succession was being decided, in his absence, by the inner circle of the Muslim community.

A tug-of-war was taking place between the early supporters from Mecca (*al-sahaba*) and the later converts from Medina (*al-ansar*). The issue was quickly settled when the influential Omar, raising the hand of Abu Bakr, declared his allegiance to the old and venerable man from the Quraysh. Nobody could object to this choice, and the acclamation was almost unanimous. After all, Abu Bakr was among the first men to accept Islam, the first to collect the revelations of the Prophet in the holy Qur'an and to name the holy book "al-Mishaf."[6] Moreover he was the Prophet's father-in-law. 'Ali was obviously left out, since he was not present when the decision was made. That did not sit well with some among the *sahaba*, who felt that the succession should have been handed over to 'Ali. For 'Ali himself, who presumably never actively aspired to the post, the rebuff was nonetheless painful. But 'Ali's devotion to the Prophet and his unflinching allegiance to Islam, as well as the nobility of his character, dictated that he should support the new order. This he did in fact and in deed. 'Ali's supporters followed suit and early Islam remained united. In time those who championed 'Ali's right to succeed the Prophet would evolve to become known as Shi'at 'Ali (Ali's followers) or simply the Shi'a.

Upon receiving the awesome responsibility, Abu Bakr revealed true humility and strength of character, illustrated by his brief inaugural remarks: "Verily, I have become the chief among you though not the best among you. If I do well help me; and set me right if I do wrong. You shall show faithfulness to me by telling me the truth. . . . As I obey God and His Messenger, obey me; but if I neglect the laws of God and His Messenger, then refuse me obedience."[7] Abu Bakr lived up to his promise, and for two years he presided over Islam as it expanded out of the Arabian Peninsula to become a regional power. Yet his life remained simple as he continued to earn his living selling cloth in the market of Medina. He also thwarted the efforts of a few renegade movements that surfaced after the death of the Prophet. Abu Bakr discharged his duties faithfully for two years, and then, longing to join the Prophet, he died. His wish was granted, and he was buried next to Muhammad. The devout, generous, and learned first caliph had in his brief reign proved that Islam would indeed survive the death of the Prophet and would continue to grow and prosper.

Omar succeeded Abu Bakr as caliph, presumably at the recommendation of Abu Bakr. Although 'Ali was bypassed for the second time, he dutifully endorsed Omar and bided his time. This, however, served to reinforce the allegiance of 'Ali's followers (Shi'a) to the legitimacy of 'Ali's right to the caliphate by his blood relationship to the Prophet. It is perhaps a testimony to the prestige and awe that

Omar commanded that ʿAliʾs supporters again pledged their allegiance. A great warrior and a paragon of justice, Omar lived up to his reputation in every detail. For ten glorious years Omar steered the state to greater heights and wider influence. At the same time he managed to maintain the purity of the message. He did not covet nor did he receive much love or adulation, but respect was another matter. That was to be his signpost. Friend and foe alike attested to the strictness of his judgment, first and foremost of himself and then of the custodians of the state that was entrusted to him to protect. The elitism of his character was mobilized to serve the egalitarian principles of the *umma* and the welfare of the state. Wearing dust-stained clothes and riding a camel, Omar presented a sharp contrast to the patriarch of Jerusalem, who was dressed in glittering robes when the two met. The Muslims had just conquered the city, and Omar permitted himself this, his first excursion outside Arabia.

Omar was invited to visit the Church of the Holy Sepulchre, but he wisely declined out of concern that the zealots among his men would convert the church into a mosque. He then knelt and prayed some distance from the church, and, sure enough, a mosque was built on that spot. By an ensuing treaty, Omar guaranteed security and rights of worship with no hindrance and no molestation of private or church property and religious symbols. There would be no compulsion in matters of faith. A poll tax was levied on the non-Muslim population, as a substitute for not serving in the armed forces. Some authorities consider such a tax to have been in lieu of the *zakat*, which was the duty of every Muslim to pay. Be that as it may, such acts of tolerance were rarely manifested by the victors of that day, or even in modern days.[8] The bigotry and fanaticism manifested in some communities of today are certainly not in tune with the magnanimity of the great Omar, nor do they, in fact, reflect the lofty message in the Qurʾan:

> O mankind, We have created you
> male and female, and appointed you
> races and tribes, that you may know
> one another. Surely the noblest
> among you in the sight of God is
> the most godfearing of you. God is
> All-knowing, All-aware. (49:12)

The display of tolerance by Omar was not lost on the people of the area, and it contributed to furthering the spread of Islam in all directions. Omar's caliphate lasted ten years. During his tenure the house or realm of Islam (*dar al-Islam*) grew stronger and more powerful. The realm began to take the shape of an empire, a feature that caused Omar palpable discomfort. However, despite the accumulation of wealth and power by the state, Omar maintained the pristine nature of governance as it had been in the days of the Prophet. Omar was assassinated by a Persian slave as he was on his way to the mosque for prayer. He died penniless and was buried, according to his request, at the side of the Prophet. His death marked a turning point in the history of Islam. The major figures of the early Muslims who had known and accompanied the Prophet were gradually dying off, while the realm of Islam, the *dar al-Islam*, was growing stronger and more widespread. No formal mechanism for succession was developed, and there was almost no time to consolidate in the frenzy of expansion.

The succession of 'Uthman as the third caliph was accomplished by a process of consultation *(shura)* among the few remaining key figures from the early days of Islam. 'Uthman was by now an old man of seventy years, devout and emotional, wealthy and generous, humble and obstinate, with a parochial mind that was ill equipped to handle the growing complexities of government. However, he was a faithful companion of the Prophet and twice his son-in-law. In addition 'Uthman projected a saintly presence that had provided comfort and peace to the Prophet. The selection of 'Uthman was endorsed by the Muslims, whose numbers by now were growing by leaps and bounds. The attention of the *umma* was more consumed by the events of daily life than by worries about the succession of power. But that was not the case for the hard core of Shi'a Muslims, who were extremely disappointed that 'Ali had been bypassed again and for the third time. 'Ali eventually endorsed 'Uthman and thus prevented, or rather postponed, a major rift that had been in the making since the death of the Prophet.

'Ali was too proud and too loyal to commit any act that would hurt Islam. Therefore, he did not openly challenge the selection process. In addition to his ample qualifications in terms of bravery, chivalry, and unflinching loyalty to Islam and to the Prophet, 'Ali was known for his wisdom and for his profound knowledge of and eloquence in the Arabic language. Commenting to a group of people on the selection of 'Uthman to the caliphate, 'Ali reputedly said: "You know that I am more entitled to it [the caliphate] than anyone else. By God I will relent as long as the well-being of Islam is safeguarded and as long as no Muslim is shortchanged in the process but me. And that is for the sake of earning the grace of God and his benevolence and not in competition for pomp and opulence."[9] 'Ali's noble demeanor, impeccable honesty, thrift, and incorruptible attachment to strict accountability stood in sharp contrast to the looser, more freewheeling style of 'Uthman. In addition, 'Uthman was weak as far his own family members were concerned, a feature of which his large and influential family took full advantage. Because of his impotence in governing, his reluctance to institute strict rule, and his resistance to advice, 'Uthman quickly became a target for criticism and even derision. The Umayyads, the powerful and rich Quraysh family to which 'Uthman belonged, were not particularly noted for their loyalty to Islam. Quite the contrary, in fact: they were latecomers who had switched allegiance and joined the winning side (Islam) more out of self-interest than piety. Yet 'Uthman appointed or promoted several members of the Umayyads to positions of power and influence. And they seemed to have his own undivided attention.[10]

Protesting voices were ignored and genuine advice was shunned by the elderly caliph as the gathering storm swirled around this once kindly figure who was unwittingly destroying the popular consensus of his caliphate. Inherent in the nascent Islamic tradition was support for the leader (caliph), but only if and when the leadership was based on justice and piety. 'Uthman's reign was being steadily undermined and his popular support eroded by his inability or unwillingness to act decisively. The *umma* could not help but compare the sorry state of affairs during his reign with that existing under his two esteemed predecessors, or for that matter with the esteem in which 'Ali was held.

As the opposition grew and became more visible and more vocal, the possibility of violence loomed on the horizon. Many of the senior members of the *umma* became alarmed and decided to ask 'Ali to confront 'Uthman with the reality of the situation. In a prophetic statement 'Ali cautioned 'Uthman not to become the first imam to open the door to internecine killing and warfare within the Muslim community. 'Uthman responded with an equally blunt message during the Friday sermon, rejecting the claims of his critics and threatening retribution. The stage was set, and there was no compromise. Expecting trouble, 'Uthman appealed for help from his appointees and relatives throughout his far-flung empire. One powerful relative was the governor of Syria, seated in Damascus, a brilliant and astute opportunist from the Umayyad clan by the name of Mu'awiya ibn Abi Sufyan. It is ironic that Mu'awiya—and indeed the Umayyad branch of the Quraysh—had been sworn enemies of the Prophet until the final and decisive victory of Islam forced them to enroll under its banner. Mu'awiya threatened dire consequences should any harm befall the caliph 'Uthman. Some members of the Umayyad family stood vigil around 'Uthman, but it was too late. The rebellion was now in full swing. 'Uthman's assassination marked the beginning of a divisive chapter in Islam, a chapter whose reverberations persist to this day. 'Uthman reigned for about ten years.

The slain caliph's successor was 'Ali, representing the fourth in line among the immediate associates of the Prophet. The first four caliphs to succeed the Prophet are collectively known as the *rashidun,* meaning roughly those on the righteous path. 'Ali's succession, however, was marked by misfortune even before his reign began. Several factors converged that led ultimately to the tragic end and schismatic sequel of 'Ali's tenure in office.

First was the cry for retribution from the killers of 'Uthman and the implicit accusation against 'Ali, his sons, and his supporters and allies in the tragedy. Such accusations were trumpeted primarily by 'Uthman's cousin Mu'awiya, the Umayyad governor of Syria. He and his followers paraded what was to become known as the blood-stained shirt of 'Uthman *(qamis 'Uthman)* as a symbol of resistance to the reign of 'Ali. They demanded that the assassins be delivered to them or subjected to swift retribution. 'Ali could not meet these terms without proper inquiry and due process. Even then, the rebellious crowd who killed 'Uthman were considered by many not as murderous thugs but as angry reformers who were removing from office a ruler who had gone astray. 'Ali was confronted with a tragic dilemma: whichever decision he made would split the community in half.[11] 'Ali temporized, and Mu'awiya, supported by the then governor of Egypt, 'Amr ibn al-'As, kept up the pressure. This strategy by Mu'awiya steadily undermined the authority and prestige of the new caliph. Ultimately Mu'awiya called for open rebellion against 'Ali's caliphate, accusing him of aiding and abetting 'Uthman's assassins, if not by direct participation, then by vocal criticism of the slain caliph. Never mind that 'Ali's sons were guarding the premises when 'Uthman was slain and that 'Ali punished them for being overwhelmed by the rebels. The picture that Mu'awiya and his followers painted of 'Ali was as one who had conspired to sabotage the legitimate rule of law through complicity in the assassination of the caliph of Islam. And they declared that 'Ali had to be held accountable for his implicit intentions and alleged contribution to the atmosphere of hate and suspicion that culminated in the crime against the caliph of Islam.

Mu'awiya was in fact playing the very role he accused 'Ali of playing, with the tables turned. Subsequent events showed that the resourceful Mu'awiya had in mind other goals besides serving justice. But he was a patient practitioner of political maneuvers, a master strategist, and a genius at exploiting controversial opportunities. The irony is that 'Ali was keenly aware of Mu'awiya's ulterior motives but could not match his rival's methods nor control the rules of the conflict that kept exploding in his face. 'Ali had watched with anguish how the house of Islam had veered from its pristine origin to an era of material extravagance and moral decay. He did not himself covet power, for he possessed an innate disregard for things material and genuine contempt for worldly possessions. On the other hand, he could not shirk the responsibility to rescue what was most important to him when duty called. He therefore stepped into the caliphate in the spirit of holy jihad to answer the command of duty and to return the state of Islam to the right path. Whether he could have succeeded had he been given a fair chance when his turn came to assume power is a debatable point. In a sense 'Ali was trying to roll back time at a moment when events had gone too far to reverse. Abu Bakr was more fortunate, governing the first two years after the death of the Prophet when Islam was still a minor player among regional powers. Omar reigned for ten years but was able to maintain control by the strength of his personality and the momentum of puritanical memory. Omar did in fact worry about the perils of growing power but did not live to see them. The combination of the weakness of 'Uthman and the growing wealth and size of the state of Islam inevitably created political corruption and moral permissiveness. 'Ali thus stepped into the fray at the wrong time and with the wrong tools to deal with the realpolitik of the day. It is no wonder that he failed at governing and succeeded at martyrdom.

'Ali was respected and feared but not universally liked. By the time he came to power, almost twenty-two years after the death of the Prophet, Islam was already a house divided. Some agreed with 'Ali that Islam should return to its initial message of purity and piety. These individuals were disappointed that 'Ali did not pursue that goal with the speed and resolve they expected of him. At the other extreme was a growing class of influential Muslims who had acquired a taste for luxury and splendor and whom 'Ali's opponents cultivated with material temptation and political influence. In fact the jinni was out of the bottle and nobody could bring it back in. The realities on the ground had outpaced the relatively stationary 'Ali, who was unwilling and evidently unable to accommodate to such massive changes. He was the right man but at the wrong time, just about twenty years too late. 'Ali had also changed physically, losing the agility and strength of his youthful days. At fifty-six and with premonitions of misfortune, he came to power beyond his prime saddled with events he could neither control nor wish away. He could not, however, avoid or shirk his devotion to Islam and the responsibility of the caliphate with which he was entrusted. Thus he proceeded in the best way he could under the circumstances.

'Ali knew that the insurrection of Mu'awiya had to be crushed before it dragged on any further. Not to deal with the crisis expeditiously would undermine his authority as the caliph of Islam. Against advice from trusted friends and his own family, 'Ali decided to leave Medina and move his capital to Kufa in Iraq.

Kufa was more cosmopolitan than the provincial Medina, and the people of Iraq were more inclined to support 'Ali than were the resurgent Quraysh in Mecca and Medina. The Ummayad branch, more powerful and more mercantile than the Hashim branch, received fresh impetus to oppose 'Ali from their favorite son, Mu'awiya. From Iraq, 'Ali planned to bring the conflict to a peaceful conclusion. Should that approach fail, 'Ali was committed to a military confrontation with the mercurial Mu'awiya.

Alas for 'Ali: another powerful voice in the *umma* had joined the chorus demanding retribution for 'Uthman's death. The voice was that of none other than 'A'isha, the youngest and most influential of the Prophet's wives. 'A'isha had harbored a personal antipathy toward 'Ali for some time. That 'Uthman's slaying provided 'A'isha with the chance to exact revenge from 'Ali is ironic since she had frequently criticized 'Uthman. Yet she joined the chorus for revenge mainly, and perhaps only, because the chorus of opposition targeted 'Ali. Initially 'Ali tried to downplay this unpleasant and somewhat embarrassing situation. However, 'Ali's hand was forced when 'A'isha, along with other ambitious figures in the community (each with a private agenda) effectively declared war on him. 'Ali's efforts at peacemaking failed and war broke out near Basra in southern Iraq.

This was no mere skirmish but a full-fledged, large-scale battle involving, according to some sources, thousands of combatants on both sides. By the end of the day 'A'isha had been defeated and was sent back to Medina under safe protection. There she lived to regret what had happened, but the damage was done. The widow of the Prophet waging a bloody war against the Prophet's cousin, son-in-law, devoted follower, and now the ruling caliph of Islam was a tragedy that was hardly believable. The fact that it did happen was an indication of the deep rift that had penetrated Islam, and the schism that would last to the present day. For now, however, 'Ali had prevailed and Iraq was pacified. There remained Mu'awiya, the head of the insurrection in Damascus. 'Ali moved with dispatch to finish the task of crushing the insurrection that had threatened the very existence of Islam. Intensive negotiations did not break the impasse, and once again Islam was plunged into civil war.

This war was more protracted and more complicated than the war with 'A'isha. Eventually the tide of battle seemed to be running in 'Ali's favor, but his victory was foiled by a ruse that prevented a decisive blow against Mu'awiya. Briefly, the ruse involved a truce and an agreement to resort to some sort of arbitration. 'Ali sensed a trap, but he could not impose his decision to continue the fight when an offer for peace was on the table. Nevertheless, his premonition was correct; in the end, arbitration worked against him through deceptive technicalities employed by his opponent. The result was confusion and desertion from 'Ali's ranks and a virtual victory for Mu'awiya. The attempt to recoup was harder than 'Ali had envisioned, and this added to his bitterness and pessimism about human nature and life in general. Mu'awiya eventually declared himself caliph, and 'Ali could do nothing about it. Finally, 'Ali was assassinated by a member of a group of dissidents (al-Khawarij) who wanted to rid Islam of 'Ali, Mu'awiya, and Mu'awiya's main accomplice and advocate, 'Amr ibn al-'As. When the group's attempts to assassinate the other two failed, 'Ali's death left Mu'awiya unchallenged and Mu'awiya's caliphate an accomplished reality. Acceptance was another matter. Islam now was heading toward an irrevocable schism.

Under Mu'awiya the caliphate became a hereditary institution. The Umayyad dynasty, as it came to be known, was more like the empires of the day. It stood in sharp contrast to the preceding era, when the caliphate was decided by a serendipitous method of consultation and consensus. Mu'awiya shifted the emphasis from a state that would serve Islam to an Islam that would promote and serve a worldly empire, with an Arab aristocracy at the helm. The empire expanded in all directions and brought untold wealth and opulence. It also promoted a cosmopolitan civilization along with corruption, greed, and intrigue.

Although they had secured the reins of power in Damascus, Mu'awiya and his successors could not ignore the lingering threat from 'Ali's two sons by Fatima, al-Hasan and al-Husayn, and from a core group of Shi'a devotees whose allegiance to 'Ali and his seed grew in intensity with every misfortune that befell them.

Shi'a Muslims adhered to the belief that the caliphate should have been exclusively reserved for the house of the Prophet (ahl-al-bayt). These were 'Ali and his progeny by Fatima, his wife (and the daughter of the Prophet), since they were the only surviving seed of the Prophet. The Shi'a therefore considered that 'Ali should have succeeded the Prophet Muhammad directly and the lineage maintained ad infinitum. They had regarded the passage of the caliphate to Abu Bakr, bypassing 'Ali, as an unfortunate usurpation but they had tolerated it out of respect for Abu Bakr's age, piety, and closeness to the Prophet. They had likewise endured the caliphate of Omar because of the firmness and justice that were hallmarks of Omar's reign. When the caliphate was entrusted to 'Uthman, the Shi'a were deeply upset and probably would have caused trouble had it not been for 'Ali himself, who pledged loyalty to the prevailing order. It was only when that prevailing order abandoned the spirit of the mission for which it existed that the revolt broke out and 'Uthman was assassinated.

The caliphate that ʿAli finally inherited was far more complicated than had existed in the days of early Islam. ʿAli would have been eminently suited to lead Islam in the simpler early days, but ʿAli was an idealist, and idealists are ill equipped to govern. Their forte lies in awakening the conscience and stirring the emotions and in championing the cause of truth, beauty, and justice, but not in the art of governing. The strength of the idealist does not lie in implementing policies, tolerating intrigue, or accepting compromise. That is the role of the pragmatist. ʿAli was by no means a pragmatist, and he knew it. Hence his sense of foreboding when finally the caliphate came to him.

Idealists present their followers with the prospect of disappointment in success and guilt in failure. ʿAli's followers suffered from both. The guilt for letting ʿAli down in the hour of need was compounded at a later date with the tragic events of his son, al-Husayn, in the infamous battle of Karbala. For now ʿAli was dead and buried in Najaf in Iraq. Some of his followers retreated to Medina to re-assess the enormity of what had befallen them. Muʾawiya had gained control of the realm, but ʿAli had gained the accolade of martyrdom. Thus, in death, ʿAli had achieved an exalted position in Islam that he could not have attained during life. His progeny, despite all the persecution that they were to endure, would be elevated to even higher positions. To some in the Islamic community, ʿAli's progeny by Fatima would in time attain a stature closer to divinity than humanity. Such is the case when colossal events create in violent death the living symbol that grows with time.

ʿAli's death marked the end of the line of successors to the Prophet known as the *rashidun* caliphs. By now most of the companions of the Prophet had died or grown old and were no longer a factor in the political equation of Islam. In the Muslim collective conscience this era is especially revered as the time when Islam was at its best. While this contention may be true in that Islam had not yet entered into its dynastic phases and had retained a certain consultative process in choosing the caliph, it was not an era of peace and harmony. Only the first out of four successors to the Prophet died of natural causes. One was murdered by a disgruntled Persian slave, while the second and third, more poignantly, were assassinated in the context of political turmoil. During the reign of the last one, ʿAli, full-fledged civil war broke out, first between ʿAli and ʿAʾisha, the young and influential widow of the Prophet, and then between ʿAli and Muʾawiya. The trend toward conflict is clearly seen in the escalation of violence with each succeeding caliphate. Thus to claim that the era of the four original caliphs was pure and pristine is to stretch the imagination. Nevertheless, the era perhaps deserves to be idealized in light of future developments, particularly the establishment of hereditary dynasties. With

Mu'awiya, the baton may have passed to the wrong hands, as the era of Umayyad rule became established, but pass it did.

Mu'awiya wasted no time in expanding and organizing Islamic rule. Islam by now had grown into one of the major powers of the day. However, even though Mu'awiya's conquests were legendary, he was unable either to extinguish the memories of 'Ali or to control the growing myth surrounding the martyrdom of the great imam. Although not fully realized at the time, Islam the worldly power no longer marched in full harmony with Islam the religious message. One ultimately had to become subservient to the other as it became virtually impossible to reconcile the realities of imperial expansion with the spiritual message that had ignited such expansion. 'Ali's attempt to return Islam to the purity of the message succumbed to the more powerful forces that were pulling Islam in the other direction. Although he possessed considerable political skills and determination to match, 'Ali could not assume the role of a pragmatic head of state, if that role was to be realized at the expense of the essence of Islam. But Mu'awiya could and did. The irony is that 'Ali was aware of the dilemma he faced and the virtual impossibility of success as he defined it. Yet he persevered and gave it his best. Martyrdom was a fitting finale for 'Ali's dedication to his faith and for the nobility of his character.

3 Dynastic Islam

UNTIL THE DEATH OF ʿALI, transfer of power in Islam had been accomplished by a process of consultation leading to consensus (shura) largely reserved to the senior members of the Muslim umma, many of whom had been close companions of the Prophet. As time went on, however, conditions changed, with the old guard dying off or aging to the point of marginality. With that Islam lost its own version of democracy (succession by consensus), and for good. Instead, Islam adopted the dynastic practices of the day and continued the momentum of empire building for more than five hundred years. However, the empire could not be maintained for long as one state stretching from the Atlantic to the Indian Oceans. Different dynasties would appear and disappear in the vast realm of Islam, presiding over different sections as historical events played out. In any event, governance from now on would be patterned along hereditary lines instead of consensus and consultation.

The Umayyads and the Abbasids

The first dynasty, the Umayyads, centered in Damascus, started with Muʾawiya in 661 C.E. and ended with Marwan II (ibn Muhammad) in 750 C.E. The second dynasty, the Abbasids, centered in Baghdad, started with Abu al-ʿAbbas Abdallah, known as al-Saffah (the one who sheds blood), in 750 C.E. and ended in 1258 C.E. when the Mongol invader Hulagu captured Baghdad and razed it. Although some of the caliphs in both dynasties were competent and effective rulers (particularly in the early stages of the caliphates), this was not always the case. The early zeal of the founders invariably gave way to the decadence of easy inheritance. Incompetent caliphs set the stage for palace intrigue and for insubordination of authority and usurpation of power. Nonetheless the Islamic realm continued to expand, bringing untold wealth to the elite and to those who ingratiated themselves with the ruling class. And there were always the sycophants and opportunists who cur-

41

ried the favor of whoever was in power. During the Umayyad rule Damascus became the capital of one of the most powerful empires that the world had known up to that time.

The Umayyads brought on their own downfall by failing to realize the magnitude of the social changes they themselves had brought about by their success in empire building. They ruled as an Arab aristocracy over a dominion in which the Arabs had become a minority. Large-scale demographic changes are hard to deal with in modern times. In antiquity the task was even more prohibitive; and so it was for the Umayyads. The distance between the rulers and their subjects, the diversity of their subjects, and disparities between different groups quickly grew to the extent that they could no longer be bridged. Not surprisingly, open rebellion broke out, starting in Persia and spreading to engulf the entire realm. Damascus succumbed to the Abbasids, and the Umayyads were virtually exterminated after a rule that had lasted roughly ninety years.

One of the Umayyads, a man by the name of 'Abd-al-Rahman, survived and eluded the Abbasids by escaping all the way to Andalusia, the western province of the Umayyad Empire at that time (and the southern province in modern-day Spain). 'Abd-al-Rahman rallied enough support among the Berber and Arab tribes in North Africa to split Andalusia from the Abbasids and establish an independent kingdom. That kingdom lasted for almost six hundred years. Although the Andalusian caliphate lost its Umayyad character in time, it produced a flourishing civilization that competed with and, in many instances, outshone even that of Damascus and Baghdad.

The Abbasid insurrection against the Umayyads was launched ostensibly to redress the wrong that befell the house of 'Ali at the hands of the Umayyad usurpers (*Abbasid* derives from 'Abbas, one of the paternal uncles of 'Ali). Rather than redressing wrongs, though, the Abbasids monopolized power in their own progeny and continued the policy of the Umayyads in persecuting 'Ali's progeny and their supporters. In fact, the Abbasids intensified the policy of persecution and harassment of 'Ali's progeny to such an extent that one of the poets was inspired to write a line made famous over the years: "By God, what the Umayyads did unto you ['Ali's progeny] / was less than one-tenth of what the Abbasids were doing."

In sum and substance both the Umayyad and the Abbasid rules were rife with hostility and persecution for the progeny of 'Ali. The majority of the Muslims were by now Sunni, generally orthodox in their views and supportive of the ruling caliphate. The Sunni either ignored or tolerated the persecution of 'Ali's progeny by the government of the day. Although the Sunnis revered ʿAli as the Prophet's cousin and son-in-law and as one of the *rashidun* caliphs, they did not support the idea that his progeny were entitled to the imamate or the caliphate by simple right of birth. Some of the Sunni in fact harbored resentment and hostility to ʿAli and his progeny. This contributed to a widening of the rift in the Islamic community between the Sunni majority and the Shiʾa minority. Since the Druze emerged from one of the major branches of the Shiʾa, the Ismaʿili branch, our story will focus mainly on the events pertaining to that sect.

Shiʾa Islam from al-Husayn to Ismaʿil

Dazed by the death of ʿAli, his followers quickly had to regroup and deal with the aftermath of this tragic loss. They could not accept the caliphate of Muʾawiya, with whom they had been at war and whom they reviled as the enemy of God and of God's prophet. In short order, al-Hasan, ʿAli's elder son, was pronounced caliph, and he along with his dwindling retinue returned to Medina to take stock of what had happened and to plan the next step. Al-Hasan was fun loving and rather apolitical. Perhaps he was more of a realist than he was given credit for since he recognized that as far as the caliphate was concerned, the game was up for the house of ʿAli. Making peace with Muʾawiya, al-Hasan abdicated his title and endorsed the caliphate of Muʾawiya, on condition that the post not be hereditary. The agreement stipulated that the process of selection by consensus would be resumed upon the death of Muʾawiya. Some sources claim that there were financial and other enticements to sweeten the deal between the two men. In any event, Muʾawiya could easily dispense with money but had no intention of honoring the other commitments.

Within a few years al-Hasan died (some believed that he was poisoned) in relative obscurity. Naturally, Muʾawiya was accused of poisoning the son of ʿAli, and a legend of another martyr was born. However, as long as Muʾawiya was alive he kept a firm but resilient hand at the helm. His enormous gifts included not only intrigue and ambition but also tact, diplomacy, and a certain measure of respect for his enemies. His son and successor, Yazid, did not possess any of his father's qualities; he was arrogant and spoiled, and had little taste for sound advice. Upon assuming authority of the caliphate he demanded allegiance from al-Husayn, the younger and more gifted brother of al-Hasan. While al-Hasan was easygoing and lightweight, al-Husayn was cut from a different cloth. Al-Husayn was more like his father ʿAli, in character and in determination. He would not endorse the caliphate that had been usurped by a devious father, Mu'awiya, and bequeathed to a corrupt and incompetent son, Yazid, in flagrant violation of the accepted traditions in Islam.

Al-Husayn's posture provided the Shi'a with the needed rallying point for opposition to the caliphate of Mu'awiya and the passage of the caliphate to his son Yazid. A movement was begun to install al-Husayn as the legitimate caliph of Islam in Kufa, Iraq, where 'Ali had been assassinated and where his elder son al-Hasan had been declared caliph. In the eyes of the Shi'a, this would restore the caliphate to where it belonged (the house of 'Ali) and would repair the damage inflicted by Mu'awiya and the emerging Umayyad dynasty. Pointedly, such a move would pacify the conscience of the Shi'a, particularly in Iraq. The guilt of the Iraqis at having forsaken 'Ali in his hour of need was compounded by the harsh treatment that befell them at the hands of Mu'awiya, with more to come at the hands of Mu'awiya's son, Yazid. This guilt complex grew under subsequent events and became an all-consuming feature in the collective conscience of the Shi'a community. It also contributed to a growing belief of attributing to 'Ali and his progeny an exalted status of infallibility and holiness that no one else could aspire to. At this early stage, however, their vision was more limited and their aim was twofold, to redress a wrongful act with respect to the house of 'Ali and to get rid of Umayyad rule. Their plight was made worse by the agents of the Damascus rulers who responded to the mounting unhappiness of the Shi'a in Iraq by merciless repression and cruel retribution. The Shi'a, therefore, once more turned to al-Husayn and launched a campaign to convince him to come to Iraq and accept the endorsement of his followers and his claim to the caliphate.

Al-Husayn weighed his options and decided to accept the invitation, despite advice to the contrary from family and friends. The decision, in fact, was against al-Husayn's better judgment. Even though he learned that the promised support was thin and unreliable, he refused to change course and turn back. It was as though al-Husayn was knowingly pursuing a sacred mission regardless of safety considerations or realistic hopes of success. After all, death in the cause of fighting tyranny and corruption was preferable to living under such conditions and implicitly accepting their legitimacy.[1] Such a situation ran against every grain in al-Husayn's character, and he had to seize the moment. Furthermore, he had already given his word to go to Iraq, and he could not renege on his word. If his supporters did not keep their part of the bargain, then it would be they who would bear the consequences. In addition, al-Husayn was a marked man after refusing to endorse the caliphate of Yazid. Al-Husayn left Medina for Mecca in an effort to evade Yazid's agents, who were watching his every move, and the hired assassins who were shadowing him.

A short distance before reaching his objective in Kufa, a famous poet of the era by the name of al-Farazdaq caught up with al-Husayn and implored him not to walk into the trap. It was to no avail. The irony was that al-Farazdaq was the premier poet of the Umayyad era but his sentiments were openly with ʿAli and his progeny. "Go back," al-Farazdaq implored al-Husayn, indicating that the people of Iraq were emotionally with him but their weapons and self-interest were with Yazid. Of course, al-Husayn did not heed the advise and continued on to assured destruction.

Yazid's army caught up with al-Husayn a short distance from the Euphrates River, in a desolate plain with the depressing name of Karbala, literally "sadness and disaster." The balance of power was absurd. Four to five thousand armed men had orders to kill al-Husayn and liquidate his army, which numbered no more than seventy. Additionally, al-Husayn had brought along his family, including women and children. After all, he did not come to do battle but to lead and participate in restoring the moral and religious underpinning of the caliphate in Islam. He was the one most qualified to do just that. If he succeeded he would fulfill his mission in this life, and if he failed his place was assured in the hereafter. There was a thin chance that he could succeed, but as a realist he knew that the odds weighed heavily against him.

Prevented from reaching water that was within sight, al-Husayn pleaded with Yazid's army to honor a tradition of never withholding water even from an enemy, but to no avail. He then appealed to the religious sentiments of the opposing forces, reminding them that he was the grandson of the Prophet and that he stood for all that was just and pious in the Islamic tradition. Yazid's army was not in the mood for such sentimentality, although many in Yazid's army were covertly sympathetic to al-Husayn and would have defected to his side if they could. Islam under the worldly oriented and powerful rulers in Damascus had become sharply different from what it was meant to be in the days of the Prophet. The clock could not be turned back. It was indeed amazing that such change could take place within the lifetime of many witnesses to this drama. Al-Husayn was not only denied water but was ordered to dismount and grovel to the Umayyad governor in Kufa, who might then, and at his discretion, consider sparing al-Husayn's life. Al-Husayn recognized that this was the end, which he calmly accepted with characteristic dignity and poise. By the time the battle was over al-Husayn and all his men were slain. Of the survivors were al-Husayn's sister, Zaynab, a remarkable woman, and a sickly child by the name of 'Ali Zayn al-'Abidin. He would live to carry the seed of 'Ali to future generations. More than three hundred years later one of al-Husayn's progeny (al-Hakim bi Amr Allah) would become the imam and caliph of the Fatimid Empire and the lightening rod of the Druze concept in Tawhid.

The Prophet died in 632 C.E., and al-Husayn was killed less than fifty years later, in 680 C.E., a date that is deeply ingrained in the Shi'a collective conscience. Karbala was a major tragedy, immortalized by the death of al-Husayn. In that one battle six half-brothers of al-Husayn were also killed, along with two of Husayn's children and three of al-Hasan's children. Thus one grandson and five great-grandchildren of the Prophet were slain in one day in the desolate plains of Karbala.[2] During this period we have seen how the soft and almost imperceptible beginning of the Shi'a movement following the death of the Prophet, when 'Ali was bypassed for the caliphate, grew in intensity with each succeeding generation until it culminated at Karbala.

For Islam, the tragedy of Karbala created an irrevocable divide. Karbala sealed the separation of the Shi'a, whose loyalty to the house of 'Ali had become central to their faith and indeed existence, from the rest of the Muslims (Sunnis) whose allegiance to the state took precedence over whatever misgivings they may have felt at transgressions of justice toward Ali and his children. The Sunnis also included a sizable number whose tribal allegiance to the Umayyads was expressed in terms of gut hatred of 'Ali and his progeny, as well as those who always cast their lot with the winning side, selling their allegiance to the highest bidder in return for influence and wealth. Karbala, therefore, represented a great divide between the dictates of conscience and the expediency of self-interest.

It could be debated that al-Husayn would have failed in any event, just as his father had before him. Like his father, al-Husayn was an idealist who failed to grasp or come to grips with the magnitude of change that had befallen the Islamic state within his lifetime. Al-Husayn's motives in challenging the Umayyad rule were not based on personal ambitions of governance but on reform of a governance gone astray when it was cut loose from its religious and moral underpinnings. His was a struggle (jihad) that appealed to the conscience but could not be sustained on the grounds of reality.

Shi'ism began politically with the rumblings of discontent when 'Ali was bypassed as the legitimate heir to the caliphate immediately following the death of the Prophet. It was 'Ali's destiny to bear the collective guilt of Islam and to die in martyrdom. His death did not expunge the sins of Muslims, as the crucifixion of

Jesus did for the Christians. Instead, it set the stage for further acts in the drama of tragic sacrifice. In anger laced with guilt, the Shi'a clung to the model of self-righteousness embodied in 'Ali and his progeny, a model that was as close to their hearts as it was far from practicality in daily life. Nonetheless, the myth of 'Ali grew steadily after his death, propelled by the corruption of power in everyday life that 'Ali vehemently opposed and that eventually claimed his life.

A brief respite was provided when 'Ali's elder son, al-Hasan, abdicated in favor of Mu'awiya by dropping his claim to the caliphate. This act of pragmatism did not diminish the exaltation of the memory of 'Ali, the tragedy that befell him, and the moral rectitude that he stood for. The seething dreams of the Shi'a were soon rekindled by the death of al-Hasan and, after the death of Mu'awiya, by the passage of the caliphate to his corrupt son Yazid. The Shi'a found a window of opportunity in al-Husayn, and they proceeded in a last-ditch effort to write the telling chapter in martyrdom and guilt—in the desolate plains of Karbala.[3]

If 'Ali's denial of the caliphate was the beginning of an ordained moral tragedy and sacrifice, al-Husayn's martyrdom at Karbala closed the ring with a paradoxical triumph that was internalized in direct proportion to the pain that it imparted. The Shi'a had lost the caliphate but somehow that no longer mattered. After all, the caliphate was a phenomenon of statehood and earthly government, the loss of which is measured in temporal terms in this life. The Shi'a found solace in clinging to the essence of Islam: submission to a merciful and compassionate God and acceptance of his will. The secular authorities could never deny or control a system of beliefs that was increasingly internalized and spiritually consecrated in the collective conscience of the Shi'a community. Retreat from politics was no longer as painful as it had seemed before, for no matter how long it took, justice would be served in the end. The imams were no longer a lightning rod for worldly politics. Instead, they were gradually accorded an exalted position of moral infallibility and divine blessings. This aura of holiness eventually caused some individuals and groups to push the envelope to the very edge of identification with the Divine. For now, however, Islam had finally bifurcated, splitting the common trunk into two main branches. Evolutionary laws would cause further branches to split along the way. The Shi'a lived for and dreamed of the day when justice (*'adl*) would assuredly prevail, when all wrongs that befell the community would be redressed. They waited for the expected day of redemption.

The concept of redemption worked itself slowly but surely into the Shi'a psyche and in time became part of the religious repertoire of the community. Redemption required an awaited redeemer to come at a time ordained by God and empowered by divine guidance. The expectant wait would eventually be re-warded no matter how long it took. For the Shi'a, keeping the faith was bolstered by yearly observance (Yawm 'Ashura') of—what else—the tragedy of Karbala. The observance became an enactment that allowed the Shi'a to experience the actual pain of Karbala on that fateful day when al-Husayn and his retinue were slaugh-tered. That sobering occasion and its impact on daily life became a defining mo-ment in the shaping of Shi'a identity. Analogy can be drawn with the Christian practice of reenactment of the crucifixion during Easter. The defeat at Karbala re-sulted in virtual withdrawal of the Shi'a from political aspirations and from the material temptations of worldly existence. Compensation of bliss in another world of justice and fairness awaited those who believed that a redeemer, in the person of an infallible *(ma'asum)* imam from the house of 'Ali would return, as Christians await the second coming of the Messiah. This central theme is at the core of religious developments and events that led to the emergence of the Druze concept of Tawhid.

Events that forced the Shi'a to give up the struggle for the caliphate in the house of 'Ali for the foreseeable future paradoxically strengthened their involve-ment in the religious and social aspects of Islam. Their desire to explore the deeper meaning of the heavenly message was amplified and deepened by the suc-cessive waves of escalating tragedies. They regarded their lack of success as a mere prelude to the delayed gratification reserved for those who struggled on the path of righteousness to implement the essence of God's message. The essence of God's message is not limited by the confines of literal and extrinsic meaning of the word of God in the Qur'an; the essence is encoded in subtle interpretations and inner symbolic secrets of the divine revelations. Seeking the hidden (and original) meaning became the preoccupation of the Shi'a religious order. At the head of this order stood the imams, starting with the scion 'Ali and cascading down through his progeny in a sanctified succession of luminaries who were blessed with divine guidance. Eventually the imamate would pass from father to son (usu-ally the eldest son) by written designation *(nass)*.

The schism in Islam gradually became defined along two planes; the political plane of governance and statehood, and the religious plane, including the overt as well as the covert interpretations of the Islamic message. The Sunni *(ahl al-sunna wa al-jama'a)* generally accepted the literal interpretation of God's word (Qur'an), the sayings of the Prophet (Hadith), and the tradition of the Prophet based on the way he lived and conducted the affairs of Islam. The Sunni, being a majority, were loyalists to the caliphate and to the security and protection of the Islamic state. If the caliph happened to be pious and virtuous, so much the better, but if he were the opposite, as was the case in most instances, so be it. That would be God's will, and only God will be in judgment when the time comes. The duty of the Muslim was to bear the burden, watch his own behavior, and refrain from undermining the state. Rebellion could not be easily justified on the basis of corruption of the caliph and cruelty in governance, if the rebellion threatened the collective security of the *umma*. Likewise, the message in the Qur'an was clear and unambiguous and it meant exactly what it said. The word must be taken at face value as it was transmitted from God to the Prophet through a process that can be described by the Arabic word *tanzil* (accepting the word of God in the Qur'an verbatim):

> And We have sent down on thee the Book
> making clear everything, and as a guidance
> and a mercy, and as good tidings to
> those who surrender. (16–90)

For the Sunni, as adherents of *tanzil*, the process was born complete, and there was little room for modification. Interpretation of the literal message *(ijtihad)* would be within a narrow latitude. Ultimately, four schools of jurisprudence *(fiqh)* emerged in the Sunni tradition: Hanafi, in 767 C.E.; Maliki, in 795 C.E.; Shafi'i, in 820 C.E.; and Hanbali, in 855 C.E. Political conservatism went hand in hand with religious fundamentalism that called for loyalty to the state and adherence to the tradition. This does not mean that the Sunni did not partake in the great intellectual and scientific accomplishments of the Islamic civilization, as the great centers in Baghdad and Cordoba were under Sunni rule. However, the Sunni did not pursue religious interpretations and refinements on a continual basis as the Shi'a did.

The Shi'a were driven by a combination of misfortune and spiritual curiosity to go beyond the literal expression of the word, seeking the hidden meaning that could be uncovered with diligence and research under the guidance of divinely inspired imams. The Shi'a developed a complex system of theological doctrines and jurisprudence and became the intellectual drive in Muslim theology. They also developed their own system of jurisprudence, known as Ja'fari, influenced by the sixth Shi'a imam, Ja'far (al-Sadiq). Because of their stand on the necessity of seeking the deeper meaning of the Holy Word, they became known as the proponents of *ta'wil*, an Arabic word that roughly translates as allegorical interpretation of the word or seeking its primary *(awwal)* intent. They considered it a natural progression to graduate from the primary stages of acquisition *(tanzil)* to the more developed levels of comprehension and analysis *(ta'wil)*. They referred to passages in the Qur'an that encouraged pondering the meaning of the transmitted message and stressed the use of one's mind for full comprehension of the moral behind the message. The wise and the learned have been accorded a special position of reverence, a position that the Shi'a claimed belonged to the imams in the house of 'Ali:

> It is He who sent down upon thee the Book,
> wherein are verses clear that are the Essence
> of the Book, and others ambiguous.
> . . . and none knows its interpretation, save
> only God. And those firmly rooted in
> knowledge say, "We believe in it; all
> is from our Lord"; yet none remembers, but men
> possessed of minds. (Qur'an 3:7)

This was the solace of the Shi'a in a world that had denied them what they considered a just and divinely ordained claim. It was at the same time a calling to follow the path of misfortune and martyrdom for which they were eminently prepared through a long encounter with adversity.

Following al-Husayn's martyrdom in Karbala, the imamate passed on to his son 'Ali, also known as Zayn al-'Abidin (roughly meaning "the splendor of the worshippers"). He was reported to be a handsome and learned man who pursued a life of piety and learning, thus adding to the legacy of his father and grandfather. 'Ali Zayn al-'Abidin was succeeded by his son Muhammad, also known as al-Baqir. From al-Baqir, the imamate passed on to his son Ja'far, also known as al-Sadiq.

The development of the imamate in Shi'ism evolved over a period of time, initially following several lines of descendants, all from the progeny of 'Ali. 'Ali had sired several sons from other women following the death of his first wife, Fatima, the Prophet's daughter and the mother of al-Hasan and al-Husayn. Eventually the lineage from 'Ali's son al-Husayn gained the ascendancy as the legitimate heirs to the imamate in Shi'ism. Ja'far was the sixth in that lineage, the fifth if al-Hasan's imamate is excluded. However, there are branches associated with descendents of other sons of 'Ali besides Zayn al-'Abidin. One branch in particular endorsed the imamate of a son of al-Husan by the name of Zayd. This group became entrenched largely in Yemen under a branch of the Shi'a known as Zaydiyya, or Zuyud.[4] This was a side branch, unrelated to the emergence of the Druze. The main body of the Shi'a followed the descendents of Zayn al-'Abidin to the sixth generation in the person of Ja'far al-Sadiq.

Ja'far was a scholar of the first order and one of the main pillars of Islamic jurisprudence of all times. His writings constitute some of the main treasures of Islamic thought. "Ja'far al-Sadiq, of superior intellectual quality to his Alid relatives and predecessors, had gradually acquired a widespread reputation for religious learning," states Farhad Daftary. "Abu Hanifa al-Nu'man (d. 767 C.E. [A.H. 150]) and Malik ibn Anas (d. 795 C.E. [A.H. 179]), the famous jurists and eponyms of the Hanafi and Maliki schools of law, studied or consulted with him."[5] Ja'far lived during another great convulsion in Islamic history, the destruction of the Umayyad caliphate and the inauguration of Abbasid rule, in 750 C.E. The Abbasids, ostensibly defenders of the house of the Prophet and 'Ali's rightful claim to the caliphate, turned out to be more pernicious than the Umayyads in persecution of the Shi'a. Such were the fortunes of history that served to deepen the attachment of the Shi'a to their imams almost in direct proportion to the level and intensity of persecution.

Ja'far had willed the imamate to his elder son Isma'il by writ *(nass)*, as heir apparent to carry the mission. Isma'il, however, is claimed to have died before his father, and this created a problem in succession. Some felt that the imamate should automatically be accorded to Isma'il's son Muhammad, while others felt that the imamate should go instead to Isma'il's brother Musa. The majority of the Shi'a were of the latter opinion. The imamate in this group continued through Musa (also known as al-Kazim), to 'Ali (al-Ridha), to Muhammad (al-Jawad), to 'Ali (al-Hadi), to Hassan (al-Askari), and then to Muhammad (al-Mahdi al-Muntazar), the twelfth imam. The imamate abruptly stopped at the level of the twelfth imam, Muhammad al-Mahdi al-Muntazar, who disappeared or was concealed in or around 879 C.E. (A.H. 266). Hence this group goes under the appellation of the Twelver Shi'a or simply the "Twelvers" (al-Shi'a al-Ithna 'Ashariyya). The twelfth imam was only a boy when he disappeared (became concealed). The concealed imam is destined to reappear again at the appropriate time and engulf the world, steeped in corruption and persecution, with peace and justice. Redemption and salvation would finally fulfill the dreams and aspirations of a people on the receiving end of cruelty, persecution, and grief.

Although the concept of the imamate continues in the Twelver Shi'a to the present day, it has more of a surrogate function, pending the return of the real one. Present-day Shi'a imams wield considerable power, depending on their piety and scholarship, but the real imam remains hidden and will reappear at the appointed time.

The second group became known as the Isma'ilis since they supported Isma'il's son Muhammad and his descendants to the imamate. The Isma'ilis are also known as the "Seveners" (al-Sab'iyya), pointing to the seventh imam. It was from this branch of the Shi'a that the Druze eventually emerged.

Revolts were rampant during the Umayyad and Abbasid rule, and most were brutally crushed. Many factors contributed to endemic violence in a widespread empire with numerous ethnic and racial groups, social and economic injustice, and poor means of communication. The addition of large numbers of people from other civilizations introduced the problem of dealing with the inevitable clash of diversity in a system ill equipped to meet these challenges. On the one hand there was the egalitarian message of Islam that preached equality of all believers, and on the other hand was the imperative of geopolitical realities. As the social and economic conditions deteriorated, governance became more autocratic and less responsive to the needs of the common people.

Persecution of the Shi'a as a whole under Abbasid rule moved from bad to worse, but the Isma'ilis received the brunt of Abbasid oppression. With their emphasis on justice and their profound tradition of attachment to the purity of the Islamic message, the Shi'a became a lightning rod for opposition to tyranny and for championship of the oppressed. In this they had the advantage of not being the ones in power. It was therefore natural for the Shi'a to be attracted to and to be supported by elements that did not conform to the mainstream of the prevailing ruling order. The majority of Muslims, though not denying 'Ali's exalted position, did not feel that this accolade should be extended to his progeny simply because they came from the house of 'Ali. Nor did the majority feel that 'Ali's progeny had exclusive rights to the imamate as though they were chosen by God to act as his viceroy on earth. It is no wonder that the majority of the Sunni Muslims adopted the posture of loyalists to the state and to the prevailing political order while the Shi'a were in opposition. The state, however, was anything but stable, with mounting internal and external forces pressing from all sides.

By the time the Abbasids consolidated their power, some one hundred fifty years after the death of the Prophet, the Islamic realm stretched from the Atlantic to the Indian Oceans, covering most of the known world at that time except for the Far East and northern Europe. The separate Umayyad caliphate in Spain (Andalusia) that survived the Abbasid purge lasted for almost six hundred years; but it was just as Islamic and Arabic as that seated in Baghdad. In its heyday Baghdad was at the epicenter of major influxes of populations from diverse cultures and the arena of cross-cultural fertilization.

The Challenge for Change

Massive changes were taking place in the Islamic state of the day, causing great stress and tension in all walks of Muslim life. Three major fronts of stress played a role in the eventual emergence of the Druze sect and the concept of Tawhid that this sect adopted. These three main fronts of stress were the political, philosophical, and mystical or spiritual.

First, stress on the political front found expression in revolts and bloody uprisings. The rapidly expanding realm of Islam *(dar al-Islam)*, encompassing large influxes of people from diverse ethnic and racial backgrounds, compounded by an influx of wealth and disparity in its distribution, provided the setting for a tinderbox ready to explode. And explode it did, in numerous revolts and insurrections, including a revolt by the Carmathians. The history of the Carmathians is intertwined with that of the Isma'ilis, who are in turn an important part of the Druze story.

Second, exposure to the philosophical classics of the Hellenic world raised intellectual and philosophical challenges. These classics were translated into Arabic and were preserved for posterity as treasures of Hellenic thought. The translations sparked a new and powerful philosophical movement in the Islamic world, exemplified by the Mu'tazilites, the Brothers of Purity (Ikhwan al-Safa'), and subsequent philosophers. The impact of this movement on the evolution of Islamic thought is considerable.

Third, the mystical and spiritual forces from the East, mainly those of Persia and the Indian subcontinent, led to the Sufi orders and associated movements in ascetic practices. All these movements found resonance among Muslim thinkers, scholars, activists, and malcontents in general, but they held a special attraction for the Shi'a.

The last two phenomena, philosophy and mysticism, were to have a direct impact on the Druze and their interpretation of Tawhid.

The Carmathians

One of the most famous or notorious movements on the political and military fronts was launched by a group of rebels known as the Carmathians (al-Qaramita).

The Carmathians reputedly represented the first truly socialist movement in Islam. Their movement ignited a widespread rebellion that lasted for almost a century. It is difficult to ascertain when or how the movement started, because of the veil of secrecy that surrounded such movements and the practice of dissimulation (taqiya). The Carmathians consisted of a coalition of intellectuals, malcontents, anarchists, Arab and non-Arab revolutionaries, and others who legitimately yearned for the social and economic justice that Islam preached but Islamic governance failed to deliver. Since there were no means of expression for such frustrations in the autocracy of the Abbasid caliphate, violence was inevitable. The long years of persecution of the Shi'a created an atmosphere wherein many in the umma of Islam, particularly among the Isma'ili faction, became attracted to this revolutionary movement. It is even proposed by some Isma'ili sources that the titular leaders of the Carmathians were the hidden Isma'ili imams, the progeny of Muhammad ibn Ja'far al-Sadiq. Again because of strict secrecy, this information was not available to the followers of the movement. Thus there was considerable confusion as to who was in charge, a situation that adversely affected the chain of command and the identity of the real imam. "We can safely state that the Qaramita were Isma'ilis in flesh and blood as well as doctrine," writes the Isma'ili scholar Aref Tamer. "But it was the [Sunnis] of Damascus who attached the appellation of al-Qaramita to the Isma'ilis for the purpose of denigration."[6] Tamer goes on to write that "it was socialism built on evolutionary thinking and economic realities . . . to rid society of xenophobia, backwardness, fanaticism, and slavery that flourished in the exploitative capitalistic conditions of the day."[7]

Recently, an exhaustive study of the Carmathians suggests that the issue is much more complicated than simply considering them as Isma'ilis and no more. "There are discrepancies in the opinions of Muslim historians and scholars in Orientalism as to the precise origins of the Carmathians and the Fatimids. Some claimed that they (Carmathians) are the product of a combination of Shi'a and Sufi traditions, with roots extending into old Persia, and that their emergence was facilitated by the economic, social, and religious conditions in that era of Abbasid rule."[8] There was also confusion as to where they first appeared on the scene and the exact date of such emergence, largely due to the veil of secrecy that surrounded the Isma'ili movement at that time. Security considerations of the Isma'ili imams dictated strict secrecy as to the identity of the real imam at any given time. Thus the Abbasid authorities and their propaganda machine were able to "smear" the revolutionary reformist movement unleashed by the Isma'ilis by using the appellation of al-Qaramita.[9]

When the Isma'ili Shi'a imam al-Mahdi finally had the chance to create the Isma'ili state in North Africa, he chose to name it the Fatimid Empire. This appellation was intended to stress the lineage of imam al-Mahdi and his predecessors and successors from 'Ali and Fatima, and to overcome the Abbasid propaganda aimed at discrediting such claims. The Carmathians professed allegiance to the Fatimids and promised help in the areas where they were strong, namely in eastern Arabia, including al-Bahrayn, the Basra region of Iraq, and southern and western Syria. Under pressure from the state and lacking centralized and unified leadership, the Carmathians eventually succumbed to a combination of internal and external forces that led to their fragmentation and eventual elimination as a political and military force. For more than one hundred years, however, the Carmathians wrecked havoc throughout the Abbasid Empire, disrupting communications and terrorizing many communities. They were reputed to have destroyed a number of mosques and to have attacked the Ka'ba, removing the Black Stone from the holy shrine and slaying a large number of pilgrims in Mecca.

These acts of violence were not indiscriminate but were directed against mosques and other institutions that were considered by the Carmathians to be corrupt and exploitative, or against places that initiated hostilities against the Carmathians. As for the Black Stone, the Carmathians considered sacredness of the stone a form of idolatry. One of the Carmathian leaders expressed poetically what he thought of the Ka'ba and the Black Stone:

> If this house "Ka'ba" were really the house of God
> He would have poured fire upon us
> Since we have exercised pilgrimage as the pagans did before us.
> But God, exalted be his name,
> Did not build a [physical] house, nor confine himself to a residence.[10]

In any event acts of excessive violence were condemned by many Isma'ilis and other supporters of the Carmathians who were appalled at such conduct. Even the Fatimid caliphs who enjoyed the support and allegiance of the Carmathians at intervals were eventually driven to join in the condemnation and actually resort to military force against the Carmathians in Palestine. Thus ended one of the most radical challenges to the established authority of the prevailing order.

The demise of the Carmathians did not mean the total abolition of their influence. After all, many of the issues raised by the Carmathians resonated with the hopes and despairs of large segments of the Muslim population. The issues were particularly attractive to some groups among the Shi'a and to those who were outside the coteries of the ruling circles and their supporters. Furthermore, the conditions that fostered revolution remained, possibly intensified by the increasingly cosmopolitan composition of the realm. The traditionally conservative and increasingly autocratic rule of the Abbasid caliphate was unable to respond to the increasing popular pressure by addressing legitimate needs and stemming corruption. Thus, remnants of Carmathian thinking persisted and worked their way into the customs and practices of some communities and became part of their culture. How much of this influence filtered to the Druze understanding of the Tawhid faith is difficult to assess, but it could be tangible. For example, the call for strict monogamy and the emphasis on reason in religious practices stressed by the Carmathians are incorporated into Druze traditions and codes of behavior. In addition, the Carmathians were among the early Muslims who placed emphasis on the inner meaning *(batin)* of the holy message over and above the literal interpretation *(zahir)*. This group included the Isma'ilis, the Alawites, and the Druze, among others.

The Mu'tazilites and the Introduction of Philosophy

Another group that had a great impact on future events were members of an intellectual movement known as the Mu'tazilites (al-Mu'tazila). The Mu'tazilites came into being at the hands of an intellectual by the name of Wasil ibn 'Ata', who died in 748 C.E. By that time scholars and theologians were already delving into deciphering what was beyond the literal interpretation of the written word and attempting to resolve areas of seeming ambiguity in some passages of the Qur'an. Chief among these was the issue of whether human beings enjoy the freedom of choice and therefore should be held accountable for their actions, or whether their fate is already determined a priori by God's will. The Mu'tazilites were not a political or military movement but rather an intellectual group whose approach to the interpretation and understanding of religious and worldly phenomena was based on rational thinking and philosophical discourse. In time their program was crystallized into a stress on five principles: (1) justice; (2) *tawhid*; (3) promise and warning; (4) the middle road between two extremes; and (5) call to virtue and admonition against vice.[11]

Philosophy had begun to enter the world of Islam after the invasion of Syria and Egypt, largely through exposure to Hellenic culture. The discovery of Greek thought sparked a major intellectual movement that reverberated throughout the Muslim world. The Muslim world had reached a stage of wealth and sophistication to seek and appreciate such leisurely and intellectual quests. Initiation into Hellenic philosophy was at the hands of Christian scholars who were versed in the Greek language. The translation of Greek philosophy was quickly followed by a succession of native Islamic and Arab thinkers and philosophers of high caliber. The support of philosophy by some of the Abbasid caliphs who were intellectually inclined to stimulate and be stimulated by free thought contributed significantly to the flowering of Arab philosophy. One caliph in particular, al-Ma'mun (833 C.E.), deserves mention because he put significant resources of the Abbasid caliphate at the disposal of scholars.

Basically the Mu'tazilites tried to subject Islamic doctrines to the probing dissection of rational thinking. Zuhdi Jar Allah writes, "The Mu'tazilites were the only group in Islam that had enough courage to delve into these principles . . . with the intention of defending Islamic beliefs by logic and reasoning."[12] They tried to understand the Qur'an and analyze its message in the light of reason and logic. Coming at the height of Abbasid power, the Mu'tazilites enjoyed the support of the caliphate for a period of time, and their teachings became popular throughout the Abbasid Empire. More importantly their activities encouraged the growth and proliferation of different schools of philosophy and logic.

The first native philosopher of renown in the Muslim Arab empire was al-Kindi, who was born around 803 C.E. in Kufa, Iraq, and lived in Baghdad. A courageous thinker and highly prolific writer on a wide variety of subjects, al-Kindi achieved considerable acclaim. Al-Kindi was the first Arab philosopher to make an attempt at reconciliation between faith and philosophy. He considered that knowledge leading to the truth can be obtained through multiple routes, three in particular, which had significance for the Druze interpretation of the concept of Tawhid.

The first route is through the senses and is therefore the most elementary of the three since it does not require more than intact biological senses in order for the individual to observe and learn. The second route is through analysis, deduction, and projection. This route is obviously more complex than the first since it involves a higher order of intellect and comprehension. The third route is through spiritual enlightenment *(ishraq)* and is therefore reserved for those whose hearts are pure and whose souls are receptive to divine messages. These three mechanisms represent progression from the material to the spiritual, thus providing possible reconciliation between philosophy and religion.[13] Graduation from the concrete to the abstract in philosophical thinking is analogous to the graduation from the exoteric *(zahir)* to the esoteric *(batin)* in religious thinking.

Al-Kindi exerted major influence on subsequent giants of Arab and Islamic philosophy such as Ibn Sina (Avicenna), al-Farabi, and Ibn Rushd (Averroes). Al-Kindi's association with the Mu'tazilites nearly cost him his life when the backlash took place. The fortunes of philosophy and philosophers were tied to the temperament of the caliph in power at the time. Thus after the death of supportive enlightened caliphs such as al-Ma'mun and the ascendancy to power of more conservative ones, such as al-Mutawakkil, the policy of the caliphate shifted from one of support to that of antagonism. The point was made apparent to the defenders of the faith who were beginning to assert themselves in shifting the policy of the Abbasid caliphate toward conservatism. No matter how benign it might have seemed initially, philosophical thinking, once unleashed, posed a threat to dogmatic "truths" and to the traditional religious structures, authorities, and practices. Given enough leeway, philosophy could go far beyond what was considered to be untouchable in religion. The by-product of such real or perceived excesses was a backlash of persecution and revival of fundamentalism in the courts of the Abbasid caliphate. Philosophy was banned and the books of the Mu'tazilites were burned in reprisal for the perceived blasphemy. As could be expected, the Shi'a received a fair share of the maltreatment through guilt by association.

The significance of the Mu'tazilites was in preparing the ground for other groups that followed, such as the Brothers of Purity (Ikhwan al-Safa'), who played a pivotal role in the incorporation of rational thinking and philosophical concepts into the sphere of Muslim religious beliefs and practices. The Brothers of Purity was an organization that operated secretly, for fear of persecution. It consisted of major intellectual figures who laid the foundation of Isma'ili philosophy. Admission to their ranks was highly guarded and was subject to proof of loyalty and trust in addition to high intellectual caliber. The precise date of the beginning activity of the Brothers is difficult to assert due to the secrecy that surrounded the organization. It is, however, considered that they began sometime during the era of occultation of the Isma'ili imams. This puts the onset of their activity sometime immediately following the imamate of Muhammad ibn Isma'il (d. 790 C.E. [A.H. 169]). In fifty-two letters (epistles), the Brothers touched on virtually all aspects of life and religion. They considered the "mind" as God's first and most important creation, followed by the "soul." They also stressed that for everything there is an external and an internal explanation: "And you should recognize, my brother, that for all things in existence there is an external and an internal aspect . . . and that the [revealed] Laws contain rules and limitations that are within the grasp of the public at large, but there are internal rules and secrets that are only accessible to those who are steeped in knowledge."[14] It is the esoteric aspect that one should seek through the external performance of religious practices and rituals. These two aspects complement each other because true faith is served by adherence to both. The Brothers of Purity may be considered the vanguard movement in the evolution of Isma'ili philosophy and the emergence of the Druze interpretation of Tawhid.

The success of the Brothers was such that in short order their influence had spread far and wide into all parts of the Islamic realm: "And there is no continent on earth nor a province that we do not have authorities and teachers who preach our message and who point to us and promise the fulfillment of our dreams."[15] Further evolution of the basic principles of the Brothers of Purity was to occur at the hands of major thinkers and philosophers in the Isma'ili movement.

The trend in philosophical and interpretive activity of seeking the hidden and more profound meaning of the religious message continued to flourish and to spawn further activities in the religious and philosophical domains despite periodic banning of such activities by the state and heavy reprisals at the hands of the religious establishment. The ultimate fate of these and other philosophical activities was tied to the personal convictions of the caliph in power, and the fortunes of the caliphate at any given time. Philosophy in the Sunni state of the Abbasid caliphate, therefore, waxed and waned until its fate was sealed by a powerful philosopher turned mystic and fundamentalist by the name of Abu Hamid al-Ghazzali (d. 1111 C.E.). It was under his spell that faith was finally divorced from philosophy. After more than thirty years of search for the truth through philosophy and logic, al-Ghazzali came to the conclusion that this approach is futile and advocated following the letter of the word of God. The impact of this prestigious figure was considerable throughout the Islamic world, particularly among the Sunni majority, where the interpretive approach to the Qur'anic message lost its momentum.

On the other hand the Shi'a in general and the Isma'ilis in particular continued their philosophical discourse, searching for the truth as a matter of faith regardless of the pressure from the ruling order. The edifice of knowledge continued to grow in scope and in complexity within the Isma'ili traditions for several hundred years. As an offshoot of the Isma'ilis, the Druze would push the envelope of philosophy beyond the Isma'ili boundaries and utilize it in defining their path to Tawhid.

The Mystics (al-Mutasawwifa)

The third major influence on Islamic thought and practices was that of mysticism. As in the case of philosophy, mysticism was an imported commodity introduced through the diverse population who converted to Islam or were included in the vast Islamic realm. Christian monks probably exerted some influence on Muslims in the early days of Islam. It is presumed that the Prophet himself may have been familiar with some of the Christian hermits and their mystical ways during his travels in the Syrian desert when he led Khadija's caravans to and from Damascus. Christian mysticism started in the second century in North Africa, with influences from Jewish heritage and Hellenic thought. The incorporation of an ascetic lifestyle into the practice of mystical contemplation led to the creation of Christian monasticism.[16] By the time Islam arrived on the scene, monasteries had proliferated throughout the Christian world including the Syrian desert and beyond. Syria was part of the Byzantine Empire at that time.

Mysticism was not an entirely imported commodity in Islam, although it grew in scope and complexity by incorporating ideas and practices from the ancient cultures of the East and the West. The experience of the Prophet himself during the solitary contemplative periods in the caves around Mecca may be considered as mystical in nature. Likewise, many of the companions of the Prophet lived their lives in simplicity and material rejection.[17] Figures such as Salman al-Farisi, who became a close confidant of the Prophet and may be considered among the group of early mystics in Islam, spent a considerable part of his life in Christian monasteries. In fact his conversion to Islam was reportedly due to some form of mystical vision during his sojourn in monasteries in Syria. The legend goes that unmistakable signs of the Prophet were revealed to a few chosen visionaries such as Salman al-Farisi.[18]

However, the early Muslims were too busy expanding and consolidating the realm to indulge in practices generally engaged in by societies that had graduated from the stage of dealing with primary concerns of daily life. Furthermore, Islam was primarily based on the Qur'an (God's words), which, as a concrete document, was taken literally by the rank and file especially in the formative years. The schools for esoteric and hidden interpretations developed later when Islamic society became more complex and the Islamic population more cultured.

Although Islamic mysticism was influenced by Christian as well as Jewish theology and by Hellenic philosophy, there was another source that probably played an even larger role in the development of mysticism in Islam. This source was the Middle and Far East. The long history of mystical experience in those lands, India and Persia in particular, projected heavily into the expanding world of Islam and led to the development of a uniquely Islamic form of mystical experience and practices. With the passage of time several schools of mysticism sprang up in different parts of the Islamic world and included members from all the major sects in Islam. Some of these practices, at least as far as they constituted a form of rejection of worldly materialism and the oppression of the state, would resonate with the Shi'a ideology. Moreover, mystical practices also provided another approach for understanding the real or hidden meaning of the religious experience.

At the core of mysticism is a passion for unity, whereby one is united with the One. Such unity is all-consuming, total, unconditional, and everlasting. From the East also came a philosophical interpretation of life and existence that does not visualize events as separate and isolated instances but as interconnected and interrelated phenomena. As such the whole of society and indeed humanity partakes in the mystical experience by direct participation. Practical (applied) and transcendental influences of mysticism are of the mainstream in the East and not of the esoteric. Therefore, the impact of mysticism in the lives of people is central and deep seated. It is interesting to note that the broad visionary strokes of the sages and mystics of the East are being rediscovered today by some schools of modern science, particularly in connection with the theory of relativity and quantum physics. Thus, Fritjof Capra writes in *The Tao of Physics*, "Eastern thought and more generally, mystical thought provide consistent and relevant philosophical background to the theories of contemporary science; a conception of the world in which scientific discoveries can be in perfect harmony with spiritual aims and religious beliefs." [19]

As Islam became ready in the third century to absorb the philosophical and mystical heritage from Byzantium and Greece, it was also ready to incorporate the powerful transcendental and mystical visions from the East. The ascetic demands of mystical life included rejection of worldly pleasures and the return to the simplest and purest of life's necessities. The practice of wearing coarse woolen clothes (*suf*) by the Muslim mystic gave him the label of "Sufi," meaning the one who wears wool. Perhaps the best-known Sufi in the West is Rumi (Jalal al-Din al-Rumi), who was born in Balkh (today's Afghanistan) in 1207 C.E.

Some of the early mystics in Islam, such as al-Junayd, practiced and taught Sufism as an entirely personal quest to achieve union with the One by total detachment from materialistic constraints and egotistical desires. Others, such as al-Husayn ibn Mansur (al-Hallaj), who was born in 858 C.E. (A.H. 244), also saw in Sufism a platform to condemn the evils of corruption and social injustice. Other Sufis developed certain rituals that resulted in such a state of ecstasy as to make them oblivious to pain and suffering. And also there were the usual charlatans and counterfeits, who used some of the mystical practices to swindle the innocent and exploit their vulnerability.

The reaction of the caliphate to these activities and endeavors ranged from bare tolerance and neglect to outright persecution, depending on the inclination of the caliph of the day, his degree of learning, his philosophical bent, the company he kept, and the level of influence of the religious figures in his administration. Above all the attitude of the ruling establishment depended on how secure the caliph of the day was in the cobweb of intrigue and conspiracies of the palace. Many of the Abbasid caliphs perished, in the later periods of the empire, at the hands of close relatives, army officers, confidants, or even personal servants and bodyguards. The dangers from within the palace were compounded by the danger of public uprisings, such as the Carmathian revolt discussed above. There were also the ever-present threats to the Islamic realm from enemies in the *dar al-harb*, those lands that lay outside the house of Islam. Amid all of this it is not surprising that the caliph of the day would be extremely suspicious of whatever appeared to be subversive or inciting disloyalty and disobedience.

The pretext for persecution of the Sufis varied from case to case, but it generally rested on accusations of heresy, apostasy, or defamation of the Prophet or the tenets of Islam. It also rested on the presumed role of the Sufis in creating an atmosphere that, by rejection of worldly power, promoted and encouraged subversion of the state and denigration of the caliphate. In this context the accusations leveled at the Sufis were similar to those leveled against other rebellious elements such as the philosophers or the political activists. Moreover, the Abbasid caliphate had reached an alarming state of weakness, disintegration, and corruption.[20] In the case of the noted Sufi al-Hallaj, it was not hard to drum up incriminating evidence from his own writings to accuse him of heresy. Although he carefully and scrupulously adhered to the tenets of Islam, al-Hallaj exceeded the limit by proclaiming a state of awareness during the ecstatic moments of transcendence that brought him into union with the Ultimate Reality. It is noteworthy that al-Hallaj was apprehended in the year 912 C.E. (A.H. 299), the same year that the Fatimid caliphate was proclaimed in North Africa.[21] True to his principles, al-Hallaj went through imprisonment, torture, and death with the anticipation of deliverance and self-actualization in the almighty God. In a final farewell address that is remi-

niscent of Jesus of Nazareth, al-Hallaj thanked God for his benevolence and requested forgiveness for his executioners, for they knew not what they were doing:

> Oh God . . . grant me gratitude for what you have bestowed upon me whereby
> you revealed to me the beauty of your countenance and withheld from others
> what you allowed me of your secrets. And here your worshipers have gathered to
> execute me out of extreme allegiance to your religion and of the desire to please
> you. Forgive them; for if you had revealed to them what you revealed to me, they
> would not have done what they did, and if you had held from me what you held
> from them, I would not have been invested with this affliction. Accept my grati-
> tude for what you do and what you will.[22]

With these words al-Hallaj met his maker and left behind a tremendous influence on subsequent thinkers and mystics of Islam. He was not the first nor
would he be the last to suffer such a fate and join the long list of martyrs at the
hands of rulers of the house of Islam.

The institution of the caliphate that grew out of the early Muslim community
following the death of the Prophet had over time veered sharply from the egalitarian concepts of Islamic justice and had become contaminated with material exploitation, public oppression, and palace intrigue The echoes of the past,
however, refused to fade away as the pristine message of Islam continued to develop and grow in the hearts and minds of many of the believers. The caliphate
would try to keep the lid on, but it could not control or extinguish the inner
thoughts and convictions of the opposition. The growing ferment in the Islamic
caliphate in Baghdad would in time lead to the establishment of a rival caliphate
in the Fatimid Empire. The new caliphate and empire would espouse a religious
ideology that was considerably more complex than what had been achieved thus
far. It was this milieu that led to the emergence of the Druze sect.

Isma'il to al-Mahdi

The Shi'a emerged as a large Islamic faction oppressed and persecuted during
both the Umayyad and the Abbasid caliphates. Consequently, the Shi'a assumed
the role of opposition against injustice, tyranny, and corruption, a position that
stemmed from their painful history and longing for redress. It was, therefore, natural for the Shi'a to attract activists and to explore alternative approaches to civil as
well as religious practices.

The first schism of the Shi'a from the mainstream of Islam began with 'Ali in

661 C.E. (A.H. 40) and continued to the sixth generation of imams, ending with the highly esteemed imam Ja'far al-Sadiq in 765 C.E. (A.H. 148). A second major schism started with the progeny of Imam Ja'far al-Sadiq, whereby succession, which was due to his eldest son Isma'il, was complicated when Isma'il died (or was presumed to have died) while his father was still alive. This prompted one branch of the Shi'a to endorse Isma'il's brother Musa to the line of succession; they came to be known of the Twelvers, holding allegiance to the imamate until the twelfth imam, who vanished mysteriously. They believed that the twelfth imam would return and spread justice and peace at some predestined time. Another branch of the Shi'a considered that succession should go instead to Isma'il's son Muhammad; they came to be known as the Isma'ilis. The Druze concept of Tawhid emerged from the Isma'ili movement.

While the Twelver Shi'a were committed to religious matters as they waited for the Mahdi to return and rectify the insurmountable ills of the social and political order of the day, the Isma'ilis were committed, in addition, to political and social activism. This made the Isma'ilis more of a target for persecution and liquidation by the Abbasids. In time the doggedness exhibited by the Isma'ilis paid handsome dividends when they were able to establish their own state, the Fatimid Empire. The Fatimid Empire quickly grew to rival and threaten the Abbasid Empire until both succumbed to outside forces and internal exhaustion.

After Isma'il's death in 762 C.E. (A.H. 145), his son Muhammad was next in line in the Isma'ili order. Muhammad was accorded special significance by the Isma'ili followers and by the Druze who came later. He is credited with more innovative approaches to the interpretation of the Qur'an than had hitherto been offered. Although he upheld the Pillars of Islam and maintained the traditional practices, he is credited with more esoteric interpretations of the traditions and of the Qur'an itself. In particular the concept of the cyclical nature of divine calls was introduced, bringing humanity to the concept of Tawhid in increments.

In the Isma'ili concept of divine calls, preparatory stages are needed to allow for a process of gradualism leading to maturation. In the absence of such preparation, human beings would be unable to absorb the magnitude of divine revelations and would perish from the intensity of premature exposure. The cycles began with the dawn of human existence and continued with increasing depth and complexity in successive cycles. Simultaneously with this evolving concept, the status of the imams in the Isma'ili tradition began to assume higher and higher levels of recognition and holiness.

Naturally the Abbasid caliphate viewed any deviation from the traditional stand as a threat, and intensified the use of measures of suppression and persecution of the Shiʾa in general and the Ismaʿili branch in particular. The Ismaʿilis were high on the list of subversive elements, and their imams and their followers became the target of witch hunts and intimidation. Hence, after the tenure of Ismaʿil's son Muhammad, succeeding Ismaʿili imams assumed a veil of secrecy and went underground. This practice marked the beginning of the era of occultation *(dawr al-satr)*. Secrecy did not mean suspension of activity. On the contrary, efforts were intensified, and the followers became more committed to the cause of what they considered to be a process of reform mandated by the logic of cyclical change and the imperative of advancement.

Muhammad moved from one city to another, evading the watchful eye of the Abbasid caliphs and the state agents who were on his trail. From the Hijaz in Arabia he moved to Kufa in Iraq and then to Farghana (today's Uzbekistan in central Asia) and then to Nisabur in Iran, always one step ahead of the security forces in pursuit. In all these places he left a large number of followers and converts to the cause of Ismaʿili Shiʾa and to the theosophical refinements and innovations that he introduced. Undoubtedly, some of these innovations resonated deeply with the cultures of the Far East where the Persian and Indian traditions were steeped in theology and mysticism. Finally settling in Palmyra, Syria, Muhammad allegedly took on the assumed name of Maymun al-Qaddah and the identity of a Persian eye doctor. There, known only to a trusted few, he continued to build support and gather followers until his death. He was buried in Palmyra.[23] In the Druze concept Muhammad is considered to be the seventh proclaimer, and the last of the series.

After Muhammad, the imamate passed to his elder son Abdullah, who moved his base of operations to the town of Salamiyya in Syria. As a well-recognized scholar and organizer, Abdullah established the Ismaʿili call on a firm basis, sending emissaries to different parts of the Islamic realm to preach and teach. It was during his tenure that the famous treatise known as the Epistles of the Brothers of Purity and Friends in Fidelity *(Rasaʾil Ikhwan al-Safaʾ wa Khillan al-Wafaʾ)* were written. These epistles, written by anonymous authors for reasons of security, are extremely important because they represent the first major building blocks of the Ismaʿili doctrine. In the words of a contemporary Ismaʿili scholar, "We can safely say that the Brothers of Purity are the foundation on which the Ismaʿilis built the philosophy of their doctrine, and I add that this seed was the first philosophical seed in Islamic thought."[24] Concepts like the mind and the soul and the concept of creation that the Druze adopted later had their origin in the Epistles of the Brothers of Purity. All of this took place under the veil of strict secrecy and away from the listening ears of informers and spies. One can only speculate as to the extent of danger that surrounded such activities and such activists, as well as the dedication and commitment of the devoted followers. The pressure from the caliphate was intense, and they were forced to remain underground.

Abdullah was succeeded by his son Ahmad (al-Wafi), who continued the tradition of his father, adding further refinements and interpretations to an already complex system of philosophy and beliefs. The circle of converts was widened further and activities intensified. During his tenure, the Comprehensive Message of the Brothers of Purity (*Al-risala al-jami'a*) was written, presumably by the hidden imam himself.[25] The main theme of the Isma'ili doctrine relates to the messianic message of the return of the redeemer who would be from the seed of 'Ali and Fatima. In this they agree with the Twelver Shi'a. The Isma'ilis, however, believe that redemption will be in continuation of the imamate through the progeny of Isma'il and his descendants. The redeemer would rid humanity of error, sin, and corruption and would restore justice and purity in accordance with God's commands. All of the prior religious messages and calls were in preparation for and in anticipation of this event. This philosophy is based on deciphering the inner meaning of the Qur'an and of prior holy messages.

At the core of the Isma'ili philosophy is the exaltation of God above and beyond any description or attribute. God, exalted be his name, created first and foremost the universal mind (*al-'aql al-kulli*), or the first cause. The first cause is also known as the precedent (*al-sabiq*), since it was the first among God's creation. It was through the universal mind that the soul was created as the second in line. These luminaries/limitaries (*hudud*) in the scheme of creation are mirrored in the spiritual context by the proclaimer or prophet (*al-natiq*) and the foundation (*al-asas*). The prophet is entrusted with articulation of the divine message, and the foundation is entrusted with the interpretation and development of the message. In addition to the spiritual dimensions of the divine message, there are laws and parameters of human conduct (*shari'a*) that are a prerequisite for belief to be firmly established. There are also rites and rituals to reinforce the message and to cement group solidarity.

In the absence of the prophet (proclaimer)—as a result of death, for instance, since the prophet is human—the foundation (*asas*) and his progeny (imams) become the custodians and the standard-bearers of the divine call. The Isma'ilis stress the necessity to observe the outer practices of the faith (*al-zahir*) as a prelude to delving into the inner meaning (*al-batin*) of the revealed word. Paul Walker writes, "Thus the sacred scripture is not a root in and of itself, but is rather a key to the root which lies behind it. The Koran is the wellspring of divine wisdom, but that wisdom lives hidden under it, or more precisely 'inside' and not in its external forms."[26] This concept is paramount in the Druze interpretation of the doctrine of Tawhid.

The Isma'ili imams gradually and painstakingly developed a complex system to disseminate their philosophy. A cadre of emissaries (*da'is*) were trained, and these in turn trained a pyramidal cadre of lieutenants and subordinates in a highly organized hierarchical system that ultimately converged on the sanctity of the blessed imam.

After Ahmad came al-Husayn (al-Taqi), who kept the momentum of his predecessors and stayed the course of the Isma'ili call to the faithful. The movement by now had become well established but remained within the secret fold of trusted followers. After all, the Abbasid state remained on the alert, and successive imams had to operate in strict secrecy for their own protection as well as for the safety of the devotees and their families. Al-Husayn was succeeded by 'Ali, who died at a young age, leaving behind a child too young for succession. The title of the young child was al-Qa'im bi Amr Allah. At this point enters a cousin of al-Qa'im by the name of Sa'id and the title of Ubaydullah al-Mahdi. Al-Mahdi represents a turning point in the Isma'ili movement, since during his tenure the movement crossed from secrecy to openness. He also played a dual role: that of a surrogate imam, by publicly launching the Isma'ili call, and that of a regent acting as the caretaker who later passed the baton to the real imam (al-Qa'im) once the latter achieved adulthood.

Thus the era from the time of Muhammad, the son of Isma'il, to that of al-Mahdi (762–945 C.E.) is known as the era of occultation (*dawr al-satr*). This era is full of confusion and controversy as to the exact identity and even the number of real imams, due to the veil of secrecy and the necessity for camouflage. It was customary during that time to have one or more surrogate imams or persons posing as imams to protect the real ones, whose true identity would be disclosed only to a very small group of key supporters and to the most trusted of followers. In fact there are references that indicate that al-Qa'im was actually the son of al-Mahdi and not his nephew.[27] Although the details of these issues are outside our immediate concern, the fact remains that this era was of major importance in the evolution of the imamate and the formulation of the Isma'ili doctrine. The Druze movement that emerged approximately one century later was greatly influenced by the events of this era, including the major political and philosophical movements that were in the limelight at that time.

The era of occultation was not only a major incubator for political developments culminating in the creation of the Fatimid Empire but also an era of increased complexity of religious and philosophical doctrines. Concepts like the continuity of God's revelations, as well as the role of helpers, teachers, and advisers to messengers and prophets and the repetitive cycles of religious development were all discussed, defined, and refined. Likewise, the concepts that dealt with the extension of the imamate into the future as well as into the depths of the past were further elaborated and its importance augmented beyond the traditional norms of the day. The fact that the identity of the real imams was not disclosed to the public during the era of occultation added further mystery. Thus the mystical vision of redemption was augmented by the extraordinary status of the imamate, a status that grew exponentially with time. The imams came to be viewed as being vested with extraordinary powers, as being infallible, and as possessing special qualities that almost elevated them above human mortals. They were considered the centerpiece in the long process of man's spiritual development appearing in every age and at every stage of that process. Passages from the Qur'an as well as from other holy scriptures were quoted and interpreted to refer to the centrality of the imams in human spiritual growth and salvation.

The Isma'ili theologians resorted to several approaches in order to buttress their argument with respect to the sanctity of their imams. Major figures such as Abu Ya'qub Ishak ibn Ahmad al-Sijistani (d. 971 C.E.), al-Qadi al-Nu'man (d. 974 C.E.), and Hamid al-Din al-Kirmani (d. 1021 C.E., 411 H.) were strong advocates of using philosophical arguments to validate their religious belief. Others, like the famous physician and philosopher Abu Hatem al-Razi (Rhazes), put more of their trust in philosophy, regardless of the revealed word in religion. The Isma'ili theologians also drew from the mystical tradition further support for a creed already profoundly imbedded in the hearts and minds of committed followers. Thus, by the time al-Mahdi decided to go public, the Isma'ili movement had gathered enough momentum to embark on the ambitious undertaking of launching a sovereign state of their own in direct competition with the Abbasid Empire. For several reasons al-Mahdi chose to relocate from Syria to North Africa, specifically to al-Qairawan (in modern-day Tunisia) to launch the uprising.

As is the case in major events, supporters of al-Mahdi sought validation for the undertaking from sayings, indications, and predictions from established sources and authorities in the traditions of the community. Al-Mahdi had many of these references at his disposal, particularly in his capacity as the protector of and the front man for the real imam (al-Qa'im), who was still underage at the time of the uprising. For example Salman al-Farisi, a trusted devotee of the Prophet, is reputed to have predicted that "it is certain that a descendant of Fatima will arise in the West [referring to North Africa], and prevail over the aggressors."[28]

By creating their own state, the Fatimid Empire, the Isma'ili Shi'a reentered the arena in the geopolitical world of Islam, and in full force. They had finally succeeded in redressing the wrong that had been their lot for more than three hundred years. The Fatimid Empire was expected to address the mundane affairs of the citizens and satisfy the spiritual yearnings of a once persecuted and deprived community. The head of the state would be the real caliph, and not the Abbasid usurper of the caliphate seated in Baghdad. That post, according to the Isma'ili Shi'a, belonged in perpetuity to the seed from 'Ali and Fatima, by divine will. The head of the Fatimid state was also the imam vested with divine guidance to lead the faithful in their journey to spiritual fulfillment and God's grace.

4 *The Fatimid Caliphate*

From al-Qa'im to al-Hakim

AFTER A LONG AND CIRCUITOUS ROUTE, al-Mahdi reached North Africa and publicly proclaimed the caliphate in the year 909 C.E. (A.H. 297).[1] The claim of al-Mahdi to the Fatimid caliphate in North Africa provoked immediate condemnation from the Abbasid caliphate in Baghdad and a campaign of vitriolic accusations and misinformation was launched to discredit the claim and the claimant. Adjoining tribes in North Africa that were loyal to the Western (Sunni) Islamic Empire in Andalusia embarked on a series of revolts and insurrections to wipe out the nascent Fatimid effort at empire building. However, there were also tribes that were fiercely loyal to the Fatimid cause and provided crucial support without which it would have been impossible for al-Mahdi to succeed. Chief among these were the Kutama tribes under the charismatic leadership of a man by the name of 'Abdullah al-Shi'i who had converted to Isma'ilism while he was in Yemen. Thus in spite of tremendous difficulties and some setbacks, al-Mahdi was able to prevail and to strengthen his realm. By the time of his death some twenty-four years later, al-Mahdi was able to pass on to his successor a power base from which to govern and expand. He also gave the name of Fatimid to the newly established caliphate. The name was meant to dramatize the legitimacy of this caliphate by linking it without interruption directly to Fatima, the daughter of the Prophet and the wife of 'Ali and to counteract accusations from the Abbasids aimed at undermining the veracity of the claim.

Part of the warfare waged against the nascent caliphate was in the form of propaganda and misinformation. Al-Mahdi was described by agents of the Abbasids as an impostor and a usurper with family origins in Persia. Rumors began to circulate that al-Mahdi was of Jewish ancestry and his movement was nothing but an attempt to discredit Islam. Other rumors claimed that the entire Isma'ili movement was nothing but an effort by the enemies of Islam to sabotage legitimate

70

Muslim rule. After all, some segments among the non-Arab converts to Islam, especially among the Persian population, continued to harbor a grudge against the desert nomads, who were blamed for the virtual destruction of the ancient civilization of Persia. Even in modern times we see reference to the effect that the appellation of "Fatimid" should be dissociated from the empire that was established by al-Mahdi, thereby denying the legitimacy of relating the endeavor to Fatima and 'Ali.[2] It is noteworthy that accusations of one sort or another continue to be leveled nowadays by conservative circles against persons or groups who deviate from the strict line of dogmatism in Islam. Differences of opinion have become synonymous with heresy, and opposition to unjust rule treachery. Such rigidity in condemnation of free thinking is in fact contrary to the liberal and tolerant spirit of the Qur'an. Such "phobia of free thinking," according to a modern Muslim scholar, "is the tragedy of the world of Islam."[3]

In the Fatimid Empire as in all of North Africa, most Muslims were of the Sunni persuasion. The newly established caliphate was of the Isma'ili Shi'a persuasion. Instead of pursuing a policy of coercion and intimidation, al-Mahdi and the succeeding Fatimid caliphs followed a liberal policy and avoided imposing their particular path in Islam on the majority of their subjects. Such tolerance had been rarely encountered since the days of the Prophet and the *rashidun* caliphs.

Al-Qa'im succeeded al-Mahdi by written edict and pursued a similar policy of tolerance and respect for the various Muslim sects as well as for Christians and Jews. He sought to consolidate and expand his realm by gradually inching his way to the East with Egypt as his goal. Although al-Qa'im succeeded in occupying the city of Alexandria, he could not capitalize on his victory due to threats from the tribes in North Africa. Therefore, he had to be content with consolidation instead of expansion. Al-Qa'im reigned for twelve years and is considered to be the second Fatimid caliph. He died in 946 C.E. (A.H. 334).

Al-Qa'im was succeeded by his son Isma'il, who took the title of al-Mansur, meaning "the victorious." He would be the third Fatimid caliph. Al-Mansur began his tenure by warding off the ever-lurking threats from without and from within. Accordingly, he kept the news of his father's death secret for a long time to avoid the upheavals associated with transfer of power during perilous times. Nevertheless, al-Mansur's realm survived, and his reign was consolidated to the point that it was ready for the next phase of Fatimid expansion. Al-Mansur reigned for eight years and was noted for his bravery and wisdom.[4]

Al-Mansur was succeeded by an illustrious son who took the title of al-Mu'izz

Li Din-Allah in 952 C.E. (A.H. 341). Al-Mu'izz was twenty-four years old when he assumed the burden of the caliphate and the mantle of the imamate. The task of transferring the seat of the caliphate to Egypt fell on his shoulders, and he proved to be eminently qualified for the undertaking.

Al-Mu'izz was a gifted and respected leader who had the good vision to assemble an efficient and dedicated team. Using a combination of force and diplomacy, he consolidated his realm across all of North Africa to the Atlantic, then turned his attention to the real prize, Egypt, which he and his predecessors had coveted since the Fatimids established their caliphate in North Africa. He sent his trusted commanders to conquer and pacify Egypt.

We should keep in mind that the great realm of Islam had by now split into three major centers of power. The first was the Abbasid caliphate in the East with the center of power in the capital Baghdad. By this time, though, the Abbasid caliph had become a mere puppet of and hostage to palace intrigue, with virtually no authority. Outside of Baghdad, autonomous principalities, emirates, shaykhdoms, and various other territorial combinations ran their own affairs. They competed and cooperated according to the interests of their microcosm, paying scant attention to the seat of government in Baghdad.

The second seat of power was the Western segment of the Islamic realm in Andalusia (in modern-day southern Spain), with its capital Cordoba (Qurtuba). Andalusia, too, had by now reached a state of disorganization and internal conflict similar to that of the Abbasid Empire. In between these two distant realms, there was a huge void in authority and governance. This void had to be filled, and the Fatimids capitalized on and took full advantage of the power vacuum. The weak seats of government in Baghdad and Cordoba set the stage for a daring and enterprising group to seize the initiative armed with innovative ideas and a long track record of moral and religious rectitude. The Fatimid movement came at the right time in the right place and at the hands of the right people.

Inspired by al-Mu'izz, his commanders set out to conquer Egypt, which they captured in 969 C.E. (A.H. 358). Al-Mu'izz then moved the seat of his government to Egypt. A new city was planned for such a purpose and built to accommodate the infrastructure of the caliphate and the needs of the fourth caliph. The city was named al-Qahira al-Mu'izziya, known today as Cairo. Cairo would soon rival Baghdad in the East and Cordoba in the West as a seat of learning and intellectual activity.

Since the inception of their sect, the Shi'a had been more inclined to the search for justice and for the inner meaning of the religious message than the rest of the Muslim community. The Isma'ili branch carried this further, incorporating philosophy and Hellenic logic into their spiritual repertoire. Al-Mu'izz laid the foundation of the al-Azhar Mosque, soon to become a major university (possibly the oldest in the world). It continues to be a major center of learning in all of Islam to this day. He also encouraged the incorporation of Greek thought and philosophy into the interpretation of Islamic concepts and practices. Partly in accordance with Isma'ili thought and partly out of sensitivity to the feelings of the Sunni majority ruled by the Isma'ili minority, the Fatimids pursued a policy of tolerance that was unparalleled at that time.

Christians and Jews were accorded a status almost equal to that of the Muslims, and many of them reached positions of great power and influence. A Jewish man by the name of Ya'qub ibn Killis, for example, exhibited such loyalty and courage while serving in the Egyptian campaign that he was eventually appointed vizier in the government of al-'Aziz, the son of al-Mu'izz. Ya'qub had a strong role in laying the organization of the Fatimid administration, educational system, and the sciences. He even wrote a theological treatise based on what he had heard from al-Mu'izz and al-'Aziz. When Ya'qub died, prayer was led by al-'Aziz, who also participated in his burial.[5] Al-Mu'izz died in the city that he founded, al-Qahira, after a reign of twenty-three years. He is remembered not only as a just and powerful ruler but also as an eminent scholar, poet, and astronomer. By the time of his death his realm covered all of North Africa and stretched beyond into Syria and the Hijaz, controlling both Mecca and Medina and even parts of Iraq.

In Syria and in the Arabian Peninsula, the Fatimid caliphs were helped by regional overlords who were of the Shi'a persuasion or whose fortunes were advanced through weakening of the central authority of the Abbasids in Baghdad. The role of the Carmathians was complex and oscillated between total allegiance to the Fatimids and outright hostility and bloody competition for power. The shared hatred of the Abbasids was not enough to maintain a steady alliance between the Fatimids and the Carmathians. In time the Fatimid caliphs turned on the Carmathians and contributed significantly to their elimination as a political power. The radicalism and excessive violence of the Carmathians were out of line with the Fatimid principles of tolerance and justice. For instance in 930 C.E. (A.H. 317), the Carmathians raided the holy Ka'ba in Mecca, killed a number of pilgrims, and removed the Black Stone from the shrine. The stone was later returned, but only after the direct intercession of the Fatimid caliph al-Qa'im.[6] The Friday Khutba was declared in the name of al-Hakim in several cities in Iraq (Majed, 141). It is also noted that one of the Abbasid caliphs, by the name of al-Qa'im, renounced all his rights to the caliphate in 1060 C.E. in favor of the Fatamid caliph al-Mustansir. These events throw some light on the extent of the power and influence that the Fatimid Empire achieved at this time. Equally impressive was the degree of organization of the Isma'ili movement and the sophistication of the doctrine that was continuously inoculated with the thriving cultural and philosophical atmosphere of an intellectually based realm.

Al-'Aziz bi Allah succeeded al-Mu'izz in 975 C.E. (A.H. 365) and followed faithfully in the footsteps of his father. A powerful and gracious man, al-'Aziz was a man of letters and an accomplished poet. In this he illustrates the high premium that the Fatimid caliphs placed on education and culture. Al-'Aziz set his sight on Syria as the gateway to Iraq and as a bulwark against the lurking threat of the Byzantines. After all, the Fatimids, the vanguard of Isma'ili Shi'ism, had a score to settle with the Abbasids, who had usurped their right to the caliphate and followed that with merciless persecution. A few selected lines of poetry by al-'Aziz express his sentiments with respect to the Abbasids and to the perception of Fatimids in the greater scheme of things:

> When I saw religion had deteriorated
> And had lost its light and essence . . .
> I became incensed and filled with revolutionary zeal.
> I am the son of the Prophet of God
> And the noblest of men since Adam
> It is through us [Fatimids] that the doors [to true knowledge] are opened
> And with it will be sealed.
> Tell the Abbasids that they are nothing
> But hostages in custody of aliens.[7]

A decisive military campaign led by al-'Aziz himself defeated the Carmathians and opened the doors to Damascus. With Yemen and the holy cities in Arabia acknowledging the authority of the Fatimid caliph, his realm extended all the way across Egypt and the rest of North Africa to the Atlantic. Al-'Aziz was reputed to be an able and competent administrator in addition to being tolerant and humane.[8] A long period of peace and prosperity added to the affection of his subjects. He respected other peoples' faiths and encouraged discourse among theologians and philosophers without fear or bias. The religious tolerance of al-'Aziz was further demonstrated when he married a Christian woman of the Melkite sect, two of whose brothers became patriarchs, one of Jerusalem and the other of Cairo. In the last two years of his reign, the position of vizier was occupied by a Christian by the name of 'Isa ibn Nasturus.[9]

Al-ʿAziz died while en route to Syria to confront the Byzantine threat that surfaced from time to time across a fluid frontier between the two competing powers. His rule spanned about twenty-one years, an era that was considered to be one of the most productive and progressive eras of the day. He died in the year 996 C.E. (A.H. 386) and was promptly succeeded by his eleven-year-old son, al-Mansur bi Allah, who was at the time playing like any child of his age.

Al-Mansur acquired the title of al-Hakim bi Amr Allah, which roughly translates to "the ruler by the will of God." He was at the top of a tree when he was informed of his father's death. Placing the imperial headdress on the eleven-year-old boy, the chief of the imperial staff greeted him and presented the new caliph and imam to the royal retinue. The boy did not cry or shrink from the awesome responsibility. He accompanied the cortege of his father to Cairo with courage and decorum. Immediately after the burial of his father in Cairo, al-Hakim began to attend to the matters of the state. As a caliph al-Hakim intended to assume full responsibility for governing the vast realm that he had inherited and to tackle all the secular problems of the state. As an imam he would be at the center of the religious affairs in the Ismaʿili doctrine, leading to the Druze faith.

Al-Hakim bi Amr Allah (al-Hakim)

Few rulers in Islamic history have been the subject of as much controversy as al-Hakim. Almost from his first day as a caliph al-Hakim exhibited traits and features that were most unusual for a boy of eleven years. The sudden transformation from a child at play to the caliph of a large and dynamic realm seemed to be at the time almost effortless. He took charge of funeral arrangements for his deceased father, ordering the chief magistrate of the day to wash the body and perform the prayers in accordance with Islamic law. Whatever grief he may have had was not exhibited in public or reported by the observers in private. The next day al-Hakim appeared in the palace to receive condolences and accept the allegiance of his subjects. He then issued the first proclamation of a caliph bent on reassuring the public that the government was stable and there was no cause for concern: "Security is guaranteed . . . there is no cause to fear for personal safety or that of possessions. People should resume their lives and activities in freedom and peace."[10] With that simple overture, the young caliph immediately immersed himself in conducting the affairs of the state and in addressing the multiple challenges that confronted his realm.

The Fatimid Empire by that time extended all across North Africa in the west to the Hijaz and Yemen in the east. The strategic importance of Syria in this geographical context could not be overlooked, for Syria was at the crossroads of three competing forces, the Fatimids, the Abbasids, and the Byzantines. Syria was anything but stable internally or secure externally. Contributing to this state of instability was the fact that none of the three powers was strong enough to prevail and pacify Syria once and for all. Moreover, Syria represented a multiplicity of ethnic, tribal, religious, and political affiliations. The Fatimids, cognizant of the importance of Syria as a springboard to weaken and eventually obliterate the Abbasids in Iraq, kept trying to win Syria to their side. They also needed Syria to keep the Byzantines at bay or, under the right conditions, even to invade and destroy Byzantium altogether. The trouble was that the Fatimids could not win Syria's political allegiance, nor succeed in the conversion of the majority of the Syrian population to the Isma'ili persuasion. Therefore, the Fatimid foothold in Syria remained at the mercy of unstable alliances and shifting allegiances. It was during a military campaign to control Syria that al-Hakim's father al-ʿAziz died, leaving the child monarch with the heavy responsibilities of the caliphate and of the imamate. For more than one reason the campaign had to be called off and postponed to a later date. It was in Syria, however, that the first Druze communities emerged and survive to this day.

For about four years al-Hakim was under the protection of influential and jostling palace forces that included members from competing regions and tribes, each trying to outmaneuver the others ostensibly for the good of the realm, but more likely to further their own agenda. Royal palaces, then as now, constituted a natural arena for ambition, intrigue, avarice, corruption, violence, and above all the lust for power. Al-Hakim's courtiers were no exception, and the competition was fierce on the precious turf of the young caliph. Forces from the East conflicted with those from North Africa, while some tribes took advantage of the situation and ignited rebellions in different parts of the empire. Some of the influential figures in the royal court acted with impunity, pretending to shield al-Hakim from the vicissitudes of governing and the stress of his powerful position. Little did they know that the young boy was no mere puppet or an ordinary person whom they could manipulate under the guise of protection of the throne. They did not have to wait long; at age fifteen al-Hakim moved swiftly to clean house and assert his full authority, as a caliph and as an imam.

He fired the equivalent of the chief of imperial staff and shuffled high officials in a manner that ensured a balance of forces in his administration. This enabled him to exercise control and maintain stability. Rebellions were crushed with a combination of force, diplomacy, retribution, and leniency as the situation dictated. The sophistication with which he handled these complex issues was that expected from an older and more experienced ruler. Thus, in short order, al-Hakim became the master of his realm not only in name but in fact as well. He conferred stability to his regime and credibility to his caliphate. His mother and sister were a source of counsel and loyalty that helped him during the critical period of transition.

Al-Hakim worked tirelessly to consolidate his realm and improve the living conditions of his people. He distributed land to the farmers and promoted social justice. He fought corruption and prevented hoarding and price gouging as well as usury, and he abolished slavery. He roamed the streets incognito, especially at night, to find for himself what was happening on the ground. At times he imposed a night curfew to curb the prostitution and drunken behavior that afflicted Cairo as they generally afflict thriving cities. Consequently, al-Hakim was an extremely popular ruler, and his reign of a quarter century was a period of remarkable stability.[11]

Although al-Hakim had special interests in astronomy and built an observatory to study the stars, he had no use for astrologers and various other seers and magicians. Above all he was fond of scholars and was a champion of scholarship unhampered by tradition or dogma. A huge library was appended to al-Hakim's palace and was filled with books from all corners of the empire. Scholars were accorded high esteem and enticed to work and produce in an academic atmosphere that was free from pressure or coercion.[12] An institute was created to foster scholarship and encourage learned discourse and philosophical pursuits. The institute was named House of Wisdom (Dar al-Hikma), and the appellation was most appropriate. It was a continuation of the tradition of the Fatimid caliphs, who offered the resources of the state and the prestige of the caliphate to all aspects of learning. Dar al-Hikma and Dar al-'Ilm (House of Learning) were in a sense a continuation of al-Azhar University. Established as a mosque by al-Mu'izz (al-Hakim's grandfather) upon moving the capital of the Fatimid caliphate to Cairo, al-Azhar grew beyond being only a mosque to being a major citadel of learning as well.

These academic institutes, primarily designed to further the cause of the Isma'ili "cause" or "mission" (da'wa), provided fertile ground for a tremendous renaissance in all aspects of learning. As a result they acted as a major attraction for brilliant and probing minds to flock to Cairo from all over the Islamic world. In no time Dar al-Hikma became a beehive of activity covering all the known branches of learning at that time. An intensive search for manuscripts was undertaken and books were imported and transcribed by scores of experts.

New ideas were given a chance for discussion through lectures, seminars, and various forms of dialogue and interpretation with no restrictions or fear of heretic accusation and retribution. A large support staff kept the institution well managed and maintained, funded by the caliph himself and by grants from the revenues of the realm. In addition al-Hakim frequently joined in the philosophical and scientific discussions as a participant and adviser.

It is noteworthy that the institutions of learning and research were not restricted to Muslims. The Fatimid tolerance for open and free discourse extended the invitation to scholars from other faiths to participate in and contribute to the pluralistic atmosphere of learning. Scholarship, in the Fatimid Empire, had reached its zenith during the reign of al-Hakim.

Al-Hakim invited Ibn al-Haitham (al-Hazen), the famous mathematician and engineer who had a special expertise in optics, to Cairo. Al-Hazen provided crucial advice on economic development and construction projects, particularly those related to control of the seasonal flooding of the Nile. The famous Syrian poet-philosopher Abu al-ʿAlaʾ al-Maʿarri was invited by al-Hakim to relocate to Cairo. Al-Maʾarri preferred to stay at home for health reasons, including blindness.[13] There is strong evidence that al-Maʾarri was a loyal supporter of the Fatimid caliph, and the call to Tawhid occurred under his aegis.[14] Al-Hakim also welcomed to Cairo the famous Ismaʿili philosopher Hamid al-Din al-Kirmani to lecture on the nature of the Ismaʿili imamate. As a senior Ismaʿili theologian and proselytizer *(daʿi)* and as a scholar, al-Kirmani wielded considerable influence in the community. His loyalty to al-Hakim was beyond dispute.[15] Likewise al-Hakim was in contact with the philosopher and physician Ibn Sina (Avicenna) and his father, the latter being one of al-Hakim's followers.[16] The intellectual and philosophical activities taking place during the caliphate of al-Hakim bi Amr Allah were many and wide ranging. As well, the institutes of learning such as al-Azhar and Dar al-Hikma provided the perfect setting for refinement of the interpretive skills of Ismaʿili scholars and the continuing elaboration of Ismaʿili doctrine leading to the emergence of the Druze concept of Tawhid.

As a person, al-Hakim was reputed to be physically powerful, with a commanding and intimidating presence. He was resolute in judgment, combining leniency with firmness, thrift with generosity, and elitism with modesty. He wielded and exercised the power that his position called for but renounced the trappings associated with power. He dressed modestly, gradually emulating the Sufis in his attire and way of life. The custom of kissing the ground in front of the caliph as well as kissing his hands was prohibited. All the fanfare, including ornaments and the tympani of martial music, as well as adulation of his name during religious sermons, was also dispensed with. He discouraged people from using phrases such as "our lord and master" when referring to him.[17] Later in his tenure he developed the habit of nightly visits to the arid hills on the outskirts of Cairo for contemplation and guidance, away from the din and clamor of the bustling city and the suffocating pressures of the royal palace. With deep interest in astronomy, al-Hakim built an observatory for research. However, he totally rejected astrology, fortune-telling, and other practices that dwelt on the occult.

Al-Hakim was an idealist and a mystic who aspired to a world of peace, order, and justice. Like many idealists, though, he had considerable difficulty in the world of realpolitik, where all aspects of human nature are exhibited. He was puritanical to the point of behaving like a Sufi and therefore could not easily tolerate avarice and corruption. In religious terms he was the imam who upheld the tenets of Islam. He held all members of the Muslim *umma* in high esteem and did not favor one sect of Islam over another. For example he banned the practice of some Shi'a extremists who disparaged Abu Bakr, Omar, and 'Uthman as usurpers of the right of 'Ali to the caliphate upon the death of the Prophet. Furthermore, neither he nor his predecessors tried to impose Isma'ili doctrine on the predominantly Sunni population of Egypt. Rather he tried to treat all Muslims and non-Muslims as fairly as possible, and expected likewise.[18] It was when others did not reciprocate that he exhibited a harshness considered excessive by some people. However, the response was in keeping with what was expected from a puritan and an idealist, considering the standard practices of the time.

Much has been said and written about al-Hakim and his caliphate, with considerable disagreement and differences in interpretation among chroniclers, historians, and scholars. No other caliph in Islam enjoyed as wide a spectrum of opinions as al-Hakim. Thus what appeared as cruelty to some was bravery and fortitude to others. Puritanical behavior was considered to be a form of xenophobia by some and self-denial by others. His strict rules on hygienic matters were likewise condemned or admired depending on the persuasion of the chronicler or commentator. And this dichotomy of opinions applied across the board to all the actions and traits of the sixth Fatimid caliph. The same would become applicable to the movement that was unleashed in his name by an inner circle of his followers. Not to be ignored is that the historical portrait of al-Hakim was recorded by chroniclers most of whom were hostile to the Fatimid cause, to Isma'ilism, and more pointedly to the person of al-Hakim himself. After all the Fatimid state represented minority rule, which the majority (Sunni) Islam never forgot or forgave.

Al-Hakim was caliph of Islam in a large and fluid empire at a turbulent period in Islamic history. He was also, in the Isma'ili doctrine, the acknowledged imam of Islam, a position conferred on him by right of birth as the direct descendant of the Prophet. At the time of his tenure, the Fatimid caliphate had been in existence for nearly ninety years, and the Isma'ilis, like the rest of the Shi'a, were anxiously awaiting the dawn of enlightenment and justice and the end of tyranny at the hands of a reedemer (Mahdi) from the seed of 'Ali and Fatima. After all, they had endured a long history of repression and disenfranchisement, in anticipation of such redemption. Thus when they attained the ultimate goal of a combined caliphate and imamate, the faithful wanted to declare their religious doctrine openly and promote it vigorously. They had waited for centuries for this eventuality that fulfilled their dreams of worldly power.

Yet despite the glories and successes of the Fatimid caliphate and the high intellectual caliber of the successive caliphs, the empire remained one of this world.[19] The community was very much aware of all the strengths and weaknesses of their caliphate and the challenges that it faced. The promise of an ideal world built on justice and virtue and the bliss of redemption was a dream that only their state could fulfill. After all, the caliphate was in the hands of the imams, descendants of the Prophet through 'Ali and Fatima, a condition that should have been the culmination of the messianic Isma'ili promise of redemption. Yet after ninety years and five successive Fatimid imam-caliphs, the messianic dream remained unfulfilled.[20] It was against this backdrop that al-Hakim, in the eyes of his followers, was accorded the status of the awaited redeemer. As such, his era would represent the end of the last cycle of divine manifestations and the preparatory stage for the day of judgment. When and how that day takes place will remain a secret that the Almighty shares with no one.

Al-Hakim must have struggled with these and other issues both as a ruler and as an imam. After all, he was ordained by divine guidance to lead the faithful and indeed all of humanity to the safety of God's grace.

Within this context, al-Hakim and his circle of supporters explored theological and philosophical approaches that are bolder and more daring than the limits of the Isma'ili doctrine. He kept on searching for solutions to the insurmountable challenges that faced his probing mind and restless spirit. Hence his support of Dar al-Hikma and active participation in the intellectual activities in all aspects of learning. Furthermore this may explain the extremes of opinions that historians hold with respect to this enigmatic caliph. These opinions range from outright condemnation[21] to unequivocal adulation,[22] and all the grades in between. Regardless of the view of historians, al-Hakim is a specially revered figure in the Druze interpretation of Tawhid.

The next step in the history of the Druze was an unusual event that created a significant departure from the Isma'ili doctrine: the transfer of the imamate to a personality not connected by blood to the Fatimids. As time went on, it became clear that not only the identity but also the definition and function of this neo-imamate were also different from those in the traditional Isma'ili doctrine. The person chosen to play the new role was of Persian descent and was known as Hamza ibn 'Ali, the chief architect of the Tawhid faith of the Druze in the era of al-Hakim.

Hamza and the Neo-imamate

In the year 985 C.E. (A.H. 385), a boy was born in the town of Zouzan in eastern Iran by the name of Hamza ibn 'Ali. It was the same year in which al-Hakim was born. Gifted with a brilliant mind and an insatiable thirst for knowledge, Hamza studied hard and excelled in many fields of learning. After graduating from Jund-nisabur University (in modern-day Ahwaz), he was attracted to Cairo, which was at the time the major citadel of intellectual activity and cross-cultural interactions. Hamza participated in the intellectual and philosophical ferment of the day, thereby refining his own skills and attracting the attention of al-Hakim. Al-Hakim quickly recognized the potential of the young man and began to give him more attention. On his part, Hamza's commitment to al-Hakim was total and his allegiance unconditional. Hamza decided to dedicate his life to the exalted state that al-Hakim would eventually represent in the Druze concept of Tawhid. For the time being, however, it appeared that Hamza was entrusted with the role of developing, organizing, and proclaiming a new and somewhat innovative mod-ification of the standard Isma'ili doctrine. This doctrine, which the community to be known later as the Druze would embrace, was known as the "call to Tawhid" or the Tawhid faith. The Tawhid faith was openly proclaimed in 1017 C.E. (A.H. 408). There are hints that public disclosure of the call to join the Druze faith, the *da'wa*, may have been precipitated by one or more members of the senior leader-ship to gain advantage over the others. Nonetheless, once the call to Tawhid be-came public, proselytizing activity went into full swing.

Years of meticulous preparations preceded the open proclamation of the new doctrine. Emissaries (*da'is*) were recruited and trained and then sent to different parts of the realm, paving the way for the new call. The *da'is* enlisted the support of key individuals and families and tribes who were felt to be sympathetic to the new call throughout the Muslim world. Together they built an infrastructure capable of launching the call to Tawhid and public disclosure of its tenets. Much of this effort was initially spent in areas where the ground was fertile and among individuals who were already qualified to receive the complicated new philosophical message. No attempt was made to force the population at large (who were predominantly of the Sunni persuasion) to enroll in the new faith. Practical reasons as well as concerns about the level of individual preparedness to comprehend the message of Tawhid precluded any form of coercion or excessive proselytization among the masses of people who had never ventured beyond the security of dogma in the practice of their faith. The number seven had a special significance in the interpretation and evolution of cyclical events in the Isma'ili philosophy, and this was applied to the seven-year stages of training and preparation.

The status of the imam in the Isma'ili tradition grew by leaps and bounds with the passage of time, reaching legendary proportions with the Fatimid caliphs. There were even some zealots who went so far as to confer on the Fatimid caliphs a status closer to divine than human. For example, one of the major poets at that time, Ibn Hani al-Andalusi (the Andalusian), wrote several odes that could be interpreted as portraying al-Mu'izz (al-Hakim's grandfather) in terms of the divine:

> It is your will, not that of fate
> Reign you are the one and only supreme
> It is as though you are the Prophet Muhammad
> And your supporters [ansar] are the same as his.[23]

The Fatimid caliphs for the most part looked the other way, as they were convinced of the special place they had in God's grand scheme. The basic edifice of Isma'ili doctrine rests on the sacred status of the imams who descended from the seed of the Prophet through his daughter Fatima and son-in-law 'Ali. A short poem that Prince Tammam composed addressing his brother, the caliph al-'Aziz, serves to illustrate the point:

> You are in comparison to other kings
> But a holy spirit in a human body
> An ethereal light whose essence exceeded that of the sun and the moon
> The meaning emanating from the first cause that preceded
> The creation of Earth and the skies.[24]

This degree of adulation is not merely an expression of poetic sentimentality but goes to the core of Isma'ili and subsequent Druze theosophy. The Fatimid caliphs, however, never reached the point where they would be considered as gods by their devoted followers, except for a few zealots who emerged from time to time in Shi'ism and who, in their excessive adulation, raised their imams to the level of divinity. The contention of divinity would be blasphemous in Islam, and the Fatimid caliphs were devout Muslims. In fact, the next line from the poem of Ibn Hani quoted above likens the status of the Fatimid caliph to the position of the Prophet, thereby refuting any claim of the caliphs to divinity. The imamate, exalted as it may have become, was theirs by divine right and in perpetuity, but the Fatimid caliphs were not gods. For example, a letter of chastisement sent by al-Mu'izz to al-Hasan al-Qurmuti (the Carmathian) serves to demonstrate how far the Fatimid caliphs had gone as human beings, albeit with a divinely ordained status as caliphs and imams, who were destined to preserve and propagate the Islamic message:

> And all of these phenomena, referring to his own interpretation of events and principles in the various devine messages across the eternity of cyclical revelations, contain references *(dalalat)* to us and are preludes to our reach and pretexts to show our will, gifts, testimonies, and blessed stature, and nature. . . . For there was no proclaimer who testified nor prophet who was sent. . . . that did not point to us and glorify our nature and identify us in his speech and in writing, and in the essence of his message.

Then al-Mu'izz goes on to say: "And for all to know . . . that we are the [custodians of] the eternal word of God, his perfect attributes, his dazzling light, his guiding beacon . . . and his divine will; no order except through us and *no era is without our presence.*"[25] All these claims, however, fall within the context of propagating Islam and preserving its pristine message.

Since the Abbasid caliphs had resorted to spreading misinformation accusing the Fatimids of claiming divinity, the same Fatimid caliph (al-Mu'izz) explained in another communication: "It has come to our attention that some [zealots] have resorted to excessive exaggeration of our status. . . . We completely refute their claims since we are servants of God. . . . We claim no prophecy and we profess no knowledge except what we have inherited from his Prophet (and our great-grandfather), Muhammad (PBOH). . . . We are below the claims of the zealots and above the accusations of the ignorant."[26]

At some point in the latter years of al-Hakim's reign, a new phenomenon was introduced whereby the role of imam was designated to Hamza. This constituted a departure from the tradition of almost four hundred years, since Hamza had no claims to the imamate by right of birth or by written edict *(nass)*. We do not learn of this appointment from al-Hakim himself but from epistles written by Hamza and from other epistles written by one of Hamza's junior associates (Baha' al-Din) indicating that the appointment of Hamza to the new imamate had received al-Hakim's support. The departure from keeping the imamate ad infinitum in the house of ʿAli was a major breach of the Ismaʿili tradition. In fact it represented a new definition of the imamate in the Druze interpretation of Tawhid. The new era of Tawhid, representing the culmination of the long process of spiritual evolution, necessitated redefinition of the role and function of the imamate in the new order. The traditional concept of the imamate was, therefore, superceded by a new paradigm that reflected the theosophy of the new path. In fact it represented an end to the traditional role of the imam in the new faith, and a departure from the main Ismaʿili doctrine whereby the imamate continued to the present time. This is how Hamza refers to the emergence of the new path:

> And now the culmination of the revolving cycles is at hand, and what was hidden from the noble principles [of the faith] is disclosed, and what was kept behind solid walls is now revealed for all to see, and the circle was closed by reaching its focal point *[nuqtat al-bikar]*. I composed this epistle by the grace of our master . . . and called it Disclosure of Truths *[Kashf al-Haqa'iq]*.[27]

The basic function of Hamza's imamate was to formulate, explain, and propagate the new message of Tawhid, in the era of the sixth Fatimid caliph, al-Hakim bi Amr Allah. Suffice it to say that the ending of the traditional imamate with al-Hakim would have serious repercussions on the nascent "Druze" community after his disappearance, when the community did not recognize the succession to the imamate from his bloodline. The role of the imamate in the Ismaʿili tradition was no longer applicable to the new conditions in the age of disclosure (Dawr al-Kashf) in the era of al-Hakim.

As for al-Hakim, he was elevated to a status higher than that of imam-designate since the era of a divinely guided imam from the bloodline of ʿAli and Fatima had reached its goal and a new order had begun. Al-Hakim was the centerpiece of the faith and the beacon of the faithful, while Hamza assumed the role of guide of the faithful. It was in this capacity, as imam, that Hamza became the chief architect of the Tawhid faith and the primary designated force behind the eventual emergence of the Druze path to Tawhid.

During the first year the call to join the Druze faith appeared to be on target, with a large number of notables and intellectuals proclaiming their allegiance to al-Hakim as the spiritual head of the movement and to Hamza as his chief lieutenant. However, and unexpectedly, there ensued a power struggle between Hamza and two other members of al-Hakim's inner circle. The first was a man by the name of Abu Haidara al-Farghani, also known as al-Akhram, a zealot who openly preached the divinity of al-Hakim.[28] Al-Farghani did not last long enough to leave a legacy of his thinking since he was assassinated early on. The other was Muhammad ibn Isma'il, better known as Neshtegin al-Darazi, who had ingratiated himself with al-Hakim and probably with Hamza himself. After gaining enough of a foothold, al-Darazi tried to usurp the role of Hamza as the chief architect of the faith.

Repeated admonitions to cease and desist from divisiveness and distortion went unheeded, and a confrontation became inevitable. Thus we hear Hamza addressing al-Darazi in 1019 C.E. (A.H. 410), after the latter reneged and challenged Hamza's role as the imam-designate:

> And what I have disclosed of the true and preserved doctrine neither you nor anyone else could do and that was through the support of our sovereign [al-Hakim] in what he promised to me, and he never reneges on his promise. . . . Therefore if you still claim to be faithful, declare your allegiance and publicly support my imamate as you have done before.[29]

Al-Darazi, it is implied, never did that and ended up losing the power struggle. There are no records that I know of from al-Darazi himself as to the events of this fateful period. In addition to competition with Hamza for leadership of the budding movement, al-Darazi, according to Hamza, erred in the interpretation of the tenets of Tawhid and committed moral laxities that Hamza had warned against. Al-Darazi was also probably more rash in proclaiming the *da'wa*, presumably to be ahead of Hamza.[30]

The elimination of al-Darazi and the endorsement of Hamza to the leadership of the faithful took place, according to Hamza himself, only after al-Hakim gave the nod of approval. Thus ended the first serious threat to the nascent movement before it was barely a year old. It is ironic that the Druze appellation given to the followers of Tawhid was derived from the name of a major renegade and traitor to the movement.

An alternative explanation for the Druze appellation may be related to the confusion between Neshtegin al-Darazi (the renegade) and Khatkin (al-Dayf), who was one of the trusted followers of al-Hakim. Khatkin was among those who requested the assistance of al-Kirmani in the resolution of the growing rift among the followers of al-Hakim. Another source of confusion may be related to Anoshtigin al-Dizbari, a military commander who served in the army of al-Hakim in Palestine; he subsequently fought battles against some of the warlords hostile to the Druze (for example, Saleh ibn Mirdas), thereby protecting the Druze during the era of persecution that began immediately after the disappearance of al-Hakim. Some Druze authors refer to Neshtegin al-Darazi as another Anoshtigin al-Darazi, probably due to a mix-up in names.[31] In this case the Druze appellation would make more sense. Nonetheless most of the Druze are aware of al-Darazi the renegade, which causes them considerable discomfort. In fact some members of the community even now would like to eliminate the term Druze and replace it with something like "Muwahhidun," that is, believers in Tawhid, or "Banu Ma'ruf," in view of their adulation of knowledge (*ma'rifa*, gnosis) or their tradition of generosity (*ma'ruf*). The change would be difficult to make as it would require overriding several hundred years of common usage of an admittedly controversial appellation.

The traumatic episode of the renegade al-Darazi caused a reassessment and reorganization of the movement, and all overt activities were suspended for a year. We are largely in the dark as to the events of the year and why it took so long for al-Hakim to tilt the balance in favor of Hamza during the power struggle. There may have been major efforts going on to reassess what had been set in motion in terms of openly declaring the *da'wa* and the wisdom of the timing. There is subtle reference in the Druze epistles that the call may have been prematurely launched, probably to give one party advantage over others. Be that as it may, the believers then, as now, had no difficulty in providing a rational explanation for the early and rather prolonged suspension of the call to Tawhid barely within a year of its initiation.

It is commonly thought by the Druze that the suspension of the call was meant to test the depth of the allegiance of those who had enrolled in it. The veracity of the commitment could be ascertained when tested. Reference to this contention is present in many epistles. However, it is also plausible that there may have been efforts to reexamine some aspects of the faith and clarify some of its basic tenets. It was during this time that al-Kirmani was invited to Cairo, presumably to offer advice and guidance on bridging the rift generated by the competing forces within the Isma'ili ranks. The fact remains that during the year 1018 C.E. (A.H. 409), there was virtual suspension of all outward activities of the movement.

This act became a precedent for suspension of the call and not for irrevocable closure.

With al-Darazi out of the way and the *da'is* more alert and wiser by this experience, the call to Tawhid was resumed in 1019 C.E. (A.H. 410). The door was again opened to accept the initiates and those who chose to join willingly, with their full physical and intellectual faculties and without any coercion. Al-Darazi would not be the last of the renegades, particularly during the difficult years after the disappearance of al-Hakim. For the moment it seemed that the road was clear for resumption of the call to Tawhid and for fresh recruits. The esoteric nature of the faith and the complex philosophical underpinnings made it more attractive to those who had reached a certain level of knowledge and willingness to break with tradition.

The conditions for enrollment were set according to strict and clearly defined rules. These rules stipulated that initiates must be of sound mind and body and must be fully aware of the basic tenets of the faith. Their commitment to the faith must be unequivocal with no hesitation, doubt, or second thoughts. The strict conditions for entry helped filter out all but those who fully understood the message and who gave it wholehearted allegiance. To seal their enrollment, the initiates were required to sign a covenant *(mithaq)* that they would honor as long as they lived. The Druze belief in reincarnation extended the life of the pledge indefinitely as long as the cycles of birth and death continued. After all, the soul of the individual is the repository of religious beliefs. The essence does not dissipate with the disintegration of the body, which merely serves as a physical abode of the soul. Rather, the soul continues the journey until the end of time.

Hamza had by now established a tightly knit spiritual and administrative organization based on the philosophical precepts of Tawhid as he and his lieutenants defined them. As the chief architect, Hamza defined his own role as well as the roles of his chief subordinates and associates in the movement. The extent to which al-Hakim himself was involved in the details of the new movement is not known. We know that the highly respected Isma'ili philosopher and *da'i* Hamid al-Din al-Kirmani was summoned to Cairo on behalf of al-Hakim to resolve some contentious issues and to help restore order and stability to the *da'wa*.[32]

The team that Hamza assembled consisted of five individuals, sometimes referred to in this text as apostles of Tawhid. In Arabic they are referred to as *hudud* (sing. *hadd*), or "luminaries" of Tawhid. In the physical sense the luminaries are ordinary human beings. In the abstract sense, however, they represent archetypes of cosmic principles, somewhat analogous to those in the Platonic realm of ideals.

This dual concept of the luminaries, with the ideal represented by the real, provides a link between the spiritual and the corporeal in the continuum of existence: "Can't you see . . . that for every luminary *[hadd]* in the heights of the spiritual realm *[ruhani]*, there is a representative counterpart *hadd* in the lower realm *[jismani* or corporeal]."[33]

The organizational structure of the new movement and the names and titles of the principal figures of the Tawhid faith in the era of al-Hakim were as follows:

1. At the apex of the hierarchy stood Hamza himself as the undisputed (and self-declared) imam of the faithful in the role of human representation of the first cosmic principle, the universal mind *(al-'aql al-kulli)*.

2. Next in line came the second in command and a brother-in-law of Hamza, Isma'il ibn Muhammad Ibn Hamed al-Tamimi in the role of human representation of the universal soul *(al-nafs)*.

3. Next came Muhammed ibn Wahb al-Qurashi as the human representation of the universal word *(al-kalima)*.

4. The fourth in line was Salama Bin Abdul-Wahhab al-Samarra'i, in the role of human representation of the right wing, the precedent *(al-sabiq)*.

5. The fifth and last of the luminaries was 'Ali ibn Ahmad al-Sammuqi in the role of human representation of the left wing, the follower *(al-tali)*. He also was affectionately called al-Muqtana Baha' al-Din. The terms *right wing* and *left wing* may be understood in the context of military formation offering protection to the main body of forces. They may also constitiue an allegorical reference to the past, the precedent *(sabiq)*, and the future—what is to follow *(tali)*.

These names, tongue twisters to the Western ear, are listed for orientation. The positions they occupied represented the apex of the pyramid in the Tawhid doctrine and in the organization of the call to Tawhid. Three more figures, al-Jidd, al-Fath, and al-Khayal, in the roles of *da'i*, *ma'thun*, and *mukasir* respectively, held high positions in the organizational hierarchy of the call, but they were ordinary people who played supportive roles to the five luminaries. Directly beneath those eight figures was a pyramidal structure that listed a total of 164 positions of leadership and power within the organization of the *da'wa*. The five luminaries and three subordinates make a total of eight senior figures in the Druze call to Tawhid. Eight persons may have been designated because of the Qur'anic verse: "And upon that day [the day of judgment], eight shall carry above them the Throne of thy Lord" (69:16).

Directly beneath the senior leadership were several layers of experts, lieutenants, and devotees each with a specific job description and a defined position in the chain of command. Much of this was already familiar territory from the long Isma'ili experience of almost two centuries. The difference was that this time the call to Tawhid was openly declared and was considered to represent the culmination of the long-awaited eventuality of redemption. It marked the last cycle in the transfer of the imamate from one era to the next in the Isma'ili order of succession. Thus this call pushed the envelope of Isma'ili doctrine farther from the Isma'ili mainstream than ever before. Concepts like reincarnation, and the Divine's revelation of himself through a kind of theophany *(tajalli)*, were introduced and defended. Stress was placed on the inner meaning of the message, to the extent that the outer forms of practice might no longer be necessary for those who had achieved a certain level of purity and spirituality.

In any event, after one year of suspension the call was resumed in the open, led by Hamza and protected by al-Hakim. The support of the head of the state provided the safety net that the movement needed to explain its doctrine and to cement the allegiance and loyalty of those who began to enter its ranks.

The second phase of open activities lasted almost two years, until 1021 C.E. (A.H. 411). In February of that year, al-Hakim left his palace at night riding a donkey to the hills (al-Muqattam) near Cairo. It was a habitual journey that al-Hakim had undertaken for many years. As was his habit, he had no guards, no retinue, and no courtiers. Therefore there was no eyewitness to what may have happened to the sixth Fatimid caliph, al-Hakim bi Amr Allah, during that fateful night. All we know is that al-Hakim did not return from his excursion and he vanished without a trace. It is reported that his shirt was found still buttoned, but no traces of his body. The donkey that he was riding was located with its limbs severed. Such an enigmatic ending for an already enigmatic personality added to the mystery of the occasion. The sudden disappearance *(ghayba)* of a venerated imam is not new in the Shi'a tradition. Implicit in the disappearance of al-Hakim, like that of al-Mahdi (al-Muntazar) in the Twelver Shi'a tradition, is the belief in the triumphal return of the vanished imam *(al-gha'ib)* as a redeemer and savior.

Followers of al-Hakim explain his sudden disappearance as an acid test of the metal of his supporters and the veracity of their faith. After all, the new movement of Tawhid that was initiated in al-Hakim's name at the height of his power could best be tested during his absence. Others claim conspiracies from many sides (including his ambitious sister) who may have wanted to eliminate a caliph who had become a liability and a threat to the Fatimid caliphate itself. After all, his personal behavior and his method of governance were beyond the ability of his family and his confidants to control or even influence to any appreciable degree. Still others claim that al-Hakim did not die but rather retreated to a secluded place somewhere in the Indian subcontinent to dedicate himself to spiritual pursuits away from the responsibilities of government and the tribulations of daily life.[34]

The details of what may have happened are discussed in multiple sources that address this eerie episode in Fatimid history.[35] According to a contemporary scholar in the field: "More pages are devoted to conjecture about his [al-Hakim's] disappearance than to the whole twenty-five years of his reign. Many stories were written and many assumptions have been made to clarify that mystery, but a satisfactory explanation has never been established."[36]

Needless to say, al-Hakim's disappearance triggered a cascade of events that had profound repercussions on the Tawhid movement. Three statements from Epistle 1, the document that was declared to the public at the time of al-Hakim's disappearance, provide a tantalizing view of what may have been happening. Speaking of what al-Hakim had done in his capacity as imam of the faithful: "And he [al-Hakim] opened to you the doors to his call and supported you with the wisdom that God has bestowed upon him, to lead you to God's grace." This can be construed as saying that the call to Tawhid was initiated by al-Hakim and then entrusted to Hamza to execute. The second statement follows after a short interval and portrays al-Hakim's displeasure with his subjects: "An indication of the displeasure of the imam [al-Hakim] is the closure of the doors to his call and the suspension of wisdom that was bestowed upon you." What the reasons were for the displeasure of al-Hakim, and for the withdrawal of the call to Tawhid that was launched in his name, we can only speculate. It could be that this statement was in the context of the one-year suspension of the call after the first year of disclosure.

The third and most vexing of these statements deals with al-Hakim's disappearance: "Beware, beware that any one of you should go searching for al-Hakim or try to follow any news that may lead to his whereabouts."[37] Whether this statement was based on speculation or on inside information as to what was in store for al-Hakim, we do not know. Did he (possibly in complicity with his followers) stage the whole episode, in which case we are left in the dark as to what would have prompted him (or them) to do so. Although we may never know what exactly happened to al-Hakim in connection with his disappearance, we know a fair amount of what happened to his followers.

Almost simultaneously with al-Hakim's disappearance, Hamza retired from public view. In addition, all but one (Baha' al-Din) of the five major luminaries also retired from public view and probably went into hiding. They were not heard from again. Hamza must have remained in Cairo or at least in a place that was accessible for a while, directing and advising Baha' al-Din. Speculation that he had met a violent death in exile, as suggested by some scholars (e.g., Heinz Halm), does not correspond to documentation to the contrary in Druze epistles.[38] Contrary to the claim by Halm that Hamza was killed when al-Hakim disappeared, the Druze epistles contain ample evidence that Hamza lived after the disappearance of al-Hakim and continued to direct the call for an unknown period of time. Baha' al-Din in turn continued to preside over the remaining leaders and lieutenants of the faith. For a period of time Baha' al-Din remained in touch with Hamza, indicating that the latter was still alive after his disappearance. However, for all practical purposes the call to Tawhid terminated all its public activities and went into secrecy.

Persecution *(Mihna)*

For seven years after the disappearance of al-Hakim, the followers of Tawhid were hunted down like criminals. The Tawhid doctrine stipulated that the era of the imamate ended with al-Hakim and Hamza. Thus, by definition, the new faith did not recognize the imamate of al-Hakim's successor and son 'Ali al-Zahir, and al-Zahir was quick to respond. Retribution was swift and widespread. It was unleashed forty days after the assumption of the new caliph to the seat of the caliphate. The reason for forty days is allegedly related to a commitment obtained by al-Hakim from al-Zahir consisting of an oath repeated forty times that al-Zahir would not harm the followers of Tawhid once al-Zahir assumed power. Al-Zahir honored the oath by waiting forty days before he commenced a policy of liquidation, one day for each oath.[39]

Hostile actions toward the followers of Tawhid were both massive and merciless. They and their families were in constant danger from the apparatus of the state. The caliphate that had protected them during al-Hakim's reign turned against them with a vengeance during the reign of his successor and son, 'Ali al-Zahir. Their belongings were confiscated and their means of livelihood constrained, to the point of exhaustion. During this period of time the best they could do was to lie low and hope for reprieve.

The first phase of persecution lasted seven years, during which almost all activities of the *da'wa* were suspended, as the community and its leadership were concerned with survival and damage control. Times were very difficult indeed, and the community had to resort to secrecy and discretion, using codes in communication to maintain the faith and protect the faithful. As expected there were those who broke ranks at the downturn and became renegades, exploiting the catastrophic situation to their advantage. More damage was done by opportunists who tried to usurp the leadership of the beleaguered community by means of sabotage and self-aggrandizement. These apostates caused further damage by twisting the message of Tawhid and inserting misleading and false documents, instructions, and statements. The extent to which these distortions infiltrated the message of Tawhid and contaminated its true meaning is not known. Nor has there been any serious effort to weed out the distortions that were inserted at one time or another into the epistles in the Druze Books of Wisdom. Baha' al-Din, the only one of the five luminaries to remain active after the disappearance of al-Hakim, tried desperately to combat the actions of the apostates. That he was deeply concerned with sabotage is evident in many of the epistles that he wrote. However, he had to exercise great discretion since he was a man of public visibility and stature, even during the administration of al-Zahir.

Baha' al-Din could no longer stay in Cairo; he relocated to Alexandria, the second city and a former pre-Islamic capital of Egypt, for his own safety. From there he stayed in touch with Hamza (his superior whose whereabouts were not known to the public). He also continued to communicate with leaders and influential elements in the movement who were entrusted to implement Baha' al-Din's instructions. Most of the communications during this period of time were circumspect, with the use of codes and insinuations. Such communications were not intended to attract converts but rather to exhort the ones already in to stand fast and not lose faith.

Al-Zahir died in 1036 C.E. (A.H. 427) after a reign of roughly sixteen years. His reign was catastrophic for the followers of Tawhid, particularly the first seven of these years. Open activity during this time was barely possible because of the persecution by al-Zahir and the ripple effects in several parts of the Fatimid realm. Renewed, organized activity on behalf of the *da'wa* did not start until two years after the death of al-Zahir. At that time, Hamza, still out of sight, instructed Baha' al-Din to resume his proselytizing activities. Thus a third phase of enrollment was initiated in 1037 C.E. (A.H. 429). By now Baha' al-Din had earned the respect of al-Zahir's successor and was appointed to high positions in the new administration. This gave Baha' al-Din enough protective cover to try openly to expand the base of the movement. Meanwhile he spent most of his time and effort repairing the damages of sabotage and apostasy. A man of great intellectual power and psychological stamina, Baha' al-Din carried the burden of the entire community almost single-handedly for another eight years. Finally, his resources exhausted, he bade farewell to the faithful in the year 1043 C.E. (A.H. 435) and was heard from no more. The magnitude of the persecution immediately following the disappearance of al-Hakim was such that it left an indelible mark on the Druze psyche to this day. The Druze refer to it as the tragedy or catastrophe *(Mihna)* that was visited upon them for adopting a religious path that harassed no one and did not seek to convert anyone by force. Even when the Mihna ended after seven years, the Druze continued to be harassed and persecuted for another fifteen years, until Baha' al-Din retired in 1043 C.E. The Mihna was one of the main events that contributed to solidarity and altruism among members of the Druze community to this day.

Baha' al-Din did not appoint a successor, and all overt activities of the public call to Tawhid came to a halt. This was interpreted as de facto closure of the call to Tawhid, a tradition that persists to this day. De facto closure in time became synonymous with closure of the door as an essential principle of the faith. The proponents of this school of thought argue that closure of the call to Tawhid was fair and just, since all of humanity, bar none, were given sufficient opportunity to enroll between 1017 and 1043 C.E. (A.H. 408–37), a period of more than twenty-six years. During that period there would have been enough time for every newborn to reach maturity and to exercise free will to accept or reject the call to Tawhid. Since everyone was offered a chance to choose during this period of time, and presumably made that choice, more time for further enrollment was no longer needed. Those who did not enroll simply missed their last chance. On the other hand, proponents of the opposing school argue that suspension does not mean closure but a mere temporary cessation of overt activity subject to changing opportunities and conditions that arise with the passage of time. Suspension (but not closure) was also in keeping with the accepted practices of most faiths when security is at stake.

Baha' al-Din was driven by intense faith and a firm conviction that the message of Tawhid, within the context of the Qur'an as the latest of God's revealed message, would prevail no matter how long it took. He may have harbored feelings similar to those of Paul the Apostle when the second coming of the Messiah did not take place as early as he envisioned.[40] If this was the case Baha' al-Din did not let on. However, his anguish, disappointment, and anger were expressed in one epistle after another, consisting of praise for those who stood their ground and condemnation for those who reneged.

According to the followers, Baha' al-Din retired only after he made sure that the message of Tawhid had reached all the people of the known world and that every individual had a chance to exercise his or her free will in accepting or rejecting the Tawhid faith. Moreover, acceptance was in a sense more likely to be effected by those who were prepared through a long process of spiritual growth and wisdom than by those who were exposed to its complexities for the first time. This contention is consistent with the principle of reincarnation whereby commitment to Tawhid is ensured during a virtually endless succession of life cycles. Furthermore, the duration of the latest call to Tawhid, in the era of al-Hakim, was long enough for any newborn to have reached maturity and to have gained the ability to decide.

Baha' al-Din struggled alone for almost twenty-five years after the disappearance of Hamza and the absence of protective cover from the caliphate. This required more physical and emotional endurance than most people could muster. It also attests to the intellectual power that Baha' al-Din possessed and that was displayed in his extensive writings on various topics of philosophy and religion. He was keenly aware of and repeatedly warned against lies and fabrications that were introduced into the epistles with the sole purpose of sabotage. On the other hand he must have felt somewhat rewarded that Tawhid survived the worst that its enemies had thrown at it and that the followers of Tawhid had become a coherent and viable community. Timely military assistance against the warlords who had participated in the persecution of the Druze during and subsequent to the rule of al-Zahir provided a respite to the nascent Druze community. Military leaders such as Anoshtigin al-Dizbari and Emir Rafi'h ibn Abi al-Layl played a significant role in the survival of the Druze.[41] However, it is largely due to Baha' al-Din that the Druze community and the legacy of their path in Tawhid have survived to this day. Although Hamza, as the imam-designate, broke several barriers in the tradition and dogma of Isma'ili doctrine and was the main architect of the doctrine of Tawhid, it was Baha' al-Din whose energy and commitment ensured the survival of Tawhid to this day. What this means for the followers of Tawhid in modern times will be for them to decide individually and collectively.

5   Tenets of the Tawhid Faith

The Concept of Tawhid

THE WORD *tawhid* refers to the attestation to the oneness of God as well as to the unity of the universe in all its aspects within the oneness of the Creator. The transcendence of God, being exalted above and beyond his creation, is balanced by the immanence of God in each and every aspect of creation. Thus the universe and all of creation is, in one way or another, a manifestation of the Divine and operates within the grand scheme of the Creator. Since human beings possess the ability to learn and recognize, to reflect and integrate, and to develop abstract concepts above and beyond those acquired through the senses, they occupy the apex of the pyramid of creation. Human beings carry the responsibility to explore the hidden secrets of the universe and to search for the unifying truth in the scheme of creation, each in his or her own way, and within their capacity to recognize and assimilate.

Tawhid is based on the quest for knowledge and enlightenment that every person strives for during recurring life cycles across the eternity of existence. In this quest individuals are guided by the grace of the Creator, but only to the extent of their readiness to accept and internalize what they can conceive of God's majesty. Moreover, one can only seek guidance in this quest with the exercise of free will. Free will and the heavy premium on the use of reason in Tawhid allow by necessity considerable latitude in the exercise of judgment. Although the concept of Tawhid has accompanied human development from the onset and has been repeatedly introduced throughout recurring cycles of divine revelations and messages, it was during the most recent cycle (the era of al-Hakim) that Tawhid reached a new dawn of spiritual enlightenment.

Individuals, families, and groups who accepted the call to Tawhid in that era were mostly from the Arab tribes that had already settled in the Syrian hinterland. These became known as the Druze. Other groups may also exist as isolated pockets scattered throughout the Islamic world, outwardly blending with the majority. For security reasons as well as for reasons that pertain to the complexity of the faith, the Druze became a closed community, resorting to secrecy in matters of faith. While the traditions of circumspection led to a state of dormancy, the evolutionary nature of the concept of Tawhid calls for continued analysis, assessment, and refinement of the philosophical underpinnings of the faith.

Tawhid Writings

The Druze concept of Tawhid is based mainly on the inner meaning *(batin)* of the Qur'an and the Christian and Jewish scriptures. The Druze path in Tawhid also derived input from a vanguard of pioneers in Pharaonic Egypt such as Amenhotep IV (Akhenaten), from the wisdom of the Greek philosophers, from the traditions of Gnostic groups such as the Hanifs and the Sabaeans of Harran, from the legacy of the ancient sages of the Orient, and from Eastern mysticism. The dependence on a multiplicity of religious and theosophical sources is not unique to the Tawhid faith of the Druze. Islam, as is well known, represents a continuation and a culmination of the messages in Judaism and Christianity. The luminaries of Tawhid formulated a unique philosophy based on their understanding of the meaning of God's revelations as expressed in the Qur'an, in light of a philosophical and transcendental interpretation of these revelations. The doctrine is articulated in what is known to the faithful as the Books of Wisdom (Kutub al-Hikma), a collection of letters or epistles *(rasa'il)* that were collated in the fifteenth century by an eminent Druze prince (emir) and theologian Sayyid Jamal al-Din Abdallah al-Tanukhi, who was born in 1417 C.E. (A.H. 820). These epistles explain and comment on the basic tenets of the faith. The books also include several communications relating to administrative matters, such as appointments, promotions, demotions, accolades, criticisms, rebukes, and various other issues of a seemingly mundane nature. These latter epistles, although intended for administrative purposes, also include further clarification of some aspects of the faith and are therefore useful in this regard. The primary reliance in understanding the basic tenets of the faith, however, is on the main epistles, which are totally devoted to the core subject matter.

The Books of Wisdom, six in number, contain 111 separate epistles and communications. Hamza wrote most of his epistles, numbering around thirty, during the first three years of the call *(da'wa)* and while he was still a public figure. As the chief architect of the faith, Hamza, in his capacity as the human representative of the universal mind (*al-'aql al-kulli*), provided the core curriculum of the tenets of the faith. This set the stage for further elaboration by his second in command, Isma'il Ibn Muhammad al-Tamimi, in his capacity as human representative of the universal soul (*al-nafs al-kulliya*). Al-Tamimi wrote only a handful of the epistles, always deferring to Hamza's leadership and inspiration. The bulk of the epistles were from the pen of Baha' al-Din, the fifth and last of the luminaries of Tawhid, who stayed behind when al-Hakim, Hamza, and the rest of the luminaries disappeared from public view. Baha' al-Din, the only luminary who maintained public visibility, remained in charge of the sanctity of the faith and the welfare of the faithful. Then Baha' al-Din departed from the scene in 1043 C.E. (A.H. 437), leaving the legacy of the faith, as articulated in the various communications from Hamza, Isma'il, and himself, to the followers, who had to fend for themselves and face an uncertain future. Only three of the epistles were attributed to al-Hakim himself, and these were in the form of public declarations or royal decrees. Al-Hakim issued numerous decrees (*sijillat*) during his reign, but somehow only these three made their way into the Books of Wisdom.

The epistles remained in the custody of trusted leaders, notables, and other worthy recipients during the active phase of the call. After that period, the epistles were passed from one generation to the next and hand copied by trusted scribes, for several centuries. They were compiled in the six books more than four centuries later through the efforts of the Druze emir and chief theologian Jamal al-Din Abdallah al-Tanukhi. Thus for more than four hundred years there was nothing known about the fate of these documents in terms of authenticity, accuracy, and precision in reproduction. The potential for distortion, errors in transcription, addition, deletion, or mere loss out of neglect and ignorance during this time should not be underestimated.

We know from references made in the surviving epistles that some, maybe even a significant number, of epistles were lost altogether, placing significant limitations on the comprehensive articulation of the faith. Such a state, however, can be used to advantage by allowing some latitude in interpretation of the message and in promoting reform. In any event al-Tanukhi, reverently known as Sayyid Abdallah, undertook the task of compiling the 111 surviving epistles into the six volumes of the Books of Wisdom.

Another surviving document is a book known as *Kitab al-Munfarid bi thatihi*, roughly meaning "The Unique One." Although it is considered authentic, it probably is not on the same level of theological significance as the six Books of Wisdom. Other books and publications dealing with the Tawhid faith have surfaced from time to time in different parts of the Muslim world and on the Indian sub-continent. These include *Al-Shari'a al-ruhaniyyah fi ulum al-latif wa al-basit wa al-kathif* (The Spiritual Law in Material and Spiritual Disciplines); *Rasa'il al-Hind* (The India Epistles); and *Sijil al-awwal wa al-akhir* (The First and Last Document). The last one was allegedly dictated by al-Hakim himself to trusted scribes. These documents presumably were discovered by the late Druze scholar and political leader Kamal Jumblatt, who played a major role in the Lebanese political scene for close to half a century. Jumblatt was revered for his intellectual and spiritual stature among the Druze as well as among many non-Druze communities in the world. However, these manuscripts, to the best of my knowledge, have not worked their way to the same level of acceptance as the six Books of Wisdom in the traditions of the Druze community. Moreover, there is no mechanism in the Druze religious structure, beyond that of tradition, that confers or denies legitimacy to these or other emerging documents.

A handful of religious scholars followed al-Tanukhi. Perhaps most notable was Shaykh Zayn al-Din 'Abd al-Gaffar Taqi al-Din, who was born in 1580 C.E. (A.H. 911), about ninety years after al-Tanukhi. Shaykh Zayn al-Din wrote several treatises of major significance on Druze faith and philosophy. Among these is the noted treatise *Al-nuqat wa al-dawa'ir* (The Dots and the Circles), in reference to the centrality of the faith within the cycles of existence. This book, recently published in edited form, is a significant reference for understanding the development of the Druze concept of Tawhid.

Shaykh Muhammad al-Ashrafani followed almost a hundred years later with his own scholarly work, *Umdat al-'arifin* (The Pillars of Knowledge). The book is a historical compendium *(mu'allaf)* of religions and religious figures viewed from a Druze perspective. Its value is in pointing the historical development of Tawhid from the perspective of a venerated Druze elder.

Another scholar, Shaykh Muhammad Abu Hilal (d. 1640 C.E. [A.H. 1050]), known to the community as Shaykh al-Fadil, had a widespread reputation for piety and for mysticism. He wore simple blue attire and ate sparingly. Mount Hermon, where he lived in solitude, later became known in Arab circles as Jabal al-Shaykh (Mountain of the Shaykh) in recognition. He wrote poetry mostly in praise of God and adulation of the prophets and messengers, in particular the Prophet Muhammad. The following is a representative sample of his poetry:

> Praise be to God now and forever, as long as I live
> And thanks to the chosen Prophet [Muhammad]
> The beacon of the world reposed in my heart and soul.[1]

It was not until modern times that Druze scholars and men of letters began to write and deal with substantive matters related to the Druze history and their concept of Tawhid. But that has not been without difficulties. The closed nature of the Druze traditions in matters of faith has not encouraged, or in fact has only recently allowed, objective research into domains that were off limits to any one outside a small circle of trusted and wise devotees. Such an attitude is not unique to the Druze, nor is it surprising. However, it is likely that important documents pertaining to the Druze, and other sects as well, exist in closely guarded custody within communities throughout the Arab and Muslim world away from the eyes of anyone outside the immediate circle of trusted men and women of faith. It is also likely that there are followers of the Tawhid path outside the confines of the known Druze communities of today. "It appears that Druze theosophy [Tawhid] survived not only in the eastern Mediterranean coast," according to a modern Druze author, Sahar Mua'kassa, "but also was accepted in the eastern region beyond the Arab political boundaries. Confinement of the Druze heritage in the Arab world is a historical tragedy of a great magnitude."[2] Communication between members of the known Druze communities in Greater Syria and potential coreligionists in other locations are hampered by the tradition of secrecy and by protective layers of circumspection.

Sayyid Jamal al-Din Abdallah al-Tanukhi not only collected and compiled the epistles into the six Books of Wisdom but also brought about the coalescence of the hitherto amorphous religious leadership into a more definable group. The religious leaders or *shaykhs* became known as the wise men (*'uqqal*), publicly identified by specific attire, generally starting with black baggy pants, white skull cap progressing to shaving of the head, cylindrical headdress covered with white cloth (*laffa*), and a cloak (*'aba'a*) with white and red or black stripes, as well as by their moustaches and beards. In more advanced stages, the color of the robe changes to blue, all material from coarse linen or cotton with no ornamentation whatsoever. Although there are no known written codes or regulations that govern this religious order, its members adhere to strict rules of conduct in personal and public life and remain under continuous peer review and scrutiny. Those who would join the ranks of the *'uqqal* must be initiated by their peers and must exercise strict self-discipline in terms of honesty, chastity, and credibility. They must refrain from smoking, drinking alcohol, or succumbing to any kind of sinful behavior or debasing instincts. Temperance in food, simplicity and modesty in dress, and avoidance of bad company are a must. Some of the *'uqqal* strive for self-sufficiency in order to avoid the contamination of usury or potentially corrupt sources of money and other worldly possessions. Above all they should have an abiding commitment to the Tawhid faith and an unshakable resolve to live and die by its tenets.

The Books of Wisdom were entrusted into the hands of the ʿuqqal by tradition, not by any written rule or regulation. Thus gradually the community became divided into two factions based on the practice of the traditions in Tawhid. The first faction was that of the ʿuqqal, who, acting as a religious order, informal as it might be, became de facto custodians of the tenets of Tawhid and the Books of Wisdom.

The other faction, consisting of the rest of the community, came to be known as the *juhhal*, "the ignorant," perhaps more correctly the uninitiated or the secularists *(zamaniyyun)*. This group was, by tradition, deprived of exposure to the Books of Wisdom that the ʿuqqal kept in safe custody. The *juhhal* imbibed what came their way by tradition and by association. Their passive posture with respect to religious matters contributed with the passage of time to a state of ignorance or near-ignorance of the religious writings of their faith. This state of coexistence was generally accepted and not challenged as it gave everybody enough elbow room to maneuver and a niche to fit in. It gave the ʿuqqal a sort of exclusive prerogative to maintain their hold on religious traditions and matters of faith. Although it is possible for anyone to be admitted to their ranks, the process is tedious, with demanding prerequisites that discourage most ordinary people from entering into it, at least early on in their lives. Later, with advancing age and the nearness of the end, many people shift from the mundane to the spiritual and go through the process of joining the ranks of the ʿuqqal. It is noteworthy that the word *shaykh* in Arabic has several meanings that include religious veneration and the veneration of old age or social and political stature in the community.

An additional feature of the ʿuqqal is the position of a titular chief of the order, known in Arabic as *shaykh al-ʿaql* or *shaykh al-ʿuqqal*, roughly meaning "chief of the wise." This position carries only a symbolic meaning and does not confer any other religious or significant secular authority. Recognition of the post by government authorities, including financial support, has been accorded at different times in history. Lebanon, for example, recognizes the jurisdiction of sectarian courts for eighteen different sects, including the Druze, in personal matters such as marriage, divorce, and inheritance. The staffs of these courts are experts from their community but are employed by the government, and their decisions are legally binding.

The number of individuals occupying the position of *shaykh al-ʿaql* at any one time has varied with the condition of the community and the historical and social factors of the time. At present there is only one in Lebanon, one in Syria, and one in Israel (Palestine). The person occupying such position need not be the most pious or the most educated among his peers, but he has to have enough stature to gain acceptance through a rather ill-defined process of consensus. This arrangement has allowed the *'uqqal* enough flexibility to maintain a system of control of religious matters by tradition built on consensus and peer acceptance rather than written rules or formal procedures. The *'uqqal* have not demanded from members of the community outside their ranks more than moral support and a peaceful coexistence based on respect for the invisible boundaries. The most pious among the *'uqqal* lead a virtual monastic life, rejecting all forms of material comfort and subsisting on bare necessities to stay alive. These self-sufficient mystics are known as men and women of piety and goodness, *"ajawid."* Some of them spend much of their time in seclusion in austere places called *khalwas.*

For the *juhhal* this arrangement has, over the years, provided a way out of the obligations of the puritanical course demanded by traditions of Tawhid. The *juhhal* have gone about their daily lives under a veneer of protective ignorance. And so it has gone from generation to generation, in a modus vivendi that has rarely been challenged. In fact some highly enlightened secular leaders in the Druze community consider it forbidden for them to read from the Books of Wisdom or even to look at them.[3] This of course is utterly untrue, as there is no one in the Druze community, *'uqqal* included, who has the authority to allow or forbid any member, *juhhal* included, from reading, possessing, or discussing the faith or its books.

The *'uqqal* may not share all aspects of worship with the *juhhal,* and that is the prerogative of any established order with respect to those who do not qualify to join its ranks. But it was not their prerogative to forbid anybody or any group within the faith from doing so on their own. In matter of practice, the *juhhal* are encouraged and welcome to join the *'uqqal* for an informal meeting prior to formal sessions of worship, when religious principles *(zikr)* are discussed and ethical values *(wa'z)* stressed. This takes place on Thursday evenings, usually at the home of a senior member of the family or in the simple and austere setting of a community meeting place of worship called *"majlis."* At the end of the preaching session the *juhhal* are politely excused and the inner circle of *'uqqal* resume the process of formal worship. This generally consists of reading designated passages from the Books of Wisdom and from writings of other religious scholars such as Sayyid Jamal al-Din Abdallah al-Tanukhi. Passages from holy books such as the Qur'an are read and interpreted in the light of the tenets of the faith. Those who have reached an advanced degree of learning and piety, material rejection, and mystical contemplation usually worship in the solitude of the *khalwa*. This is analogous to the tradition of hermitage that was born centuries earlier in Egypt and in the Far East.

The traditional division of the community along the *'uqqal-juhhal* fault line has had its pros and cons. On the positive side it has provided an orderly arrangement for safeguarding the faith during vulnerable periods of its history. It has also established certain traditions and guidelines that were acceptable to and utilized by the community. The *'uqqal* have also played a major role in rallying the community in times of danger and in maintaining a form of consensus and stability. Their participation in community events such as funerals, for example, is an indication of the stature of the deceased in the community. Likewise, their absence carries weight. In this context the *'uqqal* are a source of stability and supervision.

On the other hand, the *'uqqal-juhhal* division has perpetuated a status that deprives a considerable segment of the community of opportunity for active participation in the affairs of their faith. This has led to the spiritual impoverishment of the majority of the Druze, as they have remained on the outside in matters of faith. It is ironic that the call to Tawhid, by its very nature, was intended for those who were ready to embrace its tenets and live by its codes. Therefore theoretically all those who embraced Tawhid should be considered among the wise (*'uqqal*), and none should remain on the outside in matters of faith. Nevertheless, the *'uqqal-juhhal* segregation is a fact of life and remains one of the challenging issues that any future attempts at reform should address. Accusations surface from time to time that the Druze worship the Golden Calf or other idols and that they engage in sexual orgies in their places of worship.[4] These claims are absurd fabrications; such practices would be contrary to all the teachings in the Tawhid faith and the unbroken traditions of Druze behavior over the centuries.

The Druze approach to worship is more along puritanical lines with a minimum of ritualistic practices. Their emphasis is on internal resources rather than external manifestations such as elaborate displays or festivities or ornate buildings. Even when the Druze celebrate the few holy days, they do so with much less fanfare than other sects in Islam and other religions within their environment. In fact the puritanical strain in Druze religious traditions and the adherence of the Druze people to strict moral codes in their daily lives are traits that are recognized by those who have lived among them or had close contact with them.

The Principles of Tawhid Faith

While there is no standard presentation of the core principles of Tawhid, and the principles discussed herein could be presented in a different order or could be organized differently, it is likely that most of the believers would agree that three main tenets of the faith relate to the concept of God, the concept of creation, and the concept of reincarnation.

The Concept of God

The concept of God in Tawhid is one of the most complex concepts in the entire Druze doctrine. In the first place, the Druze concept of Tawhid, like the Islamic religion from which it emerged, is strictly and unequivocally monotheistic. The oneness of God is articulated in all the Druze epistles and is inculcated in all Druze traditions. God in the absolute sense in Tawhid is referred to as "Lahut," an appellation that defies definition, since to define is to know, or at least to have enough familiarity to be able to recognize in part or in whole. God, in this sense, is totally and permanently beyond the human capacity to know or to recognize, and beyond any future prospects of doing so. The epistles in the Books of Wisdom as well as other Druze theological writings leave no doubt as to the emphasis with which they state this conviction and the finality of this verdict. The following is how Hamza introduced the subject in Epistle 13, Disclosure of Truth *(Kashf al-Haqāʾiq)*:

> The Lord [Lahut] does not come under names, languages, and attributes. And I do not say that he is ancient or permanent because the state of being ancient or permanent are mere conditions created by God, exalted be his name. His true essence cannot be recognized by senses or by imagination and cannot be known through logic or analytical measurement. He is not subject to a known location because that would make him surrounded by defined boundaries and other locations would be devoid of his presence. Yet no location is devoid of his presence because that would indicate diminution of his power. He has no beginning, as that would necessitate an end, and has no end, for that would necessitate a beginning. He is not manifest, for that would demand occultation, and he is not occult, for that would demand manifestation, for each adjective by necessity needs its counterpart. And I do not say that he possesses a spirit or a soul, for that would make him like human beings and thus subject to change. And I do not say that he has an identity or a body or a ghost or an image or an essence or a description, for

each of these items is subject to boundaries such as above and below, right and left, and in front and behind. For whatever is subject to a dimension will demand a counterdimension, such that the six mentioned above will necessitate another six ad infinitum, and God is exalted from being bound by numbers and from individualism and dualism. And I do not say that he is something, for he becomes subject to destruction, yet he is not nothing, for he becomes nonexistent. He is not on something as he becomes borne by it, and he is not in something for he becomes surrounded by it, and he is not attached to something as he becomes subject to refuge. He is not sitting nor is he upright, not awake or asleep, he is not going or coming, nor concrete or ethereal, nor strong or weak. He has no likeness, God is exalted [*munazzah*] above and beyond all traits, appellations, languages, and everything else, bar none. [5]

After these rather dramatic and unequivocal statements that negate any form of attributes of the Almighty as these attributes are understood and defined by human beings, Hamza moves to another series of assertions that affirm the existence of God and the reasons for such belief. To define God's attributes only in negative terms would lead to a conclusion of nonexistence, *laysa*, an Arabic term denoting negation coined by Ismaeli philosophers. Because such negation is an obvious heresy and because ascribing positive attributes, *aysa*, subjects God to human definition, a way must be found out of this dilemma. One way would be to ascertain God's existence using double negatives such as "God does not not exist." Such concepts had already been debated and refined by Isma'ili theologians. For Hamza the fact of God's existence is established by necessity, for no existence is possible outside God's domain. Continuing in a subsequent section from the same epistle, Hamza states:

And I declare, by necessity and not by factual reasoning [*dharura la haqiqa*, "due to obligatory limitations of human reasoning"], that he [God], exalted be his name, is the originator of everything and the creator of all. From his light emanated all, in part and in whole, and to his realm and domain all will return. His absolute essence cannot be known in fact but can only be surmised. [6]

But how are we to recognize the existence of God, if God cannot be defined in any manner and cannot be confined to any form? Such a paradox is seemingly unsolvable, since one cannot be expected to know something when by definition that thing is beyond one's capacity to know. Hamza and his colleagues wrestled with this very question in numerous places in the Druze epistles. How can God expect human beings to believe in and to worship what is and will forever be utterly beyond the limits of human awareness and comprehension? In essence the question comes down to how to be aware of the unknowable without in any way diminishing the totality of the unknowable by subjecting God to human reason and definitions. The question demands an original and innovative answer. Let us see how the answer was gradually developed.

"Is it possible for anyone in the world," poses Baha' al-Din in Epistle 67, "to know what lies behind a wall that is closer than close to [an observer], if the obstructions are not removed to facilitate proper examination and accurate identification? We therefore take refuge in God from expecting us to worship while he remains totally beyond reach because of our human limitations. Divine justice will only be served when God in his grace reveals himself in an image that would be familiar for us to witness and believe." This image is referred to as *nasut* (roughly meaning 'God's countenance')."[7]

It is taken for granted that God is just and that he would not demand the impossible from man, whom he placed at the top of the pyramid of creation. Baha' al-Din continues: "And furthermore, everybody concurs that God, exalted be his power, is just. What justice is there when the spiritual world [God's domain] consists of ethereal concepts that are beyond human comprehension or awareness and yet God's domain is demanded to be known and comprehended?"[8]

Clearly a way must be found to satisfy the dual and seemingly irreconcilable concepts of God's unknowability and the obligatory assertion of his existence.

The bedrock of Tawhid, Hamza articulated, is the oneness of the absolute and only God whose essence, Lahut, is totally out of reach. Out of his divine grace he conferred upon human beings the highest accolade by making them aware of his existence through revelations that have accompanied the human race over the entire course of its existence. These revelations have occurred through proclaimers (*nutaqa'*, sing. *natiq*), messengers (*rusul*), prophets (*anbia'*), and specially gifted men and women of piety and holiness. The revelations have also included manifestations of God's countenance directly to man and in the image of man. This image, which was described by Hamza as that of the *nasut* of God, is the vehicle through which God has made it possible for man to witness God and believe in him.

Revelation in Man

The word that is used in Arabic to describe God's manifestation of himself to humans in human form is *tajalli* (theophany). This denotes a combination of revelation, reflection, and clarification of God's grace in the image of man. *Tajalli* in Tawhid should be distinguished from other concepts of God's taking on human form, such as incorporation, incarnation, and assumption. Incorporation into a human form, in relation to God, implies the union of the two into a single indivisible entity. This notion is rejected in Tawhid, since the union of God and man through incorporation puts limits on God's limitlessness by subjecting God to human conditions and definitions. Since God is exalted above and beyond human conditions and limitation of partnership, *tajalli* cannot occur through incorporation of God into a human body. "Incarnation" implies the act of the dwelling of God in a human body until the death of that body, at which point another abode is selected until the end of time. Again Tawhid rejects the physical incarnation of God in a human body because that would subject God to the same human conditions that incorporation does, and God is exalted above human conditions and limitations. God's acquisition of human form through the process of assumption of a physical body (transfiguration) comes close to the concept of *tajalli* in Tawhid. But still, this concept carries the risk of subjecting the Absolute to the conditions that affect the human form into which God is transfigured. In addition there is the risk of dualism, when two entities exist in the singularity of the oneness of God. The oneness of God, implicit in monotheism, is the most basic principle in Tawhid.

Tajalli in Tawhid is an initiative by which the Almighty reveals himself as an image *(nasut)* that is reflected in the human form. As such, the image is not physically incorporated in a human body any more than a ray of light is physically incorporated into the mirror through which the ray of light is reflected. The mirror is not the source of light; nor is it combined with the light in any way. The mirror is rather the medium that allows the recognition of the existence of light and facilitates awareness of the source of the light. Otherwise, the source of light will forever remain outside human reach and therefore technically nonexistent. Neither the ray of light nor the mirror that reflects the ray can detract from the unique exaltation of the Source, which remains above and beyond human comprehension and partnership. Awareness of the revealed image is a function of the level of spirituality of the recipient since the Source, in Tawhid, is limitless and indefinable. Thus, the individual is able to witness that reflected light emanating from the Source to the extent that he or she can absorb and assimilate it. God's revelation of aspects of himself through *tajalli* in the human image should in no way be interpreted as God being incorporated into the human image, or that the human image is synonymous with God. For God is exalted above and beyond any human definition, recognition, or imagery.

The cycles of *tajalli* start with the onset of time and continue in progressively revelatory stages commensurate with the human capacity to absorb and comprehend. God's *tajalli* in the *nasut* across the ages did not constitute mere repetitions over cycles of time. Rather the cyclical phenomenon was to introduce and develop the principle of Tawhid in a gradual manner for man to absorb and incorporate into his spiritual development. For human beings could not bear God's revelations in full force without the necessary preparatory stages:

> And the image addressed them [humans] through what they are familiar with of names, providing solace to their minds; and invited them to recognize him [God], out of love and grace for his subjects. By not revealing all of his majesty, it was possible for recognition and belief to become established. For if they were to be suddenly exposed to God's majesty without the gradual process of familiarization and preparation, they would be totally overpowered and destroyed.[9]

The *nasut* is the window through which human beings could achieve the impossible and recognize, by necessity and not by deductive reasoning, the existence of God's essence or Lahut. God's *tajalli* through the *nasut* is not, however, restricted to any one person, or to any specific time or place. In this context every person carries in him or her a spark of the Divine, implicit in the act of creation: "And by that I mean that God, exalted be his power, is present in his subjects, and that he is revealed to them through their own means [implying *nasut*]."[10]

Thus God's presence is felt at all times and by all people with varying degrees of clarity and intensity depending on the level of awareness and spirituality of any human being, at any given time and in any given place.

In addition to the continuous awareness of God's presence in his creation that human beings experience all the time, a major booster is called upon from time to time to recharge the whole system and to bring it to a higher orbit. This is achieved through the major cycles (*adwar*, sing. *dawr*) of *tajalli* that the Druze concept of Tawhid proposes as one of its basic tenets. A system of beliefs, or any other system for that matter, left alone, tends to decay and degenerate, subject to the laws of entropy. It can only be recharged through major events that herald the coming of a new messenger or a rejuvenated doctrine or discovery. Awakened from the sedative effects of parroting the past and the numbing influence of familiarity, humanity is jolted to a higher level of awareness by the advent of a new and more complex cycle of divine revelations. According to the Druze, the last and most recent of the cycles of *tajalli* represented the culmination of the process and involved al-Hakim as the "station" *(maqam)* through which God's *nasut* was revealed. "When I declare that I put my faith in God, I mean God the Absolute, who cannot be defined by intellect or intuition and cannot be comprehended by any stretch of imagination. . . . And when I say on him I rely in all matters, I mean the station of God's revelation, the image that we recognize in human station." [11]

Here, we should be aware of the clear distinction between God in the absolute sense (Lahut) and God's reflection *(nasut)* in the human station. Both Hamza and Baha' al-Din explain the distinction between the absolute (and unknowable) and the manifestation of the Absolute in the human station: "His subject [man] does not attach his fate to any one human being and does not worship any individual human or image, but he worships an exalted and absolute God and the supreme Creator, who revealed his *nasut* to the world through the station of al-Hakim. For God [Lahut] is exalted beyond definition and comprehension." [12]

"And know ye," declared Baha' al-Din, "that the king and shepherd [al-Hakim] is the one chosen by God to be the ruler and guide, and is blessed by [some aspects of] divinity as the recipient of some of God's revelations and attributes." [13]

Hamza starts Epistle 18, like most of the epistles, with a familiar supplication: "I place my reliance on God the All-knowing, exalted beyond human description or comprehension . . . revealed to us in our own image out of compassion for us and care for our well-being. He addresses us in us, profound wisdom, and miraculous messages. He reveals when he chooses and becomes occult when he decides. No one can oppose or object, and there is no God but he." [14]

The same theme recurs in Epistle 29, also by Hamza, which begins with this supplication:

> In thy name, oh God . . . the Light of lights in every location and place, the Creator and Sustainer of all things. Blessed, blessed is he who is worshipped and everlasting . . . the one and only God, beyond description and measure . . . He reveals of himself for people to believe while his absolute nature is beyond comprehension. He projects his will on the world [for all] to see and for each to witness according to the clarity of his vision, as though one is looking through the mirror. . . . He reveals himself in the *nasut* yet he is not confined to the *nasut*. [15]

Further elucidation of the same theme is presented in Epistle 12, also by Hamza:

> He has bestowed upon you his manifestation in humanity, and the revelation of his image in visible form for you to comprehend even a glimpse of his *nasut*. But I do not say of his real self, or real image, or face, or meaning, or essence, or station, except by necessity and according to the capacity of the faithful and the ability of the believers to prepare their minds to comprehend and their hearts to endure. [16]

God chose human beings to be the goal of his creation and the highest form of life in the universe, for the simple reason that humans possess the highest level of intellect among God's creatures and, therefore, the most advanced capacity to comprehend. Consequently, it would be more fitting for God to communicate with humanity in the form of human being than in other animate or inanimate forms. This does not mean that God incarnates himself physically in man, as that would be a limitation to God's limitlessness. Nor does it mean that the rest of creation is devoid of his grace, as he is the creator and sustainer of all. Rather God's revelation of himself in the *nasut* is more like an image or a reflection in the mirror. Such reflection enables man, by virtue of his mental capacity, to recognize the existence of God and to witness such existence in man himself: "The son of Adam is the purpose of God's creation, since all that exists in this world and the next are for him, and for his benefit. When people of knowledge and wisdom recognize that the son of Adam is the best of creation, then it becomes logical that God's revelation of himself be in the highest of God's creation, i.e., in the human form." [17]

In Epistle 13 *(Kashf al-Haqa'iq)*, Hamza elaborates further on the eligibility of the human medium to receive and articulate God's messages and the reasons for such eligibility:

> And for someone who asks how can it be allowed that we hear God's word from the mouth of man or witness God's reflection in the image of man, we say the following with God's help: You Muslims, Christians, and Jews believe that God, exalted be his name, addressed Moses from a bush on a bleak mountain, and you called Moses the receiver of God's word. But it was through the bush on the mountain that Moses received the word of God, and nobody denied that. . . . Yet the tree and the stone do not possess the intelligence to receive and transmit the word of God. Therefore, the one who can think and understand would be more worthy of the word of God than the tree and the stone. . . . And how would it be reasonable for God to take a tree as his station, when the tree can burn and with it his station. Exalted be God's name from description and definition, and [blessed be] his station *(al-hakim)* in every age and stage under different names and images. [18]

Baha' al-Din elaborates in other epistles on the same concept that Hamza proposed concerning the unique attributes of the human being. Such attributes make the individual most eligible to receive God's revelations:

> And after that the blessed and divine sage [referring to Plato] declares that godliness is to be found in an aspect of creation, namely the living, wise, and articulate

human being, who resembles [is in the image of] the Creator in the attributes of beneficence, purity, and truthfulness. . . . When these principles [human traits] achieved perfection in this small universe, and I mean by that the human being, it became clearly evident that God, exalted be his name, would appear [as an image in this universe] for completion.[19]

And when we ask [the people of faith] for what reason man was accorded a higher position than all other creatures and his position elevated to the level of the ultimate of creation . . . they [had to] say it is because of what has been bestowed on him of exalted illumination, divine revelation, and supreme knowledge. . . . Man's union with what is more elevated [than what physically exists] is because of his proximity to the Everlasting, and his acceptance of truth and spiritual reality.[20]

In Epistle 36, Isma'il ibn Muhammad al-Tamimi (affectionately referred to by the Druze as Abu Ibrahim), in the role of human representation of the soul (al-nafs), second in command to Hamza, goes a step further in the elucidation of the absoluteness of God and the link to the human connection. Speaking in the past tense al-Tamimi declares:

He approached us in us and comforted our minds in our own image, and appeared to us in our actions for our minds to comprehend. Thus we do not say that this image is he [God], for by doing so we limit and define him, exalted be his name (above and beyond any description). But we may say that he is revealed in the image, imparting love and warmth with no limit or similarity.[21]

Tamimi then cites from the holy Qur'an support for what may be considered a simile for the concept he was developing:

. . . as a mirage in a spacious plain
which the man athirst supposes to be water,
till, when he comes to it, he finds it is nothing,
there indeed he finds God,
And he pays him his amount in full" (24:39).

The *nasut*, according to al-Tamimi, has a dual role. On the one hand it behaves like the mirage that one sees as water when in fact it is merely the appearance of water. On the other hand, it also behaves like a two-way mirror that under certain conditions reflects the image of God in the observer:

This obvious image when viewed by the natural senses appears like your own image, but if you sense it with true vision [in your heart], you find the image of

God. Thus while God in the Lahut context is totally indescribable, the revealed image of God allows the viewer a vision that is analogous to what you see in the mirror. If you touch the image you will be touching your own image, and if you change, the image will change accordingly, always reflecting your capacity to witness and comprehend.[22]

The above concept is of extraordinary significance as it defines a set of relationships between God in the absolute sense (Lahut), and the image of God as a revelation *(nasut)*. It also introduces the role of God's image in allowing man to witness the reflection of his own real self in the image, not by physical sight but by an intuitive process that illuminates the soul as it elates the mind. It is the purest form of love that consumes the mystic in a state of ultimate ecstasy. Through the concept of *tajalli* one acquires the ability to become aware of the One, and to witness the reflection of his own image in the mirror of the One. Through *tajalli* God is witnessed in the image of man, as man witnesses his own real self in the image of the Creator.

Let us assume that you are "looking" at the mirror not with your eyes but with an inner vision associated with the depth of your conscience. What you experience at that point will be dependent upon your mental and psychological as well as physical well-being. It is conceivable that you may lose your sense of self-awareness and replace it with a holistic awareness that allows you to disconnect from the physical constraints and soar above the mundane. You will then begin to catch a glimpse of a state of being that is infinitely more real and more incredibly complete than that of the material world of the senses. It is in the awareness of this state of being that you begin to witness your own image and experience the Divine. The quality of the perception and its magnitude depend directly on your state of readiness to receive and assimilate. In the words of Farid al-Din al-Attar, a noted mystic:

> All who, reflecting as reflected, see
> Themselves in me, and me in them; not me
> But all of me that a contracted eye
> Is comprehensive of infinity;
> . . . As water lifted from the deep, again
> Falls back in individual drops of rain,
> Then melts into the universal main.[23]

The clarity of the seer's vision facilitates further clarity in a positive feedback loop and in the spiral trajectory of spiritual evolution. The converse is also true.

Impediments that cloud or distort the inner vision will detract from the ability of the individual to witness himself in the glory of the divine image. Hence Tawhid is a path *(maslak)* or a process *(madhhab)* that the traveler embarks upon in quest of the Divine. Obviously this is a long-term journey requiring long and meticulous preparation and commitment. We can discern the mystical component of the Tawhid faith in all aspects of the faith and the guidelines of the path. After all, the concept of witnessing oneself in the image of God and simultaneously witnessing God's image in oneself is at the center of the mystical experience. The theme of al-Tamimi in Epistle 36 is echoed by Muhyi-al-Din Ibn al-'Arabi, the noted Muslim mystic (1165–1240 C.E.): "Thus God is the mirror in which you see yourself, as you are his mirror in which he contemplates his names; now his names are not other than himself, so that the analogy of relations is an inversion." [24]

In the ancient world of Indian mythology we hear Sri Krishna addressing Prince Arjuna in the Bhagavad Gita as follows:

> My true being is unborn and changeless. I am the Lord who dwells in every creature Through my own Maya, I *manifest* myself in a finite form. [25]

> But these things cannot be seen with your physical eyes; therefore I give you spiritual vision to *perceive* my majesty. [26]

> As for those who seek the transcendental Reality, without name, without form, contemplating the *Unmanifested*, beyond the reach of *thought and feeling*, with their senses subdued and mind serene and striving for the good of all beings, they too will verily come unto me [emphasis added]. [27]

Clearly, one needs more than the five physical senses to develop an awareness of what is beyond and to achieve a state of transcendence on a plane that is above and beyond that of the physical world. In a much later period, in medieval Europe, we hear a similar message from the great mystic John Ruysbroek: "The image of God is found essentially and personally in all mankind. Each possesses it whole, entire and undivided, and all together not more than one alone. In this way we are all one, intimately united in our eternal image, which is the image of God and the source in us of all our life." [28]

And a similar theme comes from the Far East: "There is a self-existent reality that is the basis of our consciousness of ego. That reality is the witness of the states of ego and the bodily coverings. That reality is the knower in all states of consciousness. . . . It is your real self. That reality pervades the universe, but no one penetrates it. It alone shines." [29]

The same author (Wilber), quoting from Schroedinger (1964), illustrates the continuum of such wisdom to more modern times: "Inconceivable as it seems to ordinary reason, you—and all other conscious beings as such—are all in all. Hence this life of yours you are living is not merely a piece of the entire existence, but is in a sense the *whole*" [emphasis added].[30]

The distinguished molecular biologist Darryl Reanney goes a step further in simultaneously exploring the two sides of the consciousness, the scientific and the transcendental, and arrives at similar conclusions: "The universal reality is there now, open to the universal consciousness that is latent in all of us. However, the ego cages it in, shutting out the light as surely as grilles of iron or walls of hewn stone. . . . Whether we live in the cage or strive to break free of it is up to us."[31] In a later section the same author adds: "What happened in your flash of understanding was that your individual consciousness suddenly caught up with a truth already known. It tapped into the completed unitive consciousness that underpins the closed feedback loop of becoming. What you experienced was a faint foretaste of the final act in the evolution of consciousness, a memory of that magic future moment of total togetherness, when the distinction between observer and observed vanishes completely."[32]

Man, the diminutive creature, once illuminated grows to embody the entire universe, and to become one with the Knower. The two poles in the equation of existence, the Creator and the created, though far from being symmetrical, are complementary components in the cosmic partnership of being. Gershom Scholem, a modern Jewish thinker, describes this relationship with probing intellect and mystical vision:

> At opposite poles, both man and God encompass within their being the entire cosmos. However, whereas God contains all by virtue of being its Creator and Initiator in whom everything is rooted and all potency is hidden, man's role is to complete this process by being the agent through whom all the powers of creation are fully activated and made manifest. What exists seminally in God unfolds and develops in man. . . . Man is the perfecting agent in the structure of the cosmos.[33]

It is remarkable how such mystical vision is shared with the vision of modern science, as illustrated by one such example: "We who are all children of the universe—animated stardust—can nevertheless reflect on the nature of that same universe, even to the extent of glimpsing the rules on which it runs. How we have become linked into this cosmic dimension is a *mystery*. Yet the linkage cannot be denied" [emphasis added].[34]

Indeed the linkage is as mysterious as that of the image in the mirror, yet it cannot be denied any more than the reality of that image to the seer. The secrets may lie in the level of awareness of the seer and the way chosen to effect this experience. We are left in no doubt as to man's ability to achieve the goal of exaltation and of God's guidance toward that end. This sounds like an echo from the great Arab poet and philosopher Abu al-ʿAlaʾ al-Maʿarri addressing man's place in the scheme of creation a thousand years ago:

> And you claim to be but a small entity,
> When in you is incorporated
> The entirety of the universe.[35]

The graduated levels of knowledge, from the literal structural context of the word to the logical and philosophical frame of reference that uncovers the real meaning of the word, represent a major step in the evolution of knowledge and spiritual growth. The human being remains tied to the physical structure of the word in the first stage, and to the interpretation of that structure in the second. It is only when one goes beyond the confines of the letter to the intuitive and transcendental message in God's revelations (gnosis) that man begins to realize himself in the Creator and to witness the Creator in his own image. The act of *tajalli* of the Supreme in human station in Tawhid is the main vehicle by which human awareness of the Supreme is actualized in witnessing the Supreme in the human image.

"The evident reason for this anthropomorphism," according to Leo Schaya, "is that the Infinite, in order to establish relations with man, to make Himself understood and known by man, must necessarily enter the latter's field of vision: He must, so to say, espouse the form of man and of his universe and speak in human language. In other words the Infinite reveals Himself to man through the eternal human archetype . . . taking on—according to an expression of the Sufi al-Junayd—the 'color of His recipient.' But it is not His essence as such which assumes the colors of the receptacles: the Essence is eternally 'beyond what they attribute to Him.'"[36]

To be worthy of achieving a state of near communion with the Divine, man must be ready for the encounter; otherwise, the sheer intensity will destroy him. It involves a long and arduous process of enlightenment and purification across the span of human existence, with each cycle preparing for the next in an ever-expanding spiral of spiritual maturation. The luminaries of Tawhid devoted considerable attention to the prerequisites for those on the journey to reach their goal.

These prerequisites include a thorough understanding and acceptance of the basic tenets of the faith, as well as guidelines for personal behavior that reflect and enhance the impact of these tenets in daily life. The behavioral guidelines can be classified under moral and ethical practices and modes of action of the believers in daily life. Such practices generally reflect the applicability of the basic principles of the faith in the affairs of daily life. The real prerequisite for Tawhid, though, is an inner recognition that it is through God's grace that man was (is) able to embark on and to be aware of the meaning of the journey. It is the vertical dimension of the divine message that is felt in the heart and that transcends the limitations of the physical experience.

Man's awareness in the physical sense stems from the powerful ability of his physical senses to observe, collate, analyze, and project physical phenomena. In this context, awareness is essentially an acquired phenomenon using genetic tools and environmental resources. But those who have reached the depth of the mystical experience indicate that there is another form of awareness (call it primary awareness) that is essentially independent of physical senses and that projects beyond the data that the senses provide. "In quantum nonlocality, transcendent heaven—the kingdom of God—is everywhere. . . . We do not see it because we are so enamored of experience, of our melodramas, of our attempts to predict and control, to understand and manipulate everything rationally. In our efforts, we miss the simple thing—the simple truth that it is all God, which is the mystic's way of saying it is all consciousness. Physics explains phenomena, but consciousness is not a phenomenon; instead, all else are phenomena in consciousness."[37] This consciousness, this awareness, comes directly from God. Its secrets lie outside the domain of physical forces.

We hear sages and mystics from the East and modern thinkers from the West, including men and women of science, converge on the unique endowment of man to be aware of the mystery of being and to become aware of this awareness through some form of universal truth. Time and space, life and death, past and present, matter and energy, and so on become mere aspects that point to the indefinable, the one and only reality. Awareness of this reality becomes more and more manifest as humanity is exposed to it through repeated and progressively more intense exposure. This process serves to sharpen and intensify such awareness until the ultimate objective of existence is achieved. This ultimate destination is analogous to what Teilhard de Chardin called "Point Omega."[38] It is precisely this awareness that entitles man to recognize that he can be one with the One.

In the Tawhid faith awareness is amplified through cycles of divine revelations *(tajalli)*. After all, the physical senses, impressive as they may be, are too limited in scope and spectrum to encompass all of reality:

> The journey of the Sufi, though it may begin with ordinary [physical] awareness, after distillation and purification [of this awareness] reaches its destination in the transcendence of the physical reality in all its forms and shapes; thus, the seeker meets his maker in the reflection of God on the heart of the seeker, whereby the heart becomes the repository of awareness . . . and the seeker graduates from revelation to disclosure [of truth].[39]

This concept of revealed awareness has accompanied the development of spirituality in an incremental fashion and in doses commensurate with the ability of the recipient to accept and internalize. It has occupied the attention of a broad range of talented men and women across the ages.

If awareness and spirituality are entirely the result of sensory impulses generated objectively from the physical world, then this "simply represents an unexplainable jump from material organization to a level of reality of another order, analogous to the jump from nothing to something."[40] What the modern psychologists are alluding to is remarkably similar to the message of Tawhid a thousand years earlier. There is a reality beyond the one arrived at through derivation from the physical senses alone. Such reality can be experienced by the few who have been able to achieve maximum freedom from the physical dimension and maximum connection to what is above and beyond such dimension. In fact some modern psychologists have coined the term *absolute unitary being* to refer to the state of absolute awareness beyond physical reality. This concept is no longer considered to be the domain of the fringes in modern psychology: "The core insight of *psychologia perennis*," according to Wilber, "is that man's innermost consciousness is identical to the absolute and ultimate reality of the universe. . . . He begins to see himself as profoundly unique by virtue of being profoundly universal."[41]

This consciousness cannot be fully realized through the physical and literal context of the word, nor through logical methods and analytical procedures. It can only be made possible through man's spiritual transcendence beyond the concrete and the tangible to the internalized imagery bestowed upon man by God's revelations. The cycles of revelations facilitate graduation from knowledge to awareness, from the self to the whole, and from individuality to universality. This in essence is the message of Tawhid:

> And the first prerequisite [for the believer] is the exaltation of Tawhid above and beyond interpretations and constraints, and the awareness of the Creator. . . . And the first condition of exaltation is the distinction between knowledge and

awareness *(al-maʿrifa wa al-ʿilm)*. . . . It is through awareness that exaltation of Tawhid is made complete and sound, for it is through Tawhid that reality is defined and not the reverse.[42]

This is the real purpose for humanity's existence and the place that man is accorded in Tawhid within the scheme of God's creation. The cycles of *tajalli* represent the reflections of God's *nasut* in the image of man as a prerequisite for man's awareness of the otherwise unknown and unknowable Divine.

Kamal Jumblatt, the contemporary Druze secular and spiritual leader, was well versed in Western scientific and liberal thinking as well as Eastern mysticism. He describes Tawhid as a process of becoming: "Suffice it to say and to reiterate that we [humans] are not there yet. But we have to become that special being. We have to swing the door wide open to learning and thinking and to mobilize our feelings and intuitive faculties, and to intensify the quest in the light of history, religion, and true knowledge . . . and seek the ultimate truth. We have to keep searching for the *unknown God within us*" [emphasis added].[43]

This quest for spiritual growth and awareness is not foreign to the scientific community, many of whose members are discovering common ground between rigid scientific methodology and the transcendental spiritual approach. "What is more important in this view," states Christian de Duve, a distinguished biological scientist, "is not absolute truth, probably inaccessible at our level of development, but the search for truth."[44] The search takes multiple roads, but the destination is one. Schelling, almost a century and a half ago, asserted: "First I should like to remind the reader of the original thorough-going unity of all true religions. Since true religion cannot differ from true religion, and since mythological religion is true religion, there cannot be in it any other powers or potencies than in revealed religion; but they are present in the two in a different way." Then he goes on to say: "But the content of all true religion is eternal and hence cannot absolutely be excluded from any epoch. A religion that is not of all time, as old as the world, cannot be the true one."[45] "The God who is in a faith," says Ibn al-ʿArabi, "is the God whose form the heart contains, who discloses himself to the heart in such a way that the heart recognizes him."[46]

"Have you not heard the wise and blessed Buddha," posed Baha' al-Din, "who informed you about our sayings and those of our brethren, before we did [in the present cycle], that all beings and all creation are from one Source and converge on that Source. . . . Thus all of you reside in one house built upon the throne of God's revelation."[47]

Epistle 58, written by Baha' al-Din, deals with some of these questions:

And when we examined the beliefs of all who referred to Tawhid, the worship of the One, we found three separate categories. One category seeks him through the medium of the physical senses. . . . These are the people who adhere to the written document with no place for elaborate interpretation or even minor changes. The second category seeks him through logical methods and verbal deductions. Their approaches are vulnerable to the vagaries of language and the changes in the mode of expression. The third group seeks Tawhid in their hearts and by exaltation of God beyond definition and above attributes of human comprehension.[48]

It is evident that the third approach represents a qualitative evolutionary step in spiritual growth. It is the step that takes knowledge to a level beyond the confines of the physical character of the written line, and the logical and mental processing involved in the analysis of what the written line imparts to the brain through the medium of the physical senses. True knowledge (gnosis) is reached through transcendence, which is in the domain of heart and soul (love), in addition to the intellectual faculties. The third group would obviously be the most advanced in the evolution of spiritual development. Quoting from the Qur'an, Baha' al-Din in the same epistle provides support for his thesis:

Say: "Are they equal—those who know
and those who know not?"
Only men possessed of minds remember. (39:9)

We can perhaps use the analogy of spatial dimensions to further elucidate this point. In this context we may consider those who adhere to the strict letter of the word as one-dimensional. To them the word expresses the message directly and with no ambiguity to clarify or extrapolation to be uncovered beyond the concrete structure of the word's letters. The relation is linear and one-dimensional, the arithmetic simple, the logic straightforward. At this level of comprehension, acceptance of the sanctity of the revealed word and abiding by its laws are all that is needed for belief to be genuine and for the believer to be received into the graces of the Divine. This is what Islam is about, according to Tawhid, the first and most elemental stage in the progressive process of the spiritual journey. This category is referred to as the stage of the revealed word *(tanzil)*. At this level of spirituality individuals and societies must have laws to regulate and guide human behavior, and ritualistic practices to express and reinforce the divine message. They also need role models to emulate and refer to. Hence the crucial role of the messenger *(natiq)* and the religious jurisprudence (shari'a) that is enacted based mostly on the literal interpretation of the message. Complementing the function of the messenger or acting on his behalf in case of his absence or death is the role of the foundation *(asas)*. In relation to Islam, the Prophet Muhammad is the messenger and Ali, according to the Druze, is the foundation.

The second category, those who seek him through logical reasoning and linguistic deductions, can be considered two-dimensional. To those persons the simple direct and literal meaning of the word is not sufficient to portray its real essence. The word must be structurally interpreted and logically analyzed in order to uncover the more subtle messages encoded within the primary structure. This represents in essence graduation from the basic and rather uniform clarity of the message within the exoteric structure of the word to the more complex and variable shades of meaning that potentially exist in the esoteric interpretations. Individuals in this category are also referred to as those who believe in interpretation of the word *(ahl al-ta'wil)*. Ta'wil, however, goes beyond the process of linguistic interpretation of the word, to the primary and essential *(awwal)* purpose of the message. The followers of *ta'wil* refer to numerous passages in the Qur'an that stress the importance of using one's mind in the interpretation of the revealed word. The following passages constitute but a small sample:

> We have sent it down as an Arabic Qur'an; haply you will understand. (12:2)

> And those similitudes—We strike them
> for the people, but none understands them
> save those who know." (29:43)

> And on the earth are tracts neighbouring
> each to each,
> and gardens of vines,
> and fields sown,
> and palms in pairs, and palms single,
> watered with one water;
> and some of them We prefer in produce
> above others.
> Surely in that are signs for a people who understand. (13:4)

Naturally when the door is opened to interpretation, the vista becomes wider and the scope almost limitless. Thus the thought processes change from the static posture of the first category *(tanzil)* to the dynamic nature of the second *(ta'wil)*. Interpretation and development of the message that goes beyond the literal meaning of the revealed word *(zahir)* to the inner and deeper levels of comprehension *(batin)* is the function of the foundation. Nonetheless, both categories, *zahir* and *batin,* remain confined to the flat plane of observation and analysis. A third dimension is therefore needed to delve into the deeper level of the inner meaning *(batin al-batin),* in order to achieve a more complete awareness of the real meaning of God's message and achievement of the supreme reward, the fruits of Tawhid. This is the domain of the third category.

To continue the analogy, this category adds a third dimension to the understanding of the message of God. The third dimension allows appreciation of the vertical as well as the linear and flat perspectives of the word. Hence in addition to literal and esoteric interpretations, an intuitive and transcendental element is brought to bear in man's quest for the Sublime. Such is the journey in the eyes of the luminaries of Tawhid, a gradual and escalating process, with each stage a prelude to the next, in direct relation to man's ability to absorb and internalize. The rewards are commensurate with the intensity and magnitude of the quest. The ultimate goal for man is to get as close as is allowable to the Ultimate, the one and only God. "Islam is the gateway to belief, and belief is the gateway to Tawhid," declares Hamza, "because Tawhid is the culmination, and there is no higher quest."[49] To reach true understanding of Tawhid the seeker must go through the process of graduation, through submission *(islam)* and belief *(iman).* "Thus the stage of *islam* [submission to God] is that of the exoteric *[zahir],* and that is belief in the one and only God and the belief in God's messenger and message, and fulfilling the pillars and obligations attending such belief," declares the Druze scholar Sami Makarem, "while the stage of faith *[iman]* represents internalizing the veracity *[tasdiq]* of the religious message. . . . But the stage of grace *[ihsan]* . . . represents the road to Tawhid . . . the ultimate knowledge to which man can aspire."[50]

It is out of God's love for his creation, at the apex of which is man, that he reveals himself in the image of man, to enable man to embark on the path of belief in God and to worship the Creator. Tawhid is a theosophy that is built on "divine emanation," in a somewhat analogous description by Scholem in relation to Jewish mysticism, "whereby God, abandoning his self-contained repose, awakens to mysterious life . . . the mysteries of creation that reflect the pulsation of this divine life."[51] Along the arc of the pendulum between God and man, God's revelation in the mirror of the human station of the *nasut* provides the guidance and illumination for the traveler along the journey of Tawhid. For God is not in need of human or any other worship; rather, it is man who needs to recognize the reality of God and to embark on the spiritual pilgrimage that leads to God, the one and only source of truth, beauty, and grace. Above all, seeking knowledge is the foundation for seeking the truth, and it is the truth that will set man on the course to the ultimate ecstasy of getting closer to the one and only God: "And know ye, brethren, that your Lord is not solicitous of your worship and is exalted above your religion(s). His reign is not augmented by your obedience nor diminished by your refusal to obey. It is what you sow in your own actions that you will eventually reap, and whatever difficulty you may encounter is from your own doing." [52]

It is clearly, a matter of choice and free will, with corresponding accountability. Man has repeatedly been given a choice, and it remains for man, always, to make the fateful decision.

Among the Druze of today one of the common sayings describing someone's special gifts in spiritual recognition is a statement that "God's *nasut* is imprinted on his (her) face." This term is conferred affectionately and reverently on a person of acclaimed piety and purity. What this implies is that the countenance of a human being can change in such a way, after reaching high levels of purity and spirituality, as to project the inner spiritual bliss upon those in attendance. The fact that such countenance can be felt by the observer indicates a level of sublime communication and interaction that goes beyond the level of the physical senses and logical deductions. It consists of the kind of love that the mystics experience in their encounter with the Divine. Moreover God's immanence in man softens the exalted state of a transcendental God above and beyond human reach or understanding.

Cycles of Revelation

Although God in the absolute Lahut is totally beyond human reach, yet human awareness of God is achieved through multiple avenues and multiple manifestations. As a matter of fact everything in nature and every activity in life points to a higher order of organization and regulation that necessitates the existence of a supreme power within whose domain existence exists and functions. Philosophers dream of arriving at the truth through complex processes of logic and deduction, and scientists through the rigorous methods of experimentation and confirmation. Artists resort to creative imagination and express their aspirations on canvas, stone, or clay, or in the vast reservoir of inexhaustible melodies. Mystics utilize various avenues of contemplation and self-denial to arrive at increasingly more advanced stages of awareness of the Supreme. The ultimate dream of the mystic is to achieve total consummation *(al-fana')* in the glow of the Supreme, whereby the individual self is totally obliterated in the ecstasy of the union. This in fact is the ultimate goal of Tawhid.

In addition to the wonders of creation that by necessity generate awareness of the Creator, God's message reaches human beings through prophets and messengers, and through gifted men and women whose actions and lives elevate the human spirit and promote awareness of the Creator. Divinely revealed messages constitute the foundation on which monotheistic religions are based. Messengers deliver God's word in accordance with his will and his commands. The purpose is to bring humanity closer to God through heightened spiritual awareness and through actions that reflect this awareness in daily life. A human being must pass through the formative and regulatory stages of the revealed message before he or she can embark on the more abstract journey in Tawhid. To this end Tawhid proposes another avenue in addition to those in the revealed monotheistic faiths, the avenue of *tajalli*, discussed above.

According to Tawhid, God, the absolute and otherwise unknowable (Lahut), also manifests aspects of himself directly through human medium. This medium, *nasut*, represents an image that reflects the glory of God, which at the same time is reflected in the soul of the seeker. Upon reaching a certain level of spiritual growth and Gnostic maturity, the seeker can achieve awareness of the majesty of the Creator without resorting to intermediaries or to elaborate forms of worship and ritual.

The various approaches to achieving awareness of the Creator complement one another in a complex and interwoven web of spiritual quest for the Source of knowledge and the Creator of the universe. Hence, we have the multiplicity of messages and of messengers and prophets across the span of human history and, indeed, human existence. Although the approaches may vary with human conditions and the particular need of human society at any given time, their aim is one and the same: to lead humanity into higher awareness of the Divine, which is the essence of Tawhid. Thus while laws that regulate human behavior may seem to address issues of the mundane, yet there is, by necessity, an esoteric meaning and a purpose behind these laws. The esoteric meaning can be appreciated by those who are initiated after long and arduous preparation. In this manner the Druze believe that the message of Tawhid is encoded in all of God's religions and revelations. The totality of these approaches is the vehicle by which man is exposed to the principle of Tawhid in a gradually increasing depth and complexity. The journey is long and the subject matter inexhaustible.

According to the Druze path in Tawhid, the theophanic vision in human form occurs in cycles *(adwar)*. The concept of cycles is rooted in antiquity as it reflects forces of change and renewal in life and existence in general. The Druze adapted the evolving cycles of Tawhid from the Isma'ilis, who had by then refined and elaborated the cyclical concept to a high degree. The Druze concept of cyclicity of God's revelations in the human medium is extended to include cyclicity of human existence through reincarnation. As such it represents a departure from linear time inherent in the historical context of the monotheistic faiths,[53] to the ahistorical context of the evolving concept of Tawhid. This is by no means a reversion to the circular time of paganism, since Tawhid is based on evolution, which is never confined to the static nature of a closed circle. It is rather a spiral of development and change beginning with creation and lasting to the end of time, however that end is defined.

The call to Tawhid, according to the Druze, began with the beginning of time and continues forever. The cycles of God's revelations in human station are given special significance by the luminaries of Tawhid. Such intermittent revelations serve to boost the awareness of the believers in Tawhid and to upgrade the level of knowledge that each has attained in his or her quest. In addition they serve to test the depth of commitment among the believers and to demonstrate the power and justice of God:

> [Furthermore, all] of humanity agrees that God is omnipotent. What if he were to leave us [and go] into a state of occultation, would that not be construed as incapacity to be revealed? Conversely, if he were to appear and not leave, would not that be construed as incapacity at occultation? And if he were to appear in the same image and the same state, that could also be construed as incapacity. . . . Furthermore, if he were to permanently disappear, that would negate his existence, and if he were to remain permanently revealed, his worship would cease being a matter of choice as it becomes an unavoidable obligation. . . . God, exalted be his name, revealed his image in different [human] forms and in different ages and stages for justice to be served, and for the contrast of opposites to become manifest.[54]

Like steps in a ladder, the cycles of revelation serve to propel the soul along the spiritual path of Tawhid. Once launched on the journey, the soul begins the long process of pilgrimage to the Source.

The Epistles of Tawhid describe the first of the known appearances of God in the image *"tajalli"* in remote antiquity. At that point in time man's faculties were rather primordial and, therefore, the process of Tawhid was at a level commensurate with those faculties. The primordial divine message has been repeated several times since the dawn of creation. Man's inability to absorb and retain the divine message has necessitated repeated cycles of *tajalli*. Due to cumulative effects of the message and the evolution of man's faculties, the complexity of the message in each cycle was gradually, progressively advanced to match the existing level of evolution.

According to Tawhid, there were seventy cycles of divine theophany, starting from the time when man was barely able to receive God's message in remote antiquity and culminating in the most recent disclosure of the concept of Tawhid in the era of al-Hakim *(dawr al-kashf)*. This *dawr* is believed by the followers of Tawhid to be the last stage in the process and the culmination of the previous stages of revelation and theophany. Hence no further revelations are expected until the final day of judgment.

What applies to God's revelation through the cyclical process of *tajalli* applies also to the articulation of God's message through messengers and prophets and through the human representation of the luminaries of Tawhid. Thus seven cycles are invoked in relation to the concrete articulation of God's messages through chosen messengers and prophets. The Druze believe that the essence of Tawhid is encoded in all the religious messages, notably those of the three monotheistic religions. Correct understanding of the Tawhid message in these religions is contingent upon the level of spirituality that the individual has achieved at any given period of time. The Qur'an is the last of God's messages, sent to the Prophet Muhammad through the angel Gabriel. The Epistles of Wisdom contain the esoteric interpretation of the deep concept of Tawhid in God's messages, most significantly in the Qur'an. The cyclical appearance of prophets and messengers is fundamental to the understanding of Tawhid and is stressed in all Druze religious writings. Al-Tamimi, in the role of the soul *(al-nafs)*, describes in Epistle 36 the sequence of events as the concept of Tawhid evolved in the messages of the monotheistic prophets and the bearers of God's word.

Al-Tamimi starts by declaring that God's message has been articulated at different times through chosen messengers or prophets. The messenger is described as the proclaimer *(natiq)*, meaning the one who publicly declares God's word as it is transmitted by divine revelation. He then proclaims the message to the public and for the benefit of those who are prepared to receive and accept it. The message invariably includes laws and instructions that regulate human behavior, collectively known as codes (shari'a) by which society lives and functions. The regulations extend into rites and rituals of worship in accordance with the revealed word of God. The declarer or proclaimer *(natiq)* is entrusted with the noble task of delivering the message, while promotion, elaboration, and propagation of the message rests on the shoulders of a trusted coworker who is referred to, in Tawhid, as the foundation *(asas)*. The foundation upholds the message in the absence of the messenger, through death, for example. The foundation, however, is subservient to the prophet since he (the foundation) does not receive God's message directly but through the Prophet. The two are organically linked to the propagation of God's message that is essential for the process of human spiritual development. For such development to take place human beings must be instructed to uphold moral and ethical codes and to perform certain rites and rituals that promote their awareness of the Divine.

The concepts of *natiq* and *asas* are inherited from the Isma'ilis. The Druze interpretation extends it further, to include, on another level, human representation of the mind, the soul, and the other luminaries who provide support and nurturance for God's message to survive and prevail. The luminaries in Tawhid are always present but not necessarily recognized, as their role is not to articulate the concrete message but rather to search for and discover the essence of that message.

This is how the thread of Tawhid grows more visible and viable within the declared word and the essence to which it points. The message may become dim due to human frailty and the passage of time, as well as the erosive effects of worldly distractions. If not properly reinforced through cyclical revelations and continually tended to through diligence, spirituality may succumb to the forces of dissolution and entropy. In the physical world neglect, disuse, and abuse subject material structures to destruction, and so it is with the spiritual world. It is said that the Buddha's last words on his deathbed were "Decay is inherent in all things; strive with diligence."[55]

The need then is evident for continuous reinforcement and upgrading of God's message, a sort of refresher course with necessary modifications to suit the level of spirituality at the time.

Al-Tamimi indicates that the first one of God's messengers was none other than Adam, the father of all humanity. However, Tawhid refers to at least three Adams as archetypes representing different role models. Their families and retinue were the earliest vanguard of believers in Tawhid. Due to the remoteness of that era nothing is known about any specific written doctrine ascribed to Adam. The concept of Tawhid at that time was so dim as to be virtually nonexistent.

According to al-Tamimi, Noah was next in line as the declarer or proclaimer of the holy message, in brief, a prophet. Noah as the prophet was assisted by his son, Sam "Shem," as the foundation. Again, in that remote era the concept of Tawhid was barely discernible.

The next era belonged to Ibrahim "Abraham" as the declarer, with Isma'il "Ishmael" as his foundation. By now we are in biblical times. The biblical and the Qur'anic versions differ in relation to the roles of Isma'il and Isaac as legitimate heir-designates of Abraham, and the identity of the one to be sacrificed following God's command. It was Isaac in the Bible and Isma'il in the Qur'an. Furthermore, Islam, according to the Qur'an, started with Abraham and continued through Jesus until Muhammad, the last of God's messengers. Be that as it may, the level of awareness of Tawhid at the time of Abraham was like the germ cell in relation to the human being. The message is encoded but the codes have not been deciphered, awaiting further development and evolution. These first three messengers were not invested in a written word or codes; the message was oral.

Al-Tamimi continues that Moses came next as the declarer, with his brother Aaron as his foundation. Moses' prophecy brought the level of Tawhid to that of the fertilized embryo. The process is unleashed, but the stage is still too early and has to follow a prescribed route to fulfillment. The law by now is written and the commandments enunciated to guide humanity into the path of righteousness and morality. Acceptance of the law and compliance with its dictates are necessary prerequisites to begin the journey to Tawhid.

Jesus of Nazareth was the next declarer, and the apostle Simon "Peter" was his foundation. The development of Tawhid had reached the stage of the skeleton in relation to the human body. It is interesting that Jesus himself referred to Peter as "the rock." Rocks were the only building blocks used in foundations at that time. Jesus expounded on the Mosaic laws, adding a dimension of love and forgiveness to the codes of behavior, and a new approach to spirituality. Enlightenment along the path of Tawhid has progressed to a higher level than before, but it is not yet complete. The process is ongoing.

The Prophet Muhammad came next as the declarer, and 'Ali was his foundation. An often-quoted hadith ascribed to the Prophet, "I am the city of learning and 'Ali is its gateway," is frequently referred to by the followers of 'Ali in confirmation of 'Ali's special status. By now the message of Tawhid had reached a high level of development as it was the word of God transmitted to Muhammed in the suras of the Qur'an. The law was transmitted to the Prophet by the angel Gabriel and subsequently documented and preserved in the holy Qur'an. The written word, however, is a symbol by which meaning can be imparted to objects, events, ideas, and feelings. Thus the message in the Qur'an needed further delving into in order to decipher the real meaning that lies within or behind the literal structure of the written or oral word. The task for the continuing development and refinement of the holy message would be reposed in the progeny of the Prophet, through ʿAli and Fatima.

Then there was another declarer, the seventh, in the Druze (and Ismaʿili) tradition after the Prophet Muhammad. The seventh declarer was Muhammad ibn Ismaʿil ibn Jaʿfar al-Sadiq. Muhammad ibn Ismaʿil was the first imam to be hidden from public exposure for fear of persecution. This tradition ushered in the era of occultation, when the Ismaʿili imams utilized dissimulation *(taqiya)* for self-preservation and the safeguarding of their faith. Muhammed ibn Ismaʿil was the great-grandfather of the Fatimid caliphs. Although Muhammad ibn Ismaʿil is considered by al-Tamimi to be the seventh proclaimer, he reportedly was not invested with a new law (shariʾa) nor did he have a foundation *(asas)*. The reason is that the message of Tawhid had reached by then a stage of development that allowed transcendence beyond the literal interpretation of the revealed messages thus far. New laws would have been redundant at this stage and were therefore no longer needed. By then the faithful were, or should have been, ready to delve into the inner and more substantive content of God's revealed messages. The skeleton in the era of Jesus had now acquired flesh and blood and was ready to come alive. The growth of the message to the level of a fully developed human body indicated that the time had come to invest the body with life, the culmination of full spiritual development. This step took place in the cycle of disclosure *(dawr al-kashf)* when the full message of Tawhid was articulated and made public by Hamza and the other luminaries under the tutelage of the Fatimid caliph and imam al-Hakim bi Amr Allah. Meanwhile we should keep in mind that the process of Tawhid evolves and grows, utilizing multiple approaches and multiple vehicles.

Throughout all of the cycles of revelations to prophets and messengers mentioned above, the universal mind and the other luminaries have provided crucial support and counsel (see below). For example, in the time of the prophet Moses it was Jethro (Shuʾayb), as the human representation of the universal mind, who provided support, while in the time of the Prophet Muhammad, the human representation was Salman al-Farisi. A saying attributed to the Prophet describes the status of Salman: "Salman is one of us, a member of our household. If religious belief were in the galaxies, then Salman would get to it." Imam ʿAli went a step further in his opinion of Salman: "Salman is from us and to us and our house. Who is there that embodies the wisdom of Luqman (the Wise), the knowledge of the Beginning and the End? Who [but Salman] read the first book and the last book and was an inexhaustible ocean?"[56]

In the Druze concept of Tawhid, each of the succeeding messages builds on the preceding ones because the incubator of Tawhid promotes Gnostic ripening and spiritual graduation from one stage to the next. This implies that the succeeding messages are not a mere repetition of the previous ones but a reflection of the stage of development of humanity and the level of intellectual and spiritual development that man has attained. As evolution carries the human race into higher and higher levels of accomplishment, so does the depth and intensity of the message carry man closer and closer to the source of truth, justice, and beauty. This idea of one message superseding another should not be confused with the notion of one message negating another. A person at age fifty is obviously much more knowledgeable than at age five, but it is the same person nonetheless, only the age and stage have changed. The past is and will continue to be an integral part of a person or a people or a doctrine, and will always remain part of that make-up.

This principle is not limited to the spiritual sphere but extends to social and anthropological aspects as well. The advancing science of genetics has shown how much humans share in their genetic heritage with more primitive forms of animal and even plant life. Whether in the physical or biological sciences or in the spiritual domain, the past will always be part of the present as it projects to the future. Thus the Druze concept of Tawhid can be understood as a common thread throughout the entirety of human spiritual development, encoded in all the revealed religions: "Through Tawhid all things can be defined; not through things can we define Tawhid."[57] Tawhid is the benchmark of knowledge and not the other way around. The goal and the reward of all believers is to arrive at the highest level of awareness in Tawhid. The methods may differ and the means may vary, but the focus is one: the attainment of God's grace through the miracles of God's creation and through the multiple and complementary revelations of God's grace and God's messages. Passing from one stage to the next over the long haul of existence and growing in knowledge and stature, the human soul reaches a level where the true meaning of Tawhid is realized and the essence of reality revealed. "The traveler [on the road of Tawhid] distills the many into the few until he arrives at unity, whereby eternity and infinity are lost in this valley . . . and when the traveler arrives at the expanse of Tawhid he will no longer be limited in time or space and the part becomes whole."[58]

It was during the tenure of al-Hakim, according to the Druze interpretation, that the most recent of the cycles of *tajalli* took place. After the Tawhid doctrine was publicly declared, this cycle became known in Druze circles as the "cycle of disclosure of the tenets of Tawhid" *(dawr al-kashf)*. All the previous cycles were in preparation for this fateful event. In fact, the era of disclosure represented, in the Druze vision, the culmination of man's spiritual quest across the eons of time.

It is a common belief among the Druze that the seeds of Tawhid are found in all religions but that most people of faith do not recognize them as they should. Such pantheistic visions may have been the dream of al-Hakim, and the stimulus to delegate the disclosure to Hamza and to his trusted colleagues. The sudden and dramatic disappearance of al-Hakim and Hamza and the rest of the luminaries except for Baha' al-Din put a de facto closure on this era. The result was suspension of a process that was based on continuity and evolution. The suspension or closure of the call to Tawhid is a crucial issue for the Druze to examine and revisit in the context of the universiality of Tawhid and the confines of Druze tradition.

The Concept of Creation

Creation in Tawhid is an emanation from God and by his divine will, for nothing exists or can exist outside God's omnipotence. It is not creation out of nothing (ex nihilo) because an emanation from God implies (potential) existence in God's will. God's will is clearly documented in the Qur'an: "When He decrees a thing / He but says to it 'Be,' and it is" (2:116).

Following this fundamental principle the luminaries of Tawhid elaborated a distinctive approach to the development of the process of creation and cosmic genesis. In this they were influenced by the ideas of the Brothers of Purity and the subsequent development of these ideas by Isma'ili theologians. The luminaries of Tawhid hypothesized that God first created cosmic principles, five in number, whose representation is somewhat analogous to the concept of ideals in the Platonic vision. Emanation of these cosmic principles known in Tawhid as luminaries preceded the creation of the universe or any other coordinate of time or space. The real appellation is *hudud al-Tawhid*, or the pillars that embody the message of Tawhid.

Whereas the concept of luminaries is in the realm of ideals or archetypes, these ideals are reflected or represented in the flesh in human counterparts. The latter are ordinary people in every sense of the word. Yet they are especially distinguished by the divine gift of reflecting in actual life the ideals they conceptually represent. Thus while the ideals are purely spiritual concepts, their representation on earth is in concrete human form. Absent human representation, the ideals remain in a state of potentiality *(wujud bi al-quwwa)* awaiting activation *(wujud bi al-fi'l)* and therefore recognition. Potential existence remains in essence nonexistent until brought to a state of recognition by activation. By linking the two aspects, Tawhid establishes a continuity between the two poles, the spiritual and the material, between the luminaries as ideals and the humans that represent these ideals in actual life. Moreover, this principle can be extended to include the integration of body and soul in every human being, the body obviously representing the material aspect while the soul represents the spiritual. In Tawhid, body and soul are codependent. In this context Tawhid reflects the totality of existence.

In Tawhid the first of God's creation is the universal mind *(al-'aql al-kulli)*, an archetype that preceded all other beings. The creation of the universal mind and of the four succeeding cosmic principles, according to Tawhid, was outside the framework of space and time, and therefore outside the possibility of characterization by space-time definitions. Thus even the term *first* is, strictly speaking, inaccurate since the term implies temporal and/or spatial definitions, neither of which existed at the advent of creation. We are faced with the paradox of assigning a sequential order of creation, which by necessity acquires a chronological status and yet remains, by definition, outside the confines of time. This is somewhat analogous to the paradox in connection with knowing the Unknowable when discussing the concept of God in Tawhid. Therefore, the process of creation has to be conceptualized in a nondimensional context and as an expression of God's will. Hamza describes the process of creation: "God, exalted be his name, emanated from his absolute light a pure and complete image, an embodiment of his will . . . and named that image 'mind' *(al-'aql)*. This [universal] mind was perfect in enlightenment and power, complete in character and action." [59]

Hamza then goes on to elaborate on the setting of the process within the philosophical underpinnings of this concept:

> And there were [at the instant of creation of the mind], no days, months, or years . . . no time or place; no night and day . . . no oceans or lands and no orbiting planets. . . . There was no heaven or hell; there were no angels real or imagined; no physical or spiritual sun; no moon complete or partial; no oceans of knowledge or of water; no physical or religious thrones, and so on . . . [most notably] no souls or spirits and no instincts." [60]

This is but a partial recounting of Hamza's description in Epistle 13 of the state of nonexistence (as defined by space and time), prior to the creation of the universal mind. That is why Hamza also describes the first of God's creation (the universal mind) as the cause of all causes, while God, exalted be his name, is the creator of the cause of all causes, for God is beyond definition.

Once the process of creation began, it evolved with each of the subsequent cosmic principles, deriving its emergence, by God's will, from the preceding one until the creation of the five cosmic principles was complete. Only then did the universe and all there is in it emerge. Such emergence took place, by God's will, from the last one of the five luminaries in Tawhid. Hamza presents the sequence of events as follows:

> God willed from his perfect luminescence the emanation of the universal mind. From the luminescence of the universal mind, God caused the emergence of the universal soul *(al-nafs al-kulliyya)*. From the luminescence of the universal soul God caused the emergence of the word *(al-kalima)*. God then caused the emergence of the precedent *(al-sabiq)*. From the luminescence of the word and from the luminescence of the precedent God caused the emergence of the follower *(al-tali)*. And from the luminescence of the follower, God created the universe and all that is in it, the orbiting skies, the twelve planets, the four vital elements (water, wind, fire, and soil), and the spirit as the fifth element.[61]

The process of creation can therefore be conceptualized in the following sequence: *mind > soul > word > precedent > follower > universe.*

Thus the physical universe and the spiritual dimension associated with the universe were created according to the cosmic order that was latent in God's conscience and came into being by his divine will. The starting point and the center of the circle is the universal mind. As such the universal mind represents the beginning of the road to Tawhid and the ultimate destination that can be reached in the human quest on the road to God's grace. Once again, the order of creation did not represent a sequence in the temporal sense, for the concept of time did not exist. Beyond that point lies the unknowable realm of the Divine. Again from Hamza, in Epistle 13:

> And God, exalted be his name, said to the cause of creation, who is the universal mind, come hither, meaning come to worship me, and the universal mind came willingly. God said: Leave, meaning leave any notion of worshipping any other but me, and the universal mind left. God then said: By my glory and grace no one will enter my paradise [my covenant] except through you [the universal mind]; and no one will suffer hell, meaning remain at a lower level of awareness of Tawhid, except those who are not true to you. Whoever obeys you [the universal mind] will have obeyed me and whoever reneges on you will have reneged on me.[62]

It is interesting that in one of the sayings attributed to the Prophet, according to al-Muhasibi, we find a striking similarity to the passage noted above:

> God will not accept prayers from his subject, nor fasting, nor alms, nor pilgrimage . . . nor any other altruistic act unless the mind is present. . . . And we are told that when God, exalted be his name, created the mind, he said to him [the mind]: stay, and he stayed. God said: leave, and he left; and God said: come hither, and he came; and God said witness, and he witnessed. Then God said: By my grace and my exalted state and my power over my creation, I have not created anyone dearer and nearer to me than you. Through you [the mind], I will be known and worshipped and through you will be reward and punishment.[63]

According to Tawhid, the Almighty bestowed four major traits on the universal mind: obedience, illumination, wisdom, and humility. These traits are referred to in Tawhid as the positive traits that denote virtue and submission to God's will. In the absence of any blemish or drawback that would mar the record, these traits would denote perfection. Perfection, however, belongs to the Creator and not to any of his creatures, including the universal mind.

Therefore, true to expectations, the universal mind was destined to exhibit the first indication that he is in fact only a creation of the Almighty and not the Almighty himself. Although the universal mind occupies the unique privilege of being the first of God's creation, yet the universal mind is not perfect. Perfection would not be the mind's because perfection is an attribute of the Almighty alone. We go back to Epistle 13 where Hamza describes what followed when the universal mind recognized God's gift and how the universal mind exhibited his imperfection by succumbing to the temptation of pride and egotism: "When the universal mind heard this [praise] from God, he reflected upon himself, and found that he had no peer to compare to, no rival to compete with, and no antagonist to oppose. He accordingly succumbed to self-aggrandizement and felt that he needed no one ever, as he would always be without challenge."[64]

This attitude of arrogance was enough for the initiation of a sequence of events consisting of action and response that set the stage for the emergence of the struggle between opposite forces in life and in nature as a whole. The principle upon which such a struggle is based started as a concept in the realm of the ideals and subsequently worked its way into concrete expression in the physical universe and in life as we know it. What happened next, as a consequence of the mind succumbing to temptation, according to Hamza, was that "God, exalted be his name, created from his [mind's] obedience recalcitrance; and from his illumination darkness; and from his humility arrogance; and from his wisdom ignorance. Thus the four positive traits were matched with four negative traits in juxtaposition."[65]

Briefly, then, God created the exact antithesis *(dhidd)* of the universal mind and endowed the antithesis with equal power. The antithesis, however, is a concept defined solely by the absence or negation of the positive traits of the universal mind; the antithesis has no primary function or existence in its own right. This point is important to the concept of heaven and hell in the Druze interpretation of Tawhid.

Several implications attend the concept of the antithesis in response to the error (sin) committed by the mind when overcome with pride and egotism. The first is that no matter how pure and perfect, the mind remains a creation of God, the seat and source of absolute perfection. A creation therefore will never equal the creator. In this manner God remains exalted above and beyond anything else, including the mind, and the mind is forever in need of God's guidance and grace.

The second implication is that the creation of the antithesis was a necessary step for the interaction of opposing forces, as a prerequisite for the subsequent emergence of the physical world and life in general. This in essence represents a state of symmetry whereby the opposing forces are evenly matched. Such symmetry is not restricted to the spiritual domain and the world of ideals; it is extended to include every aspect of existence in the physical world as well. In the words of a noted physicist: "The symmetry between matter and antimatter implies that for every particle there exists an antiparticle with equal mass and opposite charge. Pairs of particles and antiparticles can be created if enough energy is available and can be made to turn into pure energy in the reverse process of annihilation."[66]

The temptation (and fall) of the universal mind can be considered analogous to that of Adam, who fell from eternal grace when he succumbed to the temptation of the forbidden fruit. Such fall was not altogether without merit as we can argue that the human race owes its origin to this fall in the biblical tradition. Likewise, absent such temptation as that which afflicted the universal mind, life as we know it would not have started nor would have existence begun in the concept of Tawhid.

At this point the universal mind recognized that he deserved this fateful trial because he had succumbed to pride and arrogance. Admitting his mistake, the mind began supplication to the Almighty to grant him forgiveness and to help him atone. The mind also knew that he needed God's help to prevail in his struggle with the antithesis that was created as a result of the mind's own weakness. The antithesis was in fact a negation of the mind and what the mind represented in the scheme of creation.

Responding to the mind's supplication and pleas, God created the universal soul to assist the mind in the struggle with the antithesis. As second in the hierarchy, the soul derived his power from the mind and was endowed with half his strength. The soul is the seat of compassion and tenderness. The creation of the soul, however, was in response to the plea by the mind for assistance only after the antithesis was created. Thus in a sense the soul was the first product of the struggle between the mind and the antithesis. The soul is, therefore, less pure than the mind, being influenced to a minor extent by the antithesis. Still, the overwhelming influence on the soul remains that of the mind and not the antithesis. The subsequent luminaries embody features of the two opposing poles, the mind and the antithesis, obviously with more contribution from the mind than from the antithesis. The farther down the ladder, however, the more equal the contribution becomes from both sides, the mind representing enlightenment and the antithesis representing darkness (i.e., lack of enlightenment).

Next to the universal soul comes the word, followed by the precedent as the right wing. Next to the precedent comes the follower as the left wing. We should note that "precedent" in Arabic is *al-sabiq*, that is, the first to arrive, and therefore should be ahead of the other luminaries. Such is the case in the Isma'ili interpretation. However, in the Druze epistles *al-sabiq* is the fourth in line, coming before the follower. The word supersedes the precedent, the soul supersedes the word, and the mind is above them all. The precedent would also conceptually represent the past, while the follower *(al-tali)* represents the future.

God also created a second in command to the antithesis. Taken together, the five luminaries and the two negations make a total of seven cosmic principles. The number seven recurs in Tawhid as it does in Isma'ili tradition. We should remember that this scheme was until now outside the framework of space and time and existence of the universe as we recognize it. It was from the follower that the entirety of the observed universe came into being and with it the onset of the space-time parameters of existence. The event at this juncture may be considered analogous to the big bang in modern cosmic genesis.

The scheme pertaining to the mind and the soul in relation to creation in Tawhid is not totally original as it gradually evolved with some variations over two hundred years. An often-quoted statement by Ja'far al-Sadiq, the sixth descendent of Imam 'Ali, illustrates the point: "The believer is the brother of the believer from the same father and mother. Their father is *al-nur* (luminescence) or *al-'aql* (the mind), and their mother is *al-rahma* (compassion) or *al-nafs* (the soul)."[67] In this context *al-ʿaql* can also be viewed as Adam and *al-nafs* as Eve.

Since the antithesis was endowed with powers that were equal to those of the mind, the stage was set for the contrast to be recognized and for the duality to become the basis for existence. By the time the process of creation (or spiritual evolution) reached the human level, the positive traits (derived from the universal mind and expressed in the individual mind) and the negative traits from the antithesis were equally matched. The duality also established provision for free choice and for a goal. Tawhid in essence is based on a dialectic dynamic between opposing forces and across the span of existence as ordained by God.

Some elements of this philosophy can be traced to the Persian background of Hamza and his exposure to the lingering heritage of Zoroastrians and Manichaeism. The central theme in that religious heritage revolves around the struggle between creation and destruction. The creator, known as Ahura Mazda in Zoroastrianism, is analogous to the mind in Tawhid, while the destroyer, known as Ahriman, is analogous to the antithesis. The two poles representing dualism of good and evil, or light and darkness, are at the cosmic level, equals in every respect. Thus the challenge to choose one side or the other is not only forever present but is a phenomenon that is a prerequisite for life to continue.[68] Despite the analogy there are some fundamental differences. In Zoroastrianism, the creator himself (Ahura Mazda) is one of the poles in the struggle with evil, while in Tawhid God is exalted and totally above the fray. God's first creation, the mind, in Tawhid is the pole representing the forces of light and goodness, and the antithesis represents negation.

In any event, humans are called upon to respond to the challenge by supporting the forces of light against those of darkness, with the full exercise of free will. Divine justice in Tawhid rests on the twin features of the opposing forces of good and evil and the exercise of free will. Only with free will does accountability become valid: "Know that God's command [in relation to man's decision], blessed be his name, is revelation and choice, and his admonition is guidance and warning. For if his command were irrefutable, or his admonition always binding, no one would have doubted his existence, and there would have been no difference between those who believe and those who do not. Reward and punishment would lose legitimacy."[69]

This is in a way an elaboration on the theme that recurs in the Qurʾan with respect to choice and free will. There is no coercion in religion in Islam or in the various sects that emerged therefrom:

And if thy Lord had willed, whoever
is in the earth would have believed,
all of them, all together. Wouldst thou
then constrain the people, until
they are believers? (Qur'an10:99)

We find elements in the Tawhid concept of the universal mind that can be traced to the Greek philosophers, in particular Pythagoras, Plato, Aristotle, and Plotinus. These philosophers are held in high esteem in Tawhid, as they have been by the Druze community throughout its history. In fact, through the concept of cyclical recurrence of the process of Tawhid and the concept of reincarnation, Greek philosophers (Pythagoras, Plato, and Aristotle, in particular) are considered among the human representations of God's first five luminaries. In the case of Plato, the concept of ideals on which his philosophy is based is closely related to the concept of the cosmic principles in the Tawhid doctrine. The concrete and human representation of the Platonic ideals also has a similar counterpart in Tawhid. In the case of Aristotle, the concept of the prime mover is closer to the concept of God than it is to the concept of the universal mind in Tawhid, but the relationship is obvious. The concept of reincarnation is traced to Pythagoras, among others.

It is in the philosophy of Neoplatonism, though, as developed by Plotinus "Aflutin," that we find the closest congruence with that of Tawhid. In Plotinus's scheme, the mind comes as the first emanation from the One, with attributes of perfection and power as those described in Tawhid. The temptation of the mind and the creation of the antithesis are additions that are developed further in Tawhid. These steps are vital for the concept of the struggle between opposites in Tawhid, both in the spiritual and the physical sense.

The drama enacted on the cosmic scale and expressed in the realm of ideals has its counterpart in actual life. Thus the human mind exhibits in its own limited way features of the universal mind, and this applies to all human beings. In this manner every individual is a partner in the concept of the universal mind and is therefore a component in the final common pathway to the One.

The universal mind and the other luminaries accompanied all the cycles of God's manifestations through direct revelation in the image of the nasut (tajalli), as well as through the cycles where God's word was sent via prophets and messengers. Their human reflections are known by different names in the different ages of the recurring cycles. Since God's grace is never absent from his creation, the luminaries, as cosmic principles, are never absent either. Whether recognized in the human form or not, their guiding hand is never off the steering wheel of creation.

The universal mind is referred to by different appellations. Hamza is supposed to be the human reflection of the universal mind at the time of the most recent disclosure *(dawr al-kashf)* during the era of al-Hakim. In God's scheme, according to Tawhid, the world will never be bereft of the guidance and leadership of these luminaries: "And we mention in this epistle . . . the emergence of the mind for you to observe the truth and believe in Tawhid. And to realize that God, exalted be his name, will never withhold from the universe his divine light, nor his station. And that all the luminaries are present in every age and stage for [the guidance of] whoever seeks to save his soul and does not engage in idolatry."[70]

This statement tells us first that God's hand is forever there for those who seek to touch it, and, second, anyone who seeks is never excluded. References to these claims pervade many of the epistles and under various circumstances:

> And our Lord, exalted be his name, is omnipotent, his light is never turned off, yet his nature is not fully disclosed even to those in his service. He never tears down anything but to replace it with what is better and more lofty, and never abandons his creation ever. Some people say God does not close the door on anyone unless he opens many doors instead. And the door here is the authority and teacher, the conduit to Tawhid.[71]

The authority and teacher *(murshid)* in this passage is none other than the human representation of the universal mind in the person of Hamza in the era of al-Hakim. The main point here again is that God does not abandon his creation for one wink of an eye nor does he turn away anyone who seeks him at any or all times. God's will, however, is executed through the universal mind. "That bright light [the universal mind] is present in every age and stage, in times of obscurity and enlightenment, who God, exalted be his name, deploys under different names and traits, to preach Tawhid and not to blaspheme. . . . In our time he is represented by Hamza, the guide of the believers."[72]

The universal mind, no matter how high he is in the process of creation, is and will forever remain subservient to the will of the Creator. This point of distinction is stressed over and over again, since God is exalted above and beyond all creatures that owe their creation to him and him only. Only God is beyond description and comprehension *(munazzah wa mujarrad)*, while all else, the mind included, is subject to definition and cognizance: "And the cause of all causes [the universal mind] exists in every age and is present in every stage and is subservient [to God]. How can anyone say that he [the mind] cannot be defined by thought or imagination, and how can he be beyond change and definition, when he is a creation and not the creator?"[73]

In this passage Hamza was trying to clarify his position as the human re-flection of the universal mind (in this cycle). The universal mind is the primary agent in the process of Tawhid, directed by and functioning at the pleasure of the Creator.

Tawhid is an ongoing process that has accompanied human development from inception and will continue to evolve until the final hour. Tawhid, like Islam from which it emerged, conforms to the day of judgment, which will happen when God wills. No one is privy to that secret, not even the universal mind. Meanwhile, the main emphasis in Tawhid is on earning one's way in life on earth to God's graces by firm belief and by deeds that conform to that belief. The uni-versal mind and all the other luminaries provide guidance along the way but will not assume responsibility for the individual's decision nor force the decision on anyone. It is up to the individual, in full control of his or her physical and mental faculties, to make the choice and be held accountable for the belief in Tawhid, and for the actions that attend such belief.

The mind and the other luminaries are described as playing supportive roles in providing vital assistance to those chosen to carry the message of Tawhid in dif-ferent ages and stages. This message is encoded within the various religions and faiths that openly proclaim the oneness of God, and in other faiths where the proclamation is complex and needs further clarification: "And I [Hamza, repre-senting the universal mind] have shown you the way to Tawhid in our Lord, ex-alted be his name, in seventy ages. No age passes that our Lord does not send me to you under different names, images, and tongues. I know you, and you may not know me any more than you know yourselves."[74]

Since the universal mind embodies all that God intended for creation, the culmination of Tawhid at the personal level is to arrive at the totality of the uni-versal mind. Hamza in the role of the human representation of the universal mind alludes to this idea: "Thanks be to God who created me from his pure light and supported me by his grace, and reposed in me his divine knowledge, and revealed to me his secrets. I am the basis for his creation and the bearer of his secrets, and the designee for his knowledge. . . . I am the guide to the submission to God."[75]

Of course it was not Hamza the individual human being that was meant by the above passage but Hamza in his role as the universal mind. Since the univer-sal mind was created before or rather outside the framework of space and time,

Hamza can only be a human representation of that archetype and not the ideal itself. Hamza is the human agent of the universal mind in the era of al-Hakim. This is an important point to remember as it has caused some confusion within and outside the Druze community. The universal mind is the closest that human beings can get to God, for God in the absolute (Lahut) is and will forever remain exalted beyond description or reach. The concept of the universal mind as the limit to which the soul can ever reach on its way to the Creator is somewhat different from the extreme mystical visions of the Sufis, where the goal of the soul is complete dissolution in the One. The difference, however, is one of degree and not in the fundamentals. Thus the universal mind, the first luminary (Hadd) in the order of creation, is the last destination on the way back to the Creator; the beginning and the end of the circle.

When we consider the concept of the universal mind, we are tempted to think of the idea as one originating in the distant past with the sages of antiquity. The Fertile Crescent, frequently referred to as the cradle of civilization, constituted a vital connection linking the Far East with the Nile valley. Thus from the epics of Gilgamesh and the Enuma Elish we encounter references to the budding idea of the universal mind. In ancient Egypt the idea became more developed through the teachings of the god Toth, who was also known as Hermes Trismegistus because of the syncretistic identification of the Egyptian god Toth with the Greek Hermes.[76] Hermes occupies an especially revered place in Tawhid. In point of fact Hamza, representing the human reflection of the universal mind, bestowed upon his second in command and brother-in-law, Isma'il al-Tamimi (representing the human reflection of the universal soul), the title of Hermes as a special honor.[77] As to the universal mind himself, Hamza describes him as *thu ma'at* since he was the first to recognize the unity of the Lord.[78] It is interesting to note that the concept of *ma'at* was well known in ancient Egypt as representing wisdom or genuine knowledge (*haqiqa* or truth).[79] *Ma'at* signified something "more comprehensive than fairness. . . . It came to mean righteousness, truth, and justice."[80] We can only speculate as to whether Hamza used the term *ma'at* with that definition in mind, considering that Tawhid made its first public appearance in Egypt at the hands of the pharaoh Amenhotep IV, better known as Akhenaten. Akhenaten eventually succumbed to the powerful influence of the priests when their status was completely undermined by the bold universal concept.

Abu al-'Ala' al-Ma'arri, the great Arab poet-philosopher who was a contemporary of al-Hakim and Hamza, was noted for his emphasis on the prime position that the mind occupies, particularly in matters of faith. Defying the traditional religious establishment of his day (and of these days as well), al-Ma'arri thundered in one of his poems:

> People dearly hope for the emergence of an imam
> Who will articulate (and guide) when others are mute
> Hopes are dashed, there is no imam but the mind
> The beacon [of truth] in days and nights.[81]

Al-Hakim, who was deeply committed to all aspects of learning and knowledge, invited al-Ma'arri from his hometown, Ma'arrat al-Nu'man in northern Syria, to Dar al-Hikma in Cairo.[82] Al-Ma'arri declined, ostensibly for health reasons (among other things, he was blind). There are claims, though, that al-Ma'arri had joined the converts to the call to Tawhid. This would not be surprising because there was a large community of Muwahhidun in Ma'arrat al-Nu'man during his time.

Almost a century later Averroes "Ibn Rushd," the great Arab philosopher of Andalusia, delved into the issue of the mind as a common denominator between philosophy and religion. Commenting on the ideas of his idol Aristotle and expanding on his own, Averroes proposed a concept of a primary mind that is purely spiritual and everlasting as the cause of creation. (Remember how close this is to the concept of the universal mind as the cause of causes in Tawhid, while God, exalted be his name, is the Creator of the cause of all causes). The human mind, in Averroes's view, acts in a secondary capacity as a recipient of power from and affinity to the primary mind. The secondary mind, being material, is subject to dissolution with death, although its essence, inasfar as it is derived from the primary mind, is also everlasting.[83] A favorite quotation, attributed to Emir Jamal al-Din Abdallah al-Tanukhi, is "al-'Aql is the commander of both worlds, this one and the hereafter" *(al-'aql sayyid al-ahkam fi al-darayn ma'an).*

Centuries later we hear an echo of the same theme from the New World: "Mind is the only reality, of which men and all other natures are better or worse reflections. Nature, literature, history are only subjective phenomena."[84]

It is interesting to note that many thinkers, scientists, and authors in modern times have alluded to the concept of the universal mind in a manner that is quite similar to the Tawhid vision:

> The modern scientific mind has continued to consider and be fascinated by the idea of a Supreme Being, at least as a metaphor for a transcendent, immanent, and unifying ultimate reality. . . . The individual mind is immanent but not only in the body. It is immanent also in pathways and messages outside the body; and

there is a larger *Mind*, of which the individual mind is only a subsystem [emphasis added].[85]

A quotation attributed to the physicist David Darling corresponds very closely to the concept of Tawhid with respect to the universal mind:

> What we are here today will evolve to become a single universe-wide mind, so that every particle in space will be within this cosmic consciousness—free, but aware. Every particle of which you and I are made will ultimately be reconstituted in this *universal mind*, along with everything else. Given such a prospect, we need hardly fear our own personal deaths. For nothing ever dies. And in deep time we shall be as one [emphasis added].[86]

The eminent physicist Sir James Jeans reached similar conclusions: "The stream of knowledge is heading toward a non-mechanical reality; the Universe begins to look more like a great thought than a great machine. Mind no longer appears as an accidental intruder into the realm of matter; we are beginning to suspect that we ought to hail it as the creator and governor of the realm of matter."[87] And from another towering figure in modern science, Erwin Schroedinger: "So with all due acknowledgment to the fact that physical theory is at all times relative, in that it depends on some basic assumptions, we may, or so I believe, assert that physical theory in its present stage suggests the *indestructibility of Mind* by Time" [emphasis added].[88] Julian Huxley aptly points out the role of the mind in evolution not only as a product of the process but as the agent in control: "This puts the mind in all its aspects, into the business of evolution. . . . Human society generates new mental and spiritual agencies, and sets them to work in the cosmic process: it controls matter by means of mind."[89]

It is remarkable how closely scientific notions in modern physics have come to resemble what was postulated by the luminaries of Tawhid one thousand years ago. The primacy of mind over matter is a central theme in the story of creation in the Druze understanding of Tawhid.

The message of Tawhid can be traced back to the dawn of human creation and projected forward to the uncharted realm of the future. It is found in all the holy books, the last and most important of which is the Qur'an, and implied in the most advanced scientific thinking. The individual mind, however, in its capacity as a representation (microcosm) of the universal mind, must be prepared to comprehend the full meaning of the message. The revealed religions are part and parcel of this evolutionary process, providing the framework for spiritual development and growth. Such are the marvels of creation for all to see, the guiding hand of luminaries across human evolution, and the direct reflections of God's *nasut* in the human medium.

Just as the universal mind as an ideal is represented in actuality in the human mind, so is the universal soul represented in the human soul. The individual soul, therefore, is cognizant and can distinguish between right and wrong, for the basis of free choice is precisely the capacity to make such distinction. Thus the soul in any individual can go either way: "And when the soul is equally capable of accepting [enlightenment] or negation, it will follow whichever gains the upper hand. . . . And so it is that when the soul becomes deprived of continued spiritual nourishment, which is necessary for its survival and growth, it will drift to negation and degenerate into instinctive behavior and ignorance."[90]

The cyclical messages in the revealed religions and the ever-present guidance of the luminaries of Tawhid provide the necessary catalysts for the correct choices to be made, and for illumination *(ishraq)* to take place. Once launched on the path of Tawhid, the soul will proceed to graduate from one stage to the next, in accordance with its potential. The objective is to get closer and closer to the truth and to awareness of the Creator.

The human soul will achieve this advanced status when it has shed the last vestiges of doubt and egotism and has recognized and accepted God's revelations. It has to recognize the oneness of God above and beyond any human capacity to comprehend and submit to God's will in peace and humility. Submission to God leads to a state of security and bliss that can only be felt by those who have reached this state of transcendence. The Druze epistles refer to this state as *ridha* and *taslim*, meaning acceptance or satisfaction and submission:

> Brethren, accept [God's will] and submit to God in good and in bad conditions. To this you have testified and committed yourselves. Do not object to whatever may befall you of what may be in your [worldly] interest or to its detriment. The only difference between your state [of knowledge] and that of ignorance is acceptance [of God's message] and submission [to God's will]. Acceptance and submission are the culmination of learning and knowledge.[91]

There is no original sin in Tawhid. Therefore, there is no baptism to erase the presumed sin. There is, however, the temptation to which the universal mind succumbed. The upshot of that temptation is the perpetual struggle between opposite poles both in the realm of ideals and in the individual expression of these ideals. However, if the temptation of the universal mind is equated with the fall of Adam from the Garden of Eden, the remedy in the two situations is somewhat different. In the case of Adam the sin bequeathed to his progeny is wiped out through baptism after birth, while the error of the universal mind is not transmitted to the progeny. What is transmitted is the everlasting struggle between opposites and the accountability that accompanies the gift of free choice. Thus human beings are continuously facing options and confronting situations in which they must choose between right and wrong, truth and falsehood, belief and disbelief, and so on. And they are held accountable for the consequences of their decisions and choices. There is no mechanism, except God's forgiveness, that will bear the responsibility for a bad choice or absolve the individual responsible for that choice from accountability:

> Beware, beware, dear brethren, the world of oblivion, and remain committed to the everlasting world. . . . Brethren, faith can only be true when tested, for in situations of peace and stability the boundaries of distinction [between those who truly believe and those who do not] become blurred. . . . Beware, dear brethren, of letting the negative forces in your soul gain the upper hand over the positive forces, for if that were to happen, it would be to your detriment. . . . Dear brethren, purify your intentions and God will help you prevail. . . . Dear brethren, you can ascend along the path of righteousness by patience and perseverance, for the one who can remain steadfast in the face of adversity will earn rich rewards. . . . And know ye, dear brethren, that your actions will reflect back on you . . . and whatever adversity may befall you is the result of your own actions.[92]

It is quite clear from this and several other passages throughout the Epistles of Wisdom that the responsibility of free choice is tethered to accountability that attends free choice. And no one will bear the onus of rectifying the error but the individual self guided by God's messages and messengers, who point to the correct way and offer the choice. This is a feature of the Islamic teachings in general, and more pointedly in the Druze interpretation of Tawhid. We can see in this approach a different point of emphasis from that in Christianity, whereby salvation of the individual is through the suffering and crucifixion of Jesus Christ on behalf of humanity. This applies to the original sin that is erased through baptism and the absolution of subsequent sins through the suffering and sacrifice of God's only begotten Son. Surely the individual bears the primary consequence of belief and action in both Islamic and Christian traditions, but the stress on individual responsibility is more strongly emphasized in the Druze interpretation of Tawhid.

What may be the rewards for the believers in Tawhid? What could those who have chosen the right path expect in return? In the end there is a day of judgment, that unpredictable and cataclysmic event that most religions preach and anticipate. No one knows when or how it will happen, and no one is privy to any of its secrets. For the secrets of the day of judgment remain locked in the Secret of all secrets, the Almighty, the Creator. The vision of heaven and hell in Tawhid is based on metaphysical and spiritual context and not on physical characteristics. No ear has heard, no eye has seen, nor can it be imagined in the hearts of humans. Meanwhile in this world, Tawhid states that human beings build their own version of reward and punishment by their own actions and the choices they make. Moreover, the present life on earth along the span of eternity is a kind of stage for what is to come (Karma).

Thus, in a simple word, the reward lies in the process itself, in the quest for genuine knowledge *(al-ma'rifa al-ladaniyya)*, and in the pilgrimage toward the Supreme Source. It is the attainment of a state of warmth and bliss for the travelers as they approach the destination they seek. The reward is when the target of the long journey, begun in the memories of the distant past, shines brighter than ever, until it appears within reach. After all, the purpose of life is nothing more than the enlightenment of the mind, the purification of the soul, and the arrival at the source of knowledge and wisdom *(irfan)*. It is the realization of the self within the context of the broader framework of God's creation. Anwar Abi-Khzam, in his introduction to a recently published edition of *Al-nuqat wa al-dawa'ir* (The Dots and the Circles), a manuscript written by the sixteenth-century Druze sage Zayn al-Din 'Abd al-Gaffar Taqi al-Din, describes the rewards of Tawhid as follows:

> The compelling reason for Tawhid and [God's] worship is to bring the individual to a state of everlasting bliss. This state of bliss is not limited to the realm of the hereafter [(after Judgment Day), as it exists in the present world as well. Likewise, immortality does not mean the absence of death but a state of renewal that death makes possible. The Druze faith promises no greater reward than that of Tawhid in the present and no greater goal to look forward to in the hereafter.[93]

Thus one does not have to wait until the day of judgment to experience the ecstasy that attends the presence of God; rather, such experience resides in the here and now as well. It is an ongoing process of spiritual evolution that propels the seeker from one stage to the next in the eternal pilgrimage to the ultimate reality.

Philosophers and poets, scientists and theologians, and common men and women in the humdrum of daily life are visited from time to time with the sensation of being released from the state of physical being to a dreamlike state of liberation and freedom. And in moments unexpected they soar above and beyond what we call physical reality to a reality that is a thousand times clearer and more serene. Perhaps the words of Lord Tennyson come close to describing the phenomenon:

> All at once, as it were, out of the intensity of the consciousness of the Individuality, the Individuality itself seemed to dissolve and fade away into boundless being; and this is not a confused state, but the clearest of the clearest, the surest of the surest, the weirdest of the weirdest; utterly beyond words—where death was an almost laughable impossibility—the loss of personality (if so it were) being no extinction, but the only true life. I am ashamed of my feeble description. Have I not said the state is utterly beyond words.[94]

It is in moments like these that one connects, however fleetingly, with a larger self than the individual self and a more comprehensive mind than the individual mind. In the words of the poet William Blake:

> Laws of peace, of love, of unity,
> Of pity, compassion, forgiveness;
> Let each chuse one habitation,
> His ancient infinite mansion,
> One command, one joy, one desire,
> One curse, one weight, one measure,
> One King, one God, one Law.[95]

The Concept of Reincarnation

Reincarnation is the third main tenet of Tawhid. Reincarnation, in the Tawhid interpretation, refers to the act of the soul re-entering the flesh of (presumably) a newborn at the very moment that the soul departs from the body of current residence. Thus upon physical death, as defined by biological and physiological parameters such as cessation of brain function, the soul departs the body of the deceased and immediately takes residence in the flesh of a newborn. At that point the old abode becomes lifeless just like any other object, while the newborn becomes a person with a self and an identity consisting of body and soul. The life of an individual, therefore, never ceases; it merely persists as his or her soul continues on the journey of existence, always in conjunction with a human body. In the Tawhid concept of reincarnation, the human soul does not incarnate any other but a human body. This is distinctly different from some other Muslim sects and from schools of thought, particularly in the East, where souls can transmigrate across different biological species. It is also different from the Isma'ili concept whereby what happens to the soul after death depends on the actions of the individual. The souls of the believers who lead a life of virtue (ahl al-haq), in the Isma'ili vision, are released to join the celestial bodies, while the souls of those who lead a life of vice will be banished to the wilderness and the darkness of negation.[96]

The Druze belief in reincarnation rests on two fundamental principles: first, the inseparability of body and soul, and second, the imperative of divine justice. These two principles are central to the understanding of reincarnation as a main feature in the Druze interpretation of Tawhid.

Inseparability of Body and Soul

In Tawhid the ultimate aim of the soul is to seek a state of inner spirituality and real knowledge. Such achievements enable it to keep getting closer and closer to the Creator, through the first and most important of God's creation, the universal mind:

> I say that the sages of the past and our venerated ancestors [in faith] and the rest of the believers [in Tawhid] have concurred that the proper reward is the best gift that one can receive. And the noblest of the rewards is the arrival at a state of awareness of true knowledge and divine grace. This is the ultimate state of happiness and the supreme reason for the existence of the individual and the struggle for perfection. . . . And it has become ingrained in people's minds and accepted by people of faith that such divine knowledge cannot be arrived at or obtained except through the [universal] mind.[97]

Embarking on such a journey, the soul needs a vehicle through which it is transformed from a state of virtual existence to a state of active being. This vehicle is the human body with its main instrument, the human mind, the instrument of awareness and comprehension. Thus in partnership with the body the soul is transformed from a potential (quwwah) state to a kinetic (fi'l) state and embarks on the long journey to realize the purpose of its existence. Consequently in reality we cannot divorce the soul from the body, since neither can fulfill its role without the other. Without the soul the body would become an inanimate object like any other material thing on earth or in the universe. Without the body the soul remains a homeless spirit in a perpetual state of dormancy, and therefore essentially nonexistent.

Responding to comments made by the distinguished Arab philosopher Abu Nasr al-Farabi in his book *The Perfect State*,[98] Baha' al-Din tries to bring into sharp focus the difference between the concept raised by al-Farabi in relation to the separation between body and soul, and their inseparability that Tawhid advocates. Baha' al-Din points out that the physical body is not an impediment to the progress of the soul and that the two components (body and soul) have an obligatory interdependence in the vision of Tawhid:

> And if he [al-Farabi] meant that it [the soul] departs the body that it possesses and controls, and without which the soul's actions cannot be realized, then the head of the perfect state [al-Farabi's concept] has negated the edifice on which his philosophy was built. That denotes that [after attaining perfection] total disengagement of the soul from the body takes place and it departs from this body and from this world. . . . In that case there will be no virtue left in this world to lead the inhabitants of the city [humanity] to virtue and perfection. . . . And I say that if the soul of the head of the perfect state stays in this world [in the body] for a period of time after attaining a certain degree of perfection, then it can stay for an indefinite period [to the end of time]. . . . And so the soul would reach the ultimate in perfection while still united with the physical world [the body]. . . . Logic and justice dictate that the perfection of the soul [in union with the body] is more appropriate and more desirable than a process of perfection with the soul separated from the body. For in the union [of body and soul], the soul becomes the master of the two worlds [physical and spiritual] and the shining light in the two horizons [the here and now and the hereafter]. . . . And I say in that regard that the soul cannot act independently from the physical body, since if the body were to cease and separate, the soul would become powerless. . . . There is no living body without a soul, and no soul independent of a physical body.[99]

Disengagement of the soul from the body is neither feasible nor desirable for the process of activation of the soul and for its journey to perfection. Rather Baha' al-Din considers any disengagement of body and soul as disengagement between the soul and the actions of sin and negation taking place within the context of the body. In that case the soul sheds the negative vestiges as it discards the body upon death and then gets a fresh start, through the process of reincarnation.

Thus once committed the soul cannot be dissociated from the body. Therefore, death visits only the body that the soul is occupying, and the soul goes on. The body, any physical body, is alive only when inhabited by the soul. Commenting on those who espouse the idea that the soul departs upon death and does not reincarnate, Baha' al-Din asks somewhat incredulously: "Pray tell me where does this energy [the soul] go upon leaving the body, where does it reside and where does it settle? And how is it possible [for the soul] to obtain knowledge without the instrument through which such knowledge can be acquired?"[100]

On the contrary, asserts Baha' al-Din, there is no reasonable substitute for the concept of inseparability of body and soul. He sees in that concept the perfect fit in God's scheme of creation. For it is in this partnership of the physical and the metaphysical that a human being is able to grow and evolve to reach the desired destination. Speaking in the context of creation in general, Baha' al-Din continues in the same logical sequence as follows: "And thus came into being the compounds and the minerals, the plants and animals, and the human being. This human, possessed of wisdom and grace and created from the combination of a virtuous soul and a wisely crafted body, constitutes the best combination for perfection; the combination of the concrete and the spiritual."[101]

We therefore note that Tawhid clearly does not denigrate the body nor does it look at it as a sort of jail for the soul, as some of the extreme Sufis do. After all without the body, the soul has no independent state of being of its own, and therefore the body as partner of the soul cannot be vilified. This by no means should be taken as adulation of the body, whose function as an individual body at any given instant is transitory and is terminated by physical death. Yet the function of the body, generically speaking, is permanent and consists of relay stations that ensure instantaneous and permanent abode for the soul. The emphasis on the body should not detract from the status of the soul as the agent of spiritual evolution and the entity that is everlasting. It simply affirms the crucial role of the body as long as it is kept alive by the presence of the soul. Again responding to those who claim that the planets and the stars have a stronger hold on the secrets of life and existence than the physical human body, Baha' al-Din expresses a different point of view that specifically stresses the role of the body in this context:

> And I say that the body of the human is preferable to the inanimate planets and objects that lack self-determination. For it is through the human body that the virtues of mental reflections and divine knowledge are realized, as it is impossible to benefit or discern except through the mind that exists in the body. . . . The human body is the best among the observing objects and without it there is no way to recognize the hand of the Divine.[102]

> Dear brethren, this admonition is for all of you. It is for whoever is listening with an open mind, and rising above contamination by evil thoughts and distinguish-

ing his soul with immunity against the diseases of doubting and of disbelieving [in God]. Such diseases that afflict the soul are associated with weakened bodies and ugly countenance.[103]

An impure soul is associated with an impure body and vice versa.

One of the main authorities on the Druze epistles and the interpretation of Tawhid, Shaykh Zayn al-Din 'Abd al-Gaffar Taqi al-Din (d. 1557 C.E./A.H. 965) goes into great length to emphasize the role of the body in activating the potential of the soul, which would otherwise be impossible:

> And the soul cannot recite except through the power invested in the body, and cannot imagine except through the energy in the body, and cannot think except through the thinking power [the brain] in the body, and cannot remember except through the power of memory in the body. The body is its [the soul's] veil and through the body it exhibits its actions. It is through the body that the soul is recognized and in the body that the soul is actualized. The soul cannot be independent of the body and does not vacate the body [upon death], except to relocate to another. . . . There is no obstacle to this relocation and no significance for distance. Whether near or far is irrelevant, for the luminescence of the soul is not subject to the limitations of space but to the guidance of the universal mind.[104]

Another reason for the sanctity of the human body is the choice of a human image for God to reveal himself. The fact that the image in the human form was chosen over all other creatures is in itself an indication of the symbolism and a crucial vote of confidence. We hear again from Baha' al-Din: "When we found that human beings are born ignorant, not able to know except through concrete evidence, and could not observe beyond the range of the physical senses, wisdom dictated that God's revelation of himself be in the human form." [105]

This act of grace by the Divine set the stage for human beings to believe and to begin the long pilgrimage to the Source. The potential for this transformation is made possible when all the necessary elements are assembled in the right combination and work as a team. This includes the body as well as the soul.

The choice of the human being is precisely because the human being, ignorant as he or she may be at birth, is endowed with the capacity to evolve and absorb spirituality and wisdom across the long span of existence. The soul grows into perfection by adhering to the tenets of Tawhid and by incorporating the gifts of the universal mind. In this manner the soul remains healthy and pure. Likewise, the body will stay healthy if the vital organs remain healthy and functioning properly.

> And so it is with the purity of the soul that achieves perfection through the path of Tawhid . . . the path that leads to its union with the bounty of the [universal]

mind. When the soul is missing any of the positive aspects that lead to spiritual perfection, it becomes subject to error and confusion. . . . And the evidence for that eventuality is analogous to what happens to the body whose integrity is contingent upon the harmonious function of its vital organs. . . . When any of the vital organs is damaged, the whole body becomes subject to degeneration and destruction.[106]

As an abode for so precious a commodity (the soul), the body cannot be defiled nor its well-being ignored. Mutilation of the body is strictly prohibited since such defilement would impact on the sanctity of the soul. Male circumcision is standard practice, by tradition, among the Druze as it is with all other Islamic sects. Male circumcision cannot be equated with mutilation of the body since it is performed for purely hygienic reasons and not for the symbolic meaning attached to this practice in the Jewish religion. Female circumcision that is practiced in isolated animistic societies primarily in Africa has recently become associated with some fringe groups in Islam. In fact this practice is totally baseless in Islam and is strictly forbidden in the Druze traditions, as is any form of body mutilation. (I was never aware of this barbaric practice until it became known through the media in recent years.) Suicide is not specifically mentioned, but the whole tenor of respect for the body indicates that suicide would be strongly condemned. There is no written opinion on abortion, but again the sanctity of life and the importance of bodily integrity for the well-being of the soul strongly suggest a pro-life position on this subject. However, we must note that in the Druze interpretation of Tawhid, the soul inhabits (incarnates) the body at birth and not before, and, therefore, the fetus has no independent status before its live birth. The debate on this issue has not come to the forefront in the East as it has in Western societies. It is inevitable that it will have to be addressed in the future.

Because the well-being of the soul is interconnected with the well-being of the body, the Druze pay considerable attention to the basic principles of hygiene. Cleanliness is central in Tawhid, as it is in Islam, since cleanliness is a prerequisite for the veracity of faith *(al-nazafa' min al-iman)*. Excesses of any kind are frowned upon, and moderation in food intake, work, and recreation are stressed. Smoking and the drinking of alcoholic beverages are strictly prohibited, as is overindulgence in sexual activity beyond what is needed for procreation. Moderation, modesty, and self-control are passed from one generation to the next as a matter of upbringing. Moreover, these practices are anchored in the Druze system of values as they reflect the basic tenets of the faith.

It is true that some members of the *'uqqal* order adopt a lifestyle similar to that of the Sufis and mystics, but this is purely voluntary and not required by tenets or by traditions. Even for those mystics among the ʿuqqal, their ascetic practices are never associated with bodily harm or with neglect of basic hygienic principles. On the contrary, oftentimes these mystics live a longer and healthier life than average largely due to the avoidance of toxic products and abstinence from abusive practices.

For most of the common Druze folk, however, a healthy lifestyle is a matter of upbringing, along with other habits and traditions that are passed from one generation to the next. The practice of a healthy lifestyle is firmly rooted in the philosophy of Tawhid that gave rise to the traditions in the first place. Furthermore, Islam, in the bosom of which the last of the cycles of Tawhid was incubated, places a high premium on hygiene. Ablution, a washing ritual, is dictated for preparation for prayer in Islam. In Christianity, the symbolic washing of the body during baptism may be interpreted in the same context as the preservation of the sanctity of the body in Tawhid. Although the body is a physical thing after the soul departs, it is a very important partner when the soul is in residence. And the soul is always in one residence or another across the long span of its existence. Hence the inseparability of the body and the soul.

A discussion of the body's place in the Druze tradition would not be complete without reference to the disposition of the body of the deceased. The following is a brief description of funeral services in the East, with minor variations among different communities. Upon death, the body is washed, usually by the women (sometimes by men) of the immediate family, and properly dressed. The body is kept at the home of the deceased or at a more spacious home of a close family member. More recently community centers have been utilized for such purposes for the convenience of the family and of those who come to pay respect. The women of the family are quickly joined by other women from the community at large to keep vigil, chant religious refrains, recite the virtues of the deceased, and remember others who have died. In the case of those who are extremely pious, vigil is generally more silent and reflective than demonstrative. Attendance at funerals is considered a duty and is relatively easily accomplished in the tightly knit communities in the East.

When the time of burial arrives the body of the deceased is placed in a simple wooden casket and carried by men of the family or friends in a procession headed by religious figures (ʿuqqal). To be a pallbearer is considered a privilege as it is rewarding in the eyes of God. The religious leaders lead the procession as one group starts chanting: "There is no god but God. There is no god but God. There is no god but God. Eternal is the face of God." Another group just behind responds: "There is no god but God. There is no god but God. There is no god but God. Muhammad is the messenger of God."

This chanting continues until the procession reaches the burial place. The body of the deceased is laid down with the head facing toward Mecca (*qibla*), due south in Lebanon. After a short service, modified from the Islamic schools, burial takes place usually within twenty-four hours unless there are mitigating circumstances for delay. There is no embalming, and there are no funeral homes in the Druze tradition. The body is interred in the ground or more commonly in an austere and simple structure that is built to be a family burial chamber.

In a few cases a simple stone mausoleum is built at the burial site of a pious and revered figure, who may be a male or, less commonly, a female. The place becomes in time a site of pilgrimage for those seeking spirituality or favors. These shrines dot the landscape of the Druze ancestral lands and become sites for worship and visitation for pilgrims seeking favors and spirituality.

Cremation is virtually unknown in the Druze tradition. (I personally know of no cases of cremation among the Druze of the Middle East.) This practice, entrenched in the traditions of the Far East and fairly accepted in the West, has not found acceptance in the Islamic world and did not enter into the traditions of the Druze. However, I am not aware of any written injunctions in this matter, and the debate on this particular issue has not begun. Moreover, most Druze practices are based on tradition and not on doctrine. Unless and until it enters into the traditions of the community, cremation is unlikely to be incorporated in practice.

The idea of resurrection of the body on judgment day does not apply in the Druze concept of Tawhid. Since the soul is the seat of spirituality, and since the soul is always in residence in one body or another, there is no need for resurrection of the bodies that the soul has already abandoned. The soul is already in a bodily residence at that fateful hour, thus committing to total irrelevance the virtually endless procession of bodies that the soul has previously inhabited during its long sojourn. Such a concept represents a departure from the concept of resurrection of the body on judgment day in Christianity and in traditional Islam.

Divine Justice

The human soul emanated from the Creator by divine will and became energized into an active state through an obligatory and constitutive partnership with the human body. In the Druze interpretation of Tawhid, the human being, body and soul, occupies the apex of the pyramid of God's creation. The purpose of the human soul is to evolve and advance to a state whereby it gets ever closer to the Creator. The individual human souls were created at the same time and in the same context as individual expressions of the universal soul. The individual souls then immediately took residence in human bodies, and the journey was on, in accordance with the divine scheme. Thus the number of human souls, according to Druze interpretation of Tawhid, is constant and keeps recycling to the end of time. This obviously flies in the face of the increase in population on our planet, if we assume that our planet is the only planet in the universe that harbors human souls. The message is stated unambiguously and in more than one place: human souls were created all at once and they remain in this universe, passing from one body to the next and from one stage to the next until the final day.

> And what logic dictates and what cannot be contradicted by those of sane mind is that the son of Adam [human beings] represents the purpose of God's creation. And all the rest of creation . . . is to serve him. What then would be the wisdom if the purpose of creation (i.e. the human being) disappeared altogether while the objects that were created for his service and well-being lasted forever? Would that not be a mark of imperfection (God forbid) on the ability of the Creator? It becomes clear to those with sane minds . . . that human beings, meaning the vast majority of human beings, do not increase nor do they decrease, but are constant from the beginning to the end of creation. . . . Instead, they recur in different ages and stages [for the individual soul] to grow and be held accountable.[107]

In addition to the simultaneous creation and the constancy of the number of souls, there is an interesting point in the above passage: the vast majority of souls are constant and never exist without a physical body. The exceptions to this rule are the entities such as angels, luminaries of Tawhid, and others whose souls reincarnate in ordinary human bodies but not in the same obligatory manner as the souls of ordinary human beings. After all, the souls of the luminaries may also exist outside the framework of the physical world, since the creation of the five luminaries preceded the creation of the world.

For the overwhelming majority of human beings, the individual soul, at the onset of its creation, is in middle position between good and evil, knowledge and ignorance, and positiveness and negation. The start is from a position of utter neutrality, the only position that could provide the perfect setting for free choice. And only in the context of free choice can accountability be validated in a just system. God's hand is there for guidance but not for coercion or imposition. In point of fact there was absolutely no attempt on the part of the *da'is* to attract converts to Tawhid by the use of the carrot and the stick. On the contrary converts were not encouraged nor accepted until they had reached a stage of development that allowed for such commitment to be legitimate. Divine justice cannot be valid except in the context of free choice and not through favoritism on the part of the Creator. The epistles in the Books of Wisdom contain numerous passages, such as the following, that put a major premium on the exercise of free will and not on coercive methods in the individual decision to believe or not to believe.

> If the Creator of the universe is generous toward some and not generous to others, then this would constitute predetermination conferring no reward to the one receiving the favor . . . and no punishment upon the disenfranchised. . . . God, glorified be his name, is most just. Justice dictates and logic indicates that reward and punishment be delivered according to actions and decisions by the soul, but only after the soul has been properly guided and given the opportunity for free choice.[108]

Likewise there are many references in the Qur'an to free choice and the guidance of the Almighty, which the Epistles of Wisdom draw on in support of free choice and accountability:

> The truth is from your Lord; so let whosoever will
> believe, and let whosoever will disbelieve. (18:28)

> Clear proofs have come to you from your Lord
> Whoso sees clearly, it is to his own gain,
> and whoso is blind, it is to his own loss;
> I am not a watcher over you. (6:104)

Free choice and accountability necessitate a setting of equal opportunity for the implementation of justice based on uniform criteria of evaluation. The obvious question in this regard is whether such equality of opportunity is feasible or possible in one lifetime of any individual. The question may sound rhetorical, but in fact it is substantive and cuts to the core of the imperative of divine justice; it assumes that one lifetime is all that individuals get and that they do the best (or the worst) that they can in that unit of space and that span of time. It is obvious that no two individuals will be subjected to the same hereditary or environmental influences, not even in the same family. The variables are just too many to enumerate, ranging from the genetic mix to health, education, wealth, culture, historical era, home conditions, natural disasters, and so on. How then is it possible to measure performance with the same yardstick when the variables are too many for any uniform measure to be valid? It follows that either there must be different standards for judging each case in the context of the particular setting in which the events take place; or there must be a way of accounting for the variables through some other mechanism. According to the concept of Tawhid the only possible mechanism that averages the playing field is an extension of the human life span to the limits of existence through reincarnation, rather than to restrict it to one lifetime of a body destined to last for barely the wink of an eye in an ageless universe. Reincarnation in the eyes of Tawhid is a mechanism that provides a plausible answer for the validation of divine justice.

Reincarnation satisfies the multiplicity of dimensions associated with equal opportunity and divine justice. Through reincarnation, the soul goes on living from the beginning to the end of time. During the whole span of existence the human soul is virtually guaranteed to be associated with a nearly infinite variety of conditions and to have inhabited a nearly endless number of physical bodies. It will have experienced virtually all that is possible to experience and will have been tested in any and all of the possible testing conditions. Reincarnation offers the soul the opportunity to grow into Tawhid and to mature in its acquisition of real knowledge, the knowledge of self, and through that the knowledge of God. While starting from utter neutrality at creation, the soul begins to accumulate experience and develop a track record, the essence of which is carried from one cycle to the next along the infinite cycles of reincarnation. According to Druze traditions, those who accepted the call to Tawhid in the most recent era of disclosure (the era of al-Hakim) were already at a more advanced state of spiritual evolution through the cumulative growth inherent in the process of reincarnation.

Reincarnation also provides a plausible alternative to the reconstitution of all of humanity for resurrection at the day of judgment. Since the soul of any individual is the same one from the beginning to the end of time, regardless of the number or state of the physical bodies it has inhabited along the way, the current body of residence at the time is all that is needed at judgment day. The advantages of such an alternative from a practical point of view need no elaboration.

The soul in Tawhid was not sent from a better world to this world as retribution for a prior misdemeanor or punishment for a prior sin, since there is no original sin in Tawhid. Nor would that soul be denigrated to a state of perpetual bondage in hostile or inappropriate surroundings when it errs. For this would not be consistent with divine justice:

And if [according to the assumption of some] the soul has been demoted by descending to this world to be purified, ignorant of wrongdoings that it had committed [in a better world], I say . . . that justice dictates and truth indicates that the place in which the soul gets purified should be superior to the world from which it descended and in which the soul erred in the first place. And if the soul had been committed to this world only to suffer in punishment for past sins, then seeking knowledge and spiritual growth becomes pointless and worship and belief meaningless, since its fate is already sealed.[109]

Therefore the soul emanating from the Creator is not meant to suffer some form of permanent punishment for prior transgressions that necessitated its demotion from a better world to the present one. In fact the soul was never in any other world after it emerged by the will of God and in accordance with his scheme of creation. It is this world that represents for the soul the testing ground as well as the theater for growth and development: "And in that case, it becomes clear that the soul is in this world and will never depart from it and will always return [reincarnate] in it."[110]

Eventually the individual soul along with the rest of creation will return to the Source. But that is after a lifetime that is as long as the entirety of existence during which the soul will have had ample opportunity to grow and to be tested:

And it is the consequences of your actions that will rebound to you, and everyone will be judged according to [his or her] deeds. . . . And it is mentioned in the Holy Qur'an to those who are in God's graces: "O soul at peace, return unto thy Lord, well-pleased, well-pleasing! Enter thou among My servants!" Enter thou My paradise! (89:27). And to those who stayed in error: "For what your hands have forwarded, and for that God is never unjust unto His servants." (3:182)[111]

One other aspect of reincarnation deserves emphasis and that is the restriction of the process of human reincarnation to humans only. There is no mixing of the souls among different species as is the case in some of the Oriental concepts of reincarnation. Likewise there is no crossing of human souls to inanimate objects. The human soul in the Druze concept of Tawhid will always reside in a human body and nothing else. Most of all, punishment of the soul for sins, however serious, will never be in the form of transmigration from a human to a subhuman form. Let us examine the reason for such assertion in an epistle refuting those who claim otherwise:

And the one who claims that the souls of the opponents and the enemies [of Tawhid] will return to [reincarnate] in dogs, monkeys, birds, or pigs, or even go back to iron where it would be heated and pounded by hammers . . . has surely committed a major error. It does not stand to logic nor is it in God's justice to punish an intelligent human being who has disobeyed God's command by returning him to a less intelligent form of life in the form of a dog or a pig . . . because these creatures do not understand the reasons for punishment. . . . Real punishment for disobeying God is for the human being to be deprived of the means for growth and evolution across the recurring cycles of reincarnation [until he mends his ways]. Likewise real reward is in the progression along the ladder of knowledge and wisdom until he eventually . . . reaches the level of the imamate.[112]

Punishment for straying from the right path can be considered in the form of demotion from a higher level of spiritual development to a lower one, where a new bar is set for recovery and advancement. Demotion, like promotion, is always in the human context and can never be at a super- or subhuman level.

While there is no doubt in the Druze epistles about the human-to-human reincarnation of the soul, there is no definite reference as to whether the soul is free to incarnate the body of one gender or the other, or whether it maintains the same gender identity for the entirety of the road. Certainly, gender crossing would be more in keeping with the ideal of divine justice, since that would contribute to the equalization of opportunity and to the uniformity of the measuring yardstick. However, traditional thinking (taken for granted by the Druze community) stipulates that once the soul inhabits a body of either gender it remains committed to the same gender until the final day. To the best of my knowledge, this opinion is based on tradition and not on any written documentation.

Likewise, most of the Druze believe, by tradition and not by documentation, that the soul of a Druze individual will always reincarnate in a newborn of Druze parents. In this they commit the soul of a believer in Tawhid (Muwahhid) to reincarnation into a Druze individual in an obligatory biological link. The Druze have not taken into serious consideration the possibility that the soul of a Muwahhid may pass through reincarnation as a Muwahhid into any physical body, regardless of biological determinants of birth. Although this possibility of randomness is not denied, yet it is generally not as seriously considered as the obligatory Druze-to-Druze passage of the soul of the Muwahhid. The distinction is crucial, and is not foreign to the Druze intelligentsia and many others who are steeped in the concept of Tawhid. For the rank and file in the Druze community, there is blind acceptance of the obligatory biological link in reincarnation. The soul of a Druze will always reincarnate in a Druze, no questions asked. Considering divine justice as one the main reasons for reincarnation in the first place, it seems logical that there should be no built-in discrimination by accident of birth. The written record can be understood to say that reincarnation is the vehicle that allows the soul to live without interruption in the physical world, and to progress along the path of knowledge and righteousness regardless of the biographical identity of the body that it inhabits at any given time.

Reincarnation in General

As a religious and philosophical principle, reincarnation is as old as religion itself. Religious practices of ancient as well as more recent cultures are involved in one way or another with the idea of reincarnation. In the Far East, particularly the Indian subcontinent, reincarnation is an integral part of the religious and cultural landscape with major impact on daily life. In those traditions reincarnation involves the transmigration of souls not only among human beings but also across the range of all living organisms. Other ancient cultures even considered transmigration of souls of all beings, humans included, into nonliving matter as well. In ancient Egypt, the preoccupation with immortality produced a mythology that revolved around reincarnation, although in somewhat different context than in Hinduism. The Egyptian aspiration for immortality was through a combination of reincarnation of the soul, usually to the same body, and resurrection of that body. The soul could reincarnate in other human and animal forms as well. Ancient myths from Mesopotamia and Syria contain definite features of reincarnation, particularly in relation to the demise and resurrection of the multiple gods and goddesses of the era. The ancient Greeks considered reincarnation to be one of the major features in the various schools of philosophy of the time. This is not surprising considering the centrality of justice and the relevance of reincarnation to the notion of justice in ancient Greek philosophy.

While many of the philosophers of ancient Greece dealt with some aspects of reincarnation, it was Pythagoras who left the biggest imprint.[113] It is reported that Pythagoras even claimed to have remembered events and experiences from his own past lives. Pythagoras and his school of thought considered the soul to be an everlasting element that reincarnates into a physical body, which consists of physical elements. However, the soul, being spiritual, should be distinguished from and exalted above ordinary matter. The soul is to be protected from the corrupt influences that afflict the body. What type of body the soul reincarnates depends on the actions of the individual, in a manner that resembles the concept of Karma.

Thus the soul could reincarnate into lower forms of life as punishment for prior sins. Although this point is categorically denied in the Tawhid concept of reincarnation, that denial does not detract from the tremendous influence of Greek philosophers on the Druze concept of Tawhid in general and reincarnation in particular.

Reincarnation in the three great monotheistic Abrahamic or unitarian faiths (Judaism, Christianity, and Islam) has been largely ignored or perhaps deliberately avoided by religious institutions. This does not mean that reincarnation has always been totally rejected by all followers of these great faiths. It has mainly been the mystics and Gnostics in these (and other) faiths that, being generally more intuitive, have been more receptive to the idea of reincarnation. The mainstream, guided by the religious establishment and influenced by the limits of dogma, rarely ventured beyond the literal expression of the word. Thus the concept of salvation through Christs's resurrection in Christianity weakened but did not totally obliterate the idea that the soul progresses along the principles of Karma until it is ready for salvation. In a sense the journey of the soul through reincarnation can be viewed as a form of purgatory. In the opinion of Geddes MacGregor, a modern Christian thinker:

> Moreover, Christianity . . . can be hospitable to reincarnationism, because then it can encourage the notion that for the soul to find its way back to a proper vision of reality and a right relationship to it, we must expect a long evolutionary, purgatorial process. . . . Salvation, however quickly assured, is not quickly achieved. The rescue operation even with the help of those lifebelts thrown to the endangered soul . . . is likely to take a long time. . . . At first sight, at any rate, it would now seem that Christians, far from resisting reincarnation, should be ready to embrace it as one that might both enlighten their minds and add a new and exhilarating dimension to their faith. . . . That is not to say, of course, that a Christian could ever honestly take over all the paraphernalia of oriental presuppositions.[114]

The concept of reincarnation, in the opinion of MacGregor, does not jeopardize basic Christian beliefs and may well contribute to their enrichment. It may never become a central theme in Christianity, but neither does it have to be rejected a priori. It is known that several groups of Christians in the early ages of the Church may have seriously embraced reincarnation, but these groups did not survive the strong influence of the institutions of the Church once the institutions became firmly established and backed by the state.

In Judaism, reincarnation is deeply entrenched in the Kabbalistic traditions and in mystical movements such as Hasidism. Although not in the mainstream, reincarnation surfaces from time to time under the spell of charismatic leaders whose teachings continue to explore novel approaches to perplexing problems and leave a definite imprint on the traditions of the faithful. One of the main figures in this field is the author of *Zohar* (The Book of Splendor), regarded by some to be Rabbi Moses de Leon, a Spanish Kabbalist in the thirteenth century. Mysticism intertwines with reincarnation in his approach to the mysteries of life and death:

> There are hidden mysteries and secret things which are unknown to men. . . . All souls are subject to the trials of transmigration; and men do not know the designs of the Most High with regard to them; they know not how they are being at all times judged, both before coming into this world and when they leave it. They do not know how many transformations and mysterious trials they must undergo; how many souls and spirits come to this world without returning to the place of the divine king. . . . [Reincarnation] served as a rational excuse for the apparent absence of justice in this world.[115]

Islam came with a more concrete message of submission to God and codes of behavior that reflect the sanctity of the message. For the most part, there is a direct and linear relationship between action and reward or retribution. The individual chooses and bears the consequences. Reincarnation, as such, has not been accepted by the institutions of the major factions in Islam. However, there are numerous passages in the Qur'an that could be interpreted to support reincarnation, or at least not to exclude it or make it a heresy:

> How do you disbelieve in God
> Seeing you were dead, and He gave you life,
> Then He shall make you dead,
> then He shall give you life,
> then unto Him you shall be returned? (2:28)

> Then We raised you up after you were dead,
> That haply you should be thankful. (2:56)

> Out of the earth We created you,
> And We shall restore you into it,
> And bring you forth from it a second time. (20:55)

> It is He who gave you life
> then He shall make you dead,

then He shall give you life.
Surely man is ungrateful. (22:66)

These are a few passages from the Qur'an that Druze sources cite to explain the belief in reincarnation in the Islamic context. The extent to which this explanation carries validity is up to the scholars in the field, and to the degree of intellectual and spiritual latitude within the wide Islamic spectrum. On the surface it appears that such an argument may stand on the merit. It may be of interest to note that the Qur'an is vague on matters dealing with the soul:

They will question thee concerning
the Spirit. Say: "The Spirit is of
the bidding of my Lord. You have
been given of knowledge nothing
except a little." (17:85)

Perhaps this vagueness was intentional; philosophical discussions such as those dealing with the nature of the soul at the early stages in Islamic thought may have distracted from the force and clarity of the Islamic message that there is no god but God and Muhammed is his messenger and prophet. Later on, the development of Islamic thought and its interaction with the rich historical heritage of the various people and cultures of the *umma* and with Greek and Oriental influences made exploration beyond the letter of the word inevitable. Hence the proliferation of numerous sects in Islam. The Druze are not the only sect in Islam that has embraced reincarnation; the Alawites also have a concept of reincarnation, although it is somewhat different from that of the Druze.

In the West, belief in reincarnation is more widespread than is generally appreciated, particularly among poets, writers, scientists and those interested in philosophy and mysticism. According to some authorities, it is easier to make an inventory of notable writers not interested in reincarnation than of those who are (see Cranston and Williams for more details). Some of the following quotations are from Cranston and Williams's study. Estimates of the prevalence of believers in reincarnation range from 20 to 30 percent of the population in the United States and in Western countries in general.[116] This represents a staggering figure, since reincarnation is not indigenous to Western culture. It seems to be particularly attractive to young adults and teenagers. A sample opinion from a study conducted by Harold Loukes, reader in education at Oxford, includes the following opinion of a teenager: "I think when I die I will come back as someone else and carry on like that. . . . I think you kind of come back into the world again, to lead a better life, and you go on coming back until you're perfect, and then . . . I think you go to God when you're perfect."[117]

Benjamin Franklin expressed his views on the subject in a letter he wrote when he was seventy-nine years old: "When I see nothing annihilated and not a drop of water wasted, I cannot suspect . . . or believe that God will suffer the daily waste of millions of minds ready made that now exist, and put himself to the continual trouble of making new ones. Thus, finding myself to exist in the world, I believe I shall, in some shape or the other, always exist. . . . I shall not object to a new edition of mine, hoping however that the errata of the last may be corrected. . . . I look upon death to be as necessary to the constitution as sleep. We shall rise refreshed in the morning."[118]

Leo Tolstoy, tormented at the height of his fame, came close to taking his own life. It was the futility of it all, when death would inevitably obliterate everyone and everything, that understandably drove him to the pit of despair. That is, until he came to the solution when he asked the question, "Who am I?" and answered, "I am part of the infinite." As part of the infinite, he was beyond the reach of death and obliteration. His belief in reincarnation was expressed in a letter describing the experiences: "Of our present life are the environment in which we work out our impressions, thoughts, feelings, of a former life. . . . our present life is one of many thousands of such lives. . . . I am not playing, not inventing this, I believe in it, I see it without a doubt."[119]

The noted American writer Louisa May Alcott, influenced by the milieu in which she grew up, wrote to a friend about her thoughts on the subject of immortality. The views bear an eerie resemblance to the views in the Druze concept of reincarnation. It is doubtful that Alcott had any contact with Druze writings or Druze authors on the subject of reincarnation. She writes: "I think immortality is the passing of a soul through many lives or experiences, and such as are truly lived, used, and learned, help on to the next, each growing richer, happier and higher, carrying with it only the real memories of what has gone before. . . . We don't remember the lesser things. They slip away as childish trifles, and we carry on only the real experience."[120]

The subject of immortality of the soul and of reincarnation pervades many of Emerson's writings: "Every soul is by intrinsic necessity quitting its whole system of things, as the shell-fish crawls out of its beautiful and stony case, because it no longer admits its growth, and slowly forms a new house. . . . We do not believe in the riches of the soul, in its proper eternity and omnipresence. We linger in the ruins of the old tent where once we had bread and shelter and organs, nor believe that the spirit can feed, cover and serve us again. It is the secret of the world that all things subsist and do not die, but only retire a little from sight and afterwards return again."[121]

Emerson echos the sentiments of the Sufi as he soars above and beyond the confines of the physique that houses his soul: "I am become a transparent eyeball; I am nothing; I see all; the current of the Universal Being circulates through me; I am part and parcel of God."[122]

It is interesting to note that the explosive impact of the theory of evolution on the physical sciences in the latter part of the nineteenth century stimulated many to think about spiritual evolution as well. The process of reincarnation comes in handy to assist in such evolution. In the opinion of the Boston clergyman James Freeman Clark (1887), we hear a clear articulation of how evolution is linked to reincarnation: "That man has come up to his present state of development by passing through lower forms is the popular doctrine of science today. . . . The modern doctrine of bodily organisms is not complete unless we unite with it the idea of a corresponding evolution of the spiritual monad, from which every organic form derives its unity. Evolution has a satisfactory meaning only when we admit that the soul is developed and educated by passing through many bodies. If we are to believe in evolution, let us have the assistance of the soul itself in this development."[123]

Ismaʿil ibn Muhammad al-Tamimi, representing the universal soul, described the evolution of the concept of Tawhid from its primordial beginning in remote antiquity to the more developed stages at the time the call to Tawhid was publicly proclaimed in the era of al-Hakim one thousand years ago. Al-Tamimi, however, limited his analysis to the spiritual evolution of the soul in the ladder of Tawhid. We are left to wonder how the process of understanding in human beings grew from a primordial state in the twilight of history to a level of sophistication whereby humans became capable of understanding and living by the tenets of complex messages such as that of Tawhid, without invoking, in one way or another, the process of evolution.

It is pertinent to note that Ismaʿili scholars of the time had already developed a highly sophisticated thinking with respect to the concept of evolution. Muhammad ibn Ahmad al-Nakhshabi, also known as al-Nasafi, for example, is credited with formulating a theory of evolution that antedated Darwin's by a thousand years. Al-Nasafi was an Ismaʿili *daʿi* and a brilliant philosopher who is said to have introduced a form of Neoplatonism into Ismaʿili thought. He along with his chief associates was eventually executed in Bukhara in 943 C.E. (A.H. 332).[124] His book

Kitab al-mahsul was lost, but based on the extent to which others referred to it, it must have been an important publication. Al-Nasafi's treatise on evolution can be summarized as follows: "While man has sprung from sentient creatures [animals], these have sprung from vegetal beings [plants], and these in their turn from combined substances . . . and when the combined substances mix, plants are formed; these are purified, and from their quintessence sentient animals come into being. These are purified in their turn, and from them there emerge rational beings. This is the last link of the chain."[125]

Looking at reincarnation in the broader scope of the evolutionary context, Darryl Reanney, a distinguished molecular biologist, asserts that immortality is in the thread of continuity of the self, the interrelatedness with the whole, and the prospects of becoming: "You were there at every stage. There never was a time when you were not there. The vital being that is cosmos aroused and brightened into consciousness in you, in one process, real and ongoing. . . . In truth, in reality, nothing is separate, everything is united in the four-dimensional dance of becoming. The one exists in the all, and the all exists in the one. There is no boundary between the self and other. Thou art that."[126]

Henry Ford was driven to great achievements through the idea of reincarnation, which gave his life a meaning and a reason that would otherwise have remained elusive. In a series of interviews, Ford minced no words as to where he stood on this subject: "From emptiness and uselessness, it [reincarnation] changed my outlook on life to purpose and meaning. I believe we are here now for a reason and will come back again. . . . And that we go on. . . . Work is futile if we cannot utilize the experience we collect in one life in the next. When I discovered Reincarnation it was as if I had found a universal plan . . . I would like to communicate to others the calmness that the long view of life gives to us."[127]

Similarly, the musical genius of Richard Wagner flourished in the context of his deep interest in Buddhism and specifically in the concept of reincarnation. He was able to somehow meld his beliefs with the power of German mythology to produce the great musical epics in his dramatic operas. Wagner expressed his views in a letter to a friend: "In contrast to Reincarnation and Karma all other views appear petty and narrow. . . . Only the profoundly conceived idea of Reincarnation could give me any consolation, since that belief shows how all at last can reach complete redemption."[128]

Gustav Mahler, long driven by spiritual and mystical forces, believed that perfection, which is the purpose of life, is achieved through reincarnation and that is what gives life its meaning and its purpose. Understandably,

Mahler's protégé and friend, the distinguished conductor Bruno Walter, believed likewise.

A very engaging comment with respect to reincarnation is attributed to David Lloyd George, the British prime minister of World War I fame. Evidently Lloyd George was greatly disturbed in his youth by the prospect of a squeaky clean heaven with obligatory prayer services, with the Almighty sternly watching and monitoring every action: "It was a horrible nightmare," he declared. "The conventional heaven with its angels perpetually singing, nearly drove me mad in my youth, and made me an atheist for ten years. My opinion is that we shall be reincarnated."[129]

Closer to home, the farewell address of Gibran Khalil Gibran to the inhabitants of the mythical city of Orphalese in his immortal classic *The Prophet* contains unmistakable reference to reincarnation: "Fare you well, people of Orphalese. This day has ended. . . . Forget not that I shall come back to you. A little while, and my longing shall gather dust and foam for another body. A little while, a moment of rest upon the wind, and another woman shall bear me."[130]

Michael Naʿimy, a contemporary and soulmate of Gibran, is even more explicit in his belief in reincarnation and in articulating the logical basis for such belief: "And who can claim that one lifetime, however long it may be, is enough to learn and apply all that can be learned, let alone a lifetime of only a few years, hours or minutes. And so the lifetime that spans the entirety of existence . . . is not merely the same as the one limited by one cycle from the cradle to the grave." Naimy then asks somewhat incredulously: "Why is it difficult for people to accept the idea of renewal of the human self repeatedly [through reincarnation] until it acquires the necessary means for knowledge, freedom, and everlasting permanence, while they can readily believe in a one-time passage in this life after which the self can be renewed only once again with resurrection or be condemned to oblivion and total annihilation. Which of these ideas is closer to the logic of life and to justice, compassion and love?"[131]

Whenever reincarnation is discussed, the potential for transmission of memory from one lifetime to the next comes up and provides another dimension to the mystery of this already mysterious subject. In the Druze community there is almost universal conviction that some individuals do in fact carry with them memories from past lives. The Druze present anecdotal yet compelling evidence to support that conviction. The ability to recollect events and details from past lives seems to be particularly prevalent in individuals who die suddenly, and more so if the death is violent or in younger individuals. It is ironic that the Epistles of

Tawhid are explicit in denying this phenomenon and almost label such a conviction as a form of heresy:

> And if someone [asks] why we do not remember what happened in past lives and
> past eras, the response of those who know the truth and follow the right path
> would be that when you claim full knowledge of past lives, you would be sharing
> power with the Creator. That would imply limitations on the power of the Creator, exalted be his name and exalted be his power from any limitation. . . . For if
> you knew yourself across the span of many life cycles, then you would have similar knowledge of the cycles of others, and you would have similar knowledge of
> the One who created you and made you go through the cycles of existence.[132]

In other words, human beings can only go up to a certain point; beyond that point they would be infringing on the domain of God, and knowledge of events in past lives is considered beyond the limits of human potential. Despite the firm denial in the Druze epistles, the conviction that selective memory from a previous life (or lives) can be transmitted and recognized persists in the community at large to this day. This is one occasion where popular belief standing in direct contradiction of what is written in the Books of Wisdom has caused some controversy.

Some Druze scholars, Najjar, for example, concur with the content of the text and therefore vehemently deny the phenomenon of remembrance of past lives. Others are more inclined to go beyond the text in view of the overwhelming evidence for the phenomenon. Some still ignore the subject altogether and maintain a neutral attitude. Those who believe in remembrance of events of past lives base such belief not only on Druze sources, anecdotal or otherwise, but also on a growing body of evidence on a global scale. In particular, the meticulous research of Dr. Ian Stevenson over several decades has amassed a body of evidence that is hard to ignore. Dr. Stevenson's work has been published in scientific and peer-reviewed journals as well as in books that are widely circulated. In his work Dr. Stevenson not only adheres to the strict standards of scientific inquiry but also refrains from endorsing or denying the phenomenon of memory transmission. His mission consists of presenting the findings and leaving readers to draw their own conclusions. Alternative explanations that range from fraud to paramnesia, clairvoyance, telepathy, and other forms of extrasensory perception are discussed and considered unlikely, leading the reader to conclude that reincarnation is the only reasonable explanation for the phenomenon of memory transmission.[133]

Memories from past lives, vivid in childhood, usually fade with time and become totally obliterated or remain in the dim recesses of twilight recognition. As to why that happens and, more importantly, why all of us do not carry more memories from the past is an interesting question that suggests its own answer. Can we imagine what it would be like to remember all or even most of the events in one single lifetime, and what an enormous burden that would impose on our faculties? Imagine then when we extrapolate this condition to the endless cycles of human existence. The clutter would be unbearable and would paralyze rather than enhance our experience and our growth. Thus even at the end of a long life the plate is ready to be cleaned, the mind ready to be made receptive for a fresh start of a fresh cycle. Only the essence continues to the next cycle. The physical essence is carried through the software encoded in the genetic material, and the spiritual in the condensed harvest of successive cycles of reincarnation. "Youthful at heart though many of us remain," suggests MacGregor, "a time comes when no growth is conceivable without a shedding of our memory. Indeed, even in the life we know on earth, one of the greatest mercies is our capacity to forget. But for that merciful ability, we could not endure one life let alone a succession of them, and eventually we could not but stop making any moral progress at all." [134]

We find echoes of the same theme in the works of Druze intellectuals: "It is not surprising for a human being to forget events of previous lives when he [or she] is unable to remember events in the present life. We do not remember all that we learn in childhood, in school years, or during youth. We often forget what we hear from one moment to the next. How are we then to retain memory of events across the two greatest thresholds in our existence, that of death with all that entails of emotional and physical trauma; and that of birth with all that encompasses of change and renewal." [135]

Another obvious question that comes up when discussing reincarnation pertains to the increase in the human population on earth. If, as the Druze doctrine claims, the number of individual souls is constant, how do we account for the flux in world population historically and the dramatic increase in modern times? Obviously, no one has the definitive answer to this question, and it is largely outside the limits of our discussion. The Druze, however, waste no time in pointing out how gigantic is the observable universe, with its billions of galaxies each of which has billions of suns and billions of planets. Therefore some form of human-type life elsewhere in this vast universe is not altogether unreasonable. That the scientific counterpart of this view is in the mainstream is attested by the continuing attempts by space science to make contact with extraterrestrial civilizations. Reincarnation across the wide expanse of space would not be limited by physical phenomena such as the speed of light because the soul in the absolute sense is beyond the confines of time or space. After all, the individual soul is a representation of the universal soul, the creation of which preceded the creation of the physical world. However, lacking definite proof for human-type life outside our planet, the issue of exchange of souls on a cosmic scale remains a matter of faith.

Other possible explanations for the increase in world population include, among many hypotheses, the continual creation of new souls, duplication of present ones, and the possibility of drawing from a large reservoir of potential souls. These questions continue to challenge the theory of reincarnation and contribute to the interest in the subject and the need for continued research. Discussion of these and other issues is beyond our scope, since the main objective is to present reincarnation as it relates to the Druze interpretation of Tawhid and as it fits in with the other philosophical tenets of the faith. The fact that we cannot prove its existence beyond a shadow of doubt or scientifically explain all its facets and answer all of its questions does not negate its existence or detract from the overwhelming appeal of reincarnation on a universal scale. For the Druze, reincarnation is the one tenet that is most easily grasped and accepted.

The belief in reincarnation has had a profound impact on how the Druze relate to issues of life and death. The Druze individual is generally raised with the fear of death effectively overcome (for example in battle), or when the end is near in anyone's lifetime. In fact, reincarnation affirms the sanctity of life by continuity, which death does not obliterate. Death is considered a momentary change in the carriage in the uninterrupted journey of the passenger. Indestructibility of the soul and its obligatory association with the body across the span of eternity are the basis of a holistic vision, a vision that is gaining popularity in modern life.

The impact of reincarnation cuts across a wide spectrum of human society, Druze and non-Druze, and touches the feelings and beliefs of men and women from all walks of life. From the philosopher to the scientist and from the poet to the artist, from the young to the old, rich or poor, or just simple ordinary folks, reincarnation seems to answer vital questions that would otherwise remain enigmatic and perplexing.

There is some controversy among Druze scholars as to whether reincarnation is a prerequisite for development and evolution of the soul, or merely a prolonged time for testing and assessment of the performance of the individual. In my opinion, devoid of evolution and growth reincarnation becomes meaningless and irrelevant. Reincarnation provides continuity and permanence to the existence of human life instead of a fleeting moment of randomness in one lifetime that is neither long enough for sufficient growth to take place nor fair enough for proper and just evaluation of human accomplishment. It is this aspect of continuity that makes the concept of reincarnation compatible with physical laws of conservation and natural processes of evolution. It provides the optimal stage for the union of the physical with the spiritual along a trajectory that leads from the past to the future without interruption or discontinuity. The trajectory is the pilgrimage of the soul to the Source across the eternity of cyclical existence.

Reincarnation in relation to the microcosm of the individual soul fits perfectly well within the broader concept of cyclical proclamation of God's messages through prophets and messengers as well as the revelation of God's grace through the image of the *nasut*. Through reincarnation life becomes almost timeless, as the soul is no longer subject to the linearity of definable beginning and a predetermined end except in God's conscience. In the words of T. S. Eliot:

> Time present and time past
> Are both perhaps present in time future
> And time future is contained in time past . . .
> Time past and time future
> What might have been and what has been
> Point to one end, which is always present . . .
> Or say that the end precedes the beginning,
> And the end and the beginning were always there
> Before the beginning and after the end,
> And all is always now.[136]

It is only after achieving a state of near perfection that the soul would have fulfilled its mission and been truly ready to meet its Maker:

> O soul at peace,
> Return unto thy Lord
> Well-pleased, well-pleasing!
> Enter thou among My servants!
> Enter thou My Paradise! (Qur'an 89:30)

One cannot but wonder when the soul achieves eternal peace and by what criteria such an achievement is measured. What is the true meaning of well pleased and well pleasing, and does one lifetime with all the inequities in the lives of people allow enough opportunity to achieve the exalted state of satisfaction (*ridha*) and earn the appellations of pleased, pleasing, and peace? Perhaps we should look more carefully at reincarnation to explain the inner meaning of these terms rather than be content at the level of literal interpretation.

6   Expression of the Tenets in Daily Conduct

THE CORE TENETS of the Tawhid faith rest on two main underpinnings, one of transcendence and mysticism and the other of reason and logic. This synthetic product of philosophy and belief in the Druze vision of Tawhid represents a unique, although not entirely original, attempt to bridge the gap between the occult and the revealed, the mystical and the rational, the transcendent and the immanent. Recognition of the mind as the first and most important of God's creation carries more than a symbolic meaning to the Druze. It is an affirmation of the importance of the quest for truth and the use of the clearest form of thinking and logical pursuit in this quest. Spiritual growth of the human soul occurs through a long process of enlightenment and evolution across the span of eternity rather than during a very short lifetime interrupted by death. Hence the value of reincarnation in the pursuit of this goal. God's grace illuminates the road of the seeker through multiple avenues including divine messages through chosen prophets and messengers. God's essence (Lahut), totally beyond human comprehension, is manifested through revelation of his countenance *(nasut)* in the human medium. Much like a reflection in a mirror seekers can witness the presence of God as a reflection of their own reflection in the image of God. The term used by the Druze for this form of theophany is *tajalli*.

Religious faith, however, must be accompanied by concrete expression in the individual's daily life and in modes of worship, rites, and rituals of communal practices that leave a characteristic imprint in the minds of the faithful. These expressions depict a profile that oftentimes results in a more representative portrait of a religious community than the core concepts of the faith. The religious community then defines and is defined by the behavior of the believers not only in religious practices but also in the conduct of daily living. The modes of conduct can be considered as the ethical component of religion. We are all aware of the profound impact of religion-derived ethical injunctions on the prevailing societal norms. In a pluralistic society, the interaction of the different ideologies can be

170

either enriching or destructive, depending on human beneficence or human bigotry.

To begin the process of Tawhid, in the Druze vision, one has to adopt and abide by seven conditions or commands, as laid out in Epistle 7. Esoteric interpretation of religious commands depends, by necessity, on the level of spirituality and the stage of development of the individual in the long quest for Tawhid. The commands are in the form of conditions or prerequisites to guide believers and set them on the right path, a path that prepares the seeker to begin the long and demanding journey. These conditions are as follows:

1. Truthfulness in intent and in tongue *(sidq al-lisan)*;

2. Safeguarding brothers and sisters *(hifz al-ikhwan)*;

3. Renunciation of idolatry and paganism *(tark ma kuntum a'layh min' ibadat al-'adam wa al-buhtan)*;

4. Renunciation of satanic and tyrannical influences *(al-bara'a min al-abalisa wa al-tughyan)*;

5. Belief in Tawhid of our Lord in every age and stage *(Tawhid al-mawla jalla dhikruhu fi kull 'asr wa zaman)*;

6. Acceptance of God's divine acts, whatever they may be *(al-ridha bi fi'lihi kayfa ma kan)*;

7. Submission to God's will in private and in public *(al-taslim li 'amrihi fi al-sirr wa al-hadthan)*.[1]

Looking at these conditions or requirements, we notice that belief in Tawhid is the fifth and not the first requirement. This implies that there are at least four other prerequisites that individuals must meet before they become eligible for Tawhid. Absent these preconditions, eligibility for Tawhid becomes improbable and the veracity of the believer questionable. It is not difficult to see why this is the case. Belief does not take place in a vacuum but within certain human conditions and behavioral patterns. Owing to the complexity of the Tawhid path, and most faiths are complex, it demands considerable preparation on the part of the seeker physically and mentally as well as ethically and morally. It is in this context that the class of 'uqqal emerged and became de facto custodians of the faith. A common saying in the Druze community goes something like this: "The ethics of religion take precedence over religion." We can also recognize the significance of discipline in following the rigorous demands of Tawhid, where credibility is crucial for the safety and welfare of the individual and the community. Thus while the concept of Tawhid is egalitarian with respect to the inclusion of all of humanity in the overall conceptual framework, it is elitist when it comes to the prerequisites for such inclusion. Since the prerequisites of Tawhid are not readily achievable by everyone, the Tawhid faith can be considered elitist due to its stringent imperatives. It is also elitist in that it demands continuing mental and spiritual preparedness, not merely a one-time effort to acquire the necessary prerequisites for acceptance into the faith.

The moral and ethical requirements of Tawhid complement the basic tenets and are easier to understand and attain by the common individual than the more complex philosophical tenets. Consequently, they have become more integrated into the life of the Druze community and the ethos of its members. A considerable segment of the Druze are ignorant of the philosophical tenets of the faith because they have not been initiated into the circle of the 'uqqal. However, they are indoctrinated in and generally follow the codes of behavior that emerge directly from the imperatives of the faith. Furthermore, those who are outside the faith rely almost exclusively on the behavior of the Druze when attempting to define the portrait of the Druze community.

In translating the Arabic text of these commands into English, some of the nuance is either lost or becomes redundant. Condensing the seven into five may facilitate the discussion in English; thus, in the following discussion the third and fourth commands are grouped together as "Renunciation of idolatry and paganism," and the sixth and seventh commands are grouped together as "Submission to God's will in public and in private."

Truthfulness

In its simplest form, truthfulness is a straightforward concept that does not need elaboration. "Do not lie" is implicit in one of the Ten Commandments at the center of Judeo-Christian teachings. Likewise, the Qur'an places great emphasis on telling the truth; there is hardly a single sura in which truthfulness is not advocated or falsehood condemned. One of the declarations of purity in the Book of the Dead in the religious repertoire of ancient Egypt is "I have not told lies."[2] Telling the truth is a centerpiece of upbringing and social interactions across history. As such it is at the core of civic and civil duties and expectations. It is also mandatory in legal matters, where the alternative is punishable by law.

In Tawhid, though, the command for truthfulness *(sidq al-lisan)* goes beyond the state of truthfulness as described in common usage. It goes straight to the core concept of Tawhid and is incorporated into the very fabric of the concept. Seeking and living the truth, as a prerequisite in the concept of Tawhid, is more than the

absence of falsehood. It is a positive affirmation of faith and an obligatory con-
comitant of belief in the Ultimate. Truth is not restricted to the sphere of thought
and language; it must be experienced in the heart and soul of the believer. As such
truth acquires a transcendental dimension and a mystical meaning that is at the
heart of the faith and the conscience of the faithful. The Druze epistles stress this
point in many places and devote more space to this command than to the others:

> The first and most important [command] is truthfulness. This [truthfulness]
> serves to distinguish right from wrong; therefore, you should never tell lies. And
> do not be among those who claim that they hear and obey while in their hearts
> they mean otherwise. . . . You have known that Islam and other religions and
> faiths do not become whole except through this condition [truthfulness] and
> through righteous deeds. How about Tawhid in our Lord, which is the ultimate
> goal. . . . Thus when you realize that you have committed to tell [seek] the truth
> and safeguard your brethren, you would clearly distinguish right from wrong and
> belief from blasphemy.[3]

Truthfulness is not a matter of preference or a desirable objective. It is an
obligatory process and a vital condition for belief to be valid and for the commitment to Tawhid to be irrevocable.

> And if [in terms of truthfulness] you knew what you were obligated to do—help-
> ing the brethren, Tawhid of our Lord, and submission to God's will—then you
> would be able to distinguish the genuine from the false and belief from blas-
> phemy. . . . Tawhid and belief . . . consist of being truthful in tongue and heart,
> which reflect what is in the conscience. Whosoever is not truthful in tongue is
> never truthful in heart. And you should know that truth represents the entirety of
> belief in Tawhid, while falsehood represents apostasy and straying from the right
> path. For whoever lies to his brother lies to his emissary *(da'i)*, and whoever lies
> to his emissary lies to his imam, and whoever lies to his imam lies to our Lord, ex-
> alted be his name.[4]

The linkage between truthfulness and belief in Tawhid is an obligatory one,
as they represent two sides of the same coin: "Truthfulness in relation to belief is
like the head in relation to the body."[5]

Quoting Muhammad ibn Isma'il, the great-grandfather of the Fatimid
caliphs, we hear in the same epistle: "Faith consists of expression by the tongue of
truthfulness in the heart and in actions according to [God's] commandments."[6]
Truthfulness therefore should also be expressed in daily actions and interactions
and should be reinforced lest one fall onto the slippery slope of falsehood and

negation. That slope is alluring, with subtle and insidious ways that swallow the unaware like quicksand. We repeatedly hear admonitions warning the believers of the dangers of complacency and lack of vigilance:

> And be truthful and avoid falsehood; do not add or subtract [from what is true]; telling lies to your brother is an act of blasphemy. . . . And be truthful even when that entails hardship.[7]

> Brethren, beware of falsehood, since that leads to estrangement and dissolution.[8]

> Be worthy heirs to your predecessors and be united in your efforts so that you may emulate the emissaries who bear the message of truth and so that you may always uphold the truth.[9]

> And be in obedience like brothers in purity . . . and renounce false pride and arrogance that has led others before you astray . . . and point out [to your children] the distinctive traits of the believers in Tawhid, the traits of nobility in character and humility in behavior, that are distinct from those of negation and falsehood.[10]

> And know that truthfulness is belief in its entirety and falsehood is negation and blasphemy.[11]

> And there will be no exalted place on the day [of judgment] except for those who are truthful.[12]

In his treatise *The Dots and the Circles*, Shaykh Zayn al-Din Taqi al-Din obligates the Muwahhid to the imperative of truthfulness under at least ten major settings. These include:

1. Truthfulness in the belief in God, exalted be his name above and beyond description, and in God's revelation in the *nasut*;

2. Truthfulness in the belief in the universal mind as God's first creation and in the legitimacy of his guidance and his commands;

3. Truthfulness in the belief in the luminaries, whose creation followed that of the universal mind;

4. Truthfulness in belief in God's messengers and our indebtedness to them;

5. Truthfulness in the belief of the elevated status of the true believers in Tawhid;

6. Truthfulness in belief in the Wisdom of Tawhid as the path for salvation;

7. Truthfulness in the belief in reincarnation and transmigration of souls into the human body;

8. Truthfulness in belief in God's will as a manifestation of divine justice;

9. Truthfulness in belief in the day of judgment, which will come to pass without warning;

10. Truthfulness in believing the Tawhid message of trusted brethren, as this intensifies bonds of trust, whereas the opposite leads to separation and discord.

For these reasons, the shaykh continues, truthfulness, that is, seeking God's truth, can be considered in lieu of prayer because of the relational effects of truthfulness to God Almighty, to the revered imams, the luminaries, the prophets, and the brethren in faith.[13]

The weight of this first command emerges clearly as we read similar interpretations from many authorities who have dealt with this subject, and the near unanimity of their opinions. No wonder this command has made an indelible mark on the behavior of the Druze in everyday life. It is almost second nature for the Druze to refrain from assertion of events or opinions unless they are absolutely sure of their veracity. Even then, it is second nature to utter such disclaimers as "if I am not mistaken," "if my memory does not fail me," "the ultimate truth is only in God's conscience," "only God knows," and so on, all in an effort to avoid the possibility of error that would mar the truth.

A popular anecdote in Druze circles in Lebanon when I was growing up told of an elderly Druze religious figure (shaykh) who was venerated for his piety and purity. The shaykh lived from the land that he tilled with his own hands, avoiding as much as possible dependency on government services or other resources that might contaminate the purity of his lifestyle. By living frugally, he almost achieved self-sufficiency and was content to devote much of his time to contemplation and prayer. It happened that one season when he had a bountiful harvest of wheat, his mule got sick, and he asked a neighbor to lend him a mule to cart the harvest home. The neighbor was glad to oblige as he considered it an honor to help the venerable shaykh. Casually, the neighbor asked the shaykh about the quantity of the harvest, to which the shaykh gave an educated guess at what would be the equivalent of 100 kilos. The shaykh thanked the neighbor and went to his field to load the wheat harvest. To his surprise, he had underestimated the harvest; it weighed 120 instead of 100 kilos. This created a dilemma, since the shaykh had told the neighbor that the harvest was 100 kilos. With no hesitation the shaykh proceeded to load the mule with 100 kilos of wheat and to carry the remaining 20 kilos himself. None of this would have been known had the shaykh not been seen carrying the extra sack of wheat instead of loading it on the mule. The shaykh did not do this to gain recognition or notoriety, for that would be a form of arrogance and egotism that would defeat the purpose. He did what he did solely to adhere to the truth as much as is humanly possible. The monitor was the shaykh's own conscience and the credibility of his word even when uttered casually. Such degree of self-monitoring is not a rarity among the pious of the Druze and to a large extent among the rank and file.

In addition to the self-evident affirmation of the centrality of truth in the Tawhid faith both in matters of doctrine and in the daily behavior of the believer, there are reasons of safety that are linked to truthfulness and credibility. The threat that a budding community faces when it adopts a system of beliefs divergent from that of the majority calls for extra vigilance and ironclad security. Trust becomes a vital ingredient in personal interactions and group dynamics. Trust inevitably is impossible without absolute adherence to the truth. This became particularly crucial in the face of persecution that the Druze community sustained from the caliph 'Ali al-Zahir shortly after the disappearance of al-Hakim, and from others throughout its history. A representative sample of the concern of Baha' al-Din for the safety and security of the believers just before retiring from public view illustrates the emphasis that he placed on truthfulness as a strategy: "Brethren, the time has come for people to sort themselves out. And the judge of what each soul has earned will not be misled. Arm yourselves with truthfulness, fortitude, allegiance, and purity. Beware of the company of those who espouse falsehood and treachery and those who reneged after believing. I have given you the advice that is incumbent upon and expected from those who serve the call with dedication and responsibility."[14]

The Druze were and still are a minority within a minority, emerging from the Isma'ili branch of the Shi'a, while most of the subjects of Fatimid rule were of the Sunni majority in Islam. The long history of suppression and persecution of the descendants of 'Ali by the Umayyad and Abbasid rulers of the Sunni majority led to the practice of occultation of the Isma'ili imams. Occultation can be considered an extreme form of disguise or dissimulation *(taqiya)*, which is critically dependent on the trust and truthfulness of a close circle of advisers and supporters of the targeted imams. Any breach in the security would have been fatal. In this context truthfulness serves a practical and strategic purpose.

We may ask if there are situations when the truth may be concealed or even subverted. The answer is a qualified yes, but only under extreme and exceptional circumstances, when the security of the community and the survival of the faith are at stake. In what may be considered a farewell message, Baha' al-Din alludes to situations where the believer may be absolved when denying the truth: "And the humble servant [Baha' al-Din] . . . is submitting himself to our Lord, intending to retire from view and seek occultation. And he bids farewell to all the believers, far and near. . . . And should dire circumstances befall some of you whereby you are forced to deny him [Baha' al-Din] or publicly denounce him, then do so, as necessity dictates, for God knows what is in your hearts of truth or falsehood." [15]

Baha al-Din's message was a very unusual communication, as the followers of Tawhid are as a rule exhorted to stay the course and accept whatever is in store for them with dignity and fortitude. His message represents an exception that was mentioned only once and occurred at the end of Baha' al-Din's tenure. Acceptance of God's grace and submission to God's will remain the cornerstone of the believer in dealing with adversity, without objection or complaint even in the face of mortal danger. One is always exhorted to do the best and strive for survival and safety and avoid exposure to dangerous situations as much as possible. But, when faced with adversity, the believer should remain steadfast and rely on faith in God and accept whatever outcome is in store with courage and dignity:

> Have you not heard in your gatherings that the one who accepts God's will shall endure God's will and be rewarded, while one who does not accept God's will shall suffer God's will and miss the reward?[16]

> Brethren in faith, never let the fear of a human being overshadow the fear from the wrath of the Almighty, and beware of falsehood since that undermines your faith and your solidarity. . . . Brethren, whoever fears a human being allows that human being to control his fate. The true believer in God is never afraid or cowardly. . . . The veracity of true faith is confirmed if it survives when tested, for in times of peace it would be difficult to distinguish the genuine from the sham. . . . High places are reached through courage and fortitude when [one is] confronted with threats and difficulties. . . . Those who prevail in the face of danger and adversity will surely earn rich rewards.[17]

> As for the one who is solid in his belief, truthful in his word, and genuine in his deeds, the more he is subjected to adversity the deeper becomes his commitment to his faith. It is like silver whose purity increases as it is subjected to increasing intensity of fire; so is the faith of the believer in times of stress.[18]

In other words, the believer in Tawhid should adhere to the truth regardless of the consequences. Not surprisingly, adversity generally contributes to the strengthening of one's faith, and Tawhid is no exception. Thus we have to take Baha' al-Din's farewell dispensation of putting safety ahead of truthfulness as an extreme and rare exception to the otherwise inviolate rule of truthfulness in tongue.

Some of the detractors of the Druze have suggested that seeking truthfulness is limited to dealing only with fellow Druze and not across the board. Such allegations miss the point altogether in confusing the imperative of truthfulness as a vital principle in the Druze faith and the necessity of trust among the faithful for reasons of security. Telling the truth, regardless of mitigating circumstances, is central in the Druze upbringing even if it would be detrimental to the immediate interest or personal safety. Granted, in recent times there has been a global assault on values and mores across the board, particularly in the countries of origin of the Druze, and this has resulted in some attrition in the strict adherence to truthfulness. Although the Druze are not an exception to this landslide, yet it is my conviction as well as that of friends and neighbors from diverse backgrounds that the Druze community continues to enjoy a reputation for truthfulness and trust. "I have lived among these chivalrous people [the Druze] more than a third of a century," attests the eminent literary figure Marun Abbud, "and I have experienced nothing but nobility, decorum, and compassion. And I testify that I did not hear from their *ʿuqqal* one improper or coarse statement, nor from the *juhhal* a word that was out of line. Theirs is the nobility in speech and the essence in decorum." Abbud also quotes from an earlier literary giant, Ahmad Fares al-Shedyaq: "And as for the accusation that they [the Druze] are dishonest, not trustworthy, that is nothing but a false and slanderous accusation, since they have never broken a promise nor reneged on a commitment."[19] After all, truthfulness of the tongue was, is, and will remain the first and most important prerequisite on the road to the Tawhid faith.

Safeguarding of Brothers and Sisters

Care for and safeguarding of the brothers and sisters in faith is a sacred command. As such it represents a cornerstone for the safety of the community and the imperative of mutual support in a closely knit group. A budding community consisting of a minority within a potentially resentful majority had to emphasize group solidarity for survival. In this context the Druze are no different from other sects that struggle for survival and, in many instances, prevail and prosper. The early centuries in Christianity consisted of one long saga of heroism, sacrifice, altruism, and martyrdom to promote the faith and protect the faithful. Likewise early Islam would never have survived had it not been for the solidarity of the newly constructed group identity in a faith that exhorted its followers to strive for God's sacred message.

Thus the command for the safekeeping of fellow brothers and sisters in faith is neither new nor excessive. Perhaps the uniqueness of this command in the case of the Druze is in the way it fits in with and complements the others. We can imagine how dependent the early vanguard of the movement were on one another for spiritual, emotional, and physical sustenance. Truthfulness was a prerequisite for trust, and mutual support was indispensable for safety. Hence we often hear the first two commands joined together in a complementary sequence, for the achievement of the basic tenets of the faith. In Epistle 10 Hamza entreats the believers: "By God, O faithful, exercise patience and fortitude in times of stress and in easier times; awaken one another and hearken to God in binding and irrevocable faith. Ask forgiveness for whatever evil thoughts you may have harbored, or whatever sins you may have committed. Ask God to help you stay the course in Tawhid. Remain steadfast in what I have instructed you, to be truthful in tongue and supportive of your brethren in faith." And in another epistle Hamza adds:

> And be thankful to God, exalted be his name, for what he has bestowed on you of wisdom and favored you with his grace. . . . And safeguard your brethren in faith. For in their safety your faith becomes more complete. Respond to their requests and address their needs. Accept their regrets and oppose their adversaries. Visit their sick, and support the weak and infirm among them. Give them all the support you can and never let them down. . . . And peace be upon those who chose the right path and were steadfast in believing God's messages and built their belief in Tawhid on the truth. Praise be to God.[20]

Safeguarding brothers and sisters in Tawhid, however, should not be associated with an attitude of condescension or arrogance, for that will defeat the purposes of unity and egalitarianism that are the hallmarks of Tawhid. The first of God's creation, the universal mind, was not immune to the temptation of awareness of power, and that posture of self-pride led to the creation of the antithesis. One has to be constantly reminded to curb the tendency to flaunt power or wealth or other forms of egotistical manifestations, for that would encourage the forces of darkness and negation and weaken those of Tawhid. Members of the community should be ready and willing to help with humility and patience, expecting no reward in return, for in God's grace nothing is lost:

> And be aware, fellow brethren in faith, that the supreme reward is reserved for those who persevere and prevail when tested. . . . Be humble with your weaker brethren, and accept their excuse for having temporarily succumbed to the forces of negation. You would earn high accolade [in God's grace] for having

been the first and for having done the good deeds, and they would forever be grateful to you. Let the efforts be joined to combat apostasy and the enemies of the faith, and to assist and provide succor to the weak among you. . . . Purify your souls, then, by renouncing arrogance and false pride and by embracing equanimity, perseverance, and acceptance of God's message and submission to his will.[21]

The children were not forgotten in the care for brethren in Tawhid:

And be, in submission to God's commands, brothers of purity. Be kind to the children, and equate your humility, respect, generosity, and encouragement to the young with that which is reserved for the old and wise among you. Renounce arrogance and false pride, for those traits characterize the renegades and apostates. Teach the children the gentle traits that characterize those who believe in Tawhid, by being tender, humble, and chivalrous. Tame the aggressive side of your behavior, and build on endearing traits so that they [the children] learn to emulate those who are righteous and avoid those who are not. Extend all forms of protection to the children and to your sisters that they may not fall into corruption and promiscuity.[22]

Safeguarding the brethren is not restricted to passive acceptance or rejection of an errant brother's (or sister's) behavior while keeping a safe distance in order to avoid dealing with controversial or potentially confrontational situations. That would represent a form of self-serving attitude devoid of empathy and altruism. It is the duty of a Muwahhid to extend himself to his fellow Muwahhid, to advise and guide him or her into the right path. Since no one is immune to error, it is incumbent upon the believer to assist, advise, and if need be chastise and discipline those who have strayed from the path of Tawhid.

It is incumbent on you believers in Tawhid who are on the righteous path of piety and purity to be in harmony, alignment, and cooperation with fellow believers, thus facilitating nobility in character, advancement in acquisition of knowledge, and avoidance of erroneous and sinful behavior. . . . And when you find out that someone has gone astray and has fallen into the company of the corrupt and those who deviate from telling the truth and has reneged on his commitments, you have to be cognizant of the conditions that misled him into pursuing that road. . . . [In that case] you should first counsel and admonish the errant brother, and if he persists, chastise him and remind him of the consequences of his errant behavior. Should he refuse to recant, then distance yourselves from him [to allow time for reconsideration]. Should [you find] that he intends to persist in his errant ways [despite the above measures], then sever relations and distance him from your ranks.[23]

In other words one should exhaust all other avenues before giving up hope on someone who falls astray. At the same time the community should not compromise their faith, their standards, or their security for a cause that is, for all intents and purposes, beyond recovery. After all Tawhid is built upon free choice and with that comes full accountability.

It is interesting to note that the measures mentioned above are used by the *'uqqal* to this day to discipline a colleague who in their judgment has veered from the accepted norms of behavior. They start with subtle and gentle reference to the presumed error in the behavior of the person in question, and move gradually to the extreme form of severing all ties (excommunication). Since there is no formal structure in the Druze religious establishment nor an established hierarchy, excommunication is in the form of distancing between the group and the accused. The term applied to this action is distancing *(bu'd)*, whereby the offender is literally made not fit to be associated with (persona non grata) by his former friends and cohorts. The punishment is moral, but the pain and loss of face that it imparts can be devastating. It even follows the errant individual to the grave as religious leaders stay silent during funeral services when the shaykh performing the services asks for God's grace *(rahma)* on the deceased. Their silence is an indication of their reluctance to jeopardize their conscience by false testimony as they bear witness at that fateful moment. Ordinarily the shaykhs would echo with a phrase that roughly means "God's grace be upon him" *(Allah yarhamu)*, when they are convinced of the truth of their testimony. This activity is more an expression of the shaykhs' strict adherence to truth telling than an objective judgment of the deceased. The exercise of moral authority in a close-knit community such as the Druze is vital in safeguarding the brethren and protecting the integrity of the faith and the welfare of the faithful.

In fact this is the same thinking that led to the division of the community into those who are in the inner circle of the faithful *('uqqal)* and those outside *(juhhal)*. The *juhhal* are better off than those who join the *'uqqal* and then decide to opt out. They become cut off completely from the company of former associates and friends and risk losing face with the community at large (including the *juhhal)*. The dynamic of group solidarity is best served when commitments are honored and the welfare of the group is placed above individual desires and needs. Such strong bonds, virtually unchanged from inception of the faith, become hard to break and may be credited with the survival of the Druze community to this day. This group solidarity has its foundation in the duty of a Muwahhid to safeguard and protect fellow brothers and sisters.

How does the command of safeguarding the brethren in Tawhid apply to women? In a nutshell women were and are treated equally with respect to the obligations of this command. In fact the status of women in the Tawhid was seldom, if ever, matched from the time Tawhid was publicly disclosed to the present. In the first place Islam elevated the status of women to a much higher position than existed in ancient Arabia. That was a giant step when considered in the geographic and historical context of the era. Nonetheless, women remain subservient to men in some matters such as bearing witness, where the testimony of two women is equivalent to that of a man. In marriage, divorce, inheritance, and polygamy, men have the upper hand. Islam could do only so much, at least initially, to change attitudes and practices that had been ingrained in the ethos of pre-Islamic Arabia for centuries. With time there were some modifications, particularly in the Shi'a community. In the Druze concept of Tawhid, the rights of women are equal to the rights of men in marriage, divorce, and inheritance:

> And the imperative of religion dictates that when a man of faith is betrothed to a woman of faith, he should treat her as his equal and share with her all that he owns. However, in case of separation, [settlement] depends on who is the aggressor. If the woman chooses to disobey and to leave her husband, in spite of his being faithful and fair to her, and if her state of aggression is confirmed by trusted witnesses, then he would be entitled to half of what she owns. And if trusted witnesses judge that he was unfair to her and that she left him under duress, then he has no right to prevent her nor is he entitled to any compensation. . . . And if the man decides to divorce his wife out of his own free will and without cause on her part, then she would be entitled to half of whatever he owns. . . . This is how fairness and justice would be served.[24]

Regrettably, these clear instructions are not strictly enforced in the male-dominated climate of the East, where cultural factors sometimes outweigh religious injunctions.

It is only in recent times that the lot of women began to improve, but it is still far from the level of parity articulated in Epistle 25. We are all aware of the gap that separates men from women in the exercise of civil rights, participation in political and economic activities, and autonomy in decision making in some Muslim countries and societies that adhere to the most rigid interpretation of the

Qur'an. Even in Western societies it is only in recent times that the gender gap is finally closing. It is also noteworthy that present-day attitudes regarding the status of women in some rigid fundamentalist Islamic societies represent a reversal of fortunes for women when compared with their status in the days of the Prophet. This reversal has affected Druze women, but to a much lesser degree. After all, safeguarding of the brethren in Tawhid is not gender specific.

Monogamy was clearly affirmed and is strictly enforced. The Druze were not the first to advocate strict monogamy, being preceded in that by the Mu'tazilites and the Carmathians, but the Druze were the first sect in Islam to institutionalize monogamy in their civil codes. In fact the Druze refer to several passages in the Qur'an that place major constraints on the practice of polygamy. For example, the Qur'an insists on absolute equality among all the wives in case of polygamy. In the eyes of the Druze, this condition is impossible to satisfy, and so polygamy should be prohibited. In a public declaration, al-Mu'izz, the grandfather of al-Hakim, instructed his subjects: "Be faithful to the one woman who is your partner. Refrain from excessive lust, and relations with multiple women . . . as this will lead to your exhaustion physically and mentally. One man is for one woman."[25] By the time of al-Hakim this admonition had become an inviolate rule and remains so to this day.

Likewise the legal age of marriage for girls was raised to fifteen years, and commitment to marriage had to be with the full consent of the woman as an adult.[26] Preservation of the brethren was extended to include laws for divorce that were fair and equitable. Once divorced, a man or a woman can never remarry the former spouse no matter what happens to either of them, such as marrying another spouse in between. The finality of divorce and the fact that it has to be conducted in court in the presence of a presiding judge may contribute to the relatively low divorce rate among the Druze.

In case of divorce, remarriage for a woman is allowed, but only after the passage of at least three months, to make certain that the woman was not pregnant at the time of divorce. This is an Islamic practice meant to preclude the possibility of confusion with respect to the identity of the father in the event she is pregnant.[27]

Extending the principle of safeguarding the brethren to women also meant abolition of slavery and prostitution. The sanctity of the human body was upheld for both men and women, and no form of white slavery could be condoned. Sex is an act of procreation and intimacy in the sanctity of monogamous marriage, and not an untamed instinct in search of indiscriminate satisfaction. Brothers and sisters in Tawhid are commanded to treat one another with decorum, respect, and protection, away from lust and situations that lead to temptation. Men and women need not be separated even in times of worship, provided decorum is maintained with proper attire and appropriate behavior. But promiscuity is un-equivocally condemned. In a communication meant to refute accusations and misleading information from sources that intended to smear the message of Tawhid with false accusations concerning moral and ethical codes, Baha' al-Din minces no words as to how women should behave:

> Beware, beware, sisters in faith, of looking at a man, whether he is a believer or not, except as you would look at your father or son. . . . And you know that you would experience anxiety and shame if a neighbor should discover that you were in a compromising position, how would you feel then when whatever you do can never be hidden from your Creator, exalted be his name. . . . Beware, beware, dear brothers and sisters in faith, of committing sinful acts and from succumbing to animal instincts and immoral actions.[28]

> And know ye that there is no god but God; atone for your sins, brothers and sisters in faith, God knows all your secrets.[29]

> And let your tongue be truthful . . . and devote your attention to safeguarding brothers and sisters in faith, for therein lies the protection from sinfulness and im-morality.[30]

Women could lead in prayer and in battle. Men are commanded to support the education of their wives and daughters and to be active in community affairs. Druze history records many women of distinction in all walks of life.[31] Although the Druze do not place much emphasis on ritualistic manifestations such as elab-orate places for worship or magnificent mausoleums for holy figures in the com-munity, there are a few simple shrines that entomb the remains of extremely pious and spiritual individuals. It is noteworthy that some of these shrines are dedicated to women of piety and purity who were judged by the same standards as men and who received the same deserved accolade as men.[32] Even in the early phases of the call to Tawhid, Baha' al-Din entrusted his niece Sarah to lead a detachment of men on a highly dangerous mission. The purpose of the mission was to destroy a group of renegades and apostates in order to save the nascent community in Tawhid from sabotage and irreparable damage. It is reported that among the men under her command was her own father, and possibly one of her uncles as well.[33] Baha' al-Din, responding to the plight of the community of believers in a district of south Lebanon, Wadi al-Taym, who had suffered persecution, rape, and other acts of violence at the hands of enemies from without and renegades from within, said: "And I have dispatched to you daughter [niece] Sarah, known for her purity, chastity, and devotion to her faith . . . and with her my brother . . . to bolster your morale, and to cooperate with you and help you recover from your ordeal."[34]

Such a degree of women's liberation was not to be at the expense of chastity, purity, honesty, and devotion to God and to the family. Women are raised to be courageous, patient, and dignified in times of joy or sorrow. Decorum and chastity, as well as provision of succor and comfort to the needy and the infirm, are expected traits in the traditions of Druze women. This "job description" has held firm throughout history. In fact part of Sarah's mission was to heal the wounds created by the renegades in subjecting women to rape and other forms of sexual exploitation. The tenderness that Baha' al-Din exhibited when dealing with this traumatic issue is deeply touching and comforting. Thus women who were coerced into immorality and sexual promiscuity by enemies of the faith and by renegades and apostates should be treated with tenderness and compassion and rehabilitated into the community of the faithful. Their case should be distinct from those who willingly commit sinful and shameful acts:

> Be cognizant, brethren in faith, of the necessity to expunge from your conscience any misgivings and doubts concerning [the veracity of] men and women . . . who may have been forced off the righteous path as a result of persecution and coercion. The imam has surrounded these people with compassionate justice according to the teachings of the holy Qur'an "excepting him who has been compelled, and his heart is still at rest in his belief" [16:106]. . . . Do not treat those whose faith is sincere with condescension and arrogance, for even disasters can be a means to test the veracity of belief. [To prejudge] would a grave offense and an egregious and divisive act. Only when you are absolutely sure that a person is a genuine liar or a traitor or an apostate . . . with ample and irrevocable proof, can you exercise the act of distancing him [or her] from your midst.[35]

Neither hearsay nor mere suspicion is sufficient to pass judgment on a fellow brother or sister in faith. Islam is the religion of compassion, and the followers of Tawhid have remained true to their Islamic heritage with respect to safeguarding fellow humans, particularly those who are brothers and sisters in faith. Practices such as female circumcision are totally unknown among the Druze, and among most Muslim communities. This barbaric practice represents a cultural aberration imported to but not inherent in any Islamic teachings. Honor killing, that is, the killing of a woman by her father or her brother if she gets pregnant out of wedlock, is a vestige of tribal customs that has no place in the compassionate teachings of Islam. It has never been a part of the Druze concept of Tawhid but rather a cultural aberrancy in the rare instances when it occurred in the past.

Slavery was totally outlawed; slaves were ordered freed by the highest authority in the Fatimid state, al-Hakim himself. Baha' al-Din was explicit in referring to the issue of slavery and how al-Hakim dealt with it:

> And he [al-Hakim] ordered the freedom of all the slaves and those who were otherwise owned, in a special decree that was absolute, forceful, and irrevocable, such that no one could return to a state of being owned or enslaved, or being subject to summary judgment. That [decree] was meant for all races and groups, [such that] no one could object to it or deny the [civil] rights of these people in any way. Whosoever does not comply with this order would be damned as an oppressor. . . . This [measure] cuts the road on those who claim to be what they are not and who would like to return to the practice of slavery. . . . This decree was issued for no purpose except to please God.[36]

This was a remarkable declaration in that age or any age.

Renunciation of Idolatry and Paganism

The command to renounce idolatry and paganism is part and parcel of the basic tenets of the Tawhid faith. It is included among the commands that are obligatory for preparing the believer for the long journey in Tawhid. Believers are constantly reminded that they have committed themselves to irrevocable renunciation of any form of pagan ideas or practices that could be remotely associated with the worship of idols or false gods. Tawhid adheres to the cornerstone of the Islamic message, "There is no god but God," with no reservation or equivocation. It follows that renunciation of false gods has to be a prerequisite for the seeker to embark on the quest of Tawhid.

Renunciation of idolatry and the worship of false gods goes beyond the verbal declaration of such, or beyond the act of eliminating pagan structures and symbols from one's surroundings. In Tawhid, the imperative of renunciation of pagan practices must be experienced in the heart and soul of the seeker. It can be considered as a form of baptism of the soul as all the vestiges of impurities and contamination that impede vision and distort genuine knowledge are disavowed and washed away. Therefore, this step is a prerequisite for the seeker to begin the spiritual journey to the Divine. The process of Tawhid is rooted in the concept of evolutionary steps that lead the soul to the ultimate destination across the span of eternity. And with each step, knowledge becomes more profound and vision becomes purer in a positive feedback that spirals upward to the Source. However, in the process of development and evolution one cannot avoid the accumulation of consumed products and items that have outlived their usefulness. To facilitate and heighten the receptive capacity of the soul, the soul must be maintained in a state of freshness and readiness. Such a state enables the soul to be receptive to evolutionary developments and facilitates the incorporation of progress into its fabric. "It is a law of life," states Darryl Reanney, "that understanding comes only to a mind that is ready to receive it."[37]

Renunciation of false gods and idols as a prerequisite for genuine belief in God does not imply a license to destroy objects of art or historical monuments and archeological sites. Such acts as have taken place recently by some fanatics in Islam have been practiced by virtually all faiths at one time or another throughout history. These actions are rooted in ignorance and flawed logic and do not contribute one iota to spiritual progress and evolution. How can the destruction of a significant part of one's heritage, including objects of beauty and innovation, contribute to one's religiosity and enhance identification with the Divine? How can one not be moved by the magnificent contributions of artists and artisans across the span of human history in painting, sculpture, architecture, music, and poetry, all sparked by the depth of spiritual yearning for truth, beauty, and perfection? How can we overlook the role of faith in unleashing such creativity and such passion as that experienced by Bach or by Leonardo da Vinci and the legacy they left for humanity? No one in his or her right state of mind would consider the products of genius as idolatry.

What is and would be considered a form of idolatry takes place when the artifacts of art become the object of worship in themselves, often at the expense of the inner source that is the reason for the artifacts in the first place. Under these conditions it is the human being that has missed the mark by emphasizing the shell and ignoring the core. Stalling at the exterior, as it were, the individual denies himself or herself the opportunity to harvest the psychic power that art can unleash once the shell is pierced. It is said of Michelangelo that he would "see" the subject of the sculpture in a slab of rock, waiting to be delivered at his hands. Through faith any human being should be able to see the symbolic significance of art as a means to identify with and try to reach aspects of the Divine. Faith, however, cannot be an end in itself. It is only a means to an end, the road to knowledge, enlightenment, beauty, and truth. Like genuine faith, objects of art and fruits of science do not lead to idolatry as long as they enhance one's spiritual quest and identification with the Divine.

In the case of the Druze concept of Tawhid, renunciation of idolatry is expressed in the heart and soul of the faithful and not in overt expression of rejection of beauty or vandalism of objects of art. The pious among the Druze may choose to adopt the austere life of a hermit, with bare surroundings for the basic necessity for survival. Worldly and material means of comfort, as well as objects of art, are rejected by the hermit lest they detract from the spirituality he seeks. The emphasis on the inner meaning *(batin)* rather than outward manifestation of religiosity by these people can be easily understood. And this is not restricted to the Druze as it is a feature that most ascetic individuals hold in common.

An obligatory condition of the cyclical nature of spiritual progress is shedding and renewal, whereby, having fulfilled its purpose, the old garb is superseded by a renewed and more developed stage of cognizance and gnosis. Vestiges of pagan thinking and practices must be discarded on the road to spiritual development and purification. This after all is the role of reincarnation, where the essence is preserved across the recurrent cycles of birth and death. The phenotype, the physical body, is a vehicle that carries the essence but is not the essence in itself. Therefore, the body, precious and necessary as it may be, will not last forever. The body will be recycled to accommodate the soul, the essence of life and existence. Tawhid does not renounce the body since the body is and will remain a necessary vehicle. What Tawhid does is to renounce making the body the focus of interest at the expense of genuine spirituality and the well-being of the soul. In the same vein Tawhid admonishes the believers to renounce idolatry and shed the vestiges of paganism that may have lingered from previous stages of development. Thus we hear Hamza admonishing the faithful to "shed what will not hurt you to discard the vestiges of prior cycles and doctrines that have become obsolete [considering that] every messenger tried to supersede those who preceded him."[38] Or to be aware lest they, seekers in Tawhid, go backward and relapse into a lesser degree of development after having achieved a more advanced stage in Tawhid: "Beware, beware of false reports and hearsay that lead you into apostasy and blasphemy. Do not take refuge in a structure of ruins, or repose under a faulty roof, and give up what is real for mirage. [Should you do so] you risk [spiritual] deprivation and face starvation by estrangement from the sources of true knowledge and reversion to the level of overt interpretation and blind dogma."[39]

The intention is not to degrade the importance of prior calls or to undermine the message or the knowledge gathered therefrom but to beware of sliding backward and losing momentum after attaining a more advanced stage of development and evolution.

Obviously these warnings and admonitions are intended for those who have already achieved a certain level of cognition and spiritual development. In other words one should not regress after graduating to a stage that is more developed and more refined than prior stages. The warnings and admonitions do not apply across the board since people are not at the same level of spiritual development. Likewise, they do not imply that literal understanding of the message is no longer necessary. Nor do they imply that rites and rituals should be totally abandoned. On the contrary, the external manifestations of worship and religiosity should remain operative for many if not most of the believers. Exoteric practices and interpretations *(zahir)* are an indispensable foundation in the process of spiritual evolution and should be maintained and upheld as long as they are necessary. This happens to be the situation in the majority of cases. In the case of the few who have already graduated from that stage of development to a more advanced level of esoteric knowledge and awareness along the path of Tawhid *(ma'rifa)*, external manifestations and practices may no longer be necessary. Again, Hamza clarifies this point in response to a challenger from a rival Islamic sect:

> And it does not follow that whoever knows the inner meaning should discard the obvious and overt meaning, as there are certain phenomena, the overt manifestation of which should never be discarded even if the inner meaning could be interpreted in seventy different ways. . . . Take for example cleanliness, the inner meaning of which is renunciation of paganism and idolatry. . . . [However], knowing that does not imply that the literal meaning should be discarded, as cleanliness of the body is obviously necessary. Thus it behooves the one who knows the inner meaning of cleanliness to be more committed to cleanliness of his body as well.[40]
>
> And act in accordance with overt meaning, as long as it can still be of use to you and as long as it is the norm, and seek the inner meaning, as much as you can decipher of its essence. . . . It is acceptable to satisfy both and to be rewarded for so doing."[41]

As long as there is need for the primary stages, so be it. Nothing should be discarded until it is superseded and can no longer fulfill the requirements of the particular stage that the seeker has attained. Only at that stage can one shed items that no longer serve the purpose, selectively and with judicious discrimination.

To return to the emphasis on the soul, Tawhid shifts the focus from the literal understanding of the word (Qur'an) to the pursuit of its essence. If that means bypassing some aspects of ritualistic nature, so be it, but only if the seeker has graduated beyond the stages where rites and rituals are still needed to seek the truth. In this context Tawhid has gone beyond the predecessor Isma'ili doctrine that mandates adherence to the overt practice of worship by everybody in addition to the pursuit of the inner meaning of the message. The Isma'ili scholar Mustafa Ghaleb states, "As to what is being said that some of the [Isma'ili] imams have abandoned the necessity for the overt practice of worship, this is out of the question. It is impossible that such opinion would come forth from the [Isma'ili] imams as it would be contrary to rules and regulations mandated by the Prophet."[42] The Druze concept of Tawhid, on the other hand, considers overt religious practices as analogous to the body, while the essence of the message is the soul. The high premium that is attached to the soul in Tawhid tips the scales in favor of the inner content as opposed to the outer manifestation in rites and rituals. Practicing Tawhid leads to the exhilarating bliss of divine knowledge *(irfan),* which is obviously more lasting and more profound than the mere physical motions of worship.

Thus, having attained that stage of spiritual maturation, one is not expected to revert to the earlier stages of development. It does not negate those stages; it simply means that they have been superseded. "Beware, beware, brethren in faith," said Hamza, "the lures of the evanescent world, and seek that which is everlasting."[43]

> Worldly goods and pleasures are easy to get, but they are temporary, while attainment of faith is hard but is everlasting. . . . Beware, dear brethren, of letting the forces of negation gain the upper hand over the forces of enlightenment, for should they succeed they will lead you to regression and peril. But if you succeed [in gaining the upper hand over the forces of negation], your reward will be everlasting. . . . Patience and fortitude in times of stress are not permanent, but their rewards are. . . . Go back to your very depths, wake up from your slumber, and cleanse your souls by renewal of commitment and renunciation of impurities and degeneration. . . . After committing to the covenant *(mithaq)* and adopting the Tawhid faith, how is it possible to revert to worshipping idols and images. . . . Dear brethren, after disclosure of Tawhid and the revelation of [God's] image and acceptance of the image *[nasut]* as an imperative for true belief, you should not renege and divert your allegiance to another [image]. For if this were to happen it would corrupt your worship and obviate the promise of the hereafter. . . . Beware, beware of falling under the influence of Satan, for truth will always prevail.[44]

The gist of these admonitions and their real intent is to protect those who have committed themselves to the path of Tawhid from regressing into the less developed stages than the path that Hamza was preaching. Viewed superficially it could be mistaken as a derogation of prior beliefs, but the entire context discloses otherwise. "How can light be appreciated except through healthy vision, and how can truth be known except through wise and sagacious intelligence? For had you not rid yourselves of ignorance, you would not have been able to accept even elements of universal wisdom."[45]

Spiritual evolution in the Druze concept of Tawhid stipulates graduation and adaptation. Such traits imply an obligatory commitment to give up what is no longer suitable and strive to the new and upgraded level of spiritual development. Failure to recognize this principle within the proper context can be a source of confusion and misunderstanding between the Druze concept of Tawhid and how this concept relates to Islam as well as to other faiths.

Seeking God's truth in the Druze concept of Tawhid is a process that began with the beginning of human awareness, individually and collectively. At that point in remote antiquity, the concept was so faint as to be considered imperceptible, at least at the conscious level. At the subconscious level, however, it was probably maturing until it was ready to surface. As human awareness grew so too did the human concept of Tawhid. The message of Tawhid was always included, in one form or another and to varying degrees of intensity and clarity, within the messages of the various religions. With each succeeding message the human concept of Tawhid has become more mature and more developed. The seeker is led all along the way by the increasing intensity and luminescence of the message *(ishraq)* and regulated by his or her ability to witness and comprehend.

Graduating to higher and more advanced levels necessitates building on prior foundations and not remaining confined to that stage. Thus to reach the higher levels one has to have successfully completed the basic requirements and to have graduated from the formative stages to a more advanced level of awareness and gnosis. Consequently, renunciation of paganism does not negate the role that pagan practices played in the initial stages of human religiosity. It simply means that it is time to move to higher ground and to discard practices that have outlived their usefulness in human spiritual development. The Druze consider some ritualistic practices to be a carryover from pagan times and no longer needed for spiritual fulfillment. Thus the Druze may reduce emphasis on, or abandon, some practices that exist in various religions, including the monotheistic ones. Divestiture of the overt rituals is only applicable to those who can navigate without them, and not across the board. The Druze do not carry icons; do not wear pendants; do not have minarets from which to call people to prayer in their simple and austere places of worship; or use bells that toll; nor do they have steeples to display their emblems or use sculpture or painting for visual representation of holy figures. Theirs is the simplicity of the Quakers in worship and the self-reliance of the Amish in lifestyle, at least in the context of tradition.

The purpose of renunciation of idolatry and paganism in Tawhid, therefore, is to relieve the seeker from a set of practices that are no longer useful and may have become an impediment to progress once the seeker has accepted and internalized the basic tenets of the faith. Such a prerequisite obviously does not apply across the board as most people remain connected to religion through overt and ritualistic practices. On the contrary, Tawhid cannot be disparaging to the cradles in which it was incubated and that have included at one time or another idolatrous and pagan practices. How can it be otherwise, when Tawhid could not and would not have evolved without tender nurturing in the long record of human religions across the entire span of human history? In the era of al-Hakim, it was in Islam that the process of Tawhid found a womb and a cradle. In the words of a contemporary Druze scholar,

> A person's spiritual growth and belief in the unity of God should be the distinguishing factor in shaping her or his being. . . . Unism [Tawhid] . . . is considered by authors of the [Druze] manuscripts as an ahistorical or eternal phenomenon. . . . Muwahhidun (unists) are found under different titles and are distinguished from one another in the manuscripts by certain characteristics, such as their firm belief concerning truthful statements and deeds as well as their sincerity and beneficence. The essence of the Druze Tawhid teachings exists within all monotheistic traditions and is not Druze per se but is a strict and progressive unist doctrine that resides in the hearts and souls of adherents and is reflected in their actions. The unist doctrine has been considered progressive by the Druze sect since it is inclusive to some extent and builds on previous monotheistic doctrines that are viewed as paving the way for the open declaration of the Druze Tawhid reform.[46]

The last call to Tawhid, according to the Druze epistles, emerged from the Islamic incubator and represented a further refinement of the literal interpretation of the Qur'an. Does that mean that a believer in Tawhid should renounce the message of Islam or consider some of the rituals in Islam, such as pilgrimage to Mecca and stoning of the devil, a form of paganism? Or for that matter, are the liturgical and elaborate rituals of many Christian denominations a form of idolatry and a vestige of paganism? Absolutely not, for to remove them would in effect remove the skeleton from the edifice on which ordinary people rely for religious fulfillment. It is only when the essence of the message is lost or significantly blurred in the ornateness of the trappings and the convolutions of rituals, that the risk of idolatry and paganism emerges. It is this erosive risk that Tawhid warns against and demands of the seeker to renounce. By such renunciation, the Druze believe that the essence of God's messages, the most recent of which are embodied in the Qur'an, become clearer and nearer to human understanding and gnosis. "Islam is the gateway to belief *(iman)*, and *iman* is the gateway to Tawhid," a message found repeatedly in the Druze epistles, is a clear affirmation that Tawhid is firmly anchored in Islam and in the doctrine of the holy book, the Qur'an.

The fact that the doctrine of Tawhid includes an elaborate philosophy of the process of creation and religious evolution, with a distinct interpretation of the Qur'an, does not detract from the essence of Islam or the veracity of the Prophet as the bearer of the divine message. Examples of this connection in the Druze epistles are too numerous to cite; one example illustrates the point. Commenting on those who believed and then reneged, Hamza warns of the dire consequences of apostasy: "Like those who reneged and increased their vehemence in apostasy, as though they had never accepted Islam or believed in Tawhid, as mentioned in the holy Qur'an ['O believers, fear God, and be with the truthful ones' 9:120]."[47]

Belief in Tawhid in Every Age and Stage

Tawhid is the fourth command, not the first; the first three are considered prerequisites for the seeker to embark on the long journey of spiritual growth and maturation.

Having thoroughly internalized the first three prerequisites, the prospective Muwahhidun have now reached a stage whereby they can be entrusted with the message of Tawhid and can incorporate it into daily life. Once again we notice the process of graduation from one stage to the next and from one level to the next in practical terms. The graduation in practice is a prerequisite to ensure the eligibility of the seeker and provide a state of readiness for the eternal pilgrimage to the Source. The attainment of Tawhid is, after all, the purpose and culmination of human existence, and for that matter of the entirety of existence. Human beings are presumably the only ones of God's creatures chosen to comprehend the message. Because of that unique gift human beings can and are meant to undergo the hard but exhilarating task of embarking on the fateful journey, with the full opportunity for choice. Starting with an implacable commitment to the truth, without which nothing can stand, the seeker is then guided into rigorous self-discipline to tame the physical and base instincts of greed, arrogance, and avarice. Genuine concern and empathy for their fellow men and women follows in the expression of safeguarding brothers and sisters in faith, and by extension all of God's creation. Putting the welfare of others ahead of selfish considerations subdues the flesh and elevates the spirit, such that the soul becomes more receptive to the sublime message of Tawhid. Renunciation of falsehood, idolatry, and other influences that contaminate the heart and impede the vision of the seeker elevates the level of readiness to assimilate the message of Tawhid.

Failure of progression along the prerequisites of Tawhid or insufficient preparation for the long and demanding journey of seeking the truth could backfire and undermine the very purpose of the intended journey. It is, therefore, safer for the believer to take the necessary time to become firmly connected to Tawhid, not only in the domain of the intellect but also in heart and soul. This may explain why the ʿuqqal have played the role of guardians of the faith protecting the core principles from the uninitiated (juhhal), while sharing with the juhhal what was considered to be safe for both. It is the same logic that enjoins the faithful not to abandon the overt interpretation of the holy message even after understanding the more profound and esoteric meaning. For those who have not reached that mystical level of experiencing the ecstasy of connection between the Creator and the creation, exposure to a message whose intensity they cannot bear could be disastrous. Thus while divine wisdom should not be withheld from those who are eligible to receive it, care should be taken from exposing the uninitiated to it, who will not comprehend the essence without sufficient preparation. In such a situation serious damage may result to the individual and to the message itself: "And protect the wisdom [of Tawhid] from [those who are] ineligible to receive it and do not withhold it from the meritorious. [For] whoever withholds divine wisdom from those who are entitled to it dishonors and reneges on his commitment to his faith. And whoever presents it [indiscriminately] to those who are not entitled to it would have jeopardized his faith. . . . Praise be to God for what he has graced you with of his divine knowledge and wisdom."[48]

This and similar admonitions explain, at least in part, the reluctance of Druze religious and civil establishments to condone total and unlimited exposure of the faith to everyone, for fear of misunderstanding and misinterpretation. It may also explain the practice of dissimulation (taqiya), which is mainly understood in relation to security but in fact goes far beyond that. Dissimulation is not restricted to the Druze; it is prevalent in many religions. "Dissimulation is my religion and the religion of my forefathers," Ja'far al-Sadiq declared, "and whoever does not practice dissimulation has no religion."[49]

"Tawhid is the world of secrets," declares a contemporary Druze scholar, "and each and every Muwahhid is a secret in his [or her] own right. Safeguarding of secrets is a necessary requirement in the behavior of the Muwahhidun, over and above it being a general rule in Sufi traditions. Thus, safeguarding the secrecy [of the faith] is not only for reasons of safety [through dissimulation]. It is a feature of their behavior, and a fundamental requirement in their faith."[50]

Dissimulation is an issue in modern life, with the explosion of information technology and the demands of the modern mind for greater disclosure and wider dissemination of ideas, thoughts, and philosophies, in all aspects of life. How will the traditional practice of dissimulation, intended to protect the sanctity of the message from the undeserving or the unprepared, stand up to modern realities that respect no boundaries and recognize no taboos? Will the Druze community accept an open-ended system, removing all restrictions and constraints without seriously damaging the core or lowering the bar to the least common denominator? Such questions are not merely an exercise in rhetorical or theoretical speculation; they are central to the dilemma that the Druze communities face in the modern era, and especially in the West (the United States).

We may add that admonitions concerning dissimulation are not restricted to Tawhid and to its Druze constituency. A wide spectrum of philosophies and faiths have warned against indiscriminate popularization of their doctrines for fear of the misinterpretation that is likely to occur in the absence of proper initiation and orientation. Approximately one hundred years after the disclosure of Tawhid in the era of al-Hakim, Maimonides, the great Jewish physician and theologian, issued similar cautionary statements: "And as all of them [referring to common people] are incapable of comprehending the true sense of the words, tradition was considered sufficient to convey the truths that were to be established. . . . We must, therefore, begin with teaching these subjects according to the capacity of the pupil [to assimilate], on two conditions, first that he be wise, and second that he be intelligent."[51]

In his exhaustive study of *taqiya* in Islam, Makarem points out that *taqiya* has been in practice in virtually all Muslim sects and schools of thought from the days of the Prophet to modern times. 'Ali Zayn al-'Abidin, the son of Husayn, the grandson of Imam 'Ali and the great-grandson of the Prophet, through whom the imamate of the Shi'a was preserved and passed on, was also an accomplished poet. His adherence to the practice of *taqiya* is illustrated in the following lines:

> I will safeguard the jewels of my knowledge
> Which when seen by the ignorant would lead to upheavals
> And in this I am following the precedent and instructions
> Of al-Hasan, al-Husayn, and 'Ali.
> For if I were to divulge the essence of knowledge
> I would be accused of apostasy
> And that would facilitate my condemnation
> At the hands of some of the devout Muslims.[52]

While it is true that complicated concepts may be misunderstood and misinterpreted without proper initiation and diligence, it is equally true that the journey cannot be postponed until preparations are fully completed. Therefore religious concepts, however complicated they may be, should not be withheld and protected in a manner that prevents the process of initiation from taking place. Otherwise, the linkage between generations and groups will be interrupted or seriously impaired, as is the case with the *'uqqal-juhhal* divide among the Druze. Moreover, the whole question of *taqiya* and its overall contribution to protection of any doctrine remains controversial, particularly in modern times when information reigns supreme.

In the Druze vision, the road to Tawhid is cut with the theosophical tenets of the faith and paved with the concrete impact of these tenets in everyday life, with the bare minimum of rituals and fanfare. Behavior, under these conditions, becomes connected to and a reflection of the basic philosophy of the faith. While this is true for religion in general, in the case of the Druze it is more remarkable since the majority of the Druze who have not been initiated into the tenets of Tawhid still cling dearly to the behavioral profile. Be that as it may, the fact remains that the prerequisites for delving into Tawhid contain stringent conditions that are imposed by tradition and that in turn are based on considerations that emanate from the basic tenets of Tawhid.

Ideas come alive when they find expression in tangible modes of behavior. Ideas likewise grow and mature with the duration and depth of the physical experience. Experience bereft of ideas (and ideals) is chaotic and haphazard and may be counterproductive in terms of human development. Alternatively, ideas at the purely speculative level do not impact behavior and become largely irrelevant to human spiritual and physical advancement. The question of the starting point remains at the center of a crucial debate between the materialistic vision of life (and creation) and the spiritual point of onset. Religions, particularly the revealed religions of monotheism, teach of creation by a supreme power (God). The Druze concept of Tawhid, being strictly monotheistic, is no exception. However, the supreme power in the Druze interpretation is the almighty and indescribable God from whose grace the universal mind emanated as the first and most important creation. From this first cosmic principle the universal soul emanated, followed by the word, the precedent, and the follower. The universe eventually emerged from the follower, the fifth and final cosmic principle.

It is interesting to hear nowadays of the concept of intelligent design, proposed by some religious circles as a counterpart to the theory of evolution. While the theory of evolution is based on scientific data subject to verification by objective methods, the proposal of intelligent design is based on religious belief as an article of faith. The two approaches therefore cannot be compared, for obvious reasons. However, the Druze concept of Tawhid endorses evolution in the spiritual sphere and, by implication, in the physical sphere as well. Tawhid also supports scientific thinking by glorifying the mind as the first and most important of God's creation. Intelligent design in Tawhid can, therefore, be considered a function of the universal mind both conceptually in the realm of ideals and physically at the level of individual human beings, since the human mind is the seat of intelligence. The supremacy of the mind makes it the cornerstone and the focal point of life and existence. As such it represents the macrosystem that sets the standard for human behavior and religiosity but does not thwart development or impose predestination. In the microworld of the individual human being, freedom of choice and accountability are the rule and the prerogative of the individual, albeit within the grand scheme of the universal mind.

Tawhid, in the Druze vision, represents an overarching principle that enables the seeker to strive for the truth in a perpetual quest along the entirety of existence. "Tawhid [in our Lord], exalted be his essence, is the primary point of departure, and the culmination of all religions."[53] "And the first boundary of exaltation *(tajrid)* is to recognize the difference between learning and knowledge. For in the knowledge of exaltation of Tawhid, guidance and support are achieved. For it is through Tawhid that everything is defined and not the reverse."[54]

Belief in Tawhid then is a commitment that the seeker must profess in private and in public to be initiated into the community of the faithful. During the time when the call was openly pursued, it was the *da'i* who made sure that the prerequisites were met before initiating the seeker into the faith. Beyond that, it was and is an act of personal volition, not subject to any formal hierarchical process or organized authority. Therefore, the seeker is essentially autonomous in his or her desire and motivation to seek and then embark on the path to Tawhid.

Submission to God's Will in Private and in Public

Submission to God's will is one of the cornerstones of Islam. In fact, one of the many shades of meaning of the word *islam* includes the intent and the act of submitting one's entire being to God and the unconditional acceptance of God's will. The name of God is incorporated into virtually all aspects of Muslim life and daily activities. "In the name of God the compassionate, the merciful" is uttered by the Muslim prior to undertaking any task or embarking on any venture. Numerous phrases, such as "by the will of God," or "by the command of God," or "no objections to God's will," depict the extent of submission to God in the mind of the Muslim. Numerous verses in the Qur'an serve to place the idea of submission at the core of the Islamic message. *Islam* in Arabic also means peace *(salam)*, indicating that peace of mind is to be achieved by the act of submission to God. Moreover, the other Abrahamic monotheistic or unitarian faiths, Judaism and Christianity, involve similar declarations in one form or another that stress the importance of submission to God. However, submission to God's will carries several implications that can be interpreted in different ways and that serve to distinguish one school of theosophy from another.

In Christianity, the concept of submission acquires a specific connotation, due to the centrality of Jesus Christ in the process of salvation and resurrection. Submission to God in this context is achieved through God's one and only begotten Son, whose suffering and death on the cross, followed by resurrection, took place for the salvation of humanity, and indeed the universe. Thus if a person undertakes the pilgrimage on the right path and believes in Jesus Christ as the Savior, he or she will surely be rewarded with redemption from the sins that were inherited at birth or that may have been committed during a person's lifetime. Salvation of each and every one who accepts Jesus Christ as the Son of God and as the Savior is assured through the suffering, death, and resurrection of Christ. Once that commitment is made the person will enter into a state of everlasting bliss. Christians are expected to lead a moral life with love and charity as its core, in accordance with the commandments. Beyond that, Christianity today is not as involved in regulatory measures or legislative dictates as Islam was historically and continues to be in modern times. The separation of church and state that now exists in most Western societies (after substantial sacrifice and suffering) has not yet taken place in the world of Islam. Submission to God's will in traditional Islam includes acceptance of the legislative dictates in the Qur'an. These dictates can be interpreted literally, as is the case in conservative circles, or esoterically, as is the case of the Druze.

In Judaism the process is somewhat more complicated, as the belief in one and only one God took time (centuries) to become entrenched. Even then the nature of this one God also evolved from autocracy and power to compassion and justice. All through, however, the demand for strict allegiance to God's commands, adherence to his laws, and acceptance of his will was and continues to be at the center of religion. Rules and regulation governing all aspects of life are supposed to be followed by the believers as a precondition and as a proof of loyalty and submission. More liberal trends that relaxed the firm grip of orthodoxy have found their way into many segments of the Jewish faith, especially the Reform movement. However, Judaism remains a religion based on the sanctity of the law, by which God's will remains forever supreme.

Mystics in all faiths have cultivated a special relationship to God that in most instances involves total and unconditional submission. To most of the Sufis, for example, submission to God's will is part and parcel of a process of transcendence and ecstasy, the climax of which is the total disintegration *(fana')* of the one in the One. The only reality in existence is consummated in this type of union. Accordingly, the behavior of Sufis is patterned along the lines that keep them on the road to this ultimate target. Whatever happens then becomes an integral part of the pilgrimage to that coveted goal and is cheerfully accepted with no contest or complaint. Thus submission involves total surrender that places the seeker along the path to the holy union. Since the only reality is that which exists through and is reflected in the union, everything else becomes a transitory illusion. Thus the journey of the mystic involves the dissolution of the ego and elimination of the physical opacities that impede the process of spiritual illumination. It is, in the words of Corbin, "the absorption of the visible and invisible, the physical and the spiritual, into a unio mystica in which the Beloved becomes a mirror reflecting the secret face of the mystic lover, while the lover, purified of the opacity of the ego, becomes in turn a mirror of the attributes and actions of the Beloved."[55]

The Druze share with the rest of Muslims belief in God's transcendence and in total and unconditional submission to God's will. They also share with the mystics the joy and ecstasy of God's immanence in the heart and soul of the believer. Such immanence is realized in a manner that is somewhat analogous to God's theophany *(tajalli)* whereby the individual can achieve as close a position as possible to the deity. Thus, submission *(taslim)* to and cheerful acceptance *(ridha)* of

God's will are carried further to include an emphasis on reward, such that this reward does not have to be deferred until the day of judgment. Rather, the reward is realized in everyday life. Basking in God's bliss the believers can literally be in heaven while on this earth. After all, faith is validated when put to the test, and acceptance of and submission to God's will is considered to be the ultimate in the quest for human knowledge:

> Dear brethren, accept and submit to [God's will], in good times and bad; [for] that is what you have committed yourselves to do; object not to what comes your way whether it be good or bad, helpful or harmful, [for] this will reduce your anguish and dispel your fears. The only difference between your [world] and that of the ignorant is acceptance and submission [to God's will]; and acceptance and submission are the penultimate in knowledge and wisdom *(al-ridha wa al-taslim nihayat al-ʿilm wa al-taʿalim)*.[56]

Does submission and acceptance mean that man's fate is already predestined and predetermined in God's scheme and that this fate is hermetically sealed with no possibility for alteration? If so, how can the individual be held accountable for actions and events that were already predetermined by God and are, by definition, irrevocable? In this case no human being can alter what has been decreed by God Almighty. Where is the divine justice in predestination, which is by definition unalterable? Yet it is axiomatic that God is just and that humans will be judged according to their own actions and not according to an obligatory situation in which they have no say. Justice dictates that if individuals are to be held accountable, it will only be when they are given the opportunity for the exercise of free choice and when they are in possession of full physical and mental faculties. Otherwise, justice is no more than a sham, and the concept of accountability loses validity.

And yet, if God is all-knowing at all times and of all things, then God must know the fate of each and every human being and all aspects of the human's existence, past, present, and future. Can man then alter what is already in the conscience of God, without the predestination for such alteration? If the answer to the above question is in the affirmative, then God's omnipotence comes into question, and that would be a blasphemous impossibility. On the other hand, if the answer is in the negative, then such irrevocable predestination stands in the way of God's justice, and that would constitute an equally blasphemous stand. The paradox may seem as insolvable as the paradox of dealing with the inability to know God while being obliged to know that he exists. Philosophers, scholars, and theologians have struggled with this problem across history and continue to do so in modern times. Predestination versus free choice has been at the center of different schools of Islamic thought such as the Mu'tazilites and the Brothers of Purity.

Tawhid, in the vision of the Druze, is built on the premise of free choice and consequent accountability. In the opinion of the luminaries of Tawhid there is no conflict between God's omnipotence and the imperative of free choice. According to Baha' al-Din, "And if someone says that when God wills it, no one can disobey or renege on his command, so therefore if anyone should disobey that would imply a deficiency in God's omnipotence—we can respond to that by declaring that [such logic] misses the point altogether, since if God's will [in relation to free choice] was obligatory, then no one would be able to disobey or renege and there would be no value for accountability, religions would lose their relevance, and humanity would go astray."[57] The same message is even more strongly articulated by Baha' al-Din in another epistle: "Know that God's command, elevated be his station and exalted be his name, [is] free choice, and his admonition is counsel and warning."[58]

Free choice, guidance, and compassion are key items in God's grace to humanity, but along with them come warnings of pitfalls and negative influences. Acceptance and submission under these conditions means making the right choice and accepting the consequences, whatever they may be. Therefore submission to and acceptance of God's will with cheerfulness and grace is part and parcel of the concept of Tawhid and the place of man in the grand scheme of creation: "And develop [the command of] acceptance and submission into an emblem for the community [of the faithful] and an avenue to the grace of God . . . and abide by the purest of principles . . . with clean hearts and loving nature."[59]

The individual events become simply a part of a cosmic order emanating from and leading to the Creator. The Creator encompasses the totality of existence but is not subject to its confines. It is up to each individual to function, to grow, and to choose, in full freedom, the path that best fulfills his or her dreams and aspirations, within the parameters of the cosmic order. In this framework the universal system is an ordained emanation from the Creator through the universal mind, and individual management is the responsibility of the individual. Inasmuch as individuals can bring their souls and hearts into alignment with the cosmic order, and bring that commitment into fruition in daily behavior, they will be rewarded accordingly. "Spirituality is a private matter, penetrating the relationship between the individual and the cosmos," declares Laszlo. "Its temple is the mind of the individual, and its altar is the state of consciousness that comes about through deep meditation and prayer."[60] Those who embrace the holistic vision of life and creation and assume the responsibility associated with the privilege of free choice will be rewarded with the fruits of acceptance and submission. In the words of Lama Govinda: "To the enlightened man . . . whose consciousness embraces the Universe, to him the universe becomes his body, while his physical body becomes a manifestation of the Universal Mind, his inner vision an expression of the highest reality, and his speech an expression of eternal truth and mantric power."[61] Alignment with the ordained celestial order allows the individual to tap into the limitless reservoir of psychic energy that pervades the universe and transcend the vicissitudes in the daily life of physical existence. This after all is what genuine faith is about, not in a narrow parochial sense but in an encompassing cosmic order.

How can humankind, then, object to, or revolt against, acceptance of and submission to the laws that govern the entirety of existence, and still remain a major component (and perhaps the purpose) of existence? Humanity's unique endowment is the ability to reflect and the drive to assimilate, project, and grow. Hence the capacity and the imperative to seek the truth and strive for its attainment is vouchsafed to every individual. And inasmuch as striving is a command, to choose is an option. The result must then be accepted as God's will. Thus acceptance can be considered within the framework of post facto but only when the event in question has already taken place. The individual making the choice has no prior knowledge of the end result, since the result will depend on the choice itself and the manner of implementation. This of course does not include events in which the individual had no choice, such as accidents of nature or the death of a child. There is no human explanation for such events, which in the eyes of believers remain within the mysterious domain of God's will. For better or for worse we should not object to the verdict, but submit willingly and cheerfully.

In a more mundane sense, acceptance of what falls our way in terms of trials and tribulations in daily life makes it easier to deal with those trials and tribulations than if we remain at the stage of denial and rejection. Whether it is an incurable disease, an unavoidable natural disaster, or a disappointing result of an endeavor, the end result is the same. Acceptance of reality is the first and perhaps the most important attitude that can help in resolution. Again this does not mean that one should resort to dependence to escape responsibility; on the contrary, it represents the essence of responsible behavior. Acceptance and submission, in the Druze concept of Tawhid, is in a way analogous to the first noble truth in the Buddhist tradition that ascribes human suffering to the resistance of the flow of life and adherence to a fixed and egotistical view of life. Suffering can be ended by choosing the path of transcendence and liberation.

Although this interpretation does not completely settle the issue of predetermination versus free choice, it does serve as a frame of reference for the individual and the community of believers. It basically highlights the need for active diligence and true jihad in the path of righteousness and not mere reliance on passive grace and waiting for God's will to carry the day. The believers are exhorted to seek and to express what they are seeking in daily behavior: "Faith is declaration by tongue, belief in the heart, and action in accordance with the commandments," declares Ja'far al-Sadiq.[62] Although the emphasis is on spiritual growth and purity of the soul rather than on material possessions, concrete expression of such emphasis is manifested in the actions of daily life.

There is a risk of misunderstanding the concept of acceptance and submission when it is thought to lead to passivity and fatalism. Such interpretation is in fact a distortion reflecting the psychological attitudes of those who have veered from the true meaning of the command. Passivity and fatalism are symptoms of decline and do not reflect the core values of God's command for acceptance of his rule and submission to his will. "Seek learning even if that be in China" is a famous hadith attributed to the Prophet. The Islamic civilization flourished because Islam commanded believers to strive and struggle and to learn and advance: "And say, 'O my Lord, increase me in knowledge'" (Qur'an 20:114).

All aspects of learning, and all of life for that matter, must be undertaken within the framework of submission to God and acceptance of his will. "By devotion to one's own particular duty, everyone can attain perfection. By performing his own work," declares Sri Krishna, "one worships the Creator who dwells in every creature. Such worship brings that person to fulfillment."[63]

We hear Isma'il ibn Muhammad al-Tamimi (representing the second luminary in the era of al-Hakim) echoing a similar theme: "Be diligent in seeking knowledge and in keeping company with those who are wise and learned. . . . Do not slumber after awakening and be not delinquent after attaining such progress. . . . Pluck the fruits of wisdom from the trees of heavenly knowledge and quench your thirst from the purity of its waters."[64]

Several proverbs, sayings, and supplications in the Tawhid tradition illustrate the balance between actively seeking and striving for spiritual growth and fulfillment and accepting God's command and submission to his will. One example is that of a symbolic sermon whereby the Almighty is portrayed as one who ushers humans into a dialogue of conditional promise and fulfillment: "My child, it is for you to seek and for me to grant. . . . It is for you to request and for me to accept. . . . It is for you to worship and for me to bless. . . . It is for you to submit and for me to pardon." There is no reward without effort and there is no effort without belief, and there is no belief without commitment to the truth. Thus, far from being a simple and passive resignation, acceptance and submission represent an active process of seeking, self-monitoring, and diligence in fulfillment of God's commands and conformity with his will. Some words of guidance by the late Druze shaykh al-ʿAql Muhammad abu Shaqra depict the interdependence of learning *(maʿrifa)* and acceptance of God's will in spiritual progress along the path of Tawhid: "Know ye who is seeking the noblest of the paths that God, exalted be his name, made it the duty of his creatures [human beings] to attest that religion in the eyes of God is submission *[islam]*, and submission depicts acceptance of God's will as the gateway to belief *(iman)*, and that belief is the gateway to Tawhid. Worship God, exalted be his name beyond description and definition."[65]

7 *Challenge and Opportunity*

IN THE PRECEDING CHAPTERS I have placed the Tawhid faith in a historical and doctrinal context. I myself was introduced to this religious path as an individual born and raised in a traditional Druze home in Lebanon. As a child I was exposed to the Druze faith through the traditional practices of members of my immediate and extended family and of the tightly knit Druze community. These practices and traditions dealt more with behavioral regulations and societal norms than with actual religious education. Valuable as these traditions and social values were and are, they clearly could not, on their own, sustain a religious faith or fulfill the imperative for spirituality latent in all human beings. My perception has also been influenced by the fact that I moved from the East, largely tethered to the strong leash of dogma, to the West, where nothing is deemed unsuitable for the probing mind and everything is subject to a relentless quest for knowledge.

Driven by a lack of religious education and my innate desire for genuine spiritual growth, I became increasingly motivated to learn the basic principles of the path into which I was born but in which, like most of my coreligionists, I was never schooled. Thus I tried as best as I could to ask the proper questions and search for answers that addressed as much as possible my spiritual thirst and intellectual needs. Living in both worlds, the East and the West, added further impetus to attempt to settle the issues and questions that we confront in our daily lives. I have presented my understanding of the faith mostly for the sake of the generations who are born and raised in the West, specifically in Anglo-America. It is safe to assume that the vast majority of people living in the West, particularly in the United States, are largely ignorant of the depth and complexity of Eastern cultures. The ignorance is particularly acute in the case of Islam, where the misunderstanding with the West is a two-way street. Violent events in recent times have made it painfully obvious to all concerned that this trend must be reversed through education, dialogue, and the peaceful resolution of substantive issues, since the stakes are too high for the alternative of confrontation.

As a distant offshoot of Islam, the Druze path to Tawhid has been ignored, neglected, and misunderstood, a situation to which the Druze have contributed by closure and indifference. Lulled by the security of self-righteousness, the Druze have not been proactive in promoting understanding of their faith even among members of their own community.

For the younger generations who are born or grow up in the West, the pull of tradition quickly weakens within the American melting pot, where the commonality in daily life with members from multireligious traditions is far stronger than that of imported old-country traditions. The spiritual needs of the Druze youth are pressing because they do not have the chance to experience the traditions firsthand and they do not have the time, or for that matter, the enticement, to delve on their own into the arcane ways of the religion of their parents. Moreover, the parents who chose to migrate to the West are generally derived from the *juhhal* segment of the Druze community and therefore do not possess sufficient knowledge of the complexity of the Tawhid faith to teach their children. And there are no institutions or organizations to fill the vacuum or to respond to the needs of those who are born or raised in the West. The language factor poses another impediment; the older generation, speaking mainly Arabic, have little or no facility in the English tongue of their progeny. The result is that the Druze youth in America live in a state of spiritual vacuum and slow erosion of the traditions of their faith, mostly by default and not by enlightened choice. A quotation from one of the responders to a questionnaire in the seminal work on the Druze in America, published recently by Druze social anthropologist Intisar Azzam, will illustrate the point: "Who is teaching our children about the Druze? Certainly not us [parents]. Even if we attempt to undertake this difficult task it would be a classic case of the blind leading the blind. Our intentions may be good but our ignorance stands in the way. So we stumble along . . . as our children slip further and further away from us, until they become totally integrated into other cultures and lose what little knowledge they may have acquired."[1]

When we look at the fundamental principles of Tawhid, we recognize major components of original and progressive thinking that should have enabled the faith to thrive and grow rather than remain restricted and confined to a handful of diehards in the Middle Eastern hinterland. The fact is, however, that the faith remains almost as it was left a thousand years ago, in a state of suspended animation. Why, we may ask, did the Tawhid path of the Druze fail to thrive and grow in accordance with the universality of its basic tenets? Why was it not possible for the Druze followers of Tawhid to utilize the substantial assets encoded in the basic principles and commands of their faith and mold them into a progressive and successful enterprise? These questions have to be addressed if the Druze are to consider any serious attempt at reform and potential rejuvenation.

In my opinion, the Tawhid faith, as expressed in the Druze tradition, did not really have a chance to consolidate its hold and develop its basic tenets to a sufficient level before it was crippled by the disappearance of its main figure, al-Hakim, and the disruption of its infrastructure. Other factors include premature disclosure to the general public, as alluded to in some of the epistles that paradoxically defend the act and the timing of disclosure, as well as unresolved and profound disagreements and conflicts among the senior leadership of the faith, whose revolutionary and bold concepts were expected to create a backlash among the majority of Muslims both Shi'a and Sunni in the Fatimid realm. The resulting backlash and persecution were a vital setback that stunted the movement at a critical juncture in its life. In essence, it was not able to take off from its launching pad with enough vigor to break into the open and claim its proper place among religious approaches, particularly within the various schools of Islamic thought. Yet it managed to survive through the tenacity and dedication of the believers, protected by a combination of courage and circumspection and a sense of solidarity that discouraged outsiders from tampering with the Druze. But it survived in the raw, virtually untouched, with no edited versions and no amended texts. In addition there was considerable loss of material, neglect of the remaining documents, distortion and sabotage by the renegades, and absence of critical assessment of the contents of the surviving epistles. The result is a confused state of a jigsaw puzzle with several sections missing, errors in transcription, and the possible introduction of material that does not fit into the main themes of the faith. When we add to this state the use of symbols and coded messages in the epistles, the real meaning of which was the prerogative of the innermost circle of believers and those who were steeped in the complexity of the Isma'ili *da'wa*, we can appreciate the difficulties in deciphering what we have inherited.

The Tawhid that the Druze inherited is like a big orchard that has been left fallow for a long time. One has to look for the fruit trees among an outgrowth of weeds and thistles to extract what is useful and discard the contaminants. Otherwise, we would easily get sidetracked into blind alleys and misleading paths, and we would lose the core in the jumble of confusion and distortion. Moreover, the surviving epistles, which were codified into six books known as the Books of Wisdom, were written by human beings and do not possess the same immunity as the Qur'an. The latter is considered by the faithful to be the word of God transmitted through the angel Gabriel to the Prophet, who merely recited the message. As such the eternal validity of the Qur'an is never in question. The epistles in the Books of Wisdom, on the other hand, consist of an elaborate theosophical venture based on the interpretation *(ta'wil)* and clarification of God's message, primarily in the Qur'an but also in the revealed (Abrahamic) religions. As such, the contents of the epistles should invite discussion and discourse and encourage continuous development and refinement. Yet this did not happen. On the contrary, a doctrine that challenged dogma became itself a victim of dogma.

The reasons for this change lie in an understanding of the basic principles of Tawhid and the historical backdrop of the era of public disclosure. Merciless persecution after al-Hakim's disappearance and the retirement of the chief architects from public view immediately put brakes on elaboration of the principles of the faith or public discussion and exchange of views. An attendant problem, caused, the Druze believe, by renegades such as al-Darazi, who sought to create disruption, is the inclusion of material in several epistles that does not fit with the theosophical foundations of the faith. The precarious situation of the emerging and fragile community did not lend itself to the probing and research that would have dealt with blatantly false passages. A desire for self-preservation took precedence over the more fruitful process of crystallization of profound and potentially revolutionary thinking and philosophy. Safety first meant shelving any major effort to address nagging questions or rectify inconsistencies and contradictions in different epistles or even in the same epistle. Considerations for self-preservation that were justifiable in the past have haunted the community throughout its history into the present time. The natural consequence of deferred reform has been the entrenchment of errors and the increasing difficulty of correction with the passage of time. Reform will come only at a price, and deferment will merely increase the price.

In order to discuss the challenges that the Druze communities face in any attempt at reform or modernization, several major items must be considered as a prelude to resolution. The discussion that follows represents an individual effort on my part and may not be shared with or endorsed by some members of the community. Religion has never been a subject that invites unanimity of opinion or of approach, and Tawhid is no exception. This, however, does not alter the fact that an open and candid discussion should be undertaken. Nor does it reduce the compelling need for such an imperative. What follows is a list of some of the major items that need to be addressed by the community, with the anticipation that a candid discussion could lead to a veritable and viable consensus:

1. The precise status of al-Hakim;

2. The relation of the Druze interpretation of Tawhid to the monotheistic religions, specifically to the world of Islam; and

3. The question of closure of the Druze call *(da'wa)* to Tawhid and the potential for admission of individuals not born into the Druze faith.

As corollaries to the items listed above, other concerns arise. What is the status of children from mixed marriages? What are the prospects for development of genuine congregations in the West (North America), with governing bodies, rites, rituals, and modes of worship? How would such a step (creation of an institutional framework for the Druze community) be consistent with the simple, nonhierarchical, individualistic, and highly personal approach to religiosity that has been the hallmark of the Druze path in Tawhid? In addition, how would addressing these and other questions in the West resonate with the needs and priorities of the Druze communities elsewhere, particularly in the East?

These items obviously do not constitute an exhaustive list, nor can they be dealt with extensively in this publication. What we can do, however, is touch upon these and other concerns in a manner that heightens awareness and encourages research. Doing so should open the way for members of the community to evaluate the current situation and embrace the imperative of reform. It is up to the Druze communities in the West to lead the way in this regard in view of the climate of free speech and objectivity that Western societies enjoy and offer.

Al-Hakim bi Amr Allah and al-Hakim bi Amrihi

The sixth Fatimid caliph, al-Hakim bi Amr Allah, plays a central role in the Druze vision of Tawhid. One major issue regarding al-Hakim causes considerable confusion and uncertainty among members of the Druze community. The issue concerns God's revelation of the *nasut (tajalli)* in the station *(maqam)* of al-Hakim, and how that became confused with claims to divinity of the person of al-Hakim. It seems that this issue was in a state of flux at the time of the call, with some extremists proclaiming the divinity of al-Hakim while others refuted the claim. We know that al-Hakim himself never made such a claim nor did he condone it. He was the caliph of Islam and the imam of the faithful, and his demeanor was that of a Sufi who rejected the trappings of power and the pomp of the caliphate. He was an idealist and a scholar, and his style of governing was hands on. He was also a populist and a reformer who implemented measures viewed as radical by members of the establishment, many of whom lost their lives or possessions. Some members of that class then wrote their own biased version of history.[2]

It is extremely unlikely that al-Hakim would have encouraged or tolerated the claim of his divinity made by extremists or zealots *(ghulat)*. In fact we are told that al-Hakim invited one of the main authorities on the Isma'ili doctrine, the venerated *da'i* Hamid al-Din al-Kirmani, to Cairo to deal with the confusion and restore balance and order into the Tawhid *da'wa*. After all, zealots have ascribed varying degrees of divine status to Ali and his descendents from time to time throughout Islamic history, but Ali's descendents have always refuted such claims. These exaggerations were fueled by the degree of persecution of 'Ali's progeny at the hands of the ruling Umayyad and Abbasid dynasties.

Al-Kirmani applied himself with the vigor and insight of a scholar and philosopher who was committed to the Isma'ili faith and to the imam al-Hakim as the head and the leader of the faithful. As a *da'i* himself, al-Kirmani's loyalty could never have been in question. He stressed that al-Hakim had a special status as an imam and caliph and, in addition, was an unusual person whose messianic appearance was predicted from previous prophesies. A few lines of poetry by al-Kirmani illustrate his adulation of and devotion to al-Hakim:

> He appeared in human form and yet
> He was exalted beyond flesh and blood
> And soon about him miracles would emerge
> And reveal of him what was unmanifest
> And through him justice would fill the world
> As it was before full of oppression
> And soon the burden will be lifted
> And through his light
> Religion will reach completion
> And God's promise fulfilled.[3]

Despite the fervor and adulation that exuded from al-Kirmani's writings in support of al-Hakim and the *da'wa* to Tawhid in al-Hakim's name, there was no ambiguity about al-Kirmani's refutation of any notion that attributed divinity to al-Hakim. Thus al-Kirmani (with the approval of al-Hakim) expressed clear and forceful condemnation of the position of the *ghulat* with respect to any claim to the divinity of al-Hakim. In addition al-Kirmani refuted another claim by the *ghulat* that one could seek the inner meaning of the holy message without adhering to the outer meaning *(zahir)* and the overt practices of Islam. Al-Kirmani shared with the *ghulat* some aspects of their revolutionary thinking, since they were all schooled in the same Isma'ili doctrine. Concepts of creation, the impossibility for man to ever know God, and God's creation *(ibda')* of the first cosmic principle were some of the common grounds of agreement. On the other hand, the divinity of al-Hakim (or anyone else, for that matter) was totally out of the question.

We have no information on how al-Kirmani viewed the concept that God reveals aspects of his being *(tajalli)* in the human medium *(nasut)*, as proposed by the luminaries of Tawhid. Nor do we have any significant knowledge of any interaction between al-Kirmani and Hamza ibn 'Ali, the chief architect of the Druze vision of Tawhid. This is surprising, considering the preeminence that Hamza achieved among the inner circle of the call to Tawhid on behalf of al-Hakim. The struggle among the various groups and personalities that were competing to curry favor with al-Hakim and that would occasionally erupt into violent expression must have troubled and distressed al-Kirmani.

The first extremist to proclaim the divinity of al-Hakim was a zealot *(da'i)* by the name of Abu Haidara al-Farghani, known as al-Akhram (see chapter 4). Al-Akhram was probably the most radical in professing the divinity of al-Hakim. His attempt to beat the others to the open declaration of the call cost him his life. Al-Akhram was assassinated in 1017 C.E. (A.H. 408), the very year the Tawhid call was made public. Al-Akhram's movement was presumably one of the reasons al-Kirmani was summoned to Cairo. Hamza emerged as the principal architect of the faith. But he had to deal with another powerful renegade and competitor and (in the eyes of the Druze) an apostate and traitor by the name of Muhammad ibn Isma'il (Neshtegin al-Darazi). Al-Darazi was also a zealot. He tried to outmaneuver Hamza by being excessively ingratiating to al-Hakim. The act backfired and Hamza won the power struggle. Al-Darazi not only tried to usurp Hamza's position in the movement but also, reportedly, promoted debauchery, prostitution, incest, and other acts of immorality that led to his execution. It is ironic that the Druze community has been mistakenly associated with the aberrant behavior of what the Druze consider a renegade and apostate who defiled their faith and besmirched their name.

The early and hasty disclosure of the call to Tawhid did not allow Hamza and his team enough time or opportunity to sufficiently elaborate the complex system of God-man interaction and the concept of divinity in the Druze epistles. The traumatic affair of al-Akhram and al-Darazi must have been one of the main reasons for the first suspension of the call for one entire year in 1018 C.E. (A.H. 409).

The difficulties in streamlining the *da'wa* were not easy to overcome in an atmosphere charged with such powerful crosswinds of change and rivalry. It was also, paradoxically, an atmosphere that was hospitable to scholars and thinkers of all colors and stripes and encouraging of religious and philosophical discourse. It comes as no surprise that such an atmosphere would facilitate stretching of the boundaries between myth and reality, generating tension almost to the breaking point.

Al-Kirmani left Cairo at or around the time the call to Tawhid was made public, with no indication of the degree to which he was successful in restoring uniformity or bringing a measure of unanimity to the confused and turbulent ranks of the followers. He died shortly after leaving Cairo.

The Druze epistles are explicit in stressing the oneness of God and the utter impossibility for humans to ever comprehend God's nature or being. God in the absolute (Lahut) is exalted above and beyond any description, characterization, or association *(munazzaha'n jami al-sifat)*. No individual and no image of any kind or substance could be confused with the exalted status of the Creator. Thus neither al-Hakim, nor anyone else in the cycles before or after the appearance of al-Hakim, could ever be defined as God.

Nevertheless, God's justice is contingent upon awareness of God's presence by mandated necessity and not by factual recognition. For this to happen, the Druze epistles argue, God's theophany becomes a most effective way to achieve that goal. Since man is the most worthy prize of God's revelations, it stands to reason that *tajalli* in the image of the *nasut* would be in the human medium. In the last call to Tawhid, according to the Druze epistles, the person of al-Hakim was the station *(maqam)* that reflected the image of God's *nasut* for man to witness and comprehend. In reality each and every human being, to the extent that spiritual development allows, witnesses God's presence directly as a reflection of his or her own inner image, in the image of the *nasut*. The Books of Wisdom also refer to al-Mu'izz and al-Hakim as one and the same *(wa kulluhum wahid)*, an obviously allegorical reference to the high level of spirituality and holiness that the Fatimid caliphs reached in the eyes of their followers. The distinction between God's essence, the unknown and unknowable (Lahut), on the one hand, and the station for God's theophany in the act of *tajalli* in the human image *(nasut)*, on the other hand, was not clearly recognized by some of the fanatics. Such confusion may have led some *ghulat* to proclaim that al-Hakim was in fact God.

Another source of potential error is linguistic in nature and revolves around the meaning of the word *al-hakim*. As a title for the monarch of the realm, the appellation *al-hakim* refers to the ruler or the lord of the realm. That was the title by which the sixth Fatimid caliph and Isma'ili imam, Abu 'Ali al-Mansur bi Allah, was known. However, the same word *al-hakim* could also be used as an attribute of the Supreme Ruler and Lord of all, the Almighty God. The shades of semantic interpretation of the word *al-hakim* must have added to the confusion that surrounded and still surrounds the question of the divinity of the caliph al-Hakim, a confusion that the sixth Fatimid caliph and imam neither coveted nor endorsed. In fact, there are definite indications that this may have been one of many issues that distressed al-Hakim and caused him great concern.

Hints as to the displeasure of al-Hakim at the turn of events, presumably at the hands of disruptive and possibly extreme elements (who infiltrated the ranks of the faith including the upper echelon in the *da'wa* and introduced subversive and damaging concepts) are visible in many places in the Epistles of Wisdom. Al-Hakim was the caliph of Islam and the imam of the faithful, and trustee of God's message by virtue of his noble birth and direct lineage to the Prophet through the seed of 'Ali and Fatima. Whatever divine knowledge is vouchsafed in al-Hakim was based on the special gift from the Almighty. The gift was for al-Hakim, as it was for his predecessors, to interpret and expound on the inner message of the Qur'an, while upholding the sanctity of the word and the Pillars of Islam. Al-Hakim would never have condoned the blasphemy *(shirk)* of equating himself with God.

The call in the name of al-Hakim was an extension of the Isma'ili doctrine that had been in the making for several decades and was complemented by philosophical and mystical dimensions from the intellectual ferment in Cairo at the time. That al-Hakim encouraged and promoted the atmosphere of learning, and protected the freedom to discuss and explore whatever bold concepts would emerge from this intellectual laboratory, is well known. His aim was to direct and shepherd the quest for knowledge, not to censor or coerce. Eventually, a complex system of thought emerged through which the process of Tawhid, with its many facets, was articulated and defined. This concept, which went beyond any of its constituent components, did not enjoy the opportunity for elaboration, discussion, or development before it was interrupted with suspension and effective closure. The arrest led to a state of confusion at that time and remains with us today.

In modern times, the state of confusion can be seen among the Druze sources outside the Books of Wisdom, in the community at large, and among the intellectuals. Although there is no disagreement among Druze authors regarding the issue of the oneness of God, the unknown and unknowable Creator, exalted is his name beyond definition and comprehension, there is no clear definition of the precise status of al-Hakim. The spectrum of opinion ranges from those who believe that al-Hakim was no more and no less than the sixth Fatimid caliph and the imam of the Isma'ili sect at that time, to those who ascribe to him varying degrees and attributes of the Divine. While the assertion that there is no god but God is unequivocal and universal among the Druze community at large, the fine shades of language and nuances in interpretation leave enough room for a variety of opinions and assertions.

Some modern-day authors, such as Nabih al-Sa'di, find no ambiguity in the epistles concerning the identity of al-Hakim as an ordinary human being with an extraordinary yet not divine status. In a recent publication, *Tawhid in Ten Essays*, al-Sa'di states: "Since the individual human spirit is representative of the divine spirit in man, so is the case with al-Hakim bi Amr Allah, whose representation of the Divine is analogous to that of any other human being. And we find in that no claim of divinity of al-Hakim and no cause for blasphemy. . . . The concept in Tawhid thought of the presence of aspects of God's Lahut in the human *nasut* does not diminish the exaltation of God nor diminish from his essence."[4] Al-Sa'di finds no conflict between God's exalted state of transcendence and his immanence in each and every individual including al-Hakim as a station of God's theophany in human form. He cites many passages that depict congruency between the epistles in the Books of Wisdom, the Qur'an, and the Bible with respect to the sanctity of human spirit and the qualification of this spirit to be a recipient of manifestation of aspects of the Divine.

> We created you, then We shaped you,
> then We said to the angels: 'Bow yourselves
> to Adam'; so they bowed themselves,
> save Iblis." (Qur'an 7:11)

The angels were ordered to bow to Adam, the father of humanity, and they all did. We know the high position that is accorded to the angels in the Qur'an. After all it was an angel by the name of Gabriel (Jabra'il) who transmitted the word of God to the prophet Mohammad. To order the angels to bow (to be made subservient) to Adam puts man at a higher level than the angels. That should qualify man to receive and assimilate aspects of divinity and to get closer to God than even the angels can. Christianity elevated man to a still higher status by deifying the Son of man as the Son of God in the person of Jesus Christ. Extending that to the rest of humanity, the apostle Paul poses the question to the Corinthians: "Know ye not that ye are the temple of God, and that the spirit of God dwelled in you?" (1 Cor. 3:16).

Sami Makarem, a noted Druze Islamic scholar and authority on Tawhid, approaches the issue from a metaphysical angle. Makarem considers al-Hakim as a station whereby the spirit of God is reflected upon man and the spirit of man finds its own image in God: "The followers of Tawhid responded to the call through the station [al-hakim], each one acquiring the message of Tawhid according to the degree of purity of his soul, being suffused with the divine light which is reflected on the mirror of his own heart. The believer would in fact be witnessing himself, and in the purity and transcendence of the encounter with the station he unites with and becomes actualized in the One. . . . The believer at this stage, by witnessing his or her true self, would be witnessing God."[5] Al-Hakim, the human individual and imam, becomes analogous to a mirror through which the individual human being is transcended into a mystical union with the Divine. The mythical dimension of this mystical vision should not be taken out of context nor mistakenly construed to mean that al-Hakim is God, for God is exalted above and beyond the reach of any human definition or attribute.

The light that emanates from the candle gives us the ability to discriminate, through the sense of sight, but the light is not and cannot be equated with the candle itself. Reflection of the light through a mirror puts the reflected rays even farther away from the source of light. However, if it were not for the light, reflected or otherwise, we would never even have known that the candle exists, let alone that it is the source of light. Likewise, the phenomenon of the revelation or theophany of God in the *nasut* is not and cannot be considered to indicate that the human *nasut* is in any way equated with God.

From another contemporary Druze scholar, Anwar Abi-Khzam, we hear a message that stresses the distinction between *al-hakim* as an attribute of Almighty God and al-Hakim as the title of the sixth Fatimid caliph. In a somewhat expanded dissertation on the absoluteness of God and the theophany of aspects of the Creator in the human image, Abi-Khzam states that in the Tawhid doctrine, *nasut* is a reflection of the attributes, while Lahut is a representation of the essence of the Divine:

> Lahut is, then, an exalted state in Tawhid, whereby the concept of the Divine is stretched to the limit in negating human attributes or human knowledge of the Supreme. Yet this extreme and absolute negation of attributes cannot refer to negation of God but rather must refer to God's being. Thus awareness (by necessity) of the Lahut becomes contingent upon the knowledge of the *nasut*. . . .

Nasut is [therefore] the guide to the exalted state of the Lahut. . . . The confusion between the *nasut* in the image of the human being and the exalted state of the Divine led some researchers to the conclusion that al-Hakim is the *nasut* in whom the Lahut is reposed. Therefore, al-Hakim is [erroneously] identified as the God of believers in Tawhid.[6]

As for the repeated references to al-Hakim as a deity in many of the epistles, Abi-Khzam offers an explanation based on linguistic confusion, between the word *al-Hakim*, meaning lord or master, as an attribute of God, often followed by the word *bi-amrihi*, and *al-hakim* as the title of the sixth Fatimid caliph and imam, often followed by the words *bi amr Allah*. Al-Hakim bi Amrihi is God Almighty, Lord of all by his own will, while al-Hakim bi Amr Allah is governor by the will of God. The followers of Tawhid do not worship a human being but worship God. Without diminishing his importance as the caliph and imam, as well as a remarkable person in his own right, al-Hakim bi Amr Allah, according to Abi-Khzam, is not the God of Tawhid.

Abdallah Najjar, one of the earlier Druze authors, whose book on the Druze created a stir among the Druze religious establishment in Lebanon, came to the conclusion that al-Hakim himself never claimed divinity or directed others to do so: "We do not find any sign or hint that indicates any claim or pretension by al-Hakim to personal divine nature or attribute; nor do we know the extent or nature of his relationship with the architects and propagators of the nascent faith of unitarism [Tawhid]. All that al-Hikma [the Epistles of Wisdom] tells of his acts and activities falls within the sphere of his legitimate duties and responsibilities as an imam and caliph."[7] Najjar does not deny that aspects of the Divine were attributed to al-Hakim by Hamza, the chief architect of the Tawhid, but that was within the philosophical context of the *nasut*-Lahut concept. This concept cannot be interpreted to equate al-Hakim with Almighty God.

A book about the Druze by Amin Talih preceded that of Najjar by a few years. Dealing with historical aspects of the era of al-Hakim bi Amr Allah, it does not even mention anything related to the issue of divinity with respect to al-Hakim. However, Talih credits the reign of al-Hakim with supporting intellectual and philosophical pursuits and with the encouragement and spread of the call to Tawhid:

And during the caliphate of al-Hakim, the call was met with great success politically and religiously, thanks to the supportive efforts of al-Hakim himself. . . . The tenets of the [Tawhid] doctrine were disseminated through lectures, seminars, and dialogues as well as through epistles and decrees. These tenets were built upon philosophical principles of the Mu'tazilites and the Batinis as well as the teachings of Aristotle and Plutinos. That is because philosophy in the Fatimid era had been elevated to approach the level of the Qur'an and the Sunna of the Prophet, since philosophy was necessary for the understanding of the deeper meaning of the holy message.[8]

To the noted Druze jurist the issue of divinity with respect to al-Hakim does not even arise.

Another author, Najib Israwi, who lived in Brazil, expresses his opinion openly and candidly. Al-Hakim, Israwi says, was a great caliph of Islam and imam of the faithful and nothing more. In a broader context Israwi believes that the Druze are a branch of the Islamic tree and should not separate from the great trunk. With respect to al-Hakim Israwi writes:

> From what has been discussed so far in reference to the biography of Imam al-Hakim bi Amr Allah, we can conclude that he was a devout Muslim and a Muwahhid in word and deed . . . proud of his lineage, which links him to the Prophet (peace be upon him) and to Imam 'Ali (God's blessing on him). . . . This then is [the portrait of] the imam by the will of God [al-Hakim bi Amr Allah], the Fatimid caliph, who was a believer in Islam and a Muwahhid who was truthful and pious. He forbade his subjects from kissing his hands . . . and prevented them from greeting him by more than simple phrases, such as 'Peace be upon the Prince of the Faithful.' He also forbade his subjects from indulging in the excesses that some of the *ghulat* were known for.[9]

Israwi goes even further, dismissing the whole idea of the appearance of the Divine in the human *nasut* as illogical, since God cannot be equated with man. However, some measure of such revelations as the theophany of aspects of the Divine in human form may be permissible, but only insofar as these manifestations refer to God and are not equated with him.

More recently, Shaykh Mursil Nasr, justice of the Druze Court of Appeals in Lebanon, echoed the message of Israwi. The Druze as followers of and believers in Tawhid worship God and not any human form or image. Distortions and misinformation, according to the Druze jurist, were introduced by enemies of the Fatimids (particularly the Abbasids of Baghdad) with the purpose of sabotage: "But it was the fear of the Abbasids and other parties from the Fatimid state under the rule of the imam [and caliph] al-Hakim that caused them and their allies to level at al-Hakim all sorts of false and sinister accusations, with the sole purpose of undermining the Fatimid state. . . . And we cannot imagine how al-Hakim would claim divinity when he described himself [from the beginning] to the end of his days as the servant of God and the prince of the faithful." [10] Nasr cites poetry from the pen of al-Hakim himself that can best portray what this unique Fatimid caliph and imam was all about:

> I have come not to desire nor to fear
> Except my God and to him I am indebted.
> My great-grandfather is my prophet and my father my imam
> And my faith is loyalty and justice.

> *Asbahtu la akhsha wa la attaqi*
> *Illa Ilahi wa lahu al-fadlu*
> *Jaddi al-nabi' wa imami abi*
> *Wa dini' al-iklasu wa al-adlu.* [11]

Many other Druze and non-Druze authors have dealt with al-Hakim and the nagging question of divinity. The preceding was but a sample from many Druze authors. The omission of many others, whose work and efforts deserve recognition, is only due to lack of material at my disposition and to avoid belaboring the point. Ultimately it is the members of the Druze community singly and collectively who are called upon to take a clear and definitive stand on this issue. The Druze must resolve the question of whether al-Hakim represents a station *(maqam)* for reflections or manifestations *(tajalli)* of the Divine (Lahut) in human form *(nasut)*; or is himself the Divine (Lahut) that can only be manifested to human beings in the human image *(nasut)*. The first concept maintains the exalted state of God in the absolute above and beyond description, while the second confers actual divinity on a human being. This obvious blasphemy is not and could not be compatible with the Druze interpretation of Tawhid nor with the teachings and policies of al-Hakim or any of his predecessors. The Druze worship God, the absolute and only God, and not any image or manifestation in whatever form or shape it appears. What emerges from the foregoing can be summarized as follows.

Al-Hakim was a revered and unusually gifted imam of the faithful and a Fatimid caliph. This plus his noble lineage from the seed of the Prophet through 'Ali and Fatima added to his stature among the community of the faithful. The combination of his love of philosophy and science aand the strong Sufi and mystical trends in his nature served to elevate his stature to a high degree in the eyes of his followers. It is not difficult to imagine that some extremists among his followers would ascribe supernatural powers to such a person. After all, lesser figures in history have been awarded such accolades, and the practice of hero worship continues to this day. That al-Hakim went to great lengths to combat such exaggerations is amply documented. A ruler can control many things in society, but controlling how people think is not one of them. Al-Hakim cannot be held accountable for some of the excesses and distortions that fringe elements may have committed in his name. Likewise, he could not be held responsible for the distortions and acts of sabotage that were committed by his enemies, either during his reign or after his disappearance.

From my personal perspective on the Tawhid faith of the Druze, I believe that al-Hakim was a human being with unusual privileges, gifts, and talents. This being said, however, I see no problem in people witnessing in him some aspects that heighten their awareness of the Divine. That neither makes him divine nor confers supernatural status upon him. "Believe in a stone and you may be cured" is a common proverb that we often hear and that depicts the importance of faith regardless of the subject of worship. Visiting shrines and burial places of men and women who are considered blessed with extraordinary attributes, for spiritual and material favors, is a widespread practice in all faiths and geographic locations. A halo of the Divine envelopes the shrines in the eyes and hearts of the faithful, who oftentimes make pilgrimages to these places at great personal sacrifice. Yet this practice is legitimized as simply being an act of faith, and as such it is generally accepted by society. Accordingly, those who believe in the extraordinary status of al-Hakim are certainly entitled to their view. The very nature of Tawhid is built on concepts that stress the connection between the human and the Divine. This connection is considered to be at the core of spiritual aspiration and development in many religions and faiths, as well as in mystical and Sufi ways. The claims of divine status in many of these situations is more of an allegorical frame of reference than a concrete fact. To the uninitiated, the distinction between allegory and fact may be blurred and thus become a source of confusion.

To seek a consensus *(ijtihad)* on the resolution of this issue in a clear and meaningful manner may take some time and will require an open dialogue among the members of the Druze community. Since the Druze gave up on the imamate after al-Hakim, there are no persons who are empowered to resolve this or other related religious issues by edict (fatwa). Consequently, such issues have to be addressed first by each person individually and second by the community as a whole in a democratic manner that allows participation of all segments of society.

The *'uqqal* order alone cannot be the sole source of authority in this matter because there are no formal institutions that regulate such an order and no written laws by which they are ordained. The Druze have settled their affairs historically by an informal process of consultation that leads to consensus. The sooner this process starts the better, for individuals of the Druze community and for the welfare of the community as a whole. Such a step would clarify a vital item in the Druze concept of Tawhid and go a long way in addressing misconceptions about the Druze path in Tawhid. It would also bring the Druze into a more realistic alignment with their history and with their Muslim heritage.

Clarification of the Relation of Tawhid to Islam

Tawhid is a dynamic and progressive process that is timeless, in that it started with the onset of creation and continues to evolve. It is also universal in the scope and depth of its vision. Yet its history in the current chapter, that of the Druze, was written within the Islamic context and, therefore, must be viewed within the specifics of time and place. The wide vista of Tawhid in the global and timeless sense is telescoped in the Druze interpretation to the chapter that concerns the religious sect that emerged a thousand years ago in the Fatimid era of al-Hakim. The sect survived as a minority within tightly knit communities in the hills and mountains of Lebanon, Syria, and Palestine-Israel, as well as in less distinct groups in other parts of the Eastern world. The Druze have survived to this day as a closed ethnoreligious group within the greater Islamic community. The Druze consider themselves to be members of an Islamic sect that is protective of its uniqueness and proud of its traditions. Their teachings and interpretations serve to distinguish their heterodox approach from the more orthodox approach of the majority in Islam. Deviation from orthodox approaches in Islam or any organized religion is generally looked upon with disfavor if not outright hostility. The accusation of heresy or apostasy is frequently thrown at sects that dissent from the dogmatic views of the majority. Thus the Druze have kept their association with the Islamic heritage in a relationship that has protected the particular features of the Druze personality.

Although this relationship falls short of total integration, the Druze utilized the core message of Islam as the primary source of their religiosity in the era of al-Hakim. They have kept many of the outward practices and traditions of mainstream Islam, such as prayer over the dead, marriage contract, and celebration of the feast of sacrifice ('Id al-Adha), albeit with some modifications. For example, the Druze hold valid the provisions in the will of an individual after death, yet in the absence of such will, the estate will be handled in the Sunni Hanafi tradition. On the other hand, the Druze have practically abandoned (or modified) the physical expression of some other practices enshrined in the Pillars of Islam. Therefore, stressing the esoteric meaning rather than the exoteric display of these practices has resulted in a certain degree of ambiguity as to where the Druze fit in relation to mainstream Islam, however mainstream is defined. This affects how the uninitiated among the Druze perceive themselves as well as how they are perceived.

As it stands, and as best I can describe the situation at this time, the Druze may be considered on the inside within the broad and liberal banks of the Islamic river, but they fall outside of the narrow confines of the stream of fundamentalists. In this the Druze are not alone, considering the Sunni-Shi'a schism and the outgrowth of many sects and schools of thought within those two major trunks. In fact there is a commonly quoted hadith, attributed to the Prophet: "My *umma* will be visited by what happened to the sons of Israel. The sons of Israel split into seventy-two sects, and my *umma* will become split into seventy-three sects. All but one will suffer in hell."[12] Obviously, each sect will try to claim the favored status for itself.

Espousing philosophy and mysticism and embracing bold and new concepts of interpretation of the Qur'an and other holy scriptures gave the Druze a springboard for renewal and evolution. At the same time, it set them apart from mainstream (orthodox) Islam. In fact, when the call to Tawhid was made public under the auspices of al-Hakim, the Muwahhidun had already moved even beyond the classical traditions of their immediate predecessors, the Isma'ilis. Such bold developments, promulgated by the new movement, exposed the doctrine and its followers as a visible target for accusation and suspicion. The rift opened between the Druze and the Isma'ilis when the Druze doctrine introduced what would be considered revolutionary measures in the Isma'ili movement. Some of these were initiated by al-Hakim himself. Noteworthy among these measures were the appointment of al-Hakim's cousin Abdul-Rahim ibn Ilyas instead of his son al-Zahir as successor in the caliphate, and bestowing the title of imam (according to Hamza) on a nonmember of the seed of 'Ali (Hamza himself). These developments must have confounded the Isma'ili establishment. In addition, the Druze, as seekers of Tawhid, believed that the succession of the imamate stopped at the stage of al-Hakim. Therefore they did not endorse the imamate of al-Hakim's son and successor, al-Zahir. Al-Zahir was quick to exact a full measure of revenge, with persecution and massacres of the Muwahhidun when he came to power.

The rift within the Isma'ili backbone of the Fatimid state was superimposed on a series of prior rifts in Islam starting with the Sunni-Shi'a division and then continuing with the Shi'a split into the Zaydi, Twelver, Alawite, and Isma'ili branches. Separation breeds mistrust, and with time new traditions replace the old, as autonomy invariably leads to independence. Unfortunately, these major rifts were not peaceful, and the underlying causes for the conflict were never fully resolved. Like family feuds these conflicts were intense and painful. Inevitably, disagreements and conflicts led to negative comments and accusations that were hurled by everybody at one time or another. Most were uttered in the politically generated heat of the moment and contained more bile than substance.

The extreme position of some of the zealots (fundamentalists) in all sects in modern times makes many devout Muslims squirm and shrink from the violence and the misguided rigidity of some of the extremists. Our concern here, though, relates more to the nuances of doctrinal content than to the political and confrontational aspects of inter- and intrafaith relations, and to the traits that distinguish the Druze interpretation of Tawhid from its immediate and distant sources.

Messages that hearken to the Islamic profile and standard practices are sprinkled throughout the Druze epistles. A few examples will illustrate the point. Baha' al-Din, ever cognizant of the dangers from renegades and the pitfalls in the road to Tawhid, declares:

> And know that the true believer who is faithful to the practice of prayer and fasting and who protects himself [from apostasy and immorality] is far better than any [current] emissary (da'i), since many [of those da'is] have reneged and lied and . . . misled people from the right path into a path of falsehood and negation. . . . Whoever has remained faithful as one of the true believers and has avoided falling into the trap of immorality and arrogance . . . will be among a group of equals, distinguished only by piety, humility, and depth of wisdom.[13]

In another epistle Hamza addresses anyone who reneges on the tenets and commands of Tawhid. Such a person would be "among those apostates who did not accept Islam and did not believe in Tawhid."[14]

> And those who followed in the footsteps of the believers in Islam and Tawhid will be rewarded like those who are blessed with purity and piety.[15]

> And people of justice judge us fairly and distinguish between us [believers in Tawhid] and those who reneged. . . . How can you [they] pretend to ignore the Pillars of Islam, and what you have been commanded to learn and live by, that

the Qur'an is God's revelation to the seal of the prophets [Muhammad], God's peace be upon him.[16]

And thanks be to God, and peace and prayers upon his messenger, the truthful and trustworthy [Muhammad], and his blessed family and retinue.[17]

Chastising one of the renegades, Baha' al-Din lists insulting the Prophet as one of the main items of treachery: "And in summary if you had any trace of knowledge or integrity . . . you would have refrained from insulting God's messenger . . . and besmirching the seal of the prophets . . . and opening through subterfuge a door to insult the religion of Islam." [18]

The last call to Tawhid, according to the Druze vision, was the fulfillment of a long process that began in the remote antiquity with creation and is ongoing until the end of time. It is noteworthy that this position is not at variance with Islam, where the message of submission to God preceded the official call by the prophet Mohammad by eons of time. The message in fact arches back to Adam and finds concrete expression in the act of submission of Abraham and his progeny as described in the Qur'an:

> When his Lord said to him, "Surrender,"
> he said, "I have surrendered me to
> the Lord of all Being."
> And Abraham charged his sons with this
> and Jacob likewise: "My sons, God has chosen
> for you the religion; see that you die not
> save in surrender." (2:125)

And when death came to Jacob, his sons said:

> "We will serve thy God and the God of thy fathers
> Abraham, Ishmael and Isaac, One God;
> to Him we surrender." (Qur'an 2:125)

We should remember that the definition of *islam* in Arabic is submission to God and acceptance of God's will. Therefore the concept of Islam goes back before the era of the prophet Mohammed to the dawn of human history. The same is true of the concept of Tawhid because *islam* is an obligatory prerequisite to faith (*iman*), and faith is a necessary prerequisite to Tawhid. On the merit of this particular issue the concept of Tawhid is consistent with Islam.

A more difficult concept to deal with is that, once Tawhid is actively pursued, it supersedes and, within the appropriate contexts, replaces some of the outward practices of the parent source (traditional Islam) from which it emerged. The stage at which the following of Tawhid constitutes separation of the new from the old is a matter of interpretation. The issues that attend such separation are very complex and spill beyond the confines of pure religious interpretations to other aspects in daily life.

At stake is the relationship between an offshoot that has acquired its own identity and traits as an identifiable sect, and the main trunk from which it sprang, as well as from other branches that have evolved along different paths. Does the offspring invalidate the parent, or does it build on and strengthen the foundation of the parent? Conversely, does the parent disown the offspring for what it may consider to be esoteric teachings and practices, or develop the tolerance and versatility to evolve and widen the horizon to accommodate the different schools of thought? Consideration of this issue has experienced the same turbulence that characterizes the political, religious, and socioeconomic evolution of the various institutions of the Islamic *umma*. The majority (the Sunni) may have difficulty endorsing the legitimacy of revolutionary thinking, such as that of the Druze concept of Tawhid, while the minority, including the Muwahhidun, have not always felt welcome within the extended family of Islam. Unfortunately, the Muwahhidun have not had the chance to articulate and develop their own system of tenets and practices through institutions of their own, in an atmosphere of tolerance and security. Hence the issue of the parent-offspring or trunk-offshoot relationship continues to demand attention for proper resolution.

As an ongoing and ahistorical process, Tawhid is by definition incremental and cumulative. *Tawhid is a dynamic process of becoming rather than a static state of being.* As such it cannot totally discard the old since the old is organically imbedded in the formation of the new. To supersede the old in this context is by no means to negate it or to denigrate its vital role in the totality of the process. It is interesting that, biologically, the human genome contains genes that can be traced all the way back to the beginning of life. Likewise, the genome of Tawhid contains spiritual components (genes) that go back to the earliest times of human awareness. Hence the reverence with which the Tawhid traditions hold the sages and spiritual figures at various stages in history. Thus, when reference is made in the Books of Wisdom with respect to a new belief superseding an older one, such reference has to be understood within the general context of continuity and evolution and not interruption and negation: "And [it is known that] any new proclaimer (*natiq* or prophet) supersedes (*yansakh*) the message of his predecessor. Thus the message of the sixth *natiq*, the prophet Mohammed, superseded all the previous messages and laws."[19] "And since the call to Tawhid [in the era of al-Hakim] is the last in the series of calls, and its luminaries [were] the last of the *da'is*, it therefore supersedes all the previous calls and messages."[20]

Superficial reading of these and similar passages could give the erroneous impression that the Druze concept of Tawhid negates what came before the last call and invalidates the previous messages and messengers. In fact, the reverse is true. Tawhid, in the Druze interpretation, is an ongoing process whereby its presence was encoded in all the previous messages, much like the presence of precious metal in the ore. If it were not for the ore, there would be no precious metal. Why else would the luminaries of Tawhid help and assist in all the previous calls and contribute to their success?

Referring to a prototype pattern of the contribution of the luminaries of Tawhid to the success of the proclaimer (the prophet) and his main foundation (*asas*) in the development of Tawhid, we hear from Isma'il al-Tamimi (the human representation of the universal soul):

> Yet all that was needed for the complete picture [evolving from the beginning of creation and reaching perfection in the Islamic call] was investiture with life; and life is the knowledge of Tawhid. From that we conclude that the message of the proclaimer [the prophet Mohammed] was stronger than all the preceding messages. . . . The universal mind [reflected in the person of Salman al-Farisi] and his assistant (soul) were at the disposal of the Prophet, all the time providing assistance and encouragement, so that the picture of Tawhid began to approach perfection.[21]

Misunderstanding may also arise with respect to the concept that one call or message or law supersedes *(tansakh)* the preceding ones, from the Arabic word *tansakh*. This word literally means to copy or reproduce. However, it has other shades of meaning that include "to displace or overtake or supersede." Thus what is meant by one message or law superseding its predecessors has to be judged in context and not literally. Despite the confusion and contradictions in some of the epistles in the Books of Wisdom, the overarching concept of Tawhid as a timeless process of development and evolution contradicts any idea of annulment or invalidation of previous calls on which it was built. Allegory *(ta'wil)* would not be possible if the literal were to be erased. The same logic dictates that there would be no meaning in a word that no longer physically exists. The soul cannot realize its potential or even exist outside the body. Hence, achieving the spiritual level of Tawhid remains critically dependent on the physical presence of the word of God and the concrete expression of God's commands in everyday life. Furthermore, many members of the human race, perhaps even a majority, who stayed at the level of understanding the concrete expression of God's word, did not graduate to the more complex levels of interpretation of Tawhid. This is not the fault of the message but is a reflection of the level of spiritual and Gnostic development on the part of the seeker. Moreover, in keeping with the evolutionary process of Tawhid, the opportunity is always there for the seeker to develop and progress along the path of Tawhid.

Therefore, the idea of negation of prior calls or existing religious laws and practices stands in direct contradiction with the essence of Tawhid and its evolving nature. Nowhere is this more critical than in the relation between the Druze concept of Tawhid and the Islamic foundation on which it was built. Some passages in the Books of Wisdom may appear to contradict the core principles of Tawhid mentioned above. These could be attributed to errors of omission or commission, including those attributed to subterfuge, ignorance, negligence, or a combination of all the above. Furthermore, most if not all books of religion contain statements in some sections that differ or contradict statements in other sections. In the case of the Qur'an the tradition is to accept the newest of the revelations as the most veritable since they supersede the earlier versions. The revelations with respect to prohibition of alcohol serve as an example, whereby the early revelations admonished Muslims not to approach prayer while drunk. The admonitions later on moved to advising Muslims to avoid drinking alcohol and later still to outright prohibition. It is the last injunction of total abstinence that supersedes, in the Qur'an, the earlier and milder forms of disapproval of drinking alcohol.

It is the duty and obligation of the spiritual and secular leadership of the Muwahhidun to clarify any misunderstanding from the state of confusion by proper editing of some of the ambiguous or contradictory statements in the Druze religious writings and streamlining the core concepts that are at the heart of the Tawhid faith of the Druze, in a concise and cohesive manner. The commonality of the Druze concept of Tawhid with its Islamic source was and is never in question. This commonality is manifested in multiple places and multiple forms.

Starting with al-Hakim, in whose name the Muwahhidun developed their particular vision of Tawhid, we encounter nothing that is outside the boundaries of Islam. In fact the main concern of al-Hakim, as a caliph and imam, was the unity of Islam and the healing of the historic rift that pitted him and his forefathers initially against the Umayyads and, later, the Abbasids. The Fatimids inherited the conflict with the Abbasids. Although the conflict was mainly political, it had a doctrinal dimension as well. The Fatimid *da'is* spread the teachings of Isma'ilism along with political allegiance to the Fatimid state. The Fatimids adopted religious tolerance and encouraged free thinking as a policy for the protection of the state. Al-Hakim, like his predecessors, embraced the policy of religious pluralism and freedom of worship. Moreover, he never tried to impose the Isma'ili tradition on the Sunni or the other Shi'a communities in his caliphate. In addition he outlawed the Shi'a practice of insulting the caliphs (Abu Bakr, Omar, and 'Uthman) who preceded 'Ali and, according to the Shi'a, usurped a divinely ordained right to succession of the Prophet. This practice was and is an expression of bitterness and anger and a manifestation of extreme loyalty to 'Ali among the Shi'a. The deep commitment to unite Islam under one broad banner took precedence over al-Hakim's loyalty to 'Ali, profound and irrevocable as it may have been. Therefore, al-Hakim was a true Muslim in belief and in practice.

The epistles and other texts used by the Druze (such as *Kitab al-Munfarid bi thatihi*) are full of passages from the Qur'an (more than five hundred locations in the Books of Wisdom alone), in support or refutation of points under discussion. The authenticity of God's word was never in question in any place where such references are made. On the contrary, the whole edifice of the Druze concept of Tawhid is largely based on the essence of the divine message and not on any doubt of its veracity. "Islam is the gateway to belief, and belief is the gateway to Tawhid" is a quotation found in several places in the Druze epistles.

Placing a premium on the mind is also consistent with the lofty position that the intellect occupies in the Qur'an. The refrain that the messages in the Qur'an were meant for "those who can think or judge" is repeated over and over in the holy book of God. To use one's mind is not only proper but is a command that, unfortunately, has not been held in as much favor as it deserves, at times in the past and more so now.

One may ask why the Druze community does not perform the same standard (orthodox) practices as the rest of the Muslims, and at the same time maintain the allegorical (heterodox) concepts of their creed. This is partly the result of long periods of estrangement due to early persecution and the resultant insecurity that the Druze experienced during most of their history, and partly because of the unique Druze interpretation of the meaning behind the standard practices. The process of estrangement was reinforced by rigidity on the part of the traditionalist majority and by the virtual vacuum in religious scholarship in the Druze leadership. The efforts of the eminent religious Druze scholars of the past, such as Emir

Abdallah al-Tanukhi and Shaykh Taqi al-Din, were not enough for the tradition of scholarship to take hold and grow among the religious class (the ʿuqqal), nor to attract the secular intelligentsia to tackle matters of faith. Most of the Druze villages used to have mosques, which were neglected and run down during the latter stages of the Ottoman rule. The Ottomans, on their part, contributed to the estrangement between the Druze and Sunni Islam, following the practice of divide and rule. We are told, for example, that in 1703 C.E., sixty-two Druze were assassinated by fanatics during their pilgrimage to Mecca, for no other reason than their faith in Tawhid.[22] While this and other incidents are not unique in the annals of sectarian conflicts historically (as well as tragically in modern times), their effects on small communities are decisive in shaping relations. As an already closed community, the Druze, under threat and suspicion, had no choice but to turn inward and become more cloistered and more secretive in matters of faith. Present-day conditions in the East remain precarious due in part to the militancy and fanaticism brought about by the frustration, humiliation, and oppressive rule that appear to be the lot of Muslims in modern times. In addition, the Druze ʿuqqal may have found enough solace in the transcendental aspects of their faith in Tawhid to compensate for the interruption in the physical performance of public rituals. Prayer at home or in a simple community center became a traditional substitute for the mosque-based rituals of traditional Islam. For most of the *juhhal*, the Druze traditions appear to have filled the void.

This brings us to the issue of the Pillars of Islam and the particular interpretation that the Druze concept of Tawhid attaches to these pillars. Islam is built on five pillars, with two more in the case of the Shiʾa. The five pillars are, briefly, testimony *(shahada)*, prayer *(salat)*, fasting *(sawm)*, alms giving *(zakat)*, and pilgrimage to Mecca *(hajj)*. The two additional pillars (commands) adopted by the Shiʾa are struggle in God's cause (jihad) and allegiance to the house of ʿAli and Fatima *(walaya)*. The first of these pillars, shahada), is easy to deal with, as it consists of a straightforward declaration that there is no god but God and Muhammad is the messenger of God. True to the unequivocal monotheistic principle of Tawhid, the Druze cannot but endorse this declaration and consider it the cornerstone of the tenets of their faith. In this context, there is very little room for variations in understanding or esoteric interpretations. Some degree of flexibility is allowed in the form of elaboration that fits with the main thrust of the Druze interpretation of Tawhid, but not at the expense of the clear and compelling declaration. "The first building block and the crowning stone," declares Hamza, "is the testimony [that] there is no god but God and Muhammad is the messenger of God."[23] No one can claim to be a Muslim, whether in the mainstream or in the sects that veered to some extent from mainstream orthodoxy (as defined by majority practices), without this declaration. Therefore, the first pillar of Islam stands on a different level from the other pillars and should be considered, in the Druze interpretation, with deeper emphasis than the remaining pillars.

As for the remaining pillars, four in the case of Sunni Islam or six in the case of Shi'a Islam, some liberty is taken by the Druze in placing more emphasis on what they consider to be the spirit of the message rather than, or in addition to, the literal interpretation. In this connection, there is a spectrum of opinions among those who have dealt with these issues in the Druze community. Thus we find clear instructions from the caliph and imam al-Hakim himself that indicate his strict observance of the Pillars of Islam. A document that was publicly displayed in 1021 C.E. (A.H. 411) in connection with the sudden and unexpected disappearance of al-Hakim, analogous to a royal decree, gives us an indication of where he stood with respect to the Islamic practices:

> Then [as an indication of] favoring you with his [al-Hakim's] inner grace, is his rejuvenation of the Pillars of Islam and belief. This is the essence of religion in the eyes of God, thus bestowing upon you purity, honor, and distinction from those who practiced idolatry. . . . And he erected mosques and built places for worship (*masajid*), established prayers at designated times of the day, instituted alms giving according to established schedule, facilitated pilgrimage and jihad, and rebuilt the holy Ka'ba, [thereby] implementing the Pillars of Islam.

Following this rather traditional declaration of loyalty and commitment to the accepted and standard practices expected from all Muslims and from the caliph of Islam and supreme imam of the Fatimid Empire, the declaration continues to the next phase of al-Hakim's message. That is the call to Tawhid: "And he opened the doors to his call and graced you with what God had bestowed upon him of divine wisdom to guide you to [God's] grace and lead you to His benevolence and urge your commitment to obedience to God and allegiance to His prophets and messengers."[24]

Careful reading of the above passage demonstrates clearly that al-Hakim initiated the call to Tawhid within the framework of the Pillars of Islam, by linking the two together and for the same purpose. He started by reaffirming his loyalty and commitment to traditional Islamic laws and practices and then moved on to the more esoteric and philosophical developments that formed the basis for the unique philosophy associated with the Druze interpretation of Tawhid. It would be left for Hamza and his associates to formulate, elaborate, and expound on the main articles of the faith and the basic philosophy. The process of such elaboration, by the very nature of emphasizing novel developments and interpretation, allowed considerable latitude in ascribing an inner meaning beyond the literal interpretation of God's message. This approach is in conformity with the practice of the Batini school and of the Shi'a in all its branches. We have to remember that inner meaning *(batin)* is not for the common and ordinary people. It is mainly the prerogative of those who have reached a level of awareness and gnosis that entitles them to comprehend and internalize what the authors of the Druze epistles considered the core essence of divine messages and commands. It is only when one reaches that level of spiritual and moral development that outward practices become less critical and may in fact become somewhat redundant. Against this background, it becomes easier to reconcile seemingly differing opinions on this subject in different places in the Druze epistles.

The essence of the Pillars of Islam, according to the Druze epistles, points in one direction, and that is Tawhid. Thus prayer *(salat)* is not merely an act of recitation that is repeated five times a day, leaving the rest of the day free for mundane activity. Rather it is, in addition, a state of continuous contemplation that ensures a perpetual transcendental and immanent relation *(silat)* between the heart and soul of the Muwahhid and God. This mystical dimension results in a state of ecstasy as the seeker feels the presence of God all the time and not only during the brief periods of routine prayers. In this context, everything and every action becomes a manifestation of the Divine and a testimony to his glory. In public but mostly in private, prayer should always be a true relation between the worshipper and the Worshipped.

"When you are alone by yourself, when you are awake on your couch," preaches the great Jewish theologian and philosopher Moses Maimonides (Musa Bin Maimoun), "be careful to meditate in such precious moments on nothing but the intellectual worship of God."[25] Maimonides was influenced by Ibn Rushd (Averroes) and may also have been influenced by the lingering intellectual activity in Cairo where Maimonides lived and worked some one hundred years after the reign of al-Hakim.

A parable relating to Emir Sayyid Jamal al-Din Abdallah al-Tanukhi perhaps illustrates the point. When asked by a Sunni Muslim scholar *(faqi)* about how he, the emir, prays, the emir said: "I arise in obedience, walk in silence, enter with purpose, exalt in glory [of God], recite in pleading, kneel in humility, prostrate myself in submission, and pray in my heart. I envision heaven on my right and hell on my left, and say to myself this is my final prayer." At that point the *faqi* looked at his colleagues and said: "Let us pray again, we have not been praying."[26]

After discussing the outer and inner interpretations of the meaning of prayer and what it should represent to the worshipper, Makarem describes what the Druze consider to be the true meaning of prayer as follows: "But the true meaning of prayer, according to the teachings of Hamza ibn 'Ali, is the relation between the heart [and soul] of the believer and Tawhid. And this relation will not materialize except through a station that reflects divine light on the hearts of the believers who are anxious to receive the truth, and thirsty for knowledge and goodness."[27] The station or *maqam* that Makarem refers to is, in the most recent call to Tawhid, that of Imam al-Hakim.

Prayer then, in the Druze concept of Tawhid, is a manifestation of and a reflection on the complex system of philosophical tenets of the path and not merely a traditionally defined series of rituals whose outer form may overshadow the true meaning and real intent of the command. Prayer in Tawhid becomes part and parcel of a mystical vision whereby the Divine shines through the worshipper and is reflected in the innermost fiber of his or her being. It is in the security of this communion that acceptance and submission to God's will are enshrined in the soul of the seeker and become a source of stability and strength in daily life. This is how belief and behavior are interconnected in an organic whole that defines Tawhid.

Fasting *(sawm)* in Islam literally means abstaining from food or drink from sunrise to sunset during the holy month of Ramadan, in accordance with the Qur'anic verses:

> O believers, prescribed for you is
> the Fast, even as it was prescribed for
> those that were before you. . . .
> the month of Ramadan, wherein the Koran
> was sent down to be a guidance
> to the people, and as clear signs
> of the Guidance and the Salvation. (2:183)

Taken literally, this represents a straightforward requirement that Muslims abstain from some of the physical necessities and pleasures of life for the sake of altruistic reasons and for spiritual growth. By such abstention, Muslims would remember those who are less fortunate and donate what they would have spent on food and other items of physical comfort to worthy causes. Muslims have not forgotten nor have they strayed from the intent of the message and continue to experience fasting as they should. Nonetheless, the risk of stopping at the literal level of the message remains obvious, for the real message can be lost within the physical limitations of food and drink, from sunrise to sunset. For example, fasting during the day is compensated for by indulgence during the night that in some instances more than makes up for the daytime privation. Thus while the command related to daytime observance of fasting may be met in the physical sense, its inner intention may be missed.

Going beyond the literal meaning of the message, the Muwahhidun consider fasting another manifestation of Tawhid, whereby the minds and hearts of the believers are focused on the unity of the Creator and the unity of existence in the Creator. The realm of fasting is extended to include abstinence from corruption of mind and spirit and from idolatry and apostasy. Safeguarding *(sawn)* the sanctity of the message from corruption and protecting the purity of the individual soul from negation and blasphemy are additional dimensions attached to fasting by the followers of Tawhid. In this context fasting becomes an ongoing process of worship and a daily exercise in self-restraint and self-monitoring, not only during the holy month of Ramadan but throughout the lifetime of the individual. Fasting means abrogation of arrogance and abstention from exploitation, evil intentions, false accusations, and other forms of sinful acts. Life is full of temptations, and only strict self-discipline and accountability to one's conscience can safeguard the seeker from lapsing into the easy trail of indiscriminate indulgence in physical pleasures and immorality. "O soul, those who refrain from excessive indulgence in the pleasures of the flesh become impervious to the ills of the flesh and exit from this life healthy and closer to God, while those who pursue excessive indulgence in the pleasures of the flesh invite illness and corruption and will exit as losers and farther away from God."[28]

Fasting from bodily and other physical pleasures does not mean neglect of the physical necessities such as proper nutrition, cleanliness, and so on. Nor does it mean denigrating or ignoring the miracle of life and the majesty of existence, since these are all manifestations of the Divine. The proper use of God's gifts should be the objective of the faithful and the purpose of fasting: "When they ask you what God has commanded us to avoid, say [it is] abominable actions overt or covert, sinful acts, false testimony, and knowingly withholding the truth from one another."[29]

Fasting, therefore, in Tawhid consists of a broad spectrum of commands and admonitions that graduate from the overt act of abstention from food and drink to the more substantive guidelines and expectations of self-monitoring and spiritual purification. As such, fasting becomes for the Muwahhidun an ongoing commitment and a process that is triggered by the coming of the holy month of Ramadan but does not stop at its end. The real meaning becomes infused into the heart and soul of the seeker, constantly providing him or her with proper guidance for moral rectitude and spiritual growth. Renunciation of idolatry, apostasy, and corruption are central to the process of fasting in both aspects of its meaning, *sawm* and *sawn.*

Alms giving *(zakat)* in the physical sense consists of contributing a portion of one's earnings for the assistance of those in the *umma* who are less fortunate in life. Reducing the difference between the haves and the have nots in society can be considered to be a form of social responsibility; this was particularly so among members of the fledgling community of believers in early Islam. It reflects the compassionate nature of the Muslim religion for the poor, the orphans, the travelers, and those who are otherwise left out of the mainstream of society, and can be viewed as an Islamic equivalent to voluntary social security in the secular states of modern times.

Laudatory as this practice may be in the literal sense, its mission remains confined to the physical and concrete sphere of material dimensions. The Druze epistles deal with alms only partly in the material context of the safeguarding of the brethren. In addition to the material dimension, the epistles attach a deeper and more substantive significance to the concept of alms giving. The inner meaning of the command links it, like the rest of the other commands in the Druze vision, to the process of Tawhid. The word for alms giving in Arabic is *zakat,* a form of tax that, in addition to offering material and emotional succor to those in need, also provides a kind of purification or absolution for the giver. For the act of giving itself is accompanied by a satisfaction of an inner need that tames the ego and enhances the soul in its quest for perfection and unity. Material generosity is converted into an act of soul cleansing and purification. In this light *zakat* acquires a spiritual perspective *(tahara)* in addition to its material connotation. In Makarem's opinion, "The true indicator for *zakat* is the process of Tawhid whereby falsehood and negation are expunged from the hearts of the believers and traditions and beliefs that are contrary to true knowledge discarded."[30] The process of purification provides the spiritual balance for material contribution.

Thus to satisfy the requirement of *zakat,* it is not enough to donate material goods to safeguard the brethren; the effort has to extend to the spiritual realm as well. We read in *Kitab al-Munfarid bi thatihi:*

Those who are true believers, and whom God endowed with souls that are discriminating and wise, purified through abstaining from physical indulgence and carnal temptations *(zakat)*; those souls are nourished by emanation of gnosis and enlightenment bestowed upon them by messengers from God. "O soul at peace, return unto thy Lord, well-pleased, well-pleasing! Enter thou among My servants, enter thou My Paradise" [89:30].

That is heaven, that is everlasting bliss. [89:29]

Zakat is an act of love and sacrifice in the moral and spiritual sense, above and beyond the provision of material assistance. Without such altruism, it becomes a hollow shell and is lost in the humdrum of everyday life. It also loses the baptismal effect that cleanses the soul and prepares it for communion with the Divine.

Pilgrimage to Mecca *(hajj)* to visit and circumambulate the Ka'ba, also defined as the house of God, is expected of all Muslims who are able to undertake it at least once in a lifetime. The purpose is to remind Muslims of their belief in God, allegiance to God's message, and submission to his will. This practice also reflects and deepens the solidarity of the Muslim communities *(umma)* in a collective display of commonality in belief and equality before God and fellow humans. On the ground, it represents an awesome experience where human beings, stripped of title and guild, clad in the simplest of white garments, become equal before the eyes of God and before the collective presence of the throngs of people amassed for the same purpose. The shared sense of solidarity imparts an immense feeling of security and peace. Such feelings are sorely needed, particularly during the stressful conditions of modern times. For many the holy exercise of pilgrimage to the house of God is the crowning achievement of a lifetime and a blissful preparation to meet their maker.

All this notwithstanding, if pilgrimage consists only of the physical act of traveling to Mecca, going through the prescribed rituals, and rubbing shoulders with masses of like-minded people and fellow believers, it would fall short of fulfilling the real intent of the command. Therefore one has to seek the deeper meaning of this command.

In the Druze vision of Tawhid, pilgrimage to the house of God really means an inner journey: "The house is the unity in God, exalted be his name, in Tawhid, the abode and refuge where God's realm is to be found. . . . Likewise, it is where the souls of the believers reside."[31] This is what is meant by the house of God, not merely a pile of stones. For no matter how the stones came to be what they are, they remain stones. Islam forbids idolatry, and worshipping a stone becomes idolatry if that is all there is to it. No Muslim can, therefore, be content with the *hajj* in the physical aspect only. The Muwahhidun simply extended the awareness of the inner meaning of the *hajj* to center stage and linked it directly to the concept of Tawhid. Perhaps two stanzas from a poem by al-Mansur, the third Fatimid caliph and the grandfather of al-Hakim (and a venerated figure in Isma'ili and Druze writings), illustrate this point.

> Come, let me show you the house, and you recognize,
> That the house of God is not what you imagined.
> Would a house of stones be worthy of reverence,
> Or the Chosen Guide who erected the house.

> *Halumma ureeka al-bayta tudriko annahu*
> *Huwa al-baytu baytu Allah la ma tawahhamta*
> *Abaytun min al-ahjar a'zamu hurmatan*
> *Am al-Mustafa al-Hadi allathi nasaba al-bayta.*[32]

The house is only meaningful when it serves to highlight the designer and the builder and when it points to the message for which the house was built in the first place. Otherwise, it remains lifeless and devoid of sanctity. The mystery behind pilgrimage to the house is the mystical vision of the house, and the aim of the faithful is to gain entry into the coveted mansion.

Clearly then, visiting the house of God becomes an inner journey that believers travel as they graduate from one level to another in the eternal pilgrimage to God's grace. The process of Tawhid is in itself a pilgrimage across the endless cycles of death, rebirth, and spiritual maturation. Entry into the house of God would not be possible if the soul had not been made ready through cleansing and purification. Action and belief go hand in hand in promoting spiritual growth and enlightenment. For "only after moral purification will the subject [man] be able to witness his creator. When the soul [of the individual] discards indulgence in pleasures of the flesh, and restrains its feeling of arrogance, jealousy, falsehood, and ingratiation for material gains, it would achieve a moral victory, in daily life and in the spiritual sense."[33]

What about those who have not reached a high level of development and spiritual growth, the *juhhal*, for example. Are they to be ignored or subjected to standards for which they are not qualified? The answer is obvious, and that is no, they are not ignored. After all they are the recipients of the cumulative calls to

Tawhid that all the major religions preach. The laws, the revelation, the rites, and rituals are multiple channels for religious enlightenment and are available for all of humanity. The physical act of pilgrimage to the house of God becomes a necessary first step in preparation for the long journey. It follows that for those who are uninitiated into the esoteric wisdom of Tawhid, the starting point would be the literal interpretation of God's message *(zahir)*. Along with this come the overt forms of religious practices and the exercise of prescribed modes of worship and associated rites and rituals. Access to and understanding of the esoteric essence of the message comes gradually, commensurate with the level of advancement along the spiritual ladder. Therefore, the inner meaning of the commands in no way obviates the literal interpretation of the religious message or the physical practice of any of the commands:

> And maintain the overt forms of [religious] practices as long as they are beneficial and mandatory, and seek the allegorical [interpretation] as long as that leads you to the true meaning. . . . Adherence to that is desirable with the commensurate reward expected . . . since overt practices are similar to existence in the physical sense, and allegorical understanding is like existence in the hereafter. Tawhid then becomes *batin al-batin*, or the essence of the hereafter.[34]

That is why we have all the steps in the ladder and not only the last rung. The complexity of Tawhid and the long and arduous process leading to it put the full understanding of Tawhid beyond the reach of the novice or the grasp of the uninitiated.

"In the first place," comments Nasr,

> most ordinary people are not interested in matters of the hereafter and are not inclined to sustain the physical and emotional taxation attending spiritual growth, just as they may not be interested in the latest scientific and technical discoveries. . . . And secondly, the process leading to Tawhid in every religion and creed . . . follows a path beyond that of the overt laws and practices. . . . Thus whoever lacked the opportunity to achieve that level of transcendence *(irfan)*, should maintain his [or her] belief in the traditional sense in accordance with the principles of free choice and the ability to absorb and comprehend. . . . The level of worship is proportional to the level of intellectual and emotional capacity of reception. Thus if one does not begin with [the traditional level] of belief, he [or she] would not be qualified to deal with the more complex and esoteric forms of gnosis.[35]

We should keep in mind that Islam is the gateway to belief and belief is the gateway to Tawhid. In the case of the *hajj*, as in the case of the other pillars, adherence to the overt practice, as well as to the various aspects and degrees of interpretation, is urged upon all the seekers in Tawhid.

In addition to the five pillars (commands), two additional pillars are firmly ingrained in the Shi'a traditions. The first consists of the directive to strive or struggle in the cause of Islam and in the path of righteousness that leads to God (jihad). The second is declaration of allegiance *(walaya)* to Imam 'Ali and his descendants as being specially favored to carry the message of Islam and the process of Tawhid.

The first of the two, struggle in the cause of Islam, is known in Arabic as jihad. Jihad has recently been tinged with shades of political and military overtones that have altered the intent and context of the command. "Jihad is one of the gateways to heaven that God has opened to the chosen of his subjects," declared Imam 'Ali. And then he adds a very important clarification that stresses the spiritual nature of jihad: "And it is the garment of spiritual purification and the impregnable shield of God." [36]

While jihad in early Islam was, in the physical sense, a matter of life and death in a community under siege, it was never really intended to be a mere command for war. It was rather a call to strive for perfection, starting with the mundane demands for survival in the physical sense and progressing to the higher levels of spiritual development. Due to the dangers that surrounded early Islam in the harsh and hostile environment of its birthplace, the use of physical force in self-defense was permitted under the concept of jihad. But the purpose of jihad was to protect and preserve Islam, whose only message is belief in God and submission to God's will. Otherwise, jihad becomes a form of raiding and revenge within the framework of tribal life and traditions in a pre-Islam or pre-enlightenment Arabia *('asr al-Jahiliyya)*. Thus, as the immediate physical dangers were overcome, the more profound aspects of inner jihad began to occupy center stage in the thoughts and emotions of the believers. It is indeed ironic and unfortunate that in modern times the concept of jihad has reverted, in some fundamentalist circles, to the physical sphere, to defend what is perceived to be Islam under siege. Such a step reflects political and social conditions of the day that, regrettably, serve to demote the concept of jihad from the lofty to the mundane and from the spiritual to the physical.

In the Druze concept of Tawhid, jihad has only one function, and that is the quest for spiritual advancement along the path of Tawhid. This quest represents another, more proactive aspect of pilgrimage to the Source and serves the same purpose.

"My Lord, the aim is dear and the journey is long . . . the road to salvation full of danger and the road to darkness filled with temptation. . . . And my soul is distraught with confusion and distracted with worldly promises. Help my soul in its quest [jihad] to thee and bless its endeavor, O compassionate and merciful God."[37] Jihad involves an active effort to seek a definable goal and to commit all one's resources to achieving that goal. It also means renouncing all that stands in the way of achieving that goal. Being aware of the pitfalls is a necessary prerequisite if one is to stay the course and remain on target.

> Beware, dear brethren, of letting the forces of negation gain the upper hand over the souls of the believers. For in so doing you will fall into a trap and suffer the consequences. On the other hand, if they [the forces of negation] are defeated and vanquished, the reward will be eternal grace and everlasting bliss. . . . Patience and fortitude in the face of adversity [jihad] will sooner [or later] be justly rewarded and [the rewards] will last forever.[38]

Thus, in the Druze interpretation, jihad is an inner struggle of the seeker in the conquest of the ills that plague the human soul and delay its growth and development. The believers are continuously exhorted to subdue base instincts such as greed, dishonesty, malice, extortion, and overindulgence in physical and harmful pleasures of the flesh. They are also exhorted to refine and expand their horizon in order to transcend the physical and engage the spiritual. Control of one aspect, that of the physical, will enhance growth of the other aspect, that of the spiritual. That is how strict codes of behavior were instituted to guide the seekers in their jihad in God's way. Since the individual soul is always at a crossroads, free to choose between belief and disbelief, enlightenment and negation, virtue and vice, good and evil, it is always in the perilous position of faltering and going astray. Hence, the need for continuous struggle (jihad) in order to maintain one's compass in the proper direction. Otherwise, the numerous and ever-present temptations will overpower any system with insufficient immunity against the insidious nature of worldly temptations.

Conquest of one's selfishness or rather the forces of negation within one's self is what is meant by jihad in the Druze vision of Tawhid. It is the struggle of the mystic to overcome the tangible in order to transcend to the intangible. This theme cuts across the entire spectrum of Druze teachings, from the Druze epistles to the sayings of sages and to the popular expressions in daily life and behavior. "Dear brethren," admonishes Shaykh Muhammad Abu-Hilal (Shaykh al-Fadil), one of the Druze sages in the seventeenth century, "beware of falling into the trap of arrogance and materialism, negligence and complacency that lead you to the lures of base instincts and desires, the love of excessive fame and pride, and overindulgence in the pleasures of the flesh. . . . Never lose track of the truth in belief, nor be derailed by the distraction of detractors and critics, and be forever vigilant."[39] The soul must always be reminded of its weakness and its vulnerability to pride, arrogance, and egotism. It must be reminded that the righteous path is hard, but it is the only path to God's grace. "O soul, beware of misunderstanding your true essence, for that will lead you astray. . . . Remember that you were created for a noble reason and you were summoned for a lofty goal, that you are provided with all the necessary preparation and clad in robes of righteousness and instructed in the word of truth, and that is the message of Tawhid."[40]

The coveted lofty goal is none other than the worship of God and submission to God's will. The forces of evil and negation within the soul must be vanquished (through jihad) for the soul to be liberated from the shackles of ignorance and disbelief. The soul would then be able to continue its eternal pilgrimage to the Source and progress along the ladder of spiritual ascension. No physical or worldly reward can come close to the ecstasy of believers when they begin to be enveloped with the grace of God, and no sacrifice is too great for the achievement of that goal. This internal struggle is imbedded in the psyche of the believers and integrated into the moral fiber of the community. The Druze, by and large, live and function on the edge of the mystical experience. They tend to downplay the material and disdain the temporary.

Many proverbs and figures of speech illustrate the depth of this concept in the Druze identity. Statements such as "The soul is always at risk of evildoing," "Conquest of the ego is the first indication of wisdom," "If I sit on a bed of coals I will not wipe out all the sins I have committed," or "Salvation of the soul is by self-denial" are common utterances among the Druze, sometimes without even pondering the deeper meaning.

Supplications by the faithful are seldom for material goods or worldly possessions, but rather for God's assistance in the inner and spiritual jihad: "I beg of you, O God, to grant me out of your grace and compassion the discriminating power to widen my horizon in the quest for Tawhid and to help me clarify my pronouncements of your glory and the yearning of my soul for your benevolence . . . so that it [my soul] may not cease from the pilgrimage to your sacred knowledge and from glorifying your name."[41] This does not invalidate the widespread practice among people of faith of visiting holy shrines and pledging physical or financial sacrifices (*nithr*) for mundane purposes such as the recovery of a beloved individual who is seriously ill or the birth of a healthy child in case of infertility. The main emphasis in supplication is for moral and spiritual fulfillment rather than physical rewards.

Ever since the most perfect of God's creation, the universal mind, suc-cumbed to the temptation of pride and arrogance, a fundamental process of op-posing forces struggling to gain the upper hand in all aspects of existence was unleashed. Cascading from the universal to the individual, the struggle is a fact of life in all aspects of existence. The struggle is at all levels and is going on all the time.

> Here I am, O Lord, setting my sight to thee and relying for salvation on thee. Do not banish me from proximity to thee and do not prolong my road to thy wisdom. Chastise me for my delinquency in seeking the truth and my preoccupation with arrogance and pride. In thee I seek refuge from my sins and my hope for healing and forgiveness. . . . Grant me thy grace and assist me in prevailing over thy ene-mies, help me remain steady in my allegiance to thee and my renunciation of thy adversaries. . . . To thee I pilgrim and in thee I find my point of reference, thy love is my purity and thou are my beacon in this life and the hereafter.[42]

In its most basic aspect, life itself is a struggle—against corporeal dangers in the physical sense and against spiritual and moral dangers in the metaphysical sense. The forces of light and darkness are evenly matched, and it is only through active struggle that the balance can be tilted in the right direction. Jihad in this sense remains one of the main forces in spiritual evolution in the path of Tawhid.

The second of the two additional commands is that of allegiance *(walaya)*. Allegiance means obedience to God in the first place, and to the Prophet and to those of stature after the Prophet, in accordance with God's command in the Qur'an: "O believers, obey God, and obey the Messenger / and those in authority among you" (4:59).

But who are the ones with authority among the early Muslims? The vague-ness with respect to the precise definition of authority was to have major repercus-sions on the future of the religious and secular affairs of the Muslim *umma*. Authority during the life of the Prophet was vested in his person and was total and unified. With the passage of time, however, the secular affairs of the state began to diverge from the pristine context of the religious message. The first challenge the early Muslim community faced was that of succession upon the death of the Prophet. Although the community rose to the challenge of succession at that time, yet some invisible seams of discord were already manifest. While the major-ity of Muslims in the early days felt that support of the nascent state should take precedence over the strict propriety of succession, a hard core believed otherwise. They referred to many instances when the Prophet had made overt and covert indications that 'Ali should be his successor. The fact that this did not take place intensified the allegiance to 'Ali and subsequently to his descendants. Some of the *sahaba* who never wavered in their allegiance to 'Ali are especially venerated by the Druze. These include figures like Abu Dharr al-Ghafari, al-Miqdad ibn al-Aswad, Ammar ibn Yasser, and Salman al-Farisi, who were staunch loyalists of 'Ali. They were also foremost champions of upholding the sanctity of the Islamic message when they saw it veering from its true course and becoming mired in the politics of wealth and power.

Persecution by the successive ruling Umayyad and Abbasid dynasties served to enhance rather than obliterate or diminish the depth of allegiance to the house of 'Ali. When the political road became impassable, allegiance to Imam 'Ali and his progeny found expression in the religious and philosophical spheres. This led to the emergence of the various ideological and theosophical interpretations of the Qur'an *(ta'wil)* and to the exploration of the inner and primary meaning *(awwal)* of the religious message. Allegiance to the imamate and what it stood for became, with the passage of time, more deeply ingrained in the lives and traditions of the followers of 'Ali. By the time of the Fatimid caliphate, allegiance had assumed a mystical dimension, such that it became a central component in the concept of Tawhid. The culmination of allegiance to al-Hakim as the station of God's *nasut* brought the concept of allegiance *(walaya)* to its logical conclusion in a covenant *(mithaq)* to which all those who accepted the call to Tawhid committed themselves.

Allegiance also denotes acceptance of the tenets of Tawhid, including the concept of creation that defines the universal mind as the first and the most important of the cosmic luminaries, and the subsequent emergence of physical universe and all of existence as an emanation from the Supreme. In this manner allegiance becomes an ongoing exercise in transcendence above and beyond the physical into the realm of the sublime.

It is then axiomatic that renunciation of idolatry, false beliefs, or doctrines that would otherwise impair or stand in the way of the fulfillment of the pledge of allegiance makes it possible for the believers to honor their pledge. Makarem ties all this together by integrating the concept of allegiance with the main tenets of the faith: "This, then, is the true meaning of allegiance, that which facilitates the efforts of the believer to come closer to the universal being, and that is through the guidance of God's first creation and the expression of his will, the universal mind." [43]

From this brief discussion we can get some perspective on the allegorical and mystical dimensions pertaining to the inner meaning of the Pillars of Islam in the

Druze concept of Tawhid. We can also appreciate the complexity of the relationship between the Druze concept of Tawhid in general and the Islamic trunk from which it emerged. It is probable that the vast majority of Muslims are not sufficiently informed regarding the main tenets of Tawhid embraced by the Druze. However justified the Druze may have been in terms of security in the past, the closed nature of their practices has become a source of suspicion and distrust in modern times. Attitudes of suspicion or even neglect from the Muslim community are met with caution and an inner feeling of isolation and insecurity by the minority. The practice of dissimulation *(taqiya)* can no longer serve as an operational model. Life in modern times demands a different model, whereby the vicious cycle would be broken and the relationship redefined.

Change, however, is unlikely to take place until the necessary ingredients become available, when liberal thinking can take hold in both camps. Traditional Islam must initiate a fruitful dialogue with those who have different interpretations of the Qur'anic message, including those who follow the Druze interpretation of Tawhid. The Muslim majority should invite and welcome a pluralistic approach to spiritual expression and consider such diversity a sign of strength and a source of rejuvenation. The Druze, on the other hand, must share with fellow Muslims and with the rest of the world the basic tenets of their faith, without fear of alienation or persecution.

While it is true that traditional Islamic religious institutions have occasionally sought to reach out to esoteric Islamic sects (for example, by including the Druze in the High Muslim Council in Lebanon), the process has been more formal than substantive. The Druze believe that the basic tenets of their faith in Tawhid, with the emphasis on the allegorical rather than the physical aspects of Islam, constitute a progressive step in the spiritual thinking of religion in general, and Islam in particular. To return to the confines of dogma and the physical exercise of rituals, just to fit in with the majority, would exact a price that many among the Druze may not be willing to pay. In fact there are some intellectual and spiritual members within the Druze community who feel that the Druze concept of Tawhid (as one of the liberal and innovative movements in Islam) may help to some degree in modernizing certain aspects of Islamic practices that may have become ends in themselves and out of synchrony with modern life and the requirements of adaptation. "How is it possible to confront the civilization that is built on free thinking [referring to modern Western civilization]," pleads Ahmad al-Baghdadi, a modern thinker in Islam, "with a mindset that ties one's mind with the ropes of the past?"[44]

Many intellectuals in the Druze community believe that the Druze path in

Tawhid contains ingredients that, with proper attention and interpretation, could provide avenues for reform and for renewal. Such revival would not be restricted to the Druze but would involve Muslims in general. It is recognized that claims like this one may sound heretical to those who espouse strict fundamentalism in religious thinking and for whom any prospect of change is frightening. On the other hand, such individuals might be pleasantly surprised by discovering that an intellectually challenging doctrine such as Tawhid can provide an impetus for fresh and courageous thinking without fear or accusations. After all, evolution and change are fundamental principles of life that do not spare religions or religious practices.

Perhaps it in the nature of monolithic institutions to put stability of the existing order ahead of the imperative for change that is at the basis of life and existence. Immobility creates tension that continues to build up like that of the tectonic plates, until release takes place often in the turbulent, violent, and disruptive force of an earthquake. Islam can no longer ignore the mounting tension generated by the compelling needs of modern life nor can it defer any longer a meaningful response to and a fruitful dialogue with the dominant Western civilization of today. According to a contemporary venerated Shi'a scholar, "To handcuff the [Muslim] man in static conditions claimed to be from the noble jurisprudence [Shari'a] of Islam . . . is an insult to Islam. And it is likely that this type of thinking constitutes one of the ills of Islam. How can a mind, frozen by writings that are correct but misunderstood or wrongly stated to start with, confront minds that have been liberated and released from such shackles?"[45]

Perhaps many aspects of the Druze path in Tawhid, with the emphasis on the mind and on the free will of the individual, along with attenuation of ritualistic practices and hierarchical control of religious institutions, may be what is needed to meet the evolutionary pressures of modern life. After all it is the restless elements, the idealists, the ones who cannot endure the dull cadence of monotony and the oppressive control of the establishment in any organization, who take the lead in the initiative for change. Once established the reformed state itself, if not continuously modified to adjust to life changes, will become liable to the ills of stagnation and dogma until a fresh batch picks up the challenge and the cycles continue. The Druze initiative in formulating the Tawhid concept was, at onset, a revolutionary movement in Islam. When that movement was stifled it stopped evolving and abandoned its role in championing change and promoting enlightenment.

The Druze should openly and clearly articulate the tenets of their faith and define their own portrait as a religious community whose faith in Tawhid is universal, resilient, and noncoercive, and whose emergence from Islam makes for a special bond of kinship and heritage. This will require considerable effort since the Druze at the present time do not possess the institutional structure nor the religious hierarchy to carry on such a project. But it can be done. The Druze communities have traditionally utilized the mode of informal consultations that lead to a de facto consensus that the community accepts. It may not be the most efficient mechanism, but it has stood the test of time.

Once a clear self-portrait is defined and presented by the Druze, it would then be up to the Islamic majority to recognize the legitimacy of the Druze faith within the wide stream of Islam or to reject the innovations as having gone too far beyond the limits of acceptance. The emerging relationship would be based on clearer grounds and more realistic expectations. This could build on what has been achieved thus far (by the High Muslim Council, for example) in opening windows of genuine dialogue and ongoing evolution of inter- and intrafaith relations. Alternatively, it could lead to the emergence of the Druze faith as an independent religion such as in the case of the Baha'is in the nineteenth century. In either case the relationship would be healthier than it has been up until now. We must take note that the intellectual and liberal atmosphere in the West offers a unique opportunity to deal with sensitive issues with boldness and objectivity and without fear of accusations or the threat of persecution. It follows that the initial steps at dialogue and reform are more likely to succeed if they are initiated in the West.

On a personal level, as a Druze born into the culture of Tawhid and steeped in the liberal thinking of the West, I would still feel a sense of loss if I were to be completely cut off from my Islamic roots. This feeling is contingent upon the Islamic tent being broad and liberal, with wide gates and open windows, and not a monolithic structure that is restrictive or coercive. The Druze owe much of their doctrine directly to their Islamic heritage; and even when other sources are drawn upon, the concepts that are adopted from such sources are viewed in one form or another within the Islamic paradigm. Ethnically the Druze consider themselves among the purest of Arab stock, an identity that they carry with pride and loyalty. If the epistles in the Books of Wisdom ventured beyond the literal confines of the word and developed interpretations and allegory of their own in understanding Tawhid, as they indeed have done, that should not lead to accusation and condemnation on grounds of heresy. In this context, I will cling to my Islamic heritage. On the other hand, it will be difficult, if not impossible, for me and others like me to adjust to the strict demands of ritualistic practices after having been exposed to the inner meaning and the spiritual dimensions of these practices. In a sense it would be like going back to the disciplined routine of school after having been initiated into the process of graduate work. Likewise, excesses in the actions of zealots and fanatics in some Islamic communities of today do not invite people like me to be identified with that type of thinking. In fact they do not represent Islam at all. Furthermore, concepts like strict monogamy, gender equality, and the definition of heaven and hell in nonphysical terms are cherished traditions that I would not be willing to give up. Moreover, they fit well with my secular outlook on social and cultural issues in general, and my own understanding of the purpose of Islam. After all, only the person involved can judge the veracity of his or her faith, as no other establishment or monolithic structure can ascertain what resides in one's own heart. Revelations in the holy book, the Qur'an, are "for a guidance and a mercy to the good-doers" (31:1) and not for coercion and intimidation. After all we live in a pluralistic world that is shrinking by the minute. Such a world demands from all of us mutual understanding, tolerance, and respect across racial, ethnic, and religious lines.

Spiritual awareness of the Divine *(ma'rifat al-'ulum al-tawhidiyya)* is what heaven is about in the Druze concept of Tawhid. The joy and ecstasy derived from acquisition of wisdom and advancement in spiritual growth can never be matched by any physical or mundane pleasure derived from the senses. Such ecstasy is what the mystics experience in moments of transcendence, an ecstasy that defies description. Heaven, in Tawhid, is the acquisition of heavenly knowledge during the long and various spans of life and not only after judgment day. "The most coveted and the most complete reward [that a human being can aspire to] is the acquisition of divine knowledge . . . and the resultant supreme happiness is the purpose of human existence." [46]

This is an allegorical interpretation that emphasizes the spiritual aspect of God's rewards and does not contradict the reward of heavenly bliss that is depicted in physical terms in the Qur'an. Likewise, the emphasis on the allegorical and spiritual aspects of the Pillars of Islam in the Druze concept of Tawhid does not negate or denigrate the significance of these pillars. On the contrary, it highlights the spiritual dimensions of such practices, and the real basis for their existence in the first place. The essence behind the physical expression of these pillars can be viewed in a relationship that is analogous to that of the body and the soul.

The purpose of Islam or any other religion is to lead the individual into a spiritual longing for and eventual union with the Creator. The impact of such should be positively reflected in daily life, promoting honesty, self-control, charity of heart, love for fellow humans, and awe of creation. "Spirituality does not require a particular place for its exercise, nor does it require a priesthood," according to Laszlo. "Its temple is the mind of the individual, and its altar is the state of consciousness that comes through deep meditation and prayer."[47] Religion is therefore merely a means to an end and not the end in itself. While strictly personal, it is quite likely that my own stand on this issue, possibly with minor variations, represents the view of the majority of the Druze believers in Tawhid.

Relation of Tawhid to the Other Monotheistic Faiths

What about the relation of the Druze concept in Tawhid to the other two major monotheistic religions, Christianity and Judaism? Just as they accept mainstream Islam, the Druze accept the legitimacy of the revealed religions as expressing the word and the will of God. Furthermore, the Druze concept of Tawhid is based on an evolving process, whereby each and every step on the way represents a constitutive element in the development of the spiritual edifice. As each divine call paves the way for succeeding ones, it becomes part of the growing common heritage. Thus Judaism paved the way for Christianity, and these two religions paved the way for Islam; all the while the central theme of Tawhid gained strength and recognition. When we add reincarnation to the process of evolution, we can conceive of human actors playing similar or complementary roles at different times in their capacity as human representation of the cosmic principles of Tawhid. For example the concept of the universal mind as God's first and most perfect creation is represented by different human persons at different times in history. So is the case with the universal soul and the other luminaries in Tawhid. The concept of linkage between human and divine is a central theme in Tawhid. It is within the context of this concept that we can understand and explain the Druze interpretation of the relationships among different faiths: "O ye people, come, let us agree with one another, that we worship none but the Almighty God, the true Lord of all, not begotten nor begetting, and none can be his equal, and whom you will find in your scriptures of the Qur'an, the Old and the New Testaments."[48]

The Druze epistles afford Jesus an exalted position equal to or even higher than that in traditional Islam. Attributes such as the Master, the Messiah, and the Revered are used in connection with Jesus. In fact, the role of Jesus is often equated with that of the human representation of the universal mind in the era of his appearance, just as the role was played by Hamza almost a thousand years later. Jesus taught the word of Tawhid, according to the Druze, but the process was not yet ripe at his time. Quoting from the Bible (John 6:3-9), Baha' al-Din elaborates on this point, indicating that when Jesus was doubted even by his brethren, who requested him to go public, "Jesus said unto them, 'My time is not yet come,' meaning that his day was not yet complete but would become complete, as he said that he was prepared to return again; and when he followed 'But your time is always ready,' he meant that while his time to fully disclose the message of Tawhid may not have reached maturity, the time for those who were still ignorant was always there."[49]

According to Abdallah Najjar, Jesus was the human representative of the universal mind at his time: "Epistle 54, addressed to 'all those who sought the Divine Essence by their true offerings and held steadfast to the truth, be they priests, bishops, or patriarchs, who follow in the footsteps of the disciples,' like similar epistles, reiterates that Christ is *al-'aql* [the universal mind], as was Salman al-Farisi at the time of the prophet Mohammed, and Hamza at the time of al-Hakim."[50] After all, the call to Tawhid is a continuous march whose theme is articulated in different eras by different figures.

Numerous admonitions are expressed in the Tawhid epistles for those among the Christians and Jews who stray from the right path, in a similar manner to the admonitions of the Jews by Jesus and of Jews and Christians by the prophet Mohammed. This is not surprising since those who introduce new modifications in faith tend to consider themselves as an upgrade to the old, and in the extreme a replacement. Perhaps it is more fitting to consider the innovations as a novel approach leading to a more profound understanding of the basic themes in religion. In this context, the Druze interpretation does not represent an invalidation of Jesus or the Holy Scriptures but rather an interpretation that falls within the theosophical context of Tawhid.

We hear Baha' al-Din in many epistles admonishing Christians and Jews, sometimes with tenderness and at other times with anger, and always with a strong voice urging a wake-up call to the true meaning of the biblical message. Addressing the Christian leadership of his time, he states:

> Be cognizant, you who lack awareness, that these are the documents in the Holy Bible that were sent through Jesus, the venerated Master, to lead people to the right path. Yet you repeat his words but discredit his message.[51]

> And I will clarify my response to all the apostates who veered from following the true tenets of the Christian faith, that their [claims] are contrary to the message of

the Messiah [Jesus] and his endeavors in the eternal path of Tawhid. . . . Do not deny after receiving proper knowledge the return of the Messiah.[52]

By God, you Christians, if you really believed the word of the Master [Jesus] in the Bible as an obligatory command and accepted the veracity of his return and his role in the day of judgment, you would have heeded his admonitions and would not have been disobedient and resistant to his commands.[53]

And then he said, "Verily, I say unto you, there be some standing here which shall not taste death, till they see the Son of man coming in his kingdom" [Matt. 16:28]. He meant by that the present time, but you did not know since you have discredited his message and denied his grace. . . . And in response to the query by the scribes about the signs of the coming of Elias [Elijah] after his departure, the Master said, "Elias truly shall first come and restore all things. But I say unto you that Elias is come already, and they knew him not" (Matt. 17:11–12).[54]

Baha' al-Din strove very hard to support his argument that the call to Tawhid in the era of al-Hakim had been predicted in many passages in the Bible but the signs were ignored. The passages from which he quotes are scattered throughout the Bible and offer evidence to support his own [Druze] interpretation of Tawhid. Baha' al-Din may have been exposed to the writings of Gnostic Christians who were declared heretic and whose Gospels were supposed to be destroyed after the Council of Nicea in 325 C.E. The discovery of some of these documents at Naga Hamadi (in Egypt) shed considerable light on groups of Christians whose approach to Christian spirituality was remarkably similar to Islamic spirituality of the Druze. One of the Gnostic Christian teachers of that time, quoted by Elaine Pagels, declares, "Abandon the search for God and the creation and other matters of a similar sort. . . . Look for him by taking yourself as the starting point. Learn who it is within you who makes everything his own and says, 'My God, my mind, my thought, my soul, my body. . . . If you carefully investigate these matters, you will find him in yourself."[55] Both Gnostic Christians and Druze Muslims emphasized the importance of self-knowledge, the power of the mind, the human link to God without the obligatory intercession of intermediaries, and a healthy mistrust of the monolithic power of organized religion. Both accepted the immanence of God in chosen archetypes of human medium and venerated the messenger of God, and they both had strong roots in Egypt.

Baha' al-Din affirms in no uncertain terms the pivotal role of Jesus in the growing edifice of Tawhid. Perhaps the most forthright statement in this regard is seen in an epistle directed to Jews, who refused to believe in Jesus Christ despite clear indications from the Old Testament that predicted his coming:

And the Jews [should] take it for fact, from the Torah, that Moses had indicated and brought good tidings to them concerning the coming of the Messiah, 'Isa [Jesus Christ], introducing him [Jesus] to them, and ordering them to obey his commands. . . . And so did the prophets Isaiah, Jeremiah, and Ezekiel enjoin them to obey the prophets that preach the word of God. . . . But they refused and reneged and disowned him . . . claiming that they are waiting for the real Messiah, who would bring them doom in retribution for what they have done to Jesus the Holy Spirit.[56]

Not only does the foregoing stress the importance of Jesus in the growth and development of the message of Tawhid, but it also affirms the roles of the prophets of the Jews and the validity of the biblical messages.

As for the Jews, the problem, according to Baha' al-Din, did not reside with Judaism itself but rather with those who failed to pursue the correct path within that religious tradition. The Jews, like the Christians, were exposed to the message of Tawhid because it is embedded within the teachings of their religions. Yet they, according to Baha' al-Din, somehow did not continue along the evolutionary path that, in the Druze vision of Tawhid, would have led them to accept the legitimacy of al-Hakim, the luminaries, and the philosophical tenets of Tawhid. After all, in the Druze vision previous calls pointed in this direction and predicted this eventuality.

Clearly, the Epistles of Tawhid venerate Jesus and the prophets of the monotheistic faiths. Negative comments, when encountered, generally reflect dissatisfaction with the followers of these religions who were not true to the message of Tawhid, but certainly not with the message itself, nor with the messengers who were entrusted by God to convey the message. Such is the case when Jesus berates the Jews for not living up to God's covenant and for not honoring God's commandments. In the process the followers of Jesus spawned an altogether new religion that presumably fulfilled the expectations and prophesies of the old. Similarly, the message in Islam can, in part, be considered an admonition and a reminder for the believers among the Jews and the Christians that they have not been completely faithful to God's message in their books and have not read the prophetic signs correctly. For had they done so, they would have recognized Muhammad as God's messenger and the seal of the prophets. Islam is the third in the trilogy of the monotheistic faiths and with that the circle comes to a close. According to the Druze concept, it is the message of Tawhid encoded in the allegorical interpretation of God's messages in the three great faiths and, to a varying extent, in other faiths and philosophies that is at the core of religious evolution and man's quest for spirituality and perfection. As such, the Druze vision is not and can never be at variance with prior calls or with the veracity of the preceding messages. Any notion to the contrary regardless of the context in which such notions may have arisen would be a gross and obvious misrepresentation of the true concept of Tawhid.

The preceding discussion should help in putting the basic tenets of Tawhid in proper perspective within the monotheistic milieu from which Tawhid evolved. The veil of ignorance and confusion that has shrouded the core concept of Tawhid since inception should be removed once and for all. For only when the core concept is freed from the distortions and inaccuracies that have marred its image and hindered its progress, only then can it be properly understood and accurately assessed. Perhaps the words of the noted Lebanese historian Yusuf Ibrahim Yazbek can serve as a summary of the foregoing discussion:

> The Tawhid path in essence and point of departure can be considered as an intellectual attempt to understand the phenomenon of belief in God and his divine essence and to gradually get closer to God and witness his majesty. . . . And it is high time for us to shred the veil that we all hid behind during the days of ignorance and bigotry, and to unequivocally express our opinion regarding a faith that respects all the revealed religions and preaches high standards of ethics and morality. . . . Its philosophical and spiritual tenets are complemented with human values and mystical and intellectual approaches that seek wisdom and enlightenment at the apex of which is an unwavering commitment to the truth, which is the essence of belief and the cornerstone of Tawhid.

And then he adds that this attestation is especially significant as it comes "from the mouth of a Maronite Christian [Yazbek] and from the depths of his conscience." [57]

Closure Versus Suspension of the Call to Tawhid

Whether the call to Tawhid was closed or merely suspended is in a sense a continuation of the previous discussion dealing with the relationship of the Druze faith to other religions. Discussion of this sensitive issue within the Druze community has been largely avoided because of the emotionality that surrounds the subject and the potential for divisiveness that a small and closed community can hardly afford. Nevertheless, and perhaps precisely because of the risks involved, dealing with such an issue becomes more compelling than ever, since its impact in daily life is felt by the Druze community as it sits at a critical juncture in any attempt at reform. In practical terms, it represents one of the most pressing issues that modern life poses for the Druze and challenges their ability to adapt in the open and pluralistic societies of the West. Beyond the traditional and well-defined boundaries of life in the relatively sequestered mountain ranges in the East, life in modern times has acquired a different set of parameters that are at variance with the traditions. Thus in place of segregation we find integration, in place of circumspection and secrecy we find openness and disclosure, and in place of isolation we find interaction and mixing. The resulting stress of facing up to these challenges is obvious for all of us and therefore needs no further elaboration.

In order to deal with this complicated subject, it may be advantageous for the Druze community to consider a two-track approach. One paradigm considers the Druze as a defined religious community with a distinct historical and anthropological profile. The other considers the Druze as self-appointed standard-bearers of the universal message of Tawhid that has distinct tenets and principles. These two points of departure are not identical because one deals with the profile of a people and is therefore restricted to the Druze community, while the other deals with the profile of a universal creed that is, by definition, inclusive of all humanity.

According to the Druze tradition, the most recent overlap between Tawhid as a creed and its followers as a people took place during the call to Tawhid in the era of al-Hakim. Those who responded to the call at that time declared their commitment and sealed it with a covenant, while those who did not remained on the outside. Perpetuity of this commitment is guaranteed through the concept of reincarnation, which maintains continuity of this covenant across subsequent life cycles to the end of time. The call to Tawhid in the era of al-Hakim took place, with interruptions, over a period of almost thirty-five years. That period of time, according to Druze tradition, was long enough for any newborn to reach maturity and to make a free and informed decision. In fact the tradition also suggests that those who responded positively have carried with them from previous lives and experiences enough of the distillate of Tawhid to allow proper reception of the call in the era of al-Hakim.

Baha' al-Din left the scene in 1042 C.E. and did not appoint a successor, nor did he indicate what future course the call to Tawhid or the community of Muwahhidun should take. Perhaps he felt that the end of time was at hand. This is not unusual in faiths that look for messianic deliverance from the seemingly insurmountable ills of humanity. Facing the threat to their survival and waiting for imminent deliverance, the members of the nascent Druze community circled the wagons and bided their time. The bonds formed by family ties, community traditions, and confidentiality, along with the relative isolation of the mountainous regions in Greater Syria, gradually molded the Druze into an inward-looking society closed to outsiders. The closed nature of communal life was extended to closure of the doors of the Tawhid faith. After all, according to Druze traditions, every person at one time or another was given a chance to accept or reject the call to Tawhid. For those who did not join at that time, it was now too late. The doors were closed simply by the process of discontinuing the call, when Baha' al-Din bade farewell to his followers without appointing a successor or maintaining the cadre of *da'is*. However, the evidence shows that the issue of closure is more complex than the mere shutting of doors.

In the first place there is, to the best of my knowledge, no written reference dictating the irrevocable closure of the doors to Tawhid beyond the de facto status of suspension that ensued following the retirement of Baha' al-Din. With his departure the administrative and hierarchical structure of the call came to an end and was not renewed. Thus events on the ground worked their way into the traditions of the community and, in time, were accepted without challenge. The Druze community, facing the threat of extermination, drew strength from internal solidarity, physical isolation, and endogamy, all of which served to reinforce the developing notion that the doors were already closed to newcomers.

We should remember that most Druze grew up with tradition and not religious education or scholarship. Therefore, the issue of closure of the doors was accepted as a fact of life and never questioned, even by many of the enlightened members of the community. While this posture is understandable, it should not remain a stumbling block in the path of genuine education and understanding of the essence of Tawhid by all members of the community.

Looking for evidence that supports the notion of closure of the door, we find only one passing reference to an occasion when the imam al-Hakim was upset with the behavior of his followers, presumably during the turmoil and internecine conflict, in the first three years of the call. The reference is in the document that was posted in connection with the disappearance of al-Hakim in 1021 C.E. (A.H. 411): "And among the signs of the displeasure of the imam [al-Hakim] are the [temporary] closure of the doors to his call and the suspension of the sessions dealing with [the discipline of] wisdom and the relocation of the offices and staff from his palace."[58] This statement was in the form of chastisement of the community of believers at the time, and a punishment for being untrustworthy with regard to what he had graced them with. In a sense this step is similar to revoking privileges in case of misconduct. The revocation was in the form of a temporary disciplinary measure because the call was subsequently resumed. Therefore the closure at that time was no more than a temporary suspension.

We know that the call to Tawhid in the era of al-Hakim was suspended for a full year after the first year of disclosure, presumably to repair damage and reinforce the ranks. The call was then reopened and maintained in high gear for another period of two years. The sudden and unexpected disappearance of al-Hakim after those two years put a temporary halt to overt activity in terms of the call itself. This in a sense can be considered as another period of suspension of activity of the call. After a few years, the atmosphere changed, and the call was again resumed for several years until the retirement of Baha' al-Din. Thus the closure of the door in both instances was no more than a temporary measure and did not mean that the doors to Tawhid had been permanently shut. In fact the doors were again reopened after the death of al-Zahir, when it was safe to do so. The *da'wa* was resumed, but with circumspection. Nonetheless, a precedent had been set for closure (suspension) in the face of danger. Thus the exercise of closure was no more than temporary suspension prompted by situational considerations and not doctrinal content.

We can surmise that internecine conflicts and other power struggles, as well as distortions and sabotage of the message and the withering away of the spiritual leadership, may also have contributed to an atmosphere that encouraged suspension of the call. The problems seem to have increased with time, disrupting the organizational structure of the call and introducing into the text of some epistles elements of distortion, misinformation, and sabotage. This explains the relatively large number of epistles devoted to discrediting the saboteurs: "When we found that certain parts of the letter [presumably written or delivered by one of the apostates] contradicted the other parts, we recognized that it was intended as misinformation . . . [and we found it] full of lies, distortions, and tricks. . . . Thanks be to God and prayers upon his Prophet [Muhammad] and his companions. Let the faithful know that when we find a trustworthy emissary to carry our letter [without tampering with it] we will do so." [59]

In another epistle Baha' al-Din laments the difficulties that some of the inner circle of the faithful were experiencing in relation to distortions and sabotage: "It has pained me in the heart and caused me to cry for what is happening in their domain of misinformation, distortion, and sabotage [of the message of Tawhid], some of which I have seen and some I could only imagine." [60] This is an explicit confirmation of his awareness of distortions within some of the letters, distortions that contradicted the essence of Tawhid and led to misunderstanding and confusion among the Druze and among Muslims in general. After all, the propaganda machine of the Abbasids that worked incessantly to discredit Isma'ilism targeted the Fatimids by casting doubt on the origin of the Fatimid caliphs. Agents of the Abbasids trumpeted the accusation that the Fatimid caliphs were not descendants of 'Ali and Fatima at all, but usurpers of such lineage.[61] We can assume that double agents and saboteurs bent on the destruction of the Fatimids purposely introduced damaging material into the work of the Isma'ili *da'is* in order to sow mistrust and ignite sectarian strife. There is definite reference to this in the Druze epistles.

In the last epistle, The Occultation *(Al-ghayba)*, we hear Baha' al-Din articulate a theme of exasperation, a measure of which runs throughout most of the latter epistles, along with exhortation for those who remained faithful to Tawhid to stay the course:

> And as for me, the humble servant, I declare my innocence from all the accusations of those who fabricated falsehood and distortions and related them to religion and belief [Tawhid], as God is my witness. . . . Whoever among you has acquired knowledge of wisdom *(hikma)* and purified his soul from immoralities and sins . . . safeguarding brothers and sisters in faith, enduring with fortitude to face whatever difficulties may come his way . . . will surely be rewarded with salvation at the time when everyone is held accountable for his [or her] actions. . . . And this humble servant is submitting himself to his Lord, seeking retirement and occultation, and thereby bidding farewell to the seekers of truth far and wide.[62]

With this rather terse epistle Baha' al-Din retired from public view. Since he left no further instructions and appointed no deputies, the activities of the past thirty-odd years with respect to the call in the name of al-Hakim came to a screeching halt. Does this mean that the doors to the Tawhid faith were permanently and irrevocably closed, or were they merely suspended? Before the reader makes up his or her mind let us examine further evidence from the Druze epistles, in support or refutation of permanent closure: "And we will mention in this epistle the first stage [of creation] and that is the emanation of the [universal] mind, that you may be informed of the truth and become believers in Tawhid, and that you recognize that our Lord, exalted be his name, does not withhold from his subjects his light or his station; and that all the luminaries of faith are present in every age and stage for whoever seeks salvation and does not bow to idolatry and paganism."[63] The emphasis on "every age and stage" leaves no doubt about the continuity of the Tawhid message in perpetuity and that it is never too late to embark on the path of Tawhid. In another section, Hamza, in the role of human representation of the mind, reminds the believers of the historical backdrop of the continuum of Tawhid:

> Brethren in faith, I have given you guidance and instructed [you] in the message of Tawhid across seventy cycles. There is no age in which I was [am] not there sent by our Lord in one image or another, one name or another, and one language or another. I know you and you may not know me or know yourselves.[64]

> And our Lord, exalted be his name, does not extinguish his guiding light and does not withhold [his grace] and does not tear anything down without building a better and stronger replacement and will never ever desert his creation. . . . As is commonly known God will not shut a door in the face of those who seek sustenance *(rizq)* unless he opens multiple other doors instead. And the door here refers to the point of reference and the primary teacher (mind) that is the gateway to Tawhid.[65]

In another section we hear from the second in command, Isma'il al-Tamimi, representing at that time the universal soul, describing the role of the mind in the perpetual propagation of the message of Tawhid: "that light [mind] who is present in *every age and stage* and who is delegated by the Lord *in all times and all places* in different guises to proclaim the message of Tawhid [emphasis added]." [66] Similar assertions are heard from Baha' al-Din: "The Creator and Lord of all *never deserts or ignores his subjects* and never leaves them at any time or place without a *da'i* to the message of Tawhid. . . . There was never a messenger or a prophet sent to you [by God] except with the mission of leading you to the truth and to the entrusted message of Tawhid." [67] "And this proves what I have already alluded to . . . that God does not deny his creatures [the opportunity of] witnessing; it is rather the actions of his creatures that create the barrier to witnessing his majesty." [68]

Another message that is repeatedly noted in the Druze epistles may reflect the incompatibility of closure with the core message of Tawhid. The message was probably intended as a warning in connection with the disappearance of Hamza and the threat of apostasy: "And know that my departure from you is a test for you and for *people of all religions*."[69] We are left to wonder why such a test would be necessary or even useful, if the doors were already shut and the final results of the test determined. We are also left to wonder why such a test would be offered to all people of religion (including but not limited to the Druze followers of Tawhid), if the selection process had already filtered out those who opted to stay on the outside when the doors were permanently closed. Regardless of the context the main point in the message is clear in that it was addressed not only to the followers of Hamza (Druze) but to all peoples of religion. The implication is that all people (including but not limited to the Druze) are entitled, and at all times, to be involved with the spiritual journey to the Source. Thus a pattern emerges that defines the continuity of the message of Tawhid across the ages from the distant past to the remote future.

From these passages and many others we can conclude that, in keeping with the core concept of Tawhid, the doors to Tawhid could not have been shut and that the evolutionary path has not come to a dead end. Rather, the activities of the *da'wa* in terms of proselytizing were suspended with the exit of Baha' al-Din, as they had been on prior occasions, only to be resumed when conditions became more favorable. The process of Tawhid is ongoing and is nondiscriminatory in terms of the identity of the community into which any given individual happens to be born. For if the process has reached its conclusion, what is to be gained by further trials and tests? In fact, what would be the purpose of life to continue as we know it if the day of judgment has already passed? Therefore, we have to remember that there is a clear distinction between suspension of activities promoting Tawhid, and the permanent and irrevocable closure of the doors.

One of the arguments used by the proponents of the principle of closure of the doors was alluded to earlier, yet it bears clarification. The argument goes as follows. Every person has been offered the opportunity to follow the Tawhid faith across the ages, until the most recent cycle (in the era of al-Hakim), when the final opportunity was offered. Those who joined sealed their commitment with a pledge in the form of a covenant that they freely signed to be upheld in perpetuity until the end of time. Because of reincarnation, the argument goes, the pledge continues to be upheld by the progeny of the faithful who would, in effect, be the same original signatories only in different bodies. Thus, the Druze individual, as a believer in Tawhid, would always be born to a Druze family as long as reincarnation exists. It is amazing how this tradition has been accepted at face value and the logic never challenged. A closer look is needed to examine the validity or otherwise of this widespread assumption.

It is common knowledge that a human body is formed by known physical and chemical processes, according to hereditary determinants encoded in the physical genetic makeup of the individual-to-be. The newborn becomes an individual in full, a complete human being, when the soul takes residence in the body. The soul, being nonmaterial, has nothing whatsoever to do with the physical makeup of the body since the two do not operate within the same parameters nor follow the same rules. It is the soul and not the body that defines the spirituality of the individual, and it is in the soul that spiritual development and evolution take place. The body becomes a mere physical structure when the soul departs. The error in traditional Druze thinking becomes obvious when that thinking designates the body as the determining factor in the choice of residence for the soul of the believer in Tawhid. It is the soul of the individual, no matter what body it incarnates at any given time, that carries the commitment to Tawhid and the pledge to remain forever faithful to the call. The body carries the physical genes, and the soul carries the spiritual essence. The spiritual essence cannot be subservient to the body any more than the permanent to the temporary. In fact, many among the Druze are careful to point out that the believers in Tawhid far exceed the number of Druze in the world. I have heard claims by reputed shaykhs and by common folk among the Druze that put the number of believers in Tawhid at a quarter or even a third of the human race. However, when Druze religious leaders are pressed as to where these people are and why the Druze do not communicate or connect with this large segment of humanity, they have no satisfactory answer. In a recently published book on the Druze, a prominent social anthropologist describes the dilemma that the Druze face nowadays:

> Here, in the theory of "cycles," lies the apparent dilemma of simultaneously claiming a "universalistic" approach to religion while clinging tenaciously to the practice of group exclusiveness — no conversion, no proselytism and no marriage outside of the religious community. Just as the Druze see themselves as a part of a universalistic order, with a common affinity to other religions, they contradictorily believe that they are "the people of al-mithaq," an exclusive group. Indeed their belief in the cyclic nature of divine manifestations, which is Isma'ili in origin . . . helps to bridge the apparent contradiction. . . . Although Tawhid evolved from previous religious forms — namely, Judaism, Christianity and Islam — it did not eliminate them. On the contrary, it is argued that Tawhid is inclusive of all of these religious traditions, along with Greek philosophy and Sufi Islam. Here lies the universalistic character of Tawhid.[70]

Furthermore, although the Druze are among the purest of the Arab stock in the Middle East because they marry primarily within their own faith, they have not been immune to genetic mixing by intermarriage, particularly with other Muslim groups. Nor has the door been completely closed for some families and individuals from other sects to be incorporated into the community either through

258 • The Druze and Their Faith in Tawhīd

marriage or through seeking refuge among Druze families leading to full integration. Among the most famous in this regard is the Jumblatt family, of Kurdish (and presumably Sunni) background, originally from the Aleppo region in modern-day Syria. The scion of this noted family, the late Kamal Jumblatt, does not mention the Druze origins of his family. However, since there are no known Druze among the Kurds then or now, the Jumblatts most likely became Druze through marriage into one of the Druze feudal families in Lebanon.[71] As is well known the Jumblatts were accepted into the Druze community in Lebanon and subsequently occupied a position of power for several hundred years. They continue to play a leadership role to this day.

Intermarriage particularly with other Islamic sects is a regular feature in another prominent family, the Arslans, whose members carry the title of emir. Among many other Druze families the same family may split into two or more factions, each adopting a different faith. And what about those who were Druze and left the community when their leaders converted to other faiths years or centuries ago; can they or their progeny return to the Druze faith and by what mechanism?

Finally, no matter how genetically pure a group is or how strictly its members adhere to the norms of morality with regard to sexual conduct, there are undoubtedly an unknown number of Druze born who were sired by non-Druze fathers. Some of them may have risen to great heights in spiritual growth and human achievement; what of them and of their progeny? After all, racial purity is a myth, particularly in areas that have witnessed a long history of invasion from East and West and have experienced multiple civilizations, as is the case in the Levant, the point of origin of the Druze. Therefore, there is no rational defense to subjecting spiritual identity to a biological abode.

To these and numerous other related issues, there is no answer, not even a genuine discussion. And the tradition persists without an open dialogue among the Druze people for fear of the instability inherent in change. But change is unavoidable, either by direct participation or by imposition from the outside.

The above arguments notwithstanding, to break a tradition of a thousand years without laying the groundwork for change and without taking into consideration the ripple effects would be difficult and traumatic. To reactivate the call and reestablish continuity from the point of arrest a thousand years ago, as though nothing had happened between then and now, is unwise and impractical. Thus resumption of the call to Tawhid as was done a thousand years ago may be untenable in view of the different conditions that prevail in modern times. Instead of trying to duplicate the past, the Druze should change their orientation to the future, based on the timelessness of their core beliefs. Thus what should be discussed and considered is an open-minded approach to the challenges and opportunities of the day that shifts the focus of the Druze community from the shackled monotony of tradition to the liberating power of the core concepts of Tawhid. If the solution cannot be that of new enrollment into the ranks of the Druze (since no one since suspension has been empowered to resume the call and to administer the covenant), there is nothing that stands in the way of dealing with the challenges of modern life on the plane of Tawhid. That is, if the Druze pathway is blocked or, more accurately, clogged, the pathway of Tawhid will always remain wide open. Instead of trying to roll back the clock to the time and space determinants that prevailed a thousand years ago, the Druze should look in the present and into the future for addressing the concerns of this generation and those of the future. Creative thinking once kindled can provide ample opportunities for consideration and implementation by consensus. After all Tawhid as a historical evolutionary concept antedated the Druze. And the Druze need (and should resort to) the broad concept of Tawhid to deal with issues of modern life. "Among the distinctive features of the Druze in their cultural life," according to one modern Druze intellectual,

> is that they have been in most of their endeavors proponents of enlightenment and renewal within a democratic Arab and Islamic vision that is open to the world. Their cultural creativity is [should be] free from the shackles of tradition. . . . The most important aspect of Tawhid and of the faith of the followers of Tawhid is that the path of Tawhid did not appear suddenly at any one time in history; rather the contrary is true, since Tawhid extends over the entirety of history.[72]

The Druze community, particularly in the West (where freedom of speech is guaranteed), can resort to this cultural creativity in bold and constructive ways. Persecution for religious beliefs or even religious heresies is a thing of the past in the West, but unfortunately continues to be a formidable obstacle to freedom of expression in the East. Until now orthodoxy continues to reign supreme in Muslim societies, denying these societies the benefit (and the risk) of the stimulating and rejuvenating forces associated with provocative thinking and esoteric interpretations. Therefore, it is the West with its pluralistic societies, freedom of expression, and religious tolerance that offers the ideal arena for Druze intellectuals to experiment with reform. The West, for the same reasons, can swallow small communities in its cultural melting pot. On the other hand, the overwhelming force of homogenization in the melting pot has led to reactivation of interest in ethnicity among different communities and in preservation of distinctive cultural traits that they bring to the table. The Druze community is no exception. Perhaps the words of Abdallah Najjar, a distinguished elder of the Druze and Arab-American community in the United States, illustrate the point: "As a Druze, the East and West merged in me. For a thousand years I have been in the midst of the stream of human history, championing the dignity of man and fighting for his freedom. As a Druze, I am a Muslim influenced by Oriental theology and Western thought, by Christian witness, Judaic law, and esoteric practice. As a Druze, I am a proud mountaineer reared in the puritan and tribal tradition of an austere and devout society."[73]

This leads us to another pressing issue that the Druze people and their children face in daily life: the issue of mixed marriages. In fact the impact of other, more substantive issues on Druze emotionality pales in comparison when it comes to the question of mixed marriages. To be fair the emotional reaction surrounding mixed marriage is not restricted to the Druze; it is a significant feature of most ethnic and religious communities. In fact, even marriages within the same community in any society are not always condoned since these marriages are frequently subject to economic considerations and other factors such as the level of education and social standing. In addition, many religious communities do not look with favor on marriage with a person of another faith because this may lead to conflicts of allegiance, child upbringing, and sense of belonging. However, the degree of antipathy (and sometimes sympathy) varies considerably and the solutions vary accordingly.

In general, Western democratic societies, being more secular than societies in the East and with a long experience in liberalism and pluralistic traditions, are more tolerant and therefore can be more innovative in handling this issue. It is not uncommon nowadays, for instance, to encounter wedding ceremonies conducted jointly by representatives of different religious traditions. Likewise couples from different faiths often expose their children to more than one religious tradition, and the change from one to the other is not considered catastrophic, except in the more conservative segments within a given tradition. Furthermore, many religious traditions not only accept but in fact welcome newcomers. Finally, there is the option of civil marriage, where the potential for conflict on the basis of religious background is avoided altogether. Thus the issue of mixed marriages in the West is largely solved through the availability of multiple options.

When it comes to the Druze we find that there are no established mechanisms to deal with the issue of mixed marriages, outside that of civil marriage.

Civil marriage is not available in the East, and its availability in the West does not obviate the need for the Druze community to address the issue of mixed marriages from the perspective of the traditions of the community and its religious tenets. For a Druze female marrying a non-Druze, the practical consequence is likely to be a one-way exit from the Druze tradition to whatever tradition her husband happens to belong. In the case of a Druze male, exogamous marriage does not necessarily follow the same path as that of the Druze female, in that most Druze families, particularly in the West, accept the spouse and the children into the Druze traditions. However, this is by no means universal, and in many cases it could still lead to the same exit. The exit may be by voluntary choice and by mutual agreement of the parties concerned, or it may be imposed by the party with the stronger backing. The absence of mechanisms to address this issue on the part of the existing Druze institutions leaves the Druze individual in a weak position, since he or she does not offer practical options. In some cases, the Druze individual will have to decide between two painful choices: give up identity or give up marriage. Not even the genuine willingness of the prospective mate to adopt the Druze tradition can save the situation, since the Druze tradition proscribes entry into the Druze path in Tawhid. This is especially poignant when other religious traditions roll out the red carpet for newcomers or potential converts.

Should it be the lot of young Druze to be faced with options that force a choice between allegiance to family and clan, and the denial of emotional and marital fulfillment? The dilemma for parents is portrayed in the response of one interviewee in a recent study by a Druze anthropologist. The study was conducted among the Druze community in Southern California.

"We beget them [children] in America. We raise them in America, and we demand that they be conservative Druze, and make conservative choices. It is not fair."[74] Fair it certainly is not, yet it is a fact. What was also interesting in Azzam's study is that exogamous marriages did not necessarily threaten Druze identity to an extent that justified parents' fears that their children would be "lost" in the American melting pot: "From such response and cases [that were interviewed] . . . one cannot conclude that the increase in exogamous marriages results in rejection of Druze identity."[75]

Furthermore we all know of instances where marriage from outside the Druze contributed significantly to the welfare of the Druze community and the enrichment of the Tawhid faith. After all it is the soul of the individual that carries the spiritual legacy regardless of the accident of birth.

This may sound like a defense or an encouragement of mixed marriages, which of course is not the primary intention of this discussion. The intent is to bring these issues out into the open and move past the ostrich-like posture of avoidance. Issues of substance must be dealt with in a realistic and responsible manner even if that means challenging the practice of strict adherence to dogma and traditions. The younger generation does not understand the powerful influence of Eastern traditions and cannot adhere in humble obedience to the rigid limits defined by these traditions. They grow in the midst of the fast and pluralistic Western culture where the primary emphasis is on personal freedom and responsible choice. To the older Druze generation (most of whom immigrated as adults), even a faint tone of understanding will weaken the defense against such acts of defection (by mixed marriages) as to provide tacit encouragement. Eligible Druze men, already in short supply, will become even less available, and this will doom many Druze women to life without the prospect of marriage within the community. Therefore, they argue, maximum pressure should be applied, on Druze men in particular, not to marry outside the community.

Coercive postures of this kind may have a temporary effect, but they often backfire, particularly in societies that put a high premium on the rights of the individual. The dilemma will not be solved by ignoring the realities of modern life or by labeling any deviation from the dogma of tradition as an act of heresy. The Druze community must recognize the validity of both concerns and come up with realistic solutions that reconcile the right of choice with the protection of the heritage. The community should resort to the resources of Tawhid to devise creative approaches to a reality that cannot (and should not) be ignored nor wished away.

The marriage of Druze women to "outsiders" is even more resented than that of Druze men. This reflects the patriarchal traditions of the East where male dominance remains in full sway, despite the gender equality in the Druze epistles in all aspects of life including marriage. The beachhead of Druze immigration in the West is of recent duration. Most of the Druze pioneers who emigrated to the West (especially the United States) in the late nineteenth and early twentieth centuries are gone, and their progeny have largely melded into the culture in which they were born, before an independent and Western-oriented approach to Druze traditions could be established. More recent Druze immigrants include large numbers of educated and professional people who are anxious to maintain their identity and wish to share with fellow Americans what is noble and uplifting in their tradition. Their progeny are growing up in an environment that cherishes ethnicity and welcomes pluralism. Hence their hunger to delve into their religious background and learn about their heritage. Their need for reconciliation between their inherited traditions and their Western identity is compelling for their social and psychological well-being as well as that of their community. Such reconciliation must include resolution of the stress that may arise from marrying outside the community.

It is worth noting that recently children from the marriage of Druze men and non-Druze women have been accepted as Druze by the sectarian Druze courts in Lebanon. As a result the Lebanese government, which endorses the decisions of the sectarian courts in these areas, considers children from such mixed marriages as Druze. The same does not, at present, hold true for mixed marriages between Druze women and non-Druze men. The woman, in this case, will be considered as having opted to leave the Druze path and to follow the religious identity of her husband. To those who are secularly oriented the whole issue has become irrelevant, but to the majority of the Druze the issue of who their children marry remains a major source of concern and a potential threat to family relations.

Concerns about marriage are a reality that cannot be wished away by the Druze communities in the West or the East. In the pluralistic and open societies of the West, particularly in large urban centers, social and cultural interactions are the norm, and deep personal relations ensue naturally. Religious and ethnic barriers are easily circumvented when there is a meeting of the minds, or simply ignored in moments of passion. The heavy burden of traditions that the parents carry does not occupy the same position in the hierarchy of priorities in the lives of the descendants. Dogma and tradition are on one side, a liberal and pluralistic milieu on the other. The clash of cultures is compounded by the clash of generations, causing considerable stress on the fabric of the entire family. All of this is a direct consequence of the traditional belief that the Druze are the sole custodians of Tawhid and that to be a Muwahhid is contingent on being born into a Druze family. Closure of the doors to outsiders to the Druze faith in the current traditions of the community has meant that no one could be admitted to Tawhid except through the accident of birth. It may be difficult to become a Druze by conversion due to the long traditions of a closed community, but this in no way precludes any person from accepting and adopting Tawhid as a path to spiritual fulfillment. Thus there is a compelling need to develop novel approaches that enhance the welfare of the Druze family based on the core concept of the universality of Tawhid and that are applicable to modern life particularly in the West.

Adhering to traditional and confining practices that are virtually unchanged over a thousand years and ignoring the tremendous resources of the core concept of Tawhid is detrimental to the religious and secular health of the Druze community. As citizens in whatever society they live, the Druze should adapt to their environment with openness and involvement and not with isolation and mistrust. After all Druze particularism did not stand in the way of proactive behavior and political leadership of the Druze in the countries of origin in the East. It should not stand in the way of service and dedication to the welfare of the Western countries in which they reside.

8   *Concluding Remarks*

THIS BOOK WAS WRITTEN with two main aims in mind. The first is to lay out the core concepts of the Tawhid faith of the Druze within the historical context of its emergence from Isma'ili Shi'a Islam in the era of the sixth Fatamid caliph, al-Hakim bi Amr Allah. The second aim is to stimulate the Druze community to take a close look at what they have and initiate a process of dialogue with reform in mind. The Druze faith is a path (*maslak madhab*) to the understanding of Tawhid, a unist concept that combines the absolute oneness of God and the unity of all creatures and creation in the oneness of the Creator. Tawhid itself, according to the Druze, is a process of acquisition of knowledge and growth in wisdom through which human beings evolve spiritually, growing ever closer to the Divine. This process, having begun in the dim twilight of existence, is open-ended, being expected to continue indefinitely. It does not follow a linear trajectory such as that starting with birth and ending with death. The course is rather curved such that the beginning and the end are coordinates of one continuous process of cyclical manifestations. Death is no longer the end of one's life but a simple transition and renewal. Evolution and progress are obligatory features of this cyclical process; otherwise, it becomes nothing more than repetition within a closed circle.

Those who are known today as the Druze are the descendants of those who accepted the call to Tawhid in the era of the sixth Fatimid caliph and imam al-Hakim bi Amr Allah almost a thousand years ago. Because they have accepted the call to Tawhid, the Druze prefer to be known as Muwahhidun. Tawhid, in the era of al-Hakim, is but a recent chapter in the long spiritual journey, not the first and certainly not the last. A complex approach to the understanding of the nature of God, the mechanism of creation, and the role of reincarnation in human evolution sits at the core of the tenets of the faith. A more mundane set of prerequisites in behavioral and social spheres complements and reinforces the core beliefs. Although the starting point in this most recent chapter of Tawhid is Islam, Tawhid is in fact ahistorical in that it goes back to the earliest stages in human gnosis and projects forward to the end of time.

The esoteric nature of the path and the revolutionary concepts it proposed were too much for traditional Islam to accept or accommodate within the mono- lithic structure, creating a backlash from traditional Islam and from the Ismaeli Fa- timid caliph who succeeded al-Hakim. The ensuing period of persecution resulted in suspension of overt activity and of further refinement in the Druze vi- sion of Tawhid. Persecution forced the beleaguered Druze community to adopt policies of secrecy and dissimulation *(taqiya)* as well as a suspension of the call *(da'wa)* to Tawhid. Suspension of activity in time developed into a de facto closure of the door for enrollment of new members. Closure also meant that the majority of the Druze became ignorant of their faith, an ignorance sustained by traditions of a community under threat. The broad spectrum of Tawhid succumbed to the nar- row confines of isolation and the imperative of self-preservation. The paradox be- tween universality of the faith (Tawhid) and particularism of the faithful (Druze) as self-appointed custodians of the faith is a fact of Druze religious life. This book is intended for the benefit of the motivated parents who were not exposed to the basic tenets of the faith and do not possess enough background to explain to their chil- dren what Tawhid is about.

A second aim for writing this book is to initiate a dialogue within the Druze community, a dialogue that may pave the way to solutions to the many challenges that haunt the community and hinder its progress. It is also intended to explain the basic tenets of the Tawhid faith of the Druze to members of the non-Druze community, an explanation based on the understanding of the faith by one of its members. It is a beginning of a process to overcome ignorance among its mem- bers and potential distrust among others. Much work needs to be done to delve further into the philosophy of Tawhid and make it more accessible to the younger generations. For this to happen, the Druze community must recognize the need for reform and anticipate the trauma of breaking with long-established traditions and modes of thinking. It is a big challenge attested by many failed attempts at re- form in the past.

The present work is not intended to provide clear and definitive answers to all the questions that haunt the Druze community, since the subject at hand does not lend itself to cookbook-type formulas. It is rather an attempt to share with others of similar and dissimilar backgrounds the main features of the Tawhid faith as artic- ulated and promoted a thousand years ago by leaders of what has come to be known as the Druze sect. It is a personal perspective of the Druze faith as I understand it and in some ways as I would wish it to become. The book presents the positive aspects of this path as articulated in the Books of Wisdom and other sources and stays clear of aspects that I consider to be incongruent with the basic principles. I do not place any value on passages that either were inserted with the purpose of sabotage or do not fit with the main theme of the philosophy. Writing the book was like extracting precious metal from its ore and purifying it of the contaminants of neglect.

For security reasons and, to some extent, for doctrinal reasons as well, a tradition of secrecy enveloped the tenets of the faith, resulting in a self-contained system bereft of the possibility for renewal and accommodation to a changing world. The irony is that Tawhid is a progressive and dynamic spiritual process, based on freedom of choice and on seeking God's knowledge. The tenets of Tawhid are not only evolutionary insofar as spirituality is concerned but also revolutionary in confronting religious dogma with the challenge of reason. Consider how and why Tawhid places the mind at the top of the list of priorities in the scheme of creation, an alternative to (or esoteric interpretation of) the six-day story of creation in the biblical tradition. That alone defines a viewpoint that places a high premium on the priority of reason in religion and on the emphasis on reason in human affairs of daily life. Mind is in fact ahead of soul in Tawhid, again emphasizing the centrality of reason as a prerequisite for spiritual development. Mind leads to knowledge through awareness that is uniquely human and uniquely personal. Man's fall from the grace of God in the biblical tradition was presumably related to an act of disobedience or defiance of God's admonition not to eat from the fruits of the tree of knowledge. That sinful act resulted in the exile of man from the heavenly garden to the earthly existence. Furthermore, Adam's and Eve's mistake was permanently transmitted to all their progeny and in perpetuity. Tawhid provided an esoteric interpretation of these fateful events.

Seeking God's knowledge is the essence of spirituality in Tawhid and the basis of the human quest for heavenly bliss. Heaven is not viewed as a physical place with physically expressed modes of reward in Tawhid. Rather, heaven is closeness to God gained through diligence and struggle for the attainment of knowledge and awareness of the Divine. The "slip" of the universal mind when afflicted with a moment of pride is perhaps analogous to the fall of Adam from grace in biblical teachings. This knowledge and this awareness represent the divine aspect of man such that God, the otherwise absolute totality beyond human reach, becomes immanent in humanity. Thus God, the exalted and, in the absolute sense, unknowable and indefinable, becomes, conceptually, a presence and an awareness within each and every individual to the extent of any individual to witness and comprehend. The Gnostic dimension to the Tawhid faith becomes obvious. Tawhid, therefore, is better understood as *a perpetual state of becoming than as a static state of being.*

Since there is no sin associated with the acquisition of divine knowledge, there is no sin to transmit to the progeny, and thus no guilt associated with the accident of birth. Likewise there is no mechanism to shoulder the consequence of one's actions beyond that of personal accountability that accompanies freedom of choice starting from a position of strict neutrality. Reincarnation gives the individual perpetual opportunity to grow and learn that is far greater than the fleeting moment of one lifetime, however long it may be. It is the essence of the cumulative experience that is transmitted in the spiritual sense from one physical life span to the next, much as the genetic code serves that function in the physical sense. Interestingly, some scientists are beginning to explore analogous mechanisms for transmission of cultural aspects of human life, through what one geneticist has labeled *memes.* "The new soup is the soup of human culture," according to Richard Dawkins. "The question really means: What is it about the idea of a god that gives it its stability and penetrance in the cultural environment? The survival value of the god meme in the meme pool results from its great psychological appeal. It provides a superficially plausible answer to deep and troubling questions about existence. It suggests that injustices in this world may be rectified in the next."[1] Memes is a hypothetical concept utilized to illustrate the replication and expansion of human cultural heritage. Notice the common use of the word *heritage,* implying heredity. Thus, the continuity of evolution physically, culturally, and spiritually is assured.

Divine law (Shari'a), necessary to guide humanity in the early phases of development when divinity was remote and unreachable, becomes more related to human volition and responsibility, arising from and answerable to the Divine within. Rites and rituals to supplicate and appease can largely be dispensed and replaced with an inner communion whereby the God of immanence meets that of transcendence. It is within this context that the interpretation of the Pillars of Islam in Tawhid, for example, changes from that of physical practice to that of the intuitive and the spiritual experience. Since human beings are at different stages in the process of spiritual development, the need for different approaches becomes apparent. In some cases literal interpretation of the laws and admonitions in what is considered to be the word of God in the revealed religions may be all that is needed, or rather all that can be assimilated at that stage. On the other hand

many others may have progressed to a stage where such concrete and literal interpretations are no longer sufficient to address their spiritual needs. To those people
it is the internal awareness that is their guide as they relate more to the God within
than to the remote and disciplinary deity.

Tawhid is not and was never meant to be a closed system limited by time and
space. If, as stated repeatedly in the Tawhid epistles, "it is through Tawhid that
everything is defined," then Tawhid can never be exclusive, nor can it be static. An
overarching principle like that of Tawhid, proposing a system of creation and cosmic genesis, should not become frozen by tradition and beset by misinterpretation. The true follower of Tawhid cannot view different components of the process
that preceded the most recent call as erroneous or obsolete, any more than gradu-
ates from any program can look with condescension at the steps that made their
ascent possible. The top floors of an edifice with several floors are, by necessity,
top floors because they rest on the foundation of the floors below. Otherwise,
there can be no top floors. The totality of truth is beyond any human being or
human system to fully grasp and comprehend. Thus there is no room for negativ-
ity or derogation for what different people believe in or how they choose to practice their faith. Any reference or insinuation to the contrary in the Druze epistles
(which were copied by hand from one generation to the next and remained scattered for several hundred years) are out of place and out of context and ought to be
outright rejected. The core concepts of Tawhid, based on universality and inclusion, are utterly incompatible with distortions and misrepresentations that may
have been inserted by renegades at one time or another with the aim of sabotage
of the real message and that the years of neglect failed to excise and rectify.

We may recall that the basic tenets of Tawhid are timeless in duration, universal in scope, and evolutionary in outlook. Tawhid, therefore, cannot be restricted to the confines of family or tribe, nor to the coordinates of geographical or
temporal dimensions. The evolutionary process includes all faiths and religions
whereby the message of Tawhid, encoded in different faiths and religions and at
different times and places in the history of creation, becomes more embellished
and more apparent to the believers. "The faith reveals the measure of the heart's
capacity," according to Ibn al-ʿArabi. "That is why there are many different faiths.
To each believer the Divine Being is he who is disclosed to him in the form of his
faith."[2] Against this backdrop of universality of Tawhid we have the particularism
of the Druze, standard-bearers of the faith but with an exclusivity rooted in tradition. It is when tradition became confused with doctrine that the Druze community lost the initiative and the opportunity to evolve and grow. As a minority at

inception, in an atmosphere of insecurity and persecution, the Druze chose to seek refuge in the solidarity of family and tribe. They could not take chances with outsiders whom they did not know and with whom they had no intimate relations. In time a community with its own particularism coalesced, enclosing itself within boundaries that are intimately connected to blood ties and family affiliation. The wide scope of Tawhid was therefore compressed to the narrow-angle lens of the closed system that remains operative in the Druze community to the present time.

Although exclusivity within a closed system stunts growth and impedes progress, it is not altogether without merit. The feeling of shared roots and security in kinship can be wonderful assets, particularly in the fast and drifting currents of modern-day life. Marriage confined within a small population over a thousand years has resulted in a grid of family ties that makes almost the whole community consider itself as one large extended family. It is virtually certain that any Druze individual can establish some sort of family connection with any other Druze individual, sometimes directly and at other times through intermediary families. The blood ties and the deep-rooted traditions are characteristics that, along with other factors, have created a profile that most Druze are proud of and would not easily relinquish. Hence opening the community to outsiders through marriage or conversion is perceived as a threat. Once again it is group solidarity that is at the forefront of the Druze response to the challenge from outside. The closure is, therefore, an expression and a by-product of the need for solidarity and the imperative for survival.

Given this backdrop one can see the difficulty in becoming a Druze, not because the Tawhid faith itself is off-limits, but because of the historical traditions and solidarity of the Druze people. When this issue is understood along two separate tiers, one of faith and the other of family and clan, we may be able to give each tier the attention it deserves and discuss possible solutions to the challenges that the Druze face today and more so in the future.

Humanity is a tapestry of different colors and shades, as is the richer variety of life in general and the still richer majesty of the universe. Yet there is a common thread that runs across this awe-inspiring landscape, and that is awareness, an awareness that generates an indescribable feeling of awe and ecstasy at the unifying force of the universe. This feeling and this awareness are uniquely human. They are also uniquely personal. Everyone ultimately finds his or her own way of seeking the truth and his or her own paradigm for getting there. That is how it appears to me and to many others who have given this matter serious consideration. Many feel that the obligation of the believers in Tawhid extends beyond the confines of the Druze family and tribe, to the wider circle of Islam and the still wider circle of humanity. A message that contains elements of such rationality and depth should not be withheld from the seekers, because Tawhid is built on universality and not on exclusion. In the words of Samah Helal, an American-born Druze and scholar in Tawhid: "We dream of resurrecting Dar al-Hikma [the House of Wisdom in the era of al-Hakim]. . . . We dream of making it the center for a universal movement to unite all monotheistic faiths. . . . We dream of American Muwahhidun taking the lead to build bridges of understanding between Christianity and Islam. . . . We dream of being joined by members of all races and religions in our pilgrimage toward union with God."[3] I would add that such a vision should extend beyond monotheism to include all faiths. How feasible is the realization of such a vision, or how far away that day is remains to be determined.

What should not be far off is an open and candid dialogue among leaders of the Druze community primarily in the West concerning the pressing problems that can no longer be deferred. The advantage of living and (thinking) in the West is the freedom of speech that allows the expression of candid opinions without fear of persecution. The physical and intellectual constraint that prevails in Eastern societies nowadays does not encourage free expression to the same extent that the West enjoys at the present time. Hence the challenge, but also the opportunity that could (and should) be seized in a responsible and meaningful way.

The question is, Are the interests of the Druze people or of the Tawhid to which they lay claim best served by maintaining the status quo for fear of rocking the boat—knowing full well that the boat under the present feudal and spiritual leadership is already leaking and is in danger of sinking—or are these interests better served by exploring options and developing proposals congruent with the core principles of Tawhid but also responsive to the demands of modern life and the pressure of evolution? The Druze community in the West at the present time is an endangered species. The Druze have no viable choice but to evolve; otherwise, they face the real danger of extinction. If some of the options and proposals herein happen to be at variance with the entrenched traditions and blindly accepted dogmas, as they undoubtedly will be, so be it. The choice is essentially between retrenchment and adherence to the old garb that no longer accommodates the imperative of growth, on the one hand, and adjustment to a changing world and readjustment of the garb to accommodate the needs of the present and anticipate those of the future, on the other. "Religion is not a system of belief," declares a contemporary Christian thinker. "It is not a catalogue of revealed truth. It is not an activity designed to control behavior, to reward virtue, and to punish vice. Religion is, rather, a human attempt to process the God experience, which breaks forth from our own depths and wells up constantly within us. We must lay down, therefore, the primitive claims we have made from our religious traditions. None of them is drawn from otherworldly revelations. None of them is inerrant or infallible. None of them represents the only way to God."[4] If the necessity for evolution and renewal is crucial to the survival and well-being of the largest and most powerful religion on earth, the need for the same in the smaller (and closed) sects requires no elaboration.

It was in the New World of Cairo that the most recent chapter in Tawhid was written. The Fatimid caliphs had just moved their capital to a new city designed to fit their need and their mission. It was the New World a thousand years ago. The analogy with the New World that we live in now should not escape notice. If the forefathers in that distant era had the courage to propose a system of thought that was as innovative and as revolutionary as that of the core concept of Tawhid, the generations of modern times should be no less courageous about confronting the needs of the present and the challenges of the future.

One further comment is in order, concerning the question of reform. The word *reform* may raise the eyebrows of some conservative elements in the Druze community who may consider it a veiled attempt to tinker with a sacrosanct and untouchable subject. Inwardly, most of them know that something has to be done but are afraid to admit it. Then there is the fear that once a process of reform is embarked upon, control over the direction or speed of the process may well be lost. More pointedly, no one can predict the outcome. The threat that any change or reform poses to the vested interests of those in a position of privilege, and the magnitude of the expected backlash, can be quite traumatic. These are legitimate concerns, but they do not solve the dilemma of the Druze. The state in which the Druze community finds itself today is the result of centuries of deferring consideration of changes or reforms. There is a potential window in the West for an open and candid dialogue and the possibility of meaningful reform, in accordance with the basic tenets of Tawhid and in keeping with the evolutionary concept of its philosophy. It is this atmosphere of free thinking that provides an opportunity to preserve the core and discard the contaminants that obviously are not (and never were) compatible with the core.

All this is fine, critics may say, but how could we translate these theoretical considerations into the domain of practicality? How do we move from a mind-set of confusion and complaints, mixed with an ego-pleasing state of denial and self-righteousness, to that of planning and action? Do we have the human and mate-

rial resources to initiate and implement what amounts to revitalization and reha-
bilitation of the Druze path in Tawhid after centuries of dormancy and neglect?
And who would confer legitimacy on such endeavors?

Any community with a shared religious and cultural background needs to satisfy a few prerequisites for survival and development. These include at a minimum a place to meet, material for spiritual and moral expression, enlightened
leadership to facilitate and guide the process, and support and active participation
by the members of the community. This is only a partial list within a very brief
context, but it could be used as a start for reform.

Reform can only be accomplished when the community coalesces around a
shared vision and creates a representation that provides a frame of reference and
an authority insofar as the religious affairs of the community are concerned. It
then becomes possible for the community to establish a democratically elected
body that fulfills the spiritual needs of the community and helps in the processes
of evolution and adaptation so that the Druze can meet the challenges of modern
life. Exclusive reliance on the Druze community in the East to address the concerns and regulate the lives of the Druze in the West is, in all probability, doomed
to failure. This should not be interpreted as a call for creating a schism between
East and West. On the contrary it calls for autonomy in the decision-making
process, an autonomy that addresses the needs of the Druze community in the
West, an autonomy without which the Druze community is threatened with disintegration. Moreover, we should take note that the Druze people have not had
this kind of institutional organization in the East where tradition was the main
source of sustenance. Organizational thinking following Western models is a recent acquisition in the Druze culture, and its introduction in the Druze communities of the West may be of great service to the traditional Druze communities of
the East. In fact the lack of a hierarchical structure, religious institutions, elaborate rites and rituals, and external trappings of religious expression are considered
by many as a mark of distinction. This simplicity contributed to freeing the Druze
from the strong hold that religious leaders exert and religious institutions possess
in many other faiths. The distinctive mystical vein in Druze religiosity makes the
Druze path intensely personal and private. This characteristic has fostered the
neglect of structure and the Druze pride in the fact that their faith does not depend on hierarchical structure and exoteric manifestations.

Modern times, however, dictate a minimum degree of organization without
which chaos and disintegration supervene, denying the community the opportunity to respond and adjust. The moment for genuine reform is upon the Druze,

and how the community deals with it is entirely in its hands. The educated class and thinkers in the Druze community have shunned dealing with religion in the past, preferring to remain within the safe haven of the uninitiated *(juhhal)*, thus avoiding the burden of responsibility inherent in religious discourse. Present times, however, dictate a different posture. Otherwise, the crisis will only worsen. John Cantwell Smith's description of the Arab and Islamic world is poignantly apt as to the Druze condition as well: "Its greatest problem is the degree to which those who in the fullest sense know the religion have largely lost contact with the modern world, and those genuinely oriented to modernity have largely lost contact with their religion." [5]

The bold initiative of Tawhid that the Druze embraced almost one thousand years ago was itself a major attempt at reform and renewal in Islam. Reform in modern times should be viewed with that heritage in mind. It is another leg in the long journey in Tawhid.

The opportunity to free the mind from the shackles of dogma and the suffocating hold of tradition should not be missed or deferred. There is ample evidence that mere reliance on tradition increasingly acts as a stumbling block in the path of the evolution of the community and a detriment to its vital interests. The choice is between seizing the initiative to rehabilitate a potentially forward-looking doctrine (the core of which is suited to modern times), and maintaining the status quo, as the Druze fathers and forefathers have done. Today's Druze community has inherited the cumulative debt of centuries of neglect and deferment. If nothing is done, the present generation will bequeath a larger debt to future generations. Attempts are always accompanied by the fear of change. The fact is that rocking the boat, with all the associated risks, may be far safer than the alternative of abandoning ship.

NOTES

BIBLIOGRAPHY

INDEX

Notes

Druze Manuscripts

The following religious texts exist primarily in manuscript form, with no definitive published version. All references to epistles *(rasa'il)* in the notes are drawn from the six volumes of epistles (111 in all) making up the *Kutub al-Hikma*. These epistles, written by the luminaries of Tawhid, were collated much later, in the fifteenth century, by the eminent Druze emir and theologian al-Sayyid Jamal al-Din Abdallah al-Tanukhi (b. 1417 C.E. [A.H. 820]).

Al-Shari'a al-ruhaniyya fi ulum al-latif wa al-basit wa al-kathif [Spiritual Law in Material and Spiritual Disciplines]

Kitab al-munfarid bi thatihi [The Unique One]

Kutub al-Hikma [Books of Wisdom]; also known as *Rasa'il al-hikma* [Epistles of Wisdom]

Rasa'il al-Hind [The India Epistles]

Sijil al-awwal wa al-akhir [The First and Last Document]

Umdat al-'arifin (al-mua'llaf) [The Pillars of Knowledge]

1. Introduction

1. Pierre Teilhard de Chardin, *The Phenomenon of Man*, trans. Bernard Wall (London: William Collins Sons Ltd., and New York: Harper and Row, 1959), 13. Originally published in French as *Le phénomène humain* (Paris: Edition du Seuil, 1955). See also 224: "Transplanted by man into the thinking layer of the earth, heredity . . . finds itself . . . settled into the reflecting organism, collective and permanent. From the chain of cells it passes into the circumterrestrial layers of the noosphere."

2. Jeremy Rifkin, *Entropy* (New York: Viking Press, 1980), 204.

3. Peter B. Medawar, *The Limits of Science* (New York: Harper and Row, 1984), 60.

4. Karen Armstrong, *A History of God* (New York: Ballantine Books, 1993), 6.

5. John C. Eccles, *Evolution of the Brain: Creation of the Self* (London: Routledge, 1991), 237.

6. Huston Smith, *The Religions of Man* (New York: Harper and Row, 1958), 5.

7. Andrew H. Knoll, *Life on a Young Planet* (Princeton, N.J.: Princeton Univ. Press, 2005), 246.

8. Alexis Carrel, *Man the Unknown* (New York: Harper and Brothers, 1935), 278.

9. Sami Abu Shakra, *Manaqib al-duruz fi al-'aqida wa al-tarikh* [Druze Morals: Belief and History] (Shouf, Lebanon: Maktabat Nasif, n.d.), 111–23.

10. Nejla Abu-Izzeddin, *The Druzes: A New Study of Their History, Faith, and Society* (Leiden: E. J. Brill, 1984), 7.

11. Nadim Hamza, *Al-Tanukhiyyun* [The Tanukh Tribe] (Beirut: Dar al-Nahar, 1984), 7.

12. Abbas Abu Saleh, *Tarikh al-Muwahhidun al-Duruz al-siasi fi al-Mashriq al-arabi* [The Political History of the Muwahhidun al-Duruz in the Arab East] (Beirut: Manshurat al-Majlis al-Durzi li al-Buhuth wa al-Inma', n.d.), 61.

13. Amin Talih, *Asl al-Muwahhidun al-Duruz wa usulahum* [The Origin and Principles of the Druze] (Beirut: Dar al-Andalus, 1961), 12.

14. Kais Firro, *A History of the Druzes* (Leiden: E. J. Brill, 1992), 20.

15. Al-Tanukhi Ajaj Nuwayhid, *Dar al-Sahafa*, 2nd edition (Beirut: n.p., 1963).

16. Muhammad Kamil Husayn, *Ta'ifat al-Duruz* [The Druze Sect] (Cairo: Dar al-Ma'rifa', 1962), 147.

2. Historical Background

1. Muhammad Zafrulla Khan, *Muhammad: Seal of the Prophets* (London: Routledge and Kegan Paul, 1980), 18.

2. Emad al-Sabbagh, *Al-Ahnaf* [The Hanifs] (Damascus: Dar al-Hisad, 1998), 2.

3. Karen Armstrong, *Muhammad: A Biography of the Prophet* (New York: HarperCollins, 1992), 62.

4. Muhammad Rawwas Kala'ji, *Qira'a siyasiyya li al-sirat al-nabawiyya* [A Political Analysis of the Legacy of the Prophet] (Beirut: Dar al-Nafa'is, 1996), 38.

5. Robert Payne, *The History of Islam* (New York: Barnes and Noble, 1950), 87.

6. Jalal al-Din al-Suyuti, *Tarikh al-khulafa'* [The History of the Caliphs], authenticated by Ibrahim Saleh (Beirut: Dar Sader, 1997) 98.

7. Payne, *History of Islam*, 89.

8. Ibid., 98.

9. 'Ali ibn Abi-Taleb, *Nahj al-balagha* [The Path of Eloquence], ed. Muhammad Abdu (Cairo: Dar al-Ma'rifa, n.d.), 124.

10. Taha Hussein, *'Uthman* (Cairo: Dar al-Ma'rifa, 1947), 190, 198.

11. Abbas Mahmud al-Akkad, *'Abqariyat al-Imam 'Ali* [The Genius of Imam 'Ali] (Beirut: Dar al-Kitab al-'Arabi, 1976), 76.

3. Dynastic Islam

1. Muhammad Mahdi Shamseddin, *Thawrat al-Husayn* [The Revolt of al-Husayn] (Beirut: Dar al-Ta'aruf li al-Matbua't, 1979), 178, 179.

2. Taha Hussein, *'Ali wa banuh* ['Ali and His Sons] (Cairo: Dar al-Ma'rifa, 1980), 245.

3. Fouad Ajami, *The Vanished Imam* (Ithaca, N.Y.: Cornell Univ. Press, 1986), 138.

4. Aref Tamer, *Al-Qaramita* [The Carmathians] (Beirut: Dar Maktabat al-Hayat, n.d.), 33.

5. Farhad Daftary, *The Isma'ilis* (New York: Cambridge Univ. Press, 1990), 83.

6. Tamer, *Al-Qaramita*, 77.

7. Ibid., 80.

8. Sulayman Salim Alamuddin, *Al-Qaramita* [The Carmathians] (Beirut: Dar Nawfal, 2003), 102.

9. Mustafa Ghaleb, *Al-Qaramita* [The Carmathians] (Beirut: Dar al-Andalus, 1983), 5, 6.

10. Tamer, *Al-Qaramita*, 209.

11. Majid Fakhry, *Tarikh al-falsafa al-islamiyya* [History of Islamic Philosophy], transl. Kamal Yazigi (into Arabic) (Beirut: Al-Dar al-Muttahida li al-Nashr, 1974), 81.

12. Zuhdi Jar Allah, *Al-Mu'tazila* [The Mu'tazilites] (Beirut: Al-Mua'sasa al-Arabia li al-Tiba'a wa al-Nashr, 1990), 253.

13. Kamal Yazigi, *Ma'alim al-fikr al-'arabi fi al-asr al-wasit* [Highlights of Arab Thought in the Middle Period] (Beirut: Dar al-'Ilm li al-Malayin, 1954), 200.

14. Aref Tamer, *Jami'at al-jami'a* [Comprehensive Compendium] (Beirut: Dar al-Hayat, n.d.), 43.

15. Ibid., 21.

16. Ursula King, *Christian Mystics* (New York: Simon and Schuster, 1998), 30.

17. Jalal Sharaf al-Din, *Dirasat fi al-tasawwuf al-islami* [Studies in Islamic Mysticism] (Beirut: Dar al-Nahdha al-'Arabiyya, 1980), 45.

18. Muhammad Jawad al-Fakih, *Salman al-Farisi* (Beirut: Dar al-Funun, 1981), 29.

19. Fritjof Capra, *The Tao of Physics* (Boston: Shambhala Publications, 2000), 25.

20. Michel Farid Ghorayyeb, *Al-Hallaj* (Beirut: Dar Maktabat al-Hayat, n.d.), 78, 86.

21. Sami Makarem, *Al-Hallaj* (London: Riad el-Rayess Books, 1989), 42.

22. Ibid., 57.

23. Aref Tamer, *Al-Hakim bi Amr Allah* [The Ruler by the Will of God] (Beirut: Dar al-Afaq al-Jadida, 1982), 9.

24. Tamer, *Jami'at al-jami'a*, 10.

25. Mustafa Ghaleb, *Al-risala al-jami'a* [The Comprehensive Epistle] (Beirut: Dar al-Andalus, 1984), 12.

26. Paul E. Walker, *Abu Ya'qub al-Sijistani* (London: I. B. Tauris and Co., 1998), 28.

27. I'mad al-Din Idris, *Tarikh al-khulafa' al-fatimiyyin bi al-Maghrib* [History of the Fatimid Caliphs in the West], authenticated by Muhammad al-Ya'lawi (Beirut: Dar al-Gharb al-Islami, 1985), 144; Mustafa Ghaleb, introduction to *Rahat al-'aql* [Peace of Mind], by Hamid al-Din al-Kirmani (Beirut: Dar al-Andalus, 1983), 27.

28. Idris, *Tarikh*, 48.

4. The Fatimid Caliphate

1. Taqi al-Din al-Maqrizi, *Al-khutat al-maqriziyya* [The Maqrizi Papers], ed. Khalil Mansur (Beirut: Dar al-Kutub al-'Ilmiyya, 1998), 185.

2. Taha al-Wali, *Al-Qaramita* [The Carmathians] (Beirut: Dar al-'Ilm li al-Malayin, 1981), 88.

3. Ahmad al-Baghdadi, *Al-tajdid al-fikr al-dini* [Renewal in Religious Thought] (Cyprus: Dar al-Mada li al-Thaqafa wa al-Nashr, 1999), 67.

4. Aref Tamer, *Al-Qai'm wa al-Mansur al-fatimiyyan* [The Fatimid Caliphs: Al-Qa'im and al-Mansour] (Beirut: Dar al-Afaq al-Jadida, 1982), 77.

5. Ahmad Amin, *Zuhr al-Islam* [The Midday of Islam] (Beirut: Dar al-Kitab al-'Arabi, 1945), 189.

6. Abdallah Najjar, *Madhhab al-Duruz wa al-Tawhid* [Druze Faith and Tawhid] (Cairo: Dar al-Ma'rifa, 1965), 99.

7. Aref Tamer, *Al-khalifa al-fatimi al-khamis al-Aziz bi Allah* [The Fifth Fatimid Caliph al-Aziz bi Allah] (Beirut: Dar al-Afaq al-Jadida, 1982), 103.

8. Abu-Izzeddin, *The Druzes*, 55.

9. Amin, *Zuhr al-Islam*, 190.

10. Tamer, *Al-Hakim bi Amr Allah*, 20.

11. Heinz Halm, *The Fatimids and Their Traditions of Learning* (New York: I. B. Tauris, 1997), 36.

12. Amin, *Zuhr al-Islam*, 200.

13. Halm, *The Fatimids*, 74.

14. Marun Abbud, *Zawba'at al-duhur* [The Cyclone of the Ages] (Beirut: Dar Marun Abbud, 1980), 124.

15. Paul E. Walker, *Hamid al-Din al-Kirmani* (London: I. B. Tauris, 1999), 20.

16. Tamer, *Al-Hakim bi Amr Allah*, 74.

17. Najjar, *Madhhab al-Duruz*, 108.

18. Sadik A. Assaad, *The Reign of al-Hakim bi Amr-Allah* (Beirut: Arab Institute for Research and Publishing, 1974), 92.

19. Firro, *History of the Druzes*, 8.

20. Robert Benton Betts, *The Druze* (New Haven: Yale Univ. Press, 1988), 8.

21. Hashim 'Uthman, *Al-Isma'iliyya* [Isma'ilism] (Beirut: Al-Alami Library, 1998), 214.

22. See generally the writings of Halm, Tamer, Ghaleb, and Sadek.

23. Ibn Hani al-Andalusi, *Diwan* [Collection of Poems] (Beirut: Dar Sader, 1994), 146.

24. 'Uthman, *Al-Isma'iliyya*, 373.

25. Al-Wali, *Al-Qaramita*, 293.

26. Muhammad 'Ali al-Zu'bi, *Al-Duruz: Zahiruhum wa batinuhum* [The Overt and Covert Beliefs of the Druze] (Damascus: N.p., n.d.), 46. See also 'Uthman, *Al-Isma'iliyya*, 167.

27. Epistle 13.

28. Walker, *Hamid al-Din al-Kirmani*, 22.

29. Epistle 16.

30. Marshal H. G. Hodgson, "Al-Darazi and Hamza in the Origin of the Druze Religion," *Journal of the American Society of Oriental Studies* 82 (1962): 7.

31. Taysir Abu Hamdan, *Al-Duruz* (Amman: Sharikat al-Sharq al-Awsat li al-Tiba'a, 1992), 20.

32. Walker, *Hamid al-Din al-Kirmani*, xi.

33. Epistle 17.

34. Abu-Izzeddin, *The Druzes*, 105.

35. Abdul-Munim Majid, *Al-Hakim bi Amr Allah, al-khalifa al-muftara alayh* [Al-Hakim bi Amr Allah, the Wronged Caliph] (Cairo: n.p., 1982), 169–76.

36. Sadek, *The Reign of al-Hakim*, 182.

37. Epistle 1.

38. Halm, *The Fatimids*, 39.

39. Abu Saleh, *Tarikh al-Muwahhidun*, 67.

40. A. N. Wilson, *Paul: The Mind of the Apostle* (New York: W. W. Norton, 1997), 15.

41. Abu Saleh, *Tarikh*, 77.

5. Tenets of the Tawhid Faith

1. Mursil Nasr, *Al-Muwahhidun al-Duruz fi al-Islam* [The Muwahhidun Druze in Islam] (Beirut: Al-Dar al-Islamiyya, 1997), 164.

2. Sahar Mua'kassa, *Comprehensive Biography of the Druze Religion* (New York: Druze Research and Publications Institute, 2004), 108.

3. Najib Alamuddin, *Turmoil: The Druzes, Lebanon and the Arab-Israeli Conflict* (London: Quartet Books, 1993), 28.

4. Betts, *The Druze*, 29.

5. Epistle 13.

6. Ibid.

7. Epistle 67.

8. Ibid.

9. Epistle 35.

10. Epistle 53.

11. Epistle 14.

12. Epistle 17.

13. *Rasa'il al-Hind.*

14. Epistle 18.

15. Epistle 29.

16. Epistle 12.

17. Epistle 67.

18. Epistle 13.

19. Epistle 69.

20. Epistle 58.

21. Epistle 36.

22. Epistle 36.

23. Fariduddin al-Attar, "The Parliament of the Birds," in *The Element Book of Mystical Verse*, ed. Alan Jacobs and Michael Mann (Shaftesbury, Dorset: Element Books, 1997), 58.

24. Yusuf Ibish, "Ibn al-Arabi's Theory of Journeying," in *Contemplation and Action in World Religions*, ed. Yusuf Ibish and Ileana Marculescu (Seattle: Univ. of Washington Press, 1978), 209.

25. Eknath Esrawan, *The Bhagavad Gita* (Tomales, Calif.: Nilgiri Press, 1985), 85.

26. Ibid., 150.

27. Ibid., 162.

28. Ibid., 12.

29. Ken Wilber, "Psychologia Perennis: The Spectrum of Consciousness," *Journal of Transpersonal Psychology* 7, no. 2 (1975): 108.

30. Ibid.

31. Darryl Reanney, *After Death* (New York: William Morrow and Co., 1991), 214.

32. Ibid., 233.

33. Gershom Scholem, quoted in *Reincarnation: A New Horizon in Science, Religion, and Society*, by Sylvia Cranston and Carey Williams (Pasadena, Calif.: Theosophical Univ. Press, 1993), 191.

34. Paul Davies, *The Mind of God: The Scientific Basis for a Rational World* (New York: Simon and Schuster, 1997), 232.

35. Abu 'Ala' al-Ma'arri, *Diwan Abi al-'Ala' al-Ma'arri* [Poetry of Abu 'Ala' al-Ma'arri] (Beirut: Dar Sader, 1975).

36. Leo Schaya, "Contemplation and Action in Judaism and Islam," in *Contemplation and Action in World Religions: Selected Papers from the Rothko Chapel Colloquium "Traditional Modes of Contemplation and Action,"* ed. Yusuf Ibish and Ileana Marculescu (Seattle, Wash.: Rothko Chapel, 1978), 151–89.

37. Amit Goswami, *The Self-Aware Universe* (New York: Penguin Putnam, 1993), 215.

38. Teilhard de Chardin, *The Phenomenon of Man*, 257–60.

39. Nasr Hamid Abu Zayd, *Falsafat al-ta'wil* [The Philosophy of Esoterism] (Beirut: Al-Markaz al-Thaqafi al-'Arabi, 1998), 211.

40. Eugene G. d'Aquili and Andrew B. Newberg, "Consciousness and the Machine," *Zygon* 31, no. 2 (1966): 245.

41. Wilber, "Psychologia Perennis," 106, 122.

42. Epistle 74.

43. Kamal Jumblatt, *Fi ma yata'adda al-harf* [Beyond the Letter] (Mukhtara, Lebanon: Al-Dar al-Taqadumiyya, 1987), 92.

44. Christian de Duve, *Vital Dust: Life as a Cosmic Imperative* (New York: Basic Books, 1995), 301.

45. Quoted in Ernst Benz, "Theogony and the Transformation of Man in Friedrich Wilhelm Joseph Schelling," in *Man and Transformation: Papers from the Eranos Yearbooks* (Bollingen Series 30, vol. 5), ed. Joseph Campbell (Princeton, N.J.: Princeton Univ. Press, 1964), 225, 229.

46. Henri Corbin, *Alone with the Alone* (Princeton, N.J.: Princeton Univ. Press, 1969), 197.

47. Rasa'il al-Hind.

48. Epistle 58.

49. Epistle 9.

50. Sami Makarem, *Al-taqiya fi al-Islam* [Dissimulation in Islam] (London: Druze Heritage Foundation, 2004), 18.

51. Gershom Scholem, *Major Trends in Jewish Mysticism* (New York: Schocken Books, 1961), 206.

52. Epistle 35.

53. José Faur, *Homo Mysticus* (Syracuse, N.Y.: Syracuse Univ. Press, 1999), 144.

54. Epistle 67.

55. Capra, *Tao of Physics*, 96.

56. Al-Fakih, *Salman al-Farisi*, 9.

57. Epistle 58.

58. Fariduddin al-Attar, *Mantiq al-tayr* [The Logic of Birds], trans. Badi' Muhammad Juma'a (Beirut: Dar al-Andalus, 1996), 104.

59. Epistle 13.

60. Ibid.

61. Ibid.

62. Ibid.

63. Al-Harith ibn Assad al-Muhasibi, *Al-'aql wa fahm al-Qur'an* [The Mind in Understanding the Qur'an], authenticated by Husayn al-Quwwatli (Damascus: Dar al-Kindi, 1978), 122.

64. Epistle 13.

65. Ibid.

66. Capra, *Tao of Physics* 77.

67. Epistle 13.

68. Sandra Mackey, *The Iranians* (New York: Penguin Books, 1966), 16.

69. Epistle 53.

70. Epistle 13.

71. Epistle 16.

72. Epistle 36.

73. Epistle 14.

74. Epistle 10.

75. Epistle 33.

76. Garth Fowden, *The Egyptian Hermes* (Princeton, N.J.: Princeton Univ. Press, 1986), 23.

77. Epistle 20.

78. Epistle 10.

79. Afif Abu Farraj, "Al-masar al-ishraqi min Hermes ila Aflaton" [The Path of Illumination from Hermes to Plato], in *Maqalat fi al-Tawhid* (Beirut: Dar Isharat, 2000), 41.

80. Christopher Knight and Robert Lomas, *The Hiram Key* (New York: Barnes and Noble, 1996), 103.

81. *Al-mihrajan al-alfi li Abi al-'Ala' al-Ma'arri* [The One-Thousandth Anniversary of Abu al-'Ala' al-Ma'arri] (Beirut: Dar Sader, 1945), 205.

82. Halm, *The Fatimids*, 51, 74.

83. Anton Farah, *Ibn Rushd wa falsafatuhu* [Averroes and His Philosophy] (Beirut: Dar al-Tali'a, 1981), 67.

84. Ralph Waldo Emerson, "The Transcendentalist," in *Emerson on Transcendentalism*, ed. Edward L. Ericson (New York: Continuum Publishing, 1986), 93.

85. David Adams Leeming, *The World of Myth* (New York: Oxford Univ. Press, 1990), 133.

86. Quoted in Reanney, *After Death*, 242.

87. James Jeans, quoted in Cranston and Williams, *Reincarnation*, 36.

88. Erwin Schroedinger, *What Is Life?* (Cambridge: Cambridge Univ. Press, 1962), 52.

89. Julian Huxley, *Evolution in Action* (New York: Harper and Brothers, 1953), 118.

90. Epistle 37.

91. Epistle 35.

92. Ibid.

93. Anwar F. Abi-Khzam, introduction to *Al-nuqat wa al-dawa'ir* [The Dots and the Circles], by Zayn al-Din 'Abd al-Gaffar Taqi al-Din, ed. Sulayman Taqi ql-Din, 19–94 (Beirut: Dar Isharat, 1999).

94. Alfred Lord Tennyson, letter to B. P. Blood, 7 May 1874, Faringford, Freshwater, Isle of

4

Wight, quoted in Tennyson, Hallam T. *Alfred, Lord Tennyson: A Memoir by His Son.* 1899. Rev. ed., London: Macmillan, 1940.

95. William Blake, *Songs of Innocence and of Experience* (1795; repr., New York: Alfred A. Knopf, 1994), 209.

96. Mustafa Ghaleb, *Mafatih al-ma'rifa* [The Keys of Knowledge] (Beirut: Mua'ssasat Izzedin li al-Tiba'a wa al-Nashr, 1982), 230.

97. Epistle 69.

98. Abu Nasr al-Farabi, *Mabadi' ara' ahl al-madina al-fadila* [The Principles of Thought of the Citizens of the Virtuous City], trans. Richard Walzer (Oxford: Clarendon Press, 1985), 319.

99. Epistle 70.

100. Epistle 75.

101. Epistle 86.

102. Epistle 69.

103. Epistle 52.

104. Zayn al-Din 'Abd al-Gaffar Taqi al-Din, *Al-nuqat wa al-dawa'ir* [The Dots and the Circles] (Beirut: Dar Isharat, 1999), 117.

105. Epistle 44.

106. Epistle 85.

107. Epistle 67.

108. Epistle 70.

109. Ibid.

110. Ibid.

111. Ibid.

112. Epistle 15.

113. Yusuf Karam, *Tarikh al-falsafa al-yunaniyya* [History of Greek Philosophy] (Beirut: Dar al-Qalam, n.d.) 24.

114. Geddes MacGregor, *Reincarnation in Christianity: A New Vision of the Role of Rebirth in Christian Thought* (Wheaton, Ill.: Theosophical Publishing House/Quest Books, 1978), 19.

115. Quoted in Cranston and Williams, *Reincarnation,* 186–87.

116. Ibid., 12.

117. Ibid., 14.

118. Quoted in Cranston and Williams, *Reincarnation,* 19.

119. Ibid., 6.

120. Ibid., 10.

121. Ibid., 23.

122. Emerson, "The Transcendentalist," 6.

123. Quoted in Cranston and Williams, *Reincarnation,* 37.

124. Daftary, *The Isma'ilis,* 133.

125. Halm, *The Fatimids,* 51.

126. Reanney, *After Death,* 268.

127. Quoted in Cranston and Williams, *Reincarnation,* 333.

128. Ibid., 338.

129. Ibid., ix.

130. Gibran Khalil Gibran, *The Prophet* (New York: Alfred A. Knopf, 1963), 103.

131. Michael Na'imy, *Al-yawm al-akhir* [The Last Day] (Beirut: Mu'asasat Nawfal, 1978), 157.

132. Epistle 67.

133. Ian Stevenson, "The Exploratory Value of the Idea of Reincarnation," *Journal of Nervous and Mental Disease* 164, no. 5 (1974): 305–26.

134. MacGregor, *Reincarnation in Christianity*, 107.

135. Al-Basha Muhammad Khalil, *Al-taqammus wa asrar al-hayat wa al-mawt* [Reincarnation and the Secrets of Life and Death] (Beirut: Dar al-Nahar li al-Nashr, 1992), 186.

136. T. S. Eliot, "Burnt Norton" (No. 1 in "Four Quartets") in *Poetry Speaks*, ed. Elise Paschen and Rebekah Presson Mosby, 110–13 (Naperville, Ill. Sourcebooks, 2001).

6. Expression of the Tenets in Daily Conduct

1. Epistle 7.

2. Joseph Kaster, trans. and ed., *The Wisdom of Ancient Egypt* (New York: Barnes and Noble, 1993), 140.

3. Epistle 41.

4. Epistle 9.

5. Epistle 15.

6. Ibid.

7. Epistle 30.

8. Epistle 35.

9. Epistle 50.

10. Epistle 65.

11. Epistle 77.

12. Epistle 93.

13. Taqi al-Din, *Al-nuqat wa al-dawa'ir*, 133.

14. Epistle 98.

15. Epistle 111.

16. Epistle 18.

17. Epistle 35.

18. Epistle 16.

19. Talih, *Asl al-Muwahhidun al-Duruz*, 8, 9.

20. Epistle 33.

21. Epistle 52.

22. Epistle 65.

23. Epistle 87.

24. Epistle 25.

25. Nasr, *Al-Muwahhidun al-Duruz*, 51.

26. Halim Taqi al-Din, *Qada' al-Muwahhidun al-Duruz* [Druze Jurisprudence] (Beirut: n.p., 1979), 183.

27. Al-Shari'a al-ruhaniyya fi ulum al-latif wa al-basit wa al-kathif.

28. Epistle 15.

29. Epistle 42.

30. Epistle 45.

31. Abu-Izzeddin, *The Druzes*, 229.

32. Wahbah Sayegh, *Know Your Tawheed Faith*, vol. 4, *Messages and Shrines* (Benton Harbor, Mich.: American Druze Society Committee on Religious Affairs, 1990), 9.

33. Sami Makarem, *Maslak al-Tawhid* [The Tawhid Path] (Beirut: Majlis al-Buhuth, 1980), 74.

34. Epistle 52.

35. Epistle 52.

36. Epistle 73.

37. Reanney, *After Death*, 241.

38. Epistle 7.

39. Epistle 9.

40. Epistle 15.

41. Epistle 74.

42. Ghaleb, *Mafatih al-ma'rifa*, 205.

43. Epistle 35.

44. Epistle 15.

45. Epistle 39.

46. Sami S. Swayd, "Rethinking Druze Historiography," *Journal of Druze Studies* 1, no. 1 (2000): 129.

47. Epistle 10.

48. Epistle 33.

49. Muhammad Abdul Hamid al-Hamd, *Sabe'at Harran wa al-Tawhid al-Durzi* [Sabe'at Harran and the Tawhid of the Druze] (Damascus: Dar al-Tali'a al-Jadida, 2003), 177.

50. Anwar Abi-Khzam, *Islam al-Muwahhidin* (n.p., n.d.), 205.

51. Moses Maimonides, *The Guide for the Perplexed [Dalat al-hayrin]*, translated from the Arabic by Michael Friedlander (New York: Dover Publications, 1946), 44.

52. Makarem, *Al-taqiya fi al-Islam*, 128.

53. Epistle 58.

54. Epistle 74.

55. Corbin, *Alone with the Alone*, 71.

56. Epistle 35.

57. Epistle 42.

58. Epistle 53.

59. Epistle 50.

60. Ervin Laszlo, *Macroshift* (San Francisco: Barret-Koehler Publishers, 2001), 122.

61. Lama Govinda, quoted in Capra, *Tao of Physics*, 305.

62. Epistle 9.

63. Esrawan, *Bhagavad Gita*, 209.

64. Epistle 39.

65. Muhammad Abu Shakra, "Fi ma'rifat al-din wa qawamuhu" [Concerning Religious Knowledge and Its Basis], in *Al-Tawhid al-durzi fi madmunihi al-insani* [The Druze Tawhid in Its Human Context], ed. Sami Abu Shakra, 104 (Beirut: n.p., 1984).

7. Challenge and Opportunity

1. Intisar Azzam, *Change for Continuity: The Druze in America* (Beirut: MAJD Enterprise Universitaire, 1997), 80.

2. Walker, *Hamid al-Din al-Karmani*, 1.

3. Hamid al-Din al-Kirmani, "Risalat isbu' dawr al-satr" [The Epistle of the Anniversary of the Era of Occultation] in *Arba' rasa'il Isma'iliyya* [Four Isma'ili Epistles], ed. Aref Tamer (Beirut: Dar al-Kashaf, 1953), 66.

4. Nabih al-Sa'di, *Madhhab al-Tawhid fi maqalat 'ashr* [Tawhid Faith in Ten Essays] (Beirut: n.p., 1993), 81.

5. Makarem, *Maslak al-Tawhid*, 154.

6. Abi-Khzam, *Islam al-Muwahhidin* 178.

7. Abdallah Najjar, *The Druze: Millenium Scrolls Revealed*, trans. Fred Massey and Abdallah Najjar (N.p., 1973) 143.

8. Talih', *Asl al-Muwahhidun al-Duruz*, 77.

9. Najib al-Israwi, *Al-madhhab al-tawhidi al-durzi* [The Druze Tawhid Faith] (Brazil: n.p., 1990), 65.

10. Nasr, *Al-Muwahhidun al-Duruz*, 80.

11. Ibid., 71.

12. Taher ibn Muhammad al-Baghdadi, *Al-farq bayn al-firaq* [The Difference Between Sects], authenticated by Muhi al-Din 'Abd al-Hamid (Beirut: Dar al-Ma'rifa, n.d.), 6.

13. Epistle 78.

14. Epistle 10.

15. Epistle 57.

16. Epistle 74.

17. Epistle 78.

18. Epistle 80.

19. Epistle 7.

20. Epistle 73.

21. Epistle 36.

22. Nasr, *Al-Muwahhidun al-Duruz*, 38.

23. Epistle 6.

24. Epistle 1.

25. Maimonides, *Guide for the Perplexed*, 387.

26. Yusuf Ibrahim Yazbek, *Waliyun min Lubnan* [A Guardian from Lebanon] (Beirut: Awraq Lunahiyya, 1960), 62.

27. Makarem, *Maslak al-Tawhid*, 182.

28. *Al-Shari'a al-ruhaniyya.*

29. *Kitab al-Munfarid bi thatihi.* In this passage, *zakat* is interpreted allegorically as purification of the soul.

30. Makarem, *Maslak al-Tawhid*, 184.

31. Epistle 6.

32. Ibid.

33. Sami Abu Shaqra, *Al-Tawhid al-durzi fi madmunihi al-insani* [The Druze Tawhid in Its Human Context] (Beirut: n.p., 1984), 25.

34. Epistle 74.

35. Nasr, *Al-Muwahhidun al-Duruz* 108.

36. Abi-Taleb, *Nahj al-Balagha*, 66.

37. *Kitab al-Munfarid bi thatihi.*

38. Epistle 35.

39. Nasr, *Al-Muwahhidun al-Duruz* 163.

40. *Al-Shari'a al-ruhaniyya.*

41. Epistle 30.

42. Epistle 29.

43. Makarem, *Maslak al-Tawhid*, 199.

44. Ahmad al-Baghdadi *Al-tajdid al-fikr al-dini*, 224.

45. Muhammad Mahdi Shamseddin, *Al-tajdid fi al-fikr al-islami* [The Renewal in Islamic Thought] (Beirut: Dar al-Manhal al-Lubnani, 1997), 78.

46. Epistle 69.

47. Laszlo, *Macroshift*, 123.

48. *Kitab al-Munfarid bi thatihi.*

49. Epistle 53.

50. Najjar, *Madhhab al-Duruz*, 123.

51. Epistle 55.

52. Epistle 53.

53. Epistle 54.

54. Epistle 55.

55. Elaine Pagels, *The Gnostic Gospels* (New York: Vantage Books, 1979), xix.

56. Epistle 72.

57. Yusuf Ibrahim Yazbek, introduction to *Al-dawlah al-durziyya* [The Druze State], trans. from *Puget San Pierre* by Hafiz Abu Muslih (Beirut: Al-Maktaba al-Haditha, 1983), 8.

58. Epistle 1.

59. Epistle 81.

60. Epistle 106.

61. Daftary, *The Isma'ilis*, 109.

62. Epistle 111.

63. Epistle 13.

64. Epistle 10.

65. Epistle 16.

66. Epistle 36.

67. Epistle 53.

68. Epistle 58.

69. Epistles 34, 64, 76.

70. Fuad I. Khuri, *Being a Druze* (London: Druze Heritage Foundation, 2004), 237–38.

71. Jumblatt Kamal, *I Speak for Lebanon* (London: Zed Press 1982), 26.

72. Taqi al-Din, *Maqalat fi al-Tawhid*, 10, 30.

73. Abdallah Najjar, "The Druzes' Role in America Today," paper delivered at the 22nd annual convention of the American Druze Society, Charleston, W. Va., June 24–26, 1968.

74. Azzam, *Change for Continuity*, 100.

75. Ibid., 103.

8. Concluding Remarks

1. Richard Dawkins, *The Selfish Gene* (Oxford: Oxford Univ. Press, 1976), 192, 193.

2. Corbin, *Alone with the Alone*, 197.

3. Samah Helal, keynote address delivered at the 41st annual convention of the American Druze Society, Durango, Colo., June 30–July 5, 1987, printed in *Our Heritage* 7, no. 3 (1987).

4. John Shelby Spong, *Why Christianity Must Change or Die* (San Francisco: HarperSanFrancisco, 1998), 225.

5. Wilfred Cantwell Smith, *Islam in Modern History* (Princeton, N.J.: Princeton Univ. Press, 1957), 160.

Bibliography

Druze Manuscripts

Al-Shari'a al-ruhaniyya fi ulum al-latif wa al-basit wa al-kathif [Spiritual Law in Material and Spiritual Disciplines]

Kitab al-munfarid bi thatihi [The Unique One]

Kutub al-Hikma [Books of Wisdom]; also known as *Rasa'il al-hikma* [Epistles of Wisdom]

Rasa'il al-Hind [The India Epistles]

Sijil al-awwal wa al-akhir [The First and Last Document]

Umdat al-'arifin (al-mua'llaf) [The Pillars of Knowledge]

General

Abbud, Marun. *Zawba'at al-duhur* [The Cyclone of the Ages]. Beirut: Dar Marun Abbud, 1980.

Abi-Khzam, Anwar F. Introduction to *Al-nuqat wa al-dawa'ir* [The Dots and the Circles], by Zayn al-Din 'Abd al-Gaffar Taqi al-Din. Edited by Sulayman Taqi al-Din. Beirut: Dar Isharat, 1999.

———. *Islam al-Muwahhidin.* N.p., n.d.

Abu Farraj, Afif. "Al-masar al-ishraqi min Hermes ila Aflaton" [The Path of Illumination from Hermes to Plato]. In *Maqalat fi al-Tawhid.* Beirut: Dar Isharat, 2000.

Abu Hamdan, Taysir. *Al-Duruz* [The Druze]. Amman: Sharikat al-Sharq al-Awsat li al-Tiba'a, 1992.

Abu-Izzeddin, Nejla M. *The Druzes: A New Study of Their History, Faith, and Society.* Leiden: E. J. Brill, 1984.

Abu Saleh, Abbas. *Tarikh al-Muwahhidun al-Duruz al-siasi fi al-Mashriq al-'arabi* [The Political History of the al-Muwahhidun al-Duruz in the Arab East]. Beirut: Manshurat al-Majlis al-Durzi li al-Buhuth wa al-Inma', n.d.

Abu Shaqra, al-'Aql Muhammad. "Fi ma'rifat al-din wa qawamuhu" [Concerning Reli-

291

gious Knowledge and Its Basis]. In *Al-Tawhid al-durzi fi madmunihi al-insani*. Edited by Sami Abu Shakra. Beirut: N.p., 1984.

Abu Shaqra, Sami. *Manaqib al-duruz fi al-ʿaqida wa al-tarikh* [Druze Morals: Belief and History]. Shouf, Lebanon: Maktabat Nasif, n.d.

———, ed. *Al-Tawhid al-durzi fi madmunihi al-insani* [The Druze Tawhid in Its Human Context]. Beirut: N.p., 1984.

Abu Zayd, Nasr Hamid. *Falsafat al-taʾwil* [The Philosophy of Esoterism]. Beirut: Al-Markaz al-Thaqafi al-ʿarabi, 1998.

Ajami, Fouad. *The Vanished Imam*. Ithaca, N.Y.: Cornell Univ. Press, 1986.

Akkad, Abbas Mahmud, al-. *Abqariyat al-Imam ʿAli* [The Genius of Imam ʿAli]. Beirut: Dar al-Kitab al-ʿarabi, 1976.

Alamuddin, Najib. *Turmoil: The Druzes, Lebanon and the Arab-Israeli Conflict*. London: Quartet Books, 1993.

Alamuddin, Sulayman Salim. *Al-Qaramita* [The Carmathians]. Beirut: Dar Nawfal, 2003.

Amin, Ahmad. *Zuhr al-Islam* [The Midday of Islam]. Vols. 1–2 of 4. Beirut: Dar al-Kitab al-ʿarabi, 1945.

d'Aquili, Eugene G., and Andrew B. Newberg. "Consciousness and the Machine." *Zygon* 31, no. 2 (1996): 235–52.

Armstrong, Karen. *A History of God*. New York: Ballantine Books, 1993.

———. *Muhammad: A Biography of the Prophet*. New York: HarperCollins, 1992.

Assaad, Sadik A. *The Reign of al-Hakim bi Amr Allah*. Beirut: Arab Institute for Research and Publishing, 1974.

Attar, Fariduddin, al-. *Mantiq al-tayr* [The Logic of Birds]. Translated by Badi' Muhammad Juma'a. Beirut: Dar al-Andalus, 1996.

———. "The Parliament of the Birds." In *The Element Book of Mystical Verse*, edited by Alan Jacobs and Michael Mann, 58. Shaftesbury, Dorset: Element Books, 1997.

Azzam, Intisar. *Change for Continuity: The Druze in America*. Beirut: MAJD Enterprise Universitaire, 1997.

Baghdadi, Ahmad, al-. *Al-tajdid al-fikr al-dini* [Renewal in Religious Thought]. Cyprus: Dar al-Mada li al-Thaqafa wa al-Nashr, 1999.

Baghdadi, Taher ibn Muhammad, al-. *Al-farq bayn al-firaq* [The Difference Between Sects]. Authenticated by Muhi al-Din 'Abd al- Hamid. Beirut: Dar al-Ma'rifa, n.d.

Basha, Muhammad Khalil, al-. *Al-taqammus wa asrar al-hayat wa al-mawt* [Reincarnation and the Secrets of Life and Death]. Beirut: Dar al-Nahar li al-Nashr, 1992.

Bayat, Mangol. *Mysticism and Dissent*. Syracuse, N.Y.: Syracuse Univ. Press, 1982.

Benz, Ernst. "Theogony and the Transformation of Man in Friedrich Wilhelm Joseph Schelling." In *Man and Transformation: Papers from the Eranos Yearbooks* (Bollingen Series 30, vol. 5), edited by Joseph Campbell, 203–49. Princeton, N.J.: Princeton Univ. Press, 1964.

Betts, Robert Benton. *The Druze*. New Haven, Conn.: Yale Univ. Press, 1988.

Blake, William. *Songs of Innocence and of Experience*. 1795. Reprint, New York: Alfred A. Knopf, 1994.

Capra, Fritjof. *The Tao of Physics*. Boston: Shambhala Publications, 2000.

Carrel, Alexis. *Man the Unknown*. New York: Harper and Brothers, 1935.

Corbin, Henri. *Alone with the Alone*. Princeton, N.J.: Princeton Univ. Press, 1969.

Cranston, Sylvia, and Carey Williams. *Reincarnation: A New Horizon in Science, Religion, and Society*. Pasadena, Calif.: Theosophical Univ. Press, 1993.

Daftary, Farhad. *The Isma'ilis*. New York: Cambridge Univ. Press, 1990.

Davies, Paul. *The Mind of God: The Scientific Basis for a Rational World*. New York: Simon and Schuster, 1997.

Dawkins, Richard. *The Selfish Gene*. Oxford: Oxford Univ. Press, 1976.

de Duve, Christian. *Vital Dust: Life as a Cosmic Imperative*. New York: Basic Books, 1995.

Eccles, John C. *Evolution of the Brain: Creation of the Self*. London: Routledge, 1991.

Eliot, T. S. "Burnt Norton" (No. 1 in "Four Quartets"). In *Poetry Speaks*, edited by Elise Paschen and Rebekah Presson Mosby, 110–13. Naperville, Ill.: Sourcebooks, 2001.

Emerson, Ralph Waldo. "The Transcendentalist." In *Emerson on Transcendentalism*, edited by Edward L. Ericson, 91–109. New York: Continuum Publishing, 1986.

Esrawan, Eknath. *The Bhagavad Gita*. Tomales, Calif.: Nilgiri Press, 1985.

Fakhry, Majid. *History of Islamic Philosophy* [Tarikh al-falsafa al-islamiyya]. Translated into Arabic by Kamal Yazigi. Beirut: Al-Dar al-Muttahida li al-Nashr, 1974.

Fakih, Muhammad Jawad, al-. *Salman al-Farisi*. Beirut: Dar al-Funun, 1981.

Farabi, Abu Nasr al-. *Mabadi' ara' ahl al-madina al-fadila* [The Principles of Thought of the Citizens of the Virtuous City]. Translated by Richard Walzer. Oxford: Clarendon Press, 1985.

Farah, Anton. *Ibn Rushd wa falsafatuhu* [Averroes and His Philosophy]. Beirut: Dar al-Tali'a, 1981.

Faur, José. *Homo Mysticus*. Syracuse, N.Y.: Syracuse Univ. Press, 1999.

Firro, Kais. *A History of the Druzes*. Leiden: E. J. Brill, 1992.

Fowden, Garth. *The Egyptian Hermes*. Princeton, N.J.: Princeton Univ. Press, 1986.

Ghaleb, Mustafa. Introduction. *Rahat al-ʿAql* [Peace of Mind], by Hamid al-Din al-Kirmani. Beirut: Dar al-Andalus, 1983.

———. *Mafatih al-ma'rifa* [The Keys of Knowledge]. Beirut: Mua'sasat Izzedin li al-Tiba'a wa al-Nashr, 1982.

———. *Al-Qaramita* [The Carmathians]. Beirut: Dar al-Andalus, 1983.

———. *Al-risala al-jami'a* [The Comprehensive Epistle]. Beirut: Dar al-Andalus, 1984.

Ghorayyeb, Michel Farid. *Al-Hallaj*. Beirut: Dar Maktabat al-Hayat, n.d.

Gibran, Gibran Khalil. *The Prophet*. New York: Alfred A. Knopf, 1963.

Goswami, Amit. *The Self-Aware Universe*. New York: Penguin Putnam, 1993.

Halm, Heinz. *The Fatimids and Their Traditions of Learning.* New York: I. B. Tauris, 1997.

al-Hamd, Muhammad Abdul Hamid. *Sabe'at Harran wa al-Tawhid al-Durzi* [Sabe'at Harran and the Tawhid of the Druze]. Damascus: Dar al-Tali'a al-Jadida, 2003.

Hamza, Nadim. *Al-Tanukhiyyun* [The Tanukh Tribe]. Beirut: Dar al-Nahar, 1984.

Hariri, Abu Musa, al-. *Al-'Alawiyyun al-Nusayriyyun, bahth fi al-'aqida wa al-tarikh* [The Alawite Nusayrites: A Study in Beliefs and History]. Beirut: Dar li Ajl al-Ma'rifa, 1987.

Helal, Samah. Keynote address delivered at the 41st annual convention of the American Druze Society, Durango, Colo., June 30–July 5, 1987. Printed in *Our Heritage* 7, no. 3 (1987).

Hodgson, Marshal H.G. "Al-Darazi and Hamza in the Origin of the Druze Religion." *Journal of the American Society of Oriental Studies* 82 (1962): 5–20.

Hoeller, Stephan A. *Jung and the Lost Gospels.* Wheaton, Ill.: Theosophical Publishing House, 1989.

Husayn, Muhammad Kamil. *Ta'ifat al-Duruz* [The Druze Sect]. Cairo: Dar al-Ma'rifa', 1962.

Hussein, Taha. *'Ali wa banuh* ['Ali and His Sons]. Cairo: Dar al-Ma'rifa, 1980.

———. *'Uthman.* Cairo: Dar al-Ma'rifa, 1947.

Huxley, Julian. *Evolution in Action.* New York: Harper and Brothers, 1953.

Ibish, Yusuf. "Ibn al-Arabi's Theory of Journeying." In *Contemplation and Action in World Religions*, ed. Yusuf Ibish and Ileana Marculescu. Seattle, Wash.: Univ. of Washington Press, 1978.

Ibish, Yusuf, and Ileana Marculescu. *Contemplation and Action in World Religions: Selected Papers from the Rothko Chapel Colloquium "Traditional Modes of Contemplation and Action."* Seattle, Wash.: Univ. of Washington Press, 1978.

Ibn Abi-Taleb, 'Ali. *Nahj al-balagha* [The Path of Eloquence], ed. Muhammad Abdu. Cairo: Dar al-Ma'rifa, n.d.

———. *Nahj al-balagha.* Collated by Muhammad Abdu. N.p., n.d.

Ibn Hani al-Andalusi. *Diwan* [Collection of Poems]. Beirut: Dar Sader, 1994.

Idris, I'mad al-Din. *Tarikh al-khulafa' al-fatimiyyin bi al-Maghrib* [History of the Fatimid Caliphs in the West]. Authenticated by Muhammad al-Ya'lawi. Beirut: Dar al-Gharb al-Islami, 1985.

Israwi, Najib, al-. *Al-madhhab al-tawhidi al-durzi* (The Druze Tawhid Faith). Brazil: n.p., 1990.

Jar Allah, Zuhdi. *Al-Mu'tazila* [The Mu'tazilites]. Beirut: Al-Mua'sasa al-'Arabia li al-Tiba'a wa al-Nashr, 1990.

Jonas, Hans. *The Gnostic Religion.* Boston: Beacon Press, 1958.

Jumblatt, Kamal. *Fi ma yata'adda al-harf* [Beyond the Letter]. Mukhtara, Lebanon: Al-Dar al-Taqadumiyya, 1987.

————. *I Speak for Lebanon.* London: Zed Press, 1982.

Kala'ji, Muhammad Rawwas. *Qira'a siyasiyya li al-sirat al-nabawiyya* [A Political Analysis of the Legacy of the Prophet]. Beirut: Dar al-Nafa'is, 1996.

Karam, Yusuf. *Tarikh al-falsafa al-yunaniyya* [History of Greek Philosophy]. Beirut: Dar al-Qalam, n.d.

Kaster, Joseph, trans. and ed. *The Wisdom of Ancient Egypt.* New York: Barnes and Noble, 1993.

Khuri, Fuad I. *Being a Druze.* London: Druze Heritage Foundation, 2004.

King, Ursula. *Christian Mystics.* New York: Simon and Schuster, 1998.

Kirmani, Hamid al-Din, al-. "Risalat isbu' dawr al-satr" [The Epistle of the Anniversary of the Era of Occultation]. In *Arba' rasa'il isma'iliyya* [Four Isma'ili Epistles], edited by Aref Tamer, 66. Beirut: Dar al-Kashaf, 1953.

Knight, Christopher, and Robert Lomas. *The Hiram Key.* New York: Barnes and Noble, 1996.

Knoll, Andrew H. *Life on a Young Planet.* Princeton, N.J.: Princeton Univ. Press, 2005.

Laszlo, Ervin. *Macroshift.* San Francisco: Barret-Koehler Publishers, 2001.

Leeming, David Adams. *The World of Myth.* New York: Oxford Univ. Press, 1990.

Ma'arri, Abu al-'Ala', al-. *Diwan Abi al-'Ala' al-Ma'arri* [Poetry of Abu al-'Ala' al-Ma'arri].Beirut: Dar Sader, 1975.

MacGregor, Geddes. *Gnosis.* Wheaton, Ill.: Theosophical Publishing House, 1979.

————. *Reincarnation in Christianity: A New Vision of the Role of Rebirth in Christian Thought.* Wheaton, Ill.: Theosophical Publishing House/Quest Books, 1978.

Mackey, Sandra. *The Iranians.* New York: Penguin Books, 1966.

Maimonides, Moses. *The Guide for the Perplexed* [Dalat al-hayrin]. Translated from the Arabic by Michael FriedlÑnder. New York: Dover Publications, 1946.

Majid, Abdul-Munim. *Al-Hakim bi Amr Allah, al-khalifa al-muftara alayh* [Al-Hakim bi Amr Allah, the Wronged Caliph]. Cairo: n.p., 1982.

Makarem, Sami. *Al-Hallaj.* London: Riad el-Rayess Books, 1989.

————. *Maslak al-Tawhid* [The Tawhid Path]. Beirut: Majlis al-Buhuth, 1980.

————. *Al-taqiya fi al-Islam* [Dissimulation in Islam]. London: Druze Heritage Foundation, 2004.

Maqrizi, Taqi al-Din, al-. *Al-khutat al-maqriziyya* [The Maqrizi Papers]. Edited by Khalil Mansur. Beirut: Dar al-Kutub al-'Ilmiyya, 1998.

Medawar, Peter B. *The Limits of Science.* New York: Harper and Row, 1984.

Al-mihrajan al-alfi li Abi al-'Ala' al-Ma'arri [The One-Thousandth Anniversary of Abu al-'Ala' al-Ma'arri]. Beirut: Dar Sader, 1945.

Mua'kassa, Sahar. *Comprehensive Biography of the Druze Religion.* New York: Druze Research and Publications Institute, 2004.

Muhasibi, al-Harith ibn Assad, al-. *Al-'Aql wa fahm al-Qur'an* [The Mind in Understanding the Qur'an]. Authenticated by Husayn al-Quwwatli. Damascus: Dar al-Kindi, 1978.

Na'imy, Michael. *Al-yawm al-akhir* [The Last Day]. Beirut: Mu'assasat Nawfal, 1978.

Najjar, Abdallah. *The Druze: Millennium Scrolls Revealed.* Translated by Fred I. Massey and Abdallah Najjar. N.p., 1973.

———. *Madhhab al-Duruz wa al-Tawhid* [Druze Faith and Tawhid]. Cairo: Dar al-Ma'rifa, 1965.

———. "The Druzes' Role in America Today." Paper delivered at the 22nd annual convention of the American Druze Society, Charleston, W. Va., June 24–26, 1968.

Nasr, Mursil *Al-Muwahhidun al-Duruz fi al-Islam* [The Muwahhidun Druze in Islam]. Beirut: Al-Dar al-Islamiyya, 1997.

Nimr, Abdul-Munim, al-. *Al-Shi'a, al-Mahdi, al-Duruz: tarikh, wa watha'iq* [The Shi'a, al-Mahdi, al-Duruz: History, and Documents]. Cairo: Dar al-Hurriya, 1988.

Pagels, Elaine. *The Gnostic Gospels.* New York: Vantage Books, 1979.

Payne, Robert. *The History of Islam.* Barnes and Noble, 1950.

Reanney, Darryl. *After Death.* New York: William Morrow and Co., 1991.

Rifkin, Jeremy. *Entropy.* New York: Viking Press, 1980.

Sabbagh, Emad, al-. *Al-Ahnaf* [The Hanifs]. Damascus: Dar al-Hisad, 1998.

Sa'di, Nabih, al-. *Madhhab al-Tawhid fi maqalat 'ashr* [Tawhid Faith in Ten Essays]. Damascus: N.p., 1993.

Sayegh, Wahbah. *The Tawheed Faith.* Vol. 4, *Messages and Shrines.* Benton Harbor, Mich.: American Druze Society Committee on Religious Affairs, 1990.

Schaya, Leo. "Contemplation and Action in Judaism and Islam." In *Contemplation and Action in World Religions: Selected Papers from the Rothko Chapel Colloquium "Traditional Modes of Contemplation and Action."* Edited by Yusuf Ibish and Ileana Marculescu, 151–89. Seattle, Wash.: Rothko Chapel, 1978.

Scholem, Gershom. *Major Trends in Jewish Mysticism.* New York: Schocken Books, 1961.

Schroedinger, Erwin. *What Is Life?* 1945. Rev. ed., Cambridge: Cambridge Univ. Press, 1962.

Shamseddin, Muhammed Mahdi. *Al-tajdid fi al-fikr al-islami* [The Renewal in Islamic Thought]. Beirut: Dar al-Manhal al-Lubnani, 1997.

———. *Thawrat al-Husayn* [The Revolt of al-Husayn]. Beirut: Dar al-Ta'aruf li al-Matbua't, 1979.

Sharaf al-Din, Jalal. *Dirasat fi al-tasawwuf al-islami* [Studies in Islamic Mysticism]. Beirut: Dar al-Nahdha al-'arabiyya, 1980.

Sirin, Hamid. *Masadir al-'aqida al-durziyya* [The Sources of the Druze Faith]. Beirut: Dar li Ajl al-Ma'rifa, 1985.

Smith, Huston. *The Religions of Man.* New York: Harper and Row, 1958.

Smith, Wilfred Cantwell. *Islam in Modern History*. Princeton, N.J.: Princeton Univ. Press, 1957.

Spong, John Shelby. *Why Christianity Must Change or Die*. San Francisco: Harper SanFrancisco, 1998.

Stevenson, Ian. "The Exploratory Value of the Idea of Reincarnation." *Journal of Nervous and Mental Disease* 164, no. 5 (1974): 305–26.

Suyuti, Jalal al-Din, al-. *Tarikh al-khulafa'* [The History of the Caliphs]. Authenticated by Ibrahim Saleh. Beirut: Dar Sader, 1997.

Swayd, Sami. "Rethinking Druze Historiography." *Journal of Druze Studies* 1, no. 1 (2000): 129.

Taqi al-Din, Halim. *Qada' al-Muwahhidun al-Duruz* [Druze Jurisprudence]. Beirut: N.p., 1979.

Talih, Amin. *Asl al-Muwahhidun al-Duruz wa usulahum* [The Origin and Principles of the Druze]. Beirut: Dar al-Andalus, 1961.

Tamer, Aref. *Al-Hakim bi Amr Allah* [The Ruler by the Will of God]. Beirut: Dar al-Afaq al-Jadida, 1982.

———. *Jami'at al-jami'a* [Comprehensive Compendium]. Beirut: Dar al-Hayat, n.d.

———. *Al-khalifa al-fatimi al-khamis al-Aziz bi Allah* [The Fifth Fatimid Caliph al-Aziz bi Allah]. Beirut: Dar al-Afaq al-Jadida, 1982.

———. *Al-Qai'm wa al-Mansur al-fatimiyyan* [The Fatimid Caliphs: Al-Qa'im and al-Mansour]. Beirut: Dar al-Afaq al-Jadida, 1982.

———. *Al-Qaramita* [The Carmathians]. Beirut: Dar Maktabat al-Hayat, n.d.

Taqi al-Din, Zayn al-Din 'Abd al-Gaffar. *Al-nuqat wa al-dawa'ir* [The Dots and the Circles]. Beirut: Dar Isharat, 1999.

Teilhard de Chardin, Pierre. *The Phenomenon of Man*. Translated by Bernard Wall. New York: Harper and Row, 1959. Originally published in French as *Le phénomène humain*. Paris: Edition du Seuil, 1955.

Tennyson, Alfred. Letter to B. P. Blood, 7 May 1874, Faringford, Freshwater, Isle of Wight. Quoted in Tennyson, Hallam T. *Alfred, Lord Tennyson: A Memoir by His Son*. 1899. Rev. ed., London: Macmillan, 1940.

'Uthman, Hashim. *Al-Isma'iliyya* [Isma'ilism]. Beirut: Al-Alami Library, 1998.

Wali, Taha, al-. *Al-Qaramita* [The Carmathians]. Beirut: Dar al-'Ilm li al-Malayin, 1981.

Walker, Paul E. *Abu Ya'qub al-Sijistani*. London: I. B. Tauris and Co., 1998.

———. *Hamid al-Din al-Kirmani*. London: I. B. Tauris and Co., 1999.

Wilber, Ken. "Psychologia Perennis: The Spectrum of Consciousness." *Journal of Transpersonal Psychology* 7, no. 2 (1975): 105-32.

Wilson, A. N. *Paul: The Mind of the Apostle*. New York: W. W. Norton and Co., 1997.

Yazbek, Yusuf Ibrahim. Introduction. *Al-dawlah al-durziyya* [The Druze State]. Translated by Hafiz Abu Muslih. Beirut: Al-Maktaba al-Haditha, 1983.

———. *Waliyun min Lubnan* [A Guardian from Lebanon]. Beirut: Awraq Lunahiyya, 1960.

Yazigi, Kamal. *Ma'alim al-fikr al-'arabi fi al-asr al-wasit* [Highlights of Arab Thought in the Middle Period]. Beirut: Dar al-'Ilm li al-Malayin, 1954.

Zafrulla Khan, Muhammad. *Muhammad, Seal of the Prophets*. London: Routledge and Kegan Paul, 1980.

Zu'bi, Muhammad 'Ali, al-. *Al-Duruz: zahiruhum wa batinuhum* [The Overt and Covert Beliefs of the Druze]. Damascus: N.d., n.p.

Index

Aaron, 126

Abbasid dynasty: conflict with Fatimids, 226–27; court intrigue and, 62; Fatimid Empire as threat to, 64, 73–74; insurrection against Umayyads, 42; intellectual movement under, 56–59; loss of power, 72; persecution of Isma'ilis, 64–65, 66, 67; persecution of progeny of 'Ali/Shi'as, 42, 44, 51, 52, 58, 63, 65, 176, 210, 241, 253–54; persecution of Sufis, 62; philosophical and spiritual movements and, 53, 60–63; reaction to mystics, 62; response to Fatimid caliphate, 70–71; rule of, 41, 42–43, 52; sabotage of Druze doctrine, 217–18; socialist movement in, 54–56

Abbud, Marun, 178

'Abd al-Muttalib, 13

Abd-al-Rahman, 42

Abdullah (grandson of Isma'il), 65–66

Abdullah (father of the Prophet), 13, 15

Abdul-Rahim ibn Ilyas, 221

al-Abidin, 'Ali Zayn, 46, 195–96

Abi-Khzam, Anwar, 144, 215

ablution, 151

abortion, 150

Abraham, 126, 223

absolute unitary being, 116

Abu al-'Abbas Abdallah. See al-Saffah

Abu 'Ali al-Mansur bi Allah. See al-Hakim bi Amr Allah

Abu Bakr: as convert to Islam, 16; as first caliph, 19, 31, 36; last prayer of Muhammad and, 29; at Muhammad's death, 30; support of Muhammad, 18–19

Abu Dharr al-Ghafari, 241

Abu Hanifa al-Nu'man, 51

Abu-Hilal, Muhammad, 98, 238–39

Abu Ibrahim. See al-Tamimi, Isma'il ibn Muhammad Ibn Hamed

Abu Shaqra, al-'Aql Muhammad, 204

Abu-Talib, 13, 20, 22

Abyssinia, 19, 20

accountability: free choice essential to, 135, 153–54, 268; Islamic studies on, 56; as outcome of error of universal mind, 142, 143; as outcome of free choice, 121, 181, 201; predestination and, 200–201; reincarnation and, 154–55; rule and prerogative of individuals, 197

Adam: angels' obeisance to, 214; fall of, 133, 142, 267; as human representation of universal mind, 134; as messenger of Tawhid, 125, 223

adversity, 176–77

adwar (cycles), 123–29

Ahmad (al-Wafi), 66

Ahriman, 135

Ahura Mazda, 135

'A'isha, 29, 37, 39

Akhenaten, 96, 139

al-Akhram, 85, 211

299